PENGUIN
CUSTOM 🐧 EDITIONS
THE WESTERN WORLD

PROF. KEITH P. LURIA
EUROPE FROM THE RENAISSANCE TO
WATERLOO
HISTORY 209
NORTH CAROLINA STATE UNIVERSITY

Pearson Learning Solutions

New York   Boston   San Francisco
London   Toronto   Sydney   Tokyo   Singapore   Madrid
Mexico City   Munich   Paris   Cape Town   Hong Kong   Montreal

Senior Vice President, Editorial and Marketing: Patrick F. Boles
Senior Sponsoring Editor: Natalie Danner
Development Editor: Mary Kate Paris
Editorial Assistant: Jill Johnson
Marketing Manager: Brian T. Berkeley
Operations Manager: Eric M. Kenney
Production Manager: Jennifer Berry
Rights Manager: Jillian Santos
Art Director and Cover Designer: Renée Sartell

Cover Art: "A Fine Roman Mosaic Depicting a Head of Medusa," by Peter
Breughel the Younger, and "In the Golden Gloaming," by John Atkinson
Grimshaw, Copyright © Christie's Images. "The Looting of Jerusalem after the
Capture by the Christians in 1099," by Jean de Courcy, (Biblioteque Nationale)
and "School of Athens," by Raphael (Vatican Museums and Galleries, Vatican
City, Italy) Copyright © The Bridgeman Art Library International Ltd. "Com-
position," by Wassily Kandinsky, Copyright © 2001 Artists Rights Society (ARS),
New York/ADAGP, Paris, and Corbis Images. "Rodins Thinker" courtesy of
Musée Rodin, Paris, France/The Bridgeman Art Library.

Printed in the United States of America.

Please visit our website at *www.pearsoncustom.com.*

Attention bookstores: For permission to return any unsold stock, contact us
at *pe-uscustomreturns@pearson.com.*

Pearson Learning Solutions, 501 Boylston Street, Suite 900, Boston, MA 02116
A Pearson Education Company
www.pearsoned.com

1 2 3 4 5 6 7 8 9 10 XXXX 14 13 12 11 10 09

ISBN 10: 1-256-02809-6
ISBN 13: 978-1-256-02809-3

Acknowledgments

As anyone could well imagine, creating *Penguin Custom Editions: The Western World* was an enormous undertaking. Not only did the project involve compiling a collection of more than a thousand selections—all of which had to be identified, excerpted, introduced, categorized, copy-edited, composed, proofread, and cleared for copyright, among other things—but as a new kind of publication, it raised a new and unpredictable set of challenges that demanded the creative skills of a dedicated team. The editors owe a sincere debt of gratitude to the scholars and professionals who worked with us to hone the original concept, to shape the materials as they emerged, and to transform idea into reality.

From the start, *Penguin Custom Editions* depended on the support of key people at Penguin Putnam, Inc. and at Penguin Books. In particular, Daniel T. Lundy's enthusiasm for the project buoyed us along, and John Schline's patience and perseverance remain much appreciated. Thanks also to Mary Sunden, Margaret Bluman, Andrew Rosenheim, and Florence Eichin.

The project benefited greatly from the advice of the many teachers who reviewed the original proposal and who, in the process, identified potential pitfalls and helped us to see how to avoid them: David A. Brewer, *The Ohio State University*; Denise Z. Davidson, *Georgia State University*; Barbara B. Diefendorf, *Boston University*; Daniel Gordon, *University of Massachusetts at Amherst*; Paul Halliday, *Union College*; Susan Hult, *Houston Community College, Central*; Ethan Knapp, *The Ohio State University*; Elizabeth A. Lehfeldt, *Cleveland State University*; Katharine J. Lualdi, *University of Southern Maine*; Christopher Martin, *Boston University*; Phillip C. Naylor, *Marquette University*; Catherine F. Patterson, *University of Houston*; John Paul Riquelme, *Boston University*; Barbara H. Rosenwein, *Loyola University of Chicago*; Charles J. Rzepka, *Boston University*; John Savage, *New York University*; and Daniel R. Schwarz, *Cornell University*.

As the manuscript neared completion, we had the good fortune to garner feedback from colleagues who helped us see what was working, what needed improvement, and how best to go about it. Many thanks to Feroz

Ahmad, *University of Massachusetts, Boston*; Joseph Aieta, *Babson College*; Kathleen Shine Cain, *Merrimack College*; Paul Doherty, *Boston College*; Paul Faler, *University of Massachusetts, Boston*; Julia Genster, *Tufts University*; Patricia A. Halpin, *Assumption College*; Robert Keohan, *Merrimack College*; Mary Kramer, *University of Massachusetts, Lowell*; Matthew Lenoe, *Assumption College*; Jennifer Morrison, *Regis College*; Janice Neuleib, *Illinois State University*; Shaun O'Connell, *University of Massachusetts, Boston*; Mark O'Connor, *Boston College*; Stuart Peterfreund, *Northeastern University*; Stephen Ruffus, *Salt Lake Community College*; Maurice Scharton, *Illinois State University*; Steven Scherwatzky, *Merrimack College*; Mary Shaner, *University of Massachusetts, Boston*; Louise Z. Smith, *University of Massachusetts, Boston*; Judith A. Stanford, *Rivier College*; Elizabeth Kowaleski Wallace, *Boston College*; James D. Wallace, *Boston College*; David Wick, *Gordon College*; and Alex Wilkes, *Northeastern University*.

Penguin Custom Editions simply would not have been possible without the talented people at Pearson Custom Publishing. Ellen Kuhl suggested the project to us and became its impresario extraordinaire throughout each step of the publishing process. Her ideas, hard work, and humor were key assets in bringing this work to fruition. Katherine Gehan invented the rules and held us to them; her creativity, her almost unbelievable organizational abilities, and her willingness to laugh at an endless stream of puns made it possible for us to finish what we started. Lydia Stuart Horton skillfully copy edited more than 15,000 pages of manuscript with a keen eye for detail and consistency. Among countless other things, Amy Hurd and Stephanie Tobin monitored the whereabouts of thousands upon thousands of files and pieces of paper without losing a single one; Mary Kaiser and Vikram Savkar wrestled all of that paper into finely crafted pages with the invaluable assistance of Melanie Aswell, her proofreading team, and Jim O'Malley at Stratford Publishing. Nathan Wilbur enthusiastically spread the news and Renée Sartell made it beautiful. Finally, a nod of grateful appreciation goes to Deborah Schwartz, Francesca Marcantonio, Michael Payne, Pat Porter, Jay Schmidt, Eric Kenney, Lisa Cutler, Pat Boles, Don Kilburn, and to the many who contributed without our awareness. It has been a pleasure and we're looking forward to doing it again.

Mark Kishlansky
David Blackbourn
Virginia Brown
James Hankins

Contents

IV

GIOVANNI BOCCACCIO

The Black Death

Giovanni Boccaccio (1313–1375), poet, scholar, and writer of short stories, was one of the greatest writers of the Italian Renaissance. He was born in Tuscany, a bastard child of the general manager of the Bardi Bank of Florence, one of the greatest European banks of the day. When his father became director of the Naples branch of the bank in 1327, young Giovanni went along and there received an education in law, a subject for which he proved unsuited. Turning to literature and scholarship instead, the young Boccaccio established a reputation in the court of the Angevin Kings of Naples as an innovative poet, specializing in the transfer of popular poetic genres from French to Italian. In 1341 he was compelled to return to Florence where in 1348–9 he witnessed firsthand the effects of the Black Death, the most devastating plague in European history. In later life Boccaccio came under the influence of Francesco Petrarca, the first great humanist of the Renaissance, and spent the final decades of his life writing various learned compendia in Latin, including biographical collections of famous men and women, and erudite studies of classical mythology.

It was in the decade after the Black Death that Boccaccio composed what is by far his most famous work, The Decameron. This work is a collection of one hundred short tales, purporting to be told by young noblemen and noblewomen to each other while in the country, seeking refuge from the plague. By turns witty, satirical, ribald, and moralizing, the tales reveal the attitudes of laymen to the world of religious and social conformity that surrounds them. Boccaccio tried to excuse the license of these tales by claiming they were necessary light relief from the horrors of the plague, hence the famous description of the Black Death with which The Decameron *begins.*

Whenever, fairest ladies, I pause to consider how compassionate you all are by nature, I invariably become aware that the present work will seem to you to possess an irksome and ponderous opening. For it carries at its head the painful memory of the deadly havoc wrought by the recent plague, which brought so much heartache and misery to those who witnessed, or had experience of it. But I do not want you to be deterred, for this reason, from reading any further, on the assumption that you are to be subjected, as you read, to an endless torrent of tears and sobbing. You will be affected no differently by this grim beginning than walkers confronted by a steep and rugged hill, beyond which there lies a beautiful and delectable plain. The degree of pleasure they derive from the latter will correspond directly to the difficulty of the climb and the descent. And just as the end of mirth is heaviness, so sorrows are dispersed by the advent of joy.

This brief unpleasantness (I call it brief, inasmuch as it is contained within few words) is quickly followed by the sweetness and the pleasure which I have already promised you, and which, unless you were told in advance, you would not perhaps be expecting to find after such a beginning as this. Believe me, if I could decently have taken you whither I desire by some other route, rather than along a path so difficult as this, I would gladly have done so. But since it is impossible without this memoir to show the origin of the events you will read about later, I really have no alternative but to address myself to its composition.

I say, then, that the sum of thirteen hundred and forty-eight years had elapsed since the fruitful Incarnation of the Son of God, when the noble city of Florence, which for its great beauty excels all others in Italy, was visited by the deadly pestilence. Some say that it descended upon the human race through the influence of the heavenly bodies, others that it was a punishment signifying God's righteous anger at our iniquitous way of life. But whatever its cause, it had originated some years earlier in the East, where it had claimed countless lives before it unhappily spread westward, growing in strength as it swept relentlessly on from one place to the next.

In the face of its onrush, all the wisdom and ingenuity of man were unavailing. Large quantities of refuse were cleared out of the city by officials specially appointed for the purpose, all sick persons were forbidden entry, and numerous instructions were issued for safeguarding the people's health, but all to no avail. Nor were the countless petitions humbly directed to God by the pious, whether by means of formal processions or in all other ways, any less ineffectual. For in the early spring of the year we have mentioned, the plague began, in a terrifying and extraordinary manner, to make its disastrous effects apparent. It did not take the form it had assumed in the East, where if anyone bled from the nose it was an obvious portent of certain death. On the contrary, its earliest symptom, in men and women alike, was the appearance of certain swellings in the groin or the armpit, some of which were egg-shaped whilst others were roughly the size of the common apple. Sometimes the swellings were large, sometimes not so large, and they were referred to by the populace as *gavòccioli*. From the two areas already mentioned, this deadly *gavòcciolo* would begin to spread, and within a short time it would appear at random all over the body. Later on, the symptoms of the disease changed, and many people began to find dark blotches and bruises on their arms, thighs, and other parts of the body, sometimes large and few in number, at other times tiny and closely spaced. These, to anyone unfortunate enough to contract them, were just as infallible a sign that he would die as the *gavòcciolo* had been earlier, and as indeed it still was.

Against these maladies, it seemed that all the advice of physicians and all the power of medicine were profitless and unavailing. Perhaps the nature of the illness was such that it allowed no remedy: or perhaps those people who were treating the illness (whose numbers had increased enormously because the ranks of the qualified were invaded by people, both men and women, who had never received any training in medicine), being ignorant of its causes, were not prescribing the appropriate cure. At all events, few of those who caught it ever recovered, and in most cases death occurred within three days from the appearance of the symptoms we have described, some people dying more rapidly than others, the majority without any fever or other complications.

But what made this pestilence even more severe was that whenever those suffering from it mixed with people who were still unaffected, it would rush upon these with the speed of a fire racing through dry or oily substances that happened to come within its reach. Nor was this the full extent of its evil, for not only did it infect healthy persons who conversed or had any dealings with the sick, making them ill or visiting an equally horrible death upon them, but it also seemed to transfer the sickness to anyone touching the clothes or other objects which had been handled or used by its victims.

It is a remarkable story that I have to relate. And were it not for the fact that I am one of many people who saw it with their own eyes, I would scarcely dare to believe it, let alone commit it to paper, even though I had heard it from a person whose word I could trust. The plague I have been describing was of so contagious a nature that very often it visibly did more than simply pass from one person to another. In other words, whenever an animal other than a human being touched anything belonging to a person who had been stricken or exterminated

3

by the disease, it not only caught the sickness, but died from it almost at once. To all of this, as I have just said, my own eyes bore witness on more than one occasion. One day, for instance, the rags of a pauper who had died from the disease were thrown into the street, where they attracted the attention of two pigs. In their wonted fashion, the pigs first of all gave the rags a thorough mauling with their snouts, after which they took them between their teeth and shook them against their cheeks. And within a short time they began to writhe as though they had been poisoned, then they both dropped dead to the ground, spread-eagled upon the rags that had brought about their undoing.

These things, and many others of a similar or even worse nature, caused various fears and fantasies to take root in the minds of those who were still alive and well. And almost without exception, they took a single and very inhuman precaution, namely to avoid or run away from the sick and their belongings, by which means they all thought that their own health would be preserved.

Some people were of the opinion that a sober and abstemious mode of living considerably reduced the risk of infection. They therefore formed themselves into groups and lived in isolation from everyone else. Having withdrawn to a comfortable abode where there were no sick persons, they locked themselves in and settled down to a peaceable existence, consuming modest quantities of delicate foods and precious wines and avoiding all excesses. They refrained from speaking to outsiders, refused to receive news of the dead or the sick, and entertained themselves with music and whatever other amusements they were able to devise.

Others took the opposite view, and maintained that an infallible way of warding off this appalling evil was to drink heavily, enjoy life to the full, go round singing and merrymaking, gratify all of one's cravings whenever the opportunity offered, and shrug the whole thing off as one enormous joke. Moreover, they practised what they preached to the best of their ability, for they would visit one tavern after another, drinking all day and night to immoderate excess; or alternatively (and this was their more frequent custom), they would do their drinking in various private houses, but only in the ones where the conversation was restricted to subjects that were pleasant or entertaining. Such places were easy to find, for people behaved as though their days were numbered, and treated their belongings and their own persons with equal abandon. Hence most houses had become common property, and any passing stranger could make himself at home as naturally as though he were the rightful owner. But for all their riotous manner of living, these people always took good care to avoid any contact with the sick.

In the face of so much affliction and misery, all respect for the laws of God and man had virtually broken down and been extinguished in our city. For like everybody else, those ministers and executors of the laws who were not either dead or ill were left with so few subordinates that they were unable to discharge any of their duties. Hence everyone was free to behave as he pleased.

There were many other people who steered a middle course between the two already mentioned, neither restricting their diet to the same degree as the first group, nor indulging so freely as the second in drinking and other forms of wantonness, but simply doing no more than satisfy their appetite. Instead of incarcerating themselves, these people moved about freely, holding in their hands a posy of flowers, or fragrant herbs, or one of a wide range of spices, which they applied at frequent intervals to their nostrils, thinking it an excellent idea to fortify the brain with smells of that particular sort; for the stench of dead bodies, sickness, and medicines seemed to fill and pollute the whole of the atmosphere.

Some people, pursuing what was possibly the safer alternative, callously maintained that there was no better or more efficacious remedy against a plague than to run away from it. Swayed by this argument, and sparing no thought for anyone but themselves, large numbers of men and women abandoned their city, their homes, their relatives, their estates and their belongings, and headed for the countryside, either in Florentine territory or, better still, abroad. It was as though they imagined that the wrath of God would not unleash this plague against men for their iniquities irrespective of where they happened to be, but would only be aroused against those who found themselves within the city walls; or possibly they assumed that the whole of the population would be exterminated and that the city's last hour had come.

Of the people who held these various opinions, not all of them died. Nor, however, did they all survive. On the contrary, many of each different persuasion fell ill here, there, and everywhere, and having themselves, when they were fit and well, set an example to those who were as yet unaffected, they languished away with virtually no one to nurse them. It was not merely a question of one citizen avoiding another, and of people almost invariably neglecting their neighbours and rarely or never visiting their relatives, addressing them only from a distance; this scourge had implanted so great a terror in the hearts of men and women that brothers abandoned brothers, uncles their nephews, sisters their brothers, and in many cases wives deserted their husbands. But even worse, and almost incredible, was the fact that fathers and mothers refused to nurse and assist their own children, as though they did not belong to them.

Hence the countless numbers of people who fell ill, both male and female, were entirely dependent upon either the charity of friends (who were few and far between) or the greed of servants, who remained in short supply despite the attraction of high wages out of all proportion to the services they performed. Furthermore, these latter were men and women of coarse intellect and the majority were unused to such duties, and they did little more than hand things to the invalid when asked to do so and watch over him when he was dying. And in performing this kind of service, they frequently lost their lives as well as their earnings.

As a result of this wholesale desertion of the sick by neighbours, relatives and friends, and in view of the scarcity of servants, there grew up a practice almost never previously heard of, whereby when a woman fell ill, no matter how gracious or beautiful or gently bred she might be, she raised no objection to being attended by a male servant, whether he was young or not. Nor did she have any scruples about showing him every part of her body as freely as she would have displayed it to a woman, provided that the nature of her infirmity required her to do so; and this explains why those women who recovered were possibly less chaste in the period that followed.

Moreover a great many people died who would perhaps have survived had they received some assistance. And hence, what with the lack of appropriate means for tending the sick, and the virulence of the plague, the number of deaths reported in the city whether by day or by night was so enormous that it astonished all who heard tell of it, to say nothing of the people who actually witnessed the carnage. And it was perhaps inevitable that among the citizens who survived there arose certain customs that were quite contrary to established tradition.

It had once been customary, as it is again nowadays, for the women relatives and neighbours of a dead man to assemble in his house in order to mourn in the company of the women who had been closest to him; moreover his kinsfolk would forgather in front of his house along with his neighbours and various other citizens, and there would be a contingent of priests, whose numbers varied according to the quality of the deceased; his body would be taken thence to the church in which he had wanted to be buried, being borne on the shoulders of his peers amidst the funeral pomp of candles and dirges. But as the ferocity of the plague began to mount this practice all but disappeared entirely and was replaced by different customs. For not only did people die without having many women about them, but a great number departed this life without anyone at all to witness their going. Few indeed were those to whom the lamentations and bitter tears of their relatives were accorded; on the contrary, more often than not bereavement was the signal for laughter and witticisms and general jollification—the art of which the women, having for the most part suppressed their feminine concern for the salvation of the souls of the dead, had learned to perfection. Moreover it was rare for the bodies of the dead to be accompanied by more than ten or twelve neighbours to the church, nor were they borne on the shoulders of worthy and honest citizens, but by a kind of gravedigging fraternity, newly come into being and drawn from the lower orders of society. These people assumed the title of sexton, and demanded a fat fee for their services, which consisted in taking up the coffin and hauling it swiftly away, not to the church specified by the dead man in his will, but usually to the nearest at hand. They would be preceded by a group of four or six clerics, who between them carried one or two candles at most, and sometimes none at all. Nor did the priests go to the trouble of pronouncing solemn and lengthy funeral rites, but, with the aid of these so-called sextons, they hastily lowered the body into the nearest empty grave they could find.

As for the common people and a large proportion of the bourgeoisie, they presented a much more pathetic spectacle, for the majority of them were constrained, either by their poverty or the hope of survival, to remain in their houses. Being confined to their own parts of the city, they fell ill daily in their thousands, and since they had no one to assist them or attend to their needs, they inevitably perished almost without exception. Many dropped dead in the open streets, both by day and by night, whilst a great many others, though dying in their own houses, drew their neighbours' attention to the fact more by the smell of their rotting corpses than by any other means. And what with these, and the others who were dying all over the city, bodies were here, there and everywhere.

Whenever people died, their neighbours nearly always followed a single, set routine, prompted as much by their fear of being contaminated by the decaying corpse as by any charitable feelings they may have entertained towards the deceased. Either on their own, or with the assistance of bearers whenever these were to be had, they extracted the bodies of the dead from their houses and left them lying outside their front doors, where anyone going about the streets, especially in the early morning, could have observed countless numbers of them. Funeral biers would then be sent for, upon which the dead were taken away, though there were some who, for lack of biers, were carried off on plain boards. It was by no means rare for more than one of these biers to be seen with two or three bodies upon it at a time; on the contrary, many were seen to contain a husband and wife, two or three brothers and sisters, a father and son, or some other pair of close relatives. And times without number it happened that two priests would be on their way to bury someone, holding a cross before them, only to find that bearers carrying three or four additional biers would fall in behind them; so that whereas the priests had thought they had only one burial to attend to, they in fact had six or seven, and sometimes more. Even in these circumstances, however, there were no tears or candles or mourners to honour the dead; in fact, no more respect was accorded to dead people than would nowadays be shown towards dead goats. For it was quite apparent that the one thing which, in normal times, no wise man had ever learned to accept with patient resignation (even though it struck so seldom and unobtrusively), had now been brought home to the feeble-minded as well, but the scale of the calamity caused them to regard it with indifference.

Such was the multitude of corpses (of which further consignments were arriving every day and almost by the hour at each of the churches), that there was not sufficient consecrated ground for them to be buried in, especially if each was to have its own plot in accordance with long-established custom. So when all the graves were full, huge trenches were excavated in the churchyards, into which new arrivals were placed in their hundreds, stowed tier upon tier like ships' cargo, each layer of corpses being covered over with a thin layer of soil till the trench was filled to the top.

But rather than describe in elaborate detail the calamities we experienced in the city at that time, I must mention that, whilst an ill wind was blowing through Florence itself, the surrounding region was no less badly affected. In the fortified towns, conditions were similar to those in the city itself on a minor scale; but in the scattered hamlets and the countryside proper, the poor unfortunate peasants and their families had no physicians or servants whatever to assist them, and collapsed by the wayside, in their field, and in their cottages at all hours of the day and night, dying more like animals than human beings. Like the townspeople, they too grew apathetic in their ways, disregarded their affairs, and neglected their possessions. Moreover they all behaved as though each day was to be their last, and far from making provision for the future by tilling their lands, tending their flocks, and adding to their previous labours, they tried in every way they could think of to squander the assets already in their possession. Thus it came about that oxen, asses, sheep, goats, pigs, chickens, and even dogs (for all their deep fidelity to man) were driven away and allowed to roam freely through the fields, where the crops lay abandoned and had not even been reaped, let alone gathered in. And after a whole day's feasting, many of these animals, as though possessing the power of reason, would return glutted in the evening to their own quarters, without any shepherd to guide them.

But let us leave the countryside and return to the city. What more remains to be said, except that the cruelty of heaven (and possibly, in some measure, also that of man) was so immense and so devastating that between March and July of the year in question, what with the fury of the pestilence and the fact that so many of the sick were inadequately cared for or abandoned in their hour of need because the healthy were too terrified to approach them, it is reliably thought that over a hundred thousand human lives were extinguished within the walls of the city of Florence? Yet before this lethal catastrophe fell upon the city, it is doubtful whether anyone would have guessed it contained so many inhabitants.

Ah, how great a number of splendid palaces, fine houses, and noble dwellings, once filled with retainers, with lords and with ladies, were bereft of all who had lived there, down to the tiniest child! How numerous were the famous families, the vast estates, the notable fortunes, that were seen to be left without a rightful successor! How many gallant gentlemen, fair ladies, and sprightly youths, who would have been judged hale and hearty by Galen, Hippocrates and Aesculapius (to say nothing of others), having breakfasted in the morning with their kinfolk, acquaintances and friends, supped that same evening with their ancestors in the next world!

LEON BATTISTA ALBERTI

How to Choose a Wife

Long considered by historians a prime example of the "universal man" of the Renaissance, Leon Battista Alberti (1404–1472) was a humanist author, architect, surveyer, art theorist, poet, painter, engineer, and mathematician. He was a member of a prominent and wealthy family of merchant-bankers who had been exiled from Florence in the 1390s but were restored in 1434 with the coming of the Medici to power. Leon Battista went to the universities of Padua and Bologna with the intention of studying law, but instead developed a passionate love of the Greek and Latin classics. In 1432, while in Rome, he was appointed an abbreviator (a type of bureaucrat) in the chancery of Pope Eugene IV, a position he held until 1464. There, among the ruins of Rome's ancient architectural splendor, he elaborated the principles of his chief work, the De re architectura *(On Architecture, begun 1449, printed 1485). While moving with the papal court between Rome and Florence, Alberti also composed his two major treatises on the arts, the* De pictura *(On Painting, 1436) and* De statua *(On Statuary, undated), as well as numerous other works of fiction, poetry, and applied science. In 1441, he organized a poetical contest in Florence, known as the* Certame Coronario, *for the best work of poetry in Italian.*

While Alberti is perhaps best known for his writings on the fine arts, his Book of the Family *(1433–1439) represents an important expression of the ideals of the middle class merchants and businessmen who created and supported the Renaissance in fifteenth-century Italy. A dialogue in four books, it treats the problem of paternal responsibility and conjugal love (Book I), marriage (Book II), the economic basis of the family and estate management (Book III), and friendship (Book IV). Against some ascetic ideals of the Middle Ages, Alberti argued that wealth and marriage were not things to be despised, but were part of good citizenship. The prologue to the work presents a famously optimistic argument for the power of reason and virtue to overcome Fortune, a theme that would later be taken up and transformed by Machiavelli. The passage excerpted here, from Book II, describes the criteria to be used in choosing a wife.*

PROLOGUE

Remembering how much ancient history and the recollection of our ancestors together can teach us, how much we are able to see in our own times both in Italy and elsewhere, and how not a few families used to be most happy and glorious but have now disappeared and died out, I often marveled to myself and was saddened over how much power Fortune's unfairness and malignity wielded over men; and how Fortune was permitted with her will and temerity to seize families well provided with the most virtuous of men, abounding in everything precious, expensive, and most desired by men, and endowed with many honors, fame, great praise, authority, and public favor; and how she would deprive them of every happiness, place them in a state of poverty, loneliness, and misery, reduce them from a great number of wealthy ancestors to only a few descendants and from countless riches to the direst straits, and, from the most glorious splendor, subject them to so many calamities, casting them down into abject, dark, and tempestuous adversity. Ah! How many families we see today which are fallen and ruined! It would not be possible to count or to describe all of the noblest families among the ancients, such as the Fabii, the Decii, the Drusii, the Grachii, and the Marcelli, or others, who existed for a long time in our land, supporting the public good and the maintenance of liberty, and who conserved the authority and the dignity of their homeland both in peacetime and in wartime—very modest, prudent, and strong families, such that they were feared by their enemies and loved and revered by their friends. Of all these families, not only their magnificence and their grandeur but the very men themselves, and not only the men but their very names and their memories, have shrunk and faded away, and every trace of them has been completely blotted out and obliterated.

Thus it is not without good reason that I have always thought it well worth knowing whether or not Fortune possesses such power over human affairs and whether this supreme license is really hers that with her instability and inconstancy she may destroy the grandest and most respectable of families. I think about this question without much emotion, detached and free of every passion, and I think to myself, O, young Albertis, how our own Alberti family has been subject to so many adversities for such a long time now and how with the strongest of spirits it has persevered and with what complete reason and good counsel our Albertis have been able to cast off and with firm determination endure our own bitter misfortunes and the furious blows of our unjust fates, and I note that many blame Fortune without just cause as being most often the reason, and I observe that many who through their own stupidity have fallen upon bad times have blamed Fortune and have complained of being buffeted by her stormy waves when they themselves in their foolishness brought about their problems. And in this way, many inept people claim that some other force was the cause of their own errors.

But if anyone who would investigate with care what it is that exalts and increases the family and what it is which also maintains the family in the highest ranks of honor and happiness, that person would soon discover how men usually are the cause of their every good or their every evil, nor will they ever attribute the reasons for their acquisition of praise, greatness, or fame more to Fortune than to their own ability. This is true, and if we examine republics or recall all the past principalities, we will discover that in acquiring and increasing as well as in maintaining and conserving the majesty and the glory already achieved, Fortune was never more influential than the good and holy disciplines of living. Who can doubt this? Just laws and virtuous principles, prudent counsel, and strong and constant actions, love of country, faith, diligence, the impeccable and most laudable customs of the citizens—these have always been able, even without Fortune's favor, to earn and to acquire fame, or with Fortune's assistance, to expand and to increase one's country gloriously and to commend themselves to posterity, achieving immortality. . . .

So then, it can be said that Fortune is incapable and most weak in taking from us even the least part of our character, and we must judge ability as itself sufficient to attain and maintain every sublime and most excellent thing—the grandest of principalities, the most supreme praise, eternal fame, and immortal glory. And you can be sure that whatever you seek or hold dear, no matter what it may be, there is nothing easier for you to acquire or obtain than this nobility. Only the man who does not desire it is without it. And there, if we admit that character, discipline, and manly behavior are man's possessions insofar as they desire them, good counsel, prudence, strong, constant, and persevering spirits, reason, order and method, good arts and discipline, equity, justice, diligence are within reach and embrace so much dominion that they ultimately climb to the highest degree and heights of glory. Oh, young Albertis, who among you would think it an easy task to persuade me that, given the often observed changeability and inconstancy of weak and mortal things, ability—which cannot be denied to men insofar as their free will and willpower seize it and make it part of them—can easily be taken away from its most diligent and vigilant possessors or its many strong defenders? We shall always be of the opinion, just as I believe you also are, since you are all prudent and wise, than in political affairs and in the lives of men, reason is more important than Fortune, and prudence more powerful than blind chance. Nor would any man ever seem wise or prudent to me who placed his hope less in his own ability than in fortuitous events. Anyone will recognize that hard work, good skills, constant enterprises, mature counsel, honest endeavor, just will, and reasonable expectations have increased and enlarged, adorned, maintained, and defended both republics and principalities, and with these qualities any dominion may arise to glory, while without them, it may remain deprived of all its majesty and honor; if we recognize that desire, inertia, lasciviousness, perfidy, cupidity, inequity, libido, and the raw and unbridled passions of human spirits contaminate, divert, and undermine every grandiose, solid, and stable human accomplishment, we shall also recognize that the same rules apply to families as they do to principalities, and we must confess that families rarely fall into unhappy times for any other cause except their lack of prudence and diligence.

And thus, since I know this to be the case, Fortune with its most cruel of floods may overcome and submerge the families which, throwing themselves upon the mercies of such waves, have either not known how to control or contain themselves in times of prosperity or have not been prudent and strong in sustaining and regulating themselves when they were buffeted by adversities; and because I do not doubt in the least that solicitous and diligent fathers of families may render their families most grand and extremely happy by their careful management, good practices, honest customs, humanity, openness, and civility, it has therefore seemed worthwhile to me to investigate with every care and concern what useful precepts are appropriate for instructing fathers and the entire family on how they may finally reach the heights of supreme happiness and not be forced in time to succumb to inequitable and unforeseen Fortune. And as much free time as I have permitted to take from my other affairs, I have been delighted to have spent in searching among the ancient writers as many precepts as they have left us which are apt and useful for the good, honor, and growth of families; and since I discovered many perfect lessons there, I felt it my duty to collect them together and set them in some order so that, gathered together in one place, you might come to know them with less effort, and in coming to know them, you might follow them. I also think, after you have reviewed with me the sayings and authority of these good ancient writers on the one hand, and have considered, on the other, the excellent customs of our Alberti ancestors, you will come to this same conclusion and will conclude for yourselves that ability determines all your fortune. Nor will it delight you any the less in

13

reading me to discover the good ancient manners of our Alberti house, for when you recognize that the counsel and the remembered customs of our older Albertis are completely applicable and most perfect, you will believe their precepts and embrace them. You will learn from them in what manner the family is increased, with what skills it becomes both fortunate and blessed, and with which type of procedure it acquires grace, good will, and friendship, and by means of what discipline it grows and spreads honor, fame, and glory, and in what ways it commends the family's name to eternal praise and immortality. . . .

[After Alberti's prologue, Book I opens during a single afternoon and evening in May 1421 as a number of the Alberti family gathers at a home in Padua, where they are visiting the dying Lorenzo Alberti (Leon Battista's father). The first book contains a discourse by Lorenzo on the role of the father in the family, the relative responsibilities of the old and the young, and the importance of education for the children.]

BOOK II

[Book II discusses the important question of taking a wife, an act which was usually more concerned with economic questions than with romantic love. For the middle-class family man, the choice of a wife involved complicated issues—gaining alliances with the family and relatives of the bride, receiving the all-important dowry along with the bride, and—most important—fathering the legitimate children who would guarantee the continuity of the all important family line. In this book, the dying Lionardo offers advice to the young Leon Battista, who would have been seventeen years of age when the fictitious dialogue was supposed to have taken place—thus, a young man of marriageable age.]

. . . Let a man take a wife for two reasons: the first is to perpetuate himself with children, and the second is to have a steady and constant companion for his entire life. Therefore, you must seek to have a woman capable of bearing children and pleasing enough to serve as your perpetual companion.

It is said that in taking a wife, you must look for beauty, relatives, and wealth. . . . I think beauty in a woman may be judged not only in her charms and in the gentleness of her face but even more in her person, which should be shaped and adapted for carrying and giving birth to a great number of beautiful children. And among the beauties of a woman, above all, are her good manners; for while an unkempt, wasteful, greasy, and drunken woman may have a beautiful body, who would call her a beautiful wife? And the most important manners worthy of praise in a woman are modesty and purity. Thus Marius, that most illustrious Roman citizen, in his first speech to the Roman people declared: "Purity in women and work from men." And it certainly seems so to me as well. There is nothing more repulsive than an untidy, filthy woman. Who is so stupid as not to realize that a woman who does not take pleasure in appearing clean and neat not only in her clothes and her body but in her every act and word is not to be considered well mannered? And who cannot see that a badly mannered woman is only very rarely a virtuous one? How damaging women without virtue are to families will be considered and discussed elsewhere, but I would not know which would be the greatest misfortune for families—complete sterility or a woman without virtue. Thus, in a bride one must first look for beauty of spirit—that is, good behavior and virtue—and then one should seek in her physical appearance loveliness, grace, and charm, but also try to find someone well suited for bearing children with the kind of body that guarantees healthy and tall ones. There is an ancient proverb which says: "When you want children, pick your wife accordingly," and every virtue of hers will show forth greater in her beautiful children. This saying is very common among the poets: "A beautiful character comes from a beautiful body." Doctors urge that a wife not be too thin nor too overloaded with fat, for the latter are full of chills, menstrual occlusions, and are slow to conceive. They also prefer that a woman be by nature happy, fresh, and lively in her blood and in her whole being. Nor are they displeased if the girl is dark-complexioned. However, they do not accept girls who are too black, nor do they like small ones or praise those who are too large or too slender. They consider it most useful for the woman to have well-balanced and well-developed limbs if she is to give birth to many children. And they always prefer a young woman, for reasons which need not be explained here, but especially because they have a more adaptable character. Young girls are pure because of their age, they are not malicious by habit, and they are by nature bashful and free of all maliciousness; they are well disposed to learning quickly and they follow the habits and wishes of their husbands without stubbornness. These things, therefore, are what follows from our discussion and are the concerns that should be most usefully kept in mind when selecting the proper, prolific wife. To these considerations should be added that it would be an excellent sign if the young girl has a great number of brothers, since you can hope that when she is yours, she will be like her mother in bearing male children.

Now we have spoken about beauty. The wife's lineage is the next problem, and here we shall consider what things are proper and to be preferred. I believe that in choosing relatives, the first thing to do is to examine the lives and the customs of all one's prospective relatives. Many marriages have brought about the utter ruin of numerous families, according to what we hear or read about every day, because they involved relatives who were quarrelsome, picky, arrogant, and full of ill will. . . . Therefore, to sum up this issue in a few words, since I wish to be brief on this question, it is important to acquire new relatives who are not of vulgar birth, who can boast a patrimony which is not insignificant, who exercise a profession which is not vile, and who are modest and respectable in all their affairs, people who are not too superior to you, so that their greatness will not eclipse your own honor and dignity, or disturb your peace and tranquillity and that of your family, and also because if one of your new relatives fail, you will be able to give him your support and sustain him without too much difficulty and without sweating too much under the weight of the burden you are carrying. Nor would I wish for these same new relatives to be inferior to you, for while the first condition of superiority places you in a state of servitude to them, this second condition of inferiority will cause you expense. Let them be, therefore, your equals, and as we have already said, modest and respectable. Next is the problem of the dowry, which, it seems to me, should be not excessive but certain and prompt rather than enormous, doubtful, and remote. . . .

[With some reluctance and obvious embarrassment, the writer then turns to the actual engendering of children, the primary function of a proper bourgeois union.]

But let us consider our first topic of discussion. I have noted what kind of woman is most suitable for bearing children; now I believe we should next treat the question of how best children may be conceived, a subject which might well be avoided on account of certain considerations of modesty. But in this nevertheless vital matter, I shall be so circumspect and so very brief that anyone expecting to find this matter dealt with at this point will not be disappointed. Husbands should not couple with their wives in an agitated state of mind or when they are perturbed by fears or other like preoccupations, for such emotions as these that afflict the spirit deaden and weaken our vital spirits, and the other passions which inflame the spirit disturb and effect those vital seeds which then must produce the human image. Thus, one may observe how a father who is impetuous and strong and knowledgeable has engendered a son who is timid, weak, and foolish, on the one hand, while another father who is moderate and reasonable has given birth to a son who is crazy and brutish. In addition, it is necessary not to couple if the body and all its members are not well disposed and healthy. Doctors declare, with good reason, and offer examples to prove that if fathers and mothers are either sluggish, deadened by debauchery, or weakened by bad blood, as well as made feeble or devoid of vigor and pulse, it is reasonable to expect that their children, as is often the case, will turn out leprous, epileptic, disgusting, and misshapen or lacking in their bodily parts—all qualities which are not desirable in one's children. As a result, doctors recommend that such couplings be undertaken in a sober, tranquil, and as happy a state of mind as possible, and they believe that the best hour of the night occurs right after the first digestion is completed, at which time you are neither empty nor filled with bad foods but, rather, well along in your digestion and refreshed with sleep. They also recommend during this coupling to make yourself intensely desired by the woman. They have yet many other recommendations, such as when it is excessively hot or when seeds and roots are hidden in the soil and frozen there; then one must wait for more temperate weather. But it would take too long a time to recite all their prescriptions, and perhaps I should keep better in mind to whom I am speaking. You are only young men, after all; perhaps this argument, which can be excused by the fact that I was drawn into it accidentally by the course of my discussion, is something I should examine explicitly. But even if I am to be blamed and should excuse myself for it, I am delighted that my error may nevertheless have served some useful purpose, and because of this, I consider what I have done less offensive than if I had delved more deeply into the question. . . .

BALDESAR CASTIGLIONE

A Disputation on the Dignity of Women

The Book of the Courtier *by Baldesar Castiglione ranks as one of the supreme expressions of the Italian Renaissance. First published in 1528 in the full glory of the High Renaissance, the book encapsulates more than a century of humanistic discussions concerning the ways to perfect human nature. Though formally confined to one particular way of life—the life of courtiers at princely courts—the dialogue in fact is a virtual compendium of themes central to Italian Renaissance thought: themes such as virtue and good manners, spiritual and sensual love, religion, the nature of beauty, true nobility, the correct use of language, the active and contemplative lives, the status of women, the ideal form of the polity, and the respective truths of arms, letters, and the arts. These subjects are laid out in the form of imaginary dialogues among the most distinguished Italian noblemen and noblewomen of the day, gathered together at the famous Renaissance court in the Duchy of Urbino.*

The author of the dialogues, Baldesar Castiglione (1478–1529), was a humanist, soldier, and diplomat who spent most of his career in the service of the dukes of Urbino. In 1524 he was appointed papal nuncio to Spain and died in Toledo of the plague in 1529. The Courtier *is his only important work, but it is one of surpassing literary artistry that represents the Urbino of his youth as a model of Renaissance ideals. In the present selection from Book III, Castiglione's (male) interlocutors debate whether women are the equals of men, using philosophical arguments and historical examples.*

'I am quite surprised,' said signor Gaspare with a laugh, 'that since you endow women with letters, continence, magnanimity and temperance, you do not want them to govern cities as well, and to make laws and lead armies, while the men stay at home to cook and spin.'

The Magnifico replied, also laughing: 'Perhaps that would not be so bad, either.'

Then he added: 'Do you not know that Plato, who was certainly no great friend of women, put them in charge of the city and gave all the military duties to the men? Don't you think that we might find many women just as capable of governing cities and armies as men? But I have not imposed these duties on them, since I am fashioning a Court lady and not a queen. I'm fully aware that you would like by implication to repeat the slander that signor Ottaviano made against women yesterday, namely, that they are most imperfect creatures, incapable of any virtuous act, worth very little and quite without dignity compared with men. But truly both you and he would be very much in error if you really thought this.'

Then signor Gaspare said: 'I don't want to repeat things that have been said already; but you are trying hard to make me say something that would hurt the feelings of these ladies, in order to make them my enemies, just as you are seeking to win their favour by deceitful flattery. However, they are so much more sensible than other women that they love the truth, even if it is not all that much to their credit, more than false praises; nor are they aggrieved if anyone maintains that men are of greater dignity, and they will admit that you have made some fantastic claims and attributed to the Court lady ridiculous and impossible qualities and so many virtues that Socrates and Cato and all the philosophers in the world are as nothing in comparison. And to tell the truth I wonder that you haven't been ashamed to go to such exaggerated lengths. For it should have been quite enough for you to make this lady beautiful, discreet, pure and affable, and able to entertain in an innocent manner with dancing, music, games, laughter, witticisms and the other things that are in daily evidence at Court. But to wish to give her an understanding of everything in the world and to attribute to her qualities that have rarely been seen in men, even throughout the centuries, is something one can neither tolerate nor bear listening to. That women are imperfect creatures and therefore of less dignity than men and incapable of practising the virtues practised by men, I would certainly not claim now, for the worthiness of these ladies here would be enough to give me the lie; however, I do say that very learned men have written that since Nature always plans and aims at absolute perfection she would, if possible, constantly being forth men; and when a woman is born this is a mistake or defect, and contrary to Nature's wishes. This is also the case when someone is born blind, or lame, or with some other defect, as again with trees, when so many fruits fail to ripen. Nevertheless, since the blame for the defects of women must be attributed to Nature, who has made them what they are, we ought not to despise them or to fail to give them the respect which is their due. But to esteem them to be more than they are seems to me to be manifestly wrong.'

The Magnifico Giuliano waited for signor Gaspare to continue, but seeing that he remained silent he remarked:

'It appears to me that you have advanced a very feeble argument for the imperfection of women. And, although this is not perhaps the right time to go into subtleties, my answer, based both on a reliable authority and on the simple truth, is that the substance of anything whatsoever cannot receive of itself either more or less; thus just as one stone cannot, as far as its essence is concerned, be more perfectly stone than another stone, nor one piece of wood more perfectly wood than another piece, so one man cannot be more perfectly man than another; and so, as far as their formal substance is concerned, the male cannot be more perfect than the female, since both the one and the other are included under the species man, and they differ in their accidents and not their essence. You may then say that man is more perfect than woman if not as regards essence then at least as regards accidents; and to this I reply that these accidents must be the properties either of the body or of the mind. Now if you mean the body, because man is more robust, more quick and agile, and more able to endure toil, I say that this is an argument of very little validity since among men themselves those who possess these qualities more than others are not more highly regarded on that account; and even in warfare, when for the most part the work to be done demands exertion and strength, the strongest are not the most highly esteemed. If you mean the mind, I say that everything men can understand, women can too; and where a man's intellect can penetrate, so along with it can a woman's.'

After pausing for a moment, the Magnifico then added with a laugh:

'Do you not know that this proposition is held in philosophy: namely, that those who are weak in body are able in mind? So there can be no doubt that being weaker in body women are abler in mind and more capable of speculative thought than men.'

Then he continued: 'But apart from this, since you have said that I should argue from their acts as to the perfection of the one and the other, I say that if you will consider the operations of Nature, you will find that she produces women the way they are not by chance but adapted to the necessary end; for although she makes them gentle in body and placid in spirit, and with many other qualities opposite to those of men, yet the attributes of the one and the other tend towards the same beneficial end. For just as their gentle frailty makes women less courageous, so it makes them more cautious; and thus the mother nourishes her children, whereas the father instructs them and with his strength wins outside the home what his wife, no less commendably, conserves with diligence and care. Therefore if you study ancient and modern history (although men have always been very sparing in their praises of women) you will find that women as well as men have constantly given proof of their worth; and also that there have been some women who have waged wars and won glorious victories, governed kingdoms with the greatest prudence and justice, and done all that men have done. As for learning, cannot you recall reading of many women who knew philosophy, of others who have been consummate poets, others who prosecuted, accused and defended before judges with great eloquence? It would take too long to talk of the work they have done with their hands, nor is there any need for me to provide examples of it. So if in essential substance men are no more perfect than women, neither are they as regards accidents; and apart from theory this is quite clear in practice. And so I cannot see how you define this perfection of theirs.

'Now you said that Nature's intention is always to produce the most perfect things, and therefore she would if possible always produce men, and that women are the result of some mistake or defect rather than of intention. But I can only say that I deny this completely. You cannot possibly argue that Nature does not intend to produce the women without whom the human race cannot be preserved, which is something that Nature desires above everything else. For by means of the union of male and female, she produces children, who then return the benefits received in childhood by supporting their parents when they are old; then they renew them when they themselves have children, from whom they expect to receive in their old age what they bestowed on their own parents when they were young. In this way Nature, as if moving in a circle, fills out eternity and confers immortality on mortals. And since woman is as necessary to this process as man, I do not see how it can be that one is more the fruit of mere chance than the other. It is certainly true that Nature always intends to produce the most perfect things, and therefore always intends to produce the species man, though not male rather than female; and indeed, if Nature always produced males this would be imperfection: for just as there results from body and soul a composite nobler than its parts, namely, man himself, so from the union of male and female there results a composite that preserves the human species, and without which its parts would perish. Thus male and female always go naturally together, and one cannot exist without the other. So by very

21

definition we cannot call anything male unless it has its female counterpart, or anything female if it has no male counterpart. And since one sex alone shows imperfection, the ancient theologians attribute both sexes to God. For this reason, Orpheus said that Jove was both male and female; and we read in Holy Scripture that God made male and female in His own likeness; and very often when the poets speak of the gods they confuse the sex.'

Then signor Gaspare said: 'I do not wish us to go into such subtleties because these ladies would not understand them; and though I were to refute you with excellent arguments, they would still think that I was wrong, or pretend to at least; and they would at once give a verdict in their own favour. However, since we have made a beginning, I shall say only that, as you know, it is the opinion of very learned men that man is as the form and woman as the matter, and therefore just as form is more perfect than matter, and indeed it gives it its being, so man is far more perfect than woman. And I recall having once heard that a great philosopher in certain of his *Problems* asks: Why is it that a woman always naturally loves the man to whom she first gave herself in love? And on the contrary, why is it that a man detests the woman who first coupled with him in that way? And in giving his explanation he affirms that this is because in the sexual act the woman is perfected by the man, whereas the man is made imperfect, and that everyone naturally loves what makes him perfect and detests what makes him imperfect. Moreover, another convincing argument for the perfection of man and the imperfection of woman is that without exception every woman wants to be a man, by reason of a certain instinct that teaches her to desire her own perfection.'

The Magnifico Giuliano at once replied:

'The poor creatures do not wish to become men in order to make themselves more perfect but to gain their freedom and shake off the tyranny that men have imposed on them by their one-sided authority. Besides, the analogy you give of matter and form is not always applicable; for woman is not perfected by man in the way that matter is perfected by form. To be sure, matter receives its being from form, and cannot exist without it; and indeed the more material a form is, the more imperfect it is, and it is most perfect when separated from matter. On the other hand, woman does not receive her being from man but rather perfects him just as she is perfected by him, and thus both join together for the purpose of procreation which neither can ensure alone. Moreover, I shall attribute woman's enduring love for the man with whom she has first been, and man's detestation for the first woman he possesses, not to what is alleged by your philosopher in his *Problems* but to the resolution and constancy of women and the inconstancy of men. And for this, there are natural reasons: for because of its hot nature, the male sex possesses the qualities of lightness, movement and inconstancy, whereas from its coldness, the female sex derives its steadfast gravity and calm and is therefore more susceptible.'

At this point, signora Emilia turned to the Magnifico to say:
'In heaven's name, leave all this business of matter and form and male and female for once, and speak in a way that you can be understood. We heard and understood quite well all the evil said about us by signor Ottaviano and signor Gaspare, but now we can't at all understand your way of defending us. So it seems to me that what you are saying is beside the point and merely leaves in everyone's mind the bad impression of us given by these enemies of ours.'
'Do not call us that,' said signor Gaspare, 'for your real enemy is the Magnifico who, by praising women falsely, suggests they cannot be praised honestly.'
Then the Magnifico Giuliano continued: 'Do not doubt, madam, that an answer will be found for everything. But I don't want to abuse men as gratuitously as they have abused women; and if there were anyone here who happened to write these discussions down, I should not wish it to be thought later on, in some place where the concepts of matter and form might be understood, that the arguments and criticisms of signor Gaspare had not been refuted.'
'I don't see,' said Gaspare, 'how on this point you can deny that man's natural qualities make him more perfect than woman, since women are cold in temperament and men are hot. For warmth is far nobler and more perfect than cold, since it is active and productive; and, as you know, the heavens shed warmth on the earth rather than coldness, which plays no part in the work of Nature. And so I believe that the coldness of women is the reason why they are cowardly and timid.'

'So you still want to pursue these sophistries,' replied the Magnifico Giuliano, 'though I warn you that you get the worst of it every time. Just listen to this, and you'll understand why. I concede that in itself warmth is more perfect than cold; but this is not therefore the case with things that are mixed and composite, since if it were so the warmer any particular substance was the more perfect it would be, whereas in fact temperate bodies are the most perfect. Let me inform you also that women are cold in temperament only in comparison with men. In themselves, because of their excessive warmth, men are far from temperate; but in themselves women are temperate, or at least more nearly temperate than men, since they possess, in proportion to their natural warmth, a degree of moisture which in men, because of their excessive aridity, soon evaporates without trace. The coldness which women possess also counters and moderates their natural warmth, and brings it far nearer to a temperate condition; whereas in men excessive warmth soon brings their natural heat to the highest point where for lack of sustenance it dies away. And thus since men dry out more than women in the act of procreation they generally do not live so long; and therefore we can attribute another perfection to women, namely, that enjoying longer life than men they fulfil far better than men the intention of Nature. As for the warmth that is shed on us from the heavens, I have nothing to say, since it has only its name in common with what we are talking about and preserving as it does all things beneath the orb of the moon, both warm and cold, it cannot be opposed to coldness. But the timidity of women, though it betrays a degree of imperfection, has a noble origin in the subtlety and readiness of their senses which convey images very speedily to the mind, because of which they are easily moved by external things. Very often you will find men who have no fear of death or of anything else and yet cannot be called courageous, since they fail to recognize danger and rush headlong without another thought along the path they have chosen. This is the result of a certain obtuse insensitivity; and a fool cannot be called brave. Indeed, true greatness of soul springs from a deliberate choice and free resolve to act in a certain way and to set honour and duty above every possible risk, and from being so stout-hearted even in the face of death, that one's faculties do not fail or falter but perform their functions in speech and thought as if they were completely untroubled. We have seen and heard of great men of this sort, and also of many women, both in recent centuries and in the ancient world, who no less than men have shown greatness of spirit and have performed deeds worthy of infinite praise.'

Then Frisio said: 'These deeds had their beginning when the first woman, through her transgression, led a man to sin against God and left to the human race a heritage of death, travails and sorrows and all the miseries and calamities suffered in the world today.'

The Magnifico retorted: 'If you want to preach a sermon, don't you know that the transgression you mentioned was repaired by a woman who won for us so much more than the other had lost that the fault for which her merits atoned is called a most happy one? But I do not wish to tell you now how inferior are all other human creatures to Our Lady, since this would be to confuse divine things with these foolish discussions of ours; nor do I wish to recount how many women with such marvellous constancy have let themselves be cruelly slain by tyrants for the sake of Christ, or to speak of those who in learned disputation have confounded so many idolators. And if you should say to me that all this was supernatural and owing to the grace of the Holy Spirit, I say that no virtue is more praiseworthy than that which is approved by the testimony of God. And you can discover many more women besides, who are less talked about, especially if you read St Jerome, who celebrated certain women of his time with such marvellous praise that it would suffice for the holiest of men.

'Then think how many other women there have been who are never mentioned at all, because the poor creatures are shut away and do not have the ostentatious pride to seek a reputation for sanctity in the world, as do so many damned hypocrites among the men of today, who forget, or rather despise, the teaching of Christ which lays down that when a man fasts he should anoint his face so that he should not seem to be fasting and which commands that prayers, alms and other good works be performed not on the public square or in the synagogue but in private, so that the left hand may not know what the right is doing. Thus they affirm that the best thing in the world is to set a good example. And so, with bowed heads and downcast eyes, letting it be known that they do not wish to speak with women or eat anything except raw herbs, sweating under their torn habits, they go about deceiving the simple; and they do not hesitate to forge wills, to stir up mortal enmities between husband and wife, and sometimes, to make use of poison, employing sorceries, incantations and every sort of villainy; and then they cite, out of their own head, a certain authority which says: "*Si non caste, tamen caute*";[1] and by this, they suppose, they can cure every great evil and plausibly convince those who are not cautious that all sins, no matter how grave, are readily pardoned by God, provided they are committed in private and there is no bad example. Thus, under a veil of holiness and in this secret manner, they often devote all their thoughts to corrupting the pure mind of some woman; to sowing hatred between brothers; to controlling governments; to exalting one man at another's expense; to having men beheaded, imprisoned and proscribed; to ministering to the crimes and, as it were, serving as the repositories of the thefts many rulers commit. Others shamelessly delight in appearing dainty and gay, with their bristles well scraped, and wearing fine clothes; and as they pass by they lift their habit to display their neat hose, and bow here and there to show what fine figures of men they are. Others, even when celebrating mass, make use of certain gestures and looks which they think make them graceful and admired. Evil and wicked men, utter strangers not only to religion but to any good way of life! And when they are taken to task for their dissolute conduct, they make light of it all and mock the one who reproves them and they more or less exult in their vices.'

At this signora Emilia remarked: 'You so enjoy talking ill of friars that you have wandered right away from the subject. But you yourself do ill to murmur against men of religion, and you are burdening your conscience for nothing. For if there were not those who pray to God on our behalf, we would suffer even worse scourges than we do.'

Then the Magnifico Giuliano smiled and said:

'How did you guess so easily, madam, that I was talking about friars, since I never mentioned them by name? But truly I should not be accused of murmuring, for I am speaking quite plainly and openly; and I am referring not to the good ones but to the evil and guilty, and even then I haven't said a thousandth part of what I know.'

'Well, say no more about friars,' retorted signora Emilia, 'because I for one consider it a grave sin to listen to you, and so as not to hear I shall go elsewhere.'

'I am quite content to say no more on the subject,' the Magnifico Giuliano continued. 'But, to get to the praises of women, I maintain that for every admirable man signor Gaspare finds me, I will discover a wife, a daughter or a sister of equal worth and sometimes better; moreover, many women have been the cause of countless benefits to their men, and have often corrected their errors. Now, as we have demonstrated, women are naturally capable of the same virtues as men, and we have often seen the fruits of this. So I do not know why, when I concede simply what they can have, often have had and still have, I should be supposed to be talking about the impossible, as signor Gaspare has alleged. For there have always been in the world and there still are women resembling the Court lady I have fashioned as closely as some men resemble the man fashioned by these gentlemen.'

Then signor Gaspare said: 'I think very little of arguments that run counter to experience. And surely if I were to ask you who were these great women as worthy of praise as the men to whom they were wives, sisters or daughters, or that have been the cause of some good, or have set men's errors to rights, I think you would be rather at a loss.'

'Indeed,' answered the Magnifico Giuliano, 'I would only be at a loss because of the great numbers involved. And if the time were available, I would cite for my purpose the story of Octavia, wife of Mark Antony and sister of Augustus; of Portia, Cato's daughter and wife of Brutus; of Caia Caecilia, wife of Tarquinius Priscus; of Cornelia, Scipio's daughter, and of countless other most remarkable women. . . .

. . .

'Really,' said the Magnifico, 'these arguments of yours are very remarkable, and I do not know why you don't put them down in writing. But tell me why it is not made the rule that men may be condemned for a dissolute way of life as much as women, seeing that if they are naturally of higher worth and virtue, they can all the more easily practise the virtue of continence; and then doubts about one's children would be neither greater nor less. For even if women were unchaste, if the men stayed pure and did not give in to the unchastity of women, they could not produce offspring all on their own. But if you wish to be truthful, you must also recognize that we have granted ourselves the licence by which we want the same sins that are trivial and sometimes even praiseworthy when committed by men to be so damnable in women that they cannot be punished enough, save by a shameful death or at least everlasting infamy. Therefore since this opinion is so widespread, I think it only proper to punish harshly those who defame women with their lies; and I consider that every noble knight is bound when it is necessary to take up arms in defence of the truth, and especially when he hears a woman falsely accused of being unchaste.'

'And I,' answered signor Gaspare with a smile, 'not only affirm that what you say is indeed the duty of every noble knight but also consider it chivalrous and gentlemanly to conceal the fault which a woman may have committed either through mischance or excessive love; and so you can see that when it is right and proper I am a greater champion of women than you. Indeed, I do not deny that men have arrogated to themselves a certain liberty; and this because they know that it is commonly accepted that a dissolute life does not bring them the infamous reputation that it does to women, who, because of the frailty of their sex, are far more influenced by their passions than men. And if they do sometimes refrain from satisfying their desires, they do so out of shame and not because they lack a very ready will to do so. And so men have instilled in them the fear of infamy as a bridle to preserve their chastity almost by force, and without which, to be honest, they would be little esteemed; for women bring no benefit to the world, save the bearing of children. This is not, however, the case with men, who govern cities and command armies and perform so many other important things: all of which, since you will have it so, I will not dispute women know how to do, but which, quite simply, they do not do. And when men have chanced to be models of continence, then they have surpassed women in this virtue just as in the others, though you do not agree. . . .

. . .

After Cesare had fallen silent, signor Gaspare started to reply, but he was interrupted by signor Ottaviano, who said with a smile:

'For God's sake, grant him the victory, for I know you will gain little from this; indeed, I think you will make not only all these ladies your enemies but most of the men as well.'

Signor Gaspare laughed and said: 'On the contrary, the women have every reason to thank me; because if I had not contradicted the Magnifico and Cesare, we would not have heard all that they had to say in their praise.'

'What the Maginifico and I had to say in praise of women,' remarked Cesare, 'and much else besides, was very well known: so it was all superfluous. Who does not realize that without women we can get no pleasure or satisfaction out of life, which but for them would lack charm and be more uncouth and savage than that of wild beasts? Who does not realize that it is only women who rid our hearts of all vile and base thoughts, anxieties, miseries and the wretched ill humours that often accompany them? And if we really consider the truth, we shall also recognize that in our understanding of great issues far from distracting us they awaken our minds, and in warfare they make men fearless and bold beyond measure. Certainly, once the flame of love is burning in a man's heart, cowardice can never possess it. For a lover always wishes to make himself as lovable as possible, and he always fears lest some disgrace befall him which can make him less esteemed by the woman whose esteem he craves; neither does he flinch from risking his life a thousand times a day in order to deserve her love. Indeed, if anyone were to recruit an army of lovers, to fight before the eyes of the women they love, it would conquer the entire world, unless, of course, it were opposed by an army of the same sort. And you may rest assured that Troy held out for ten years against the Greeks for no other reason than that a few lovers, before they went to fight, armed themselves in the presence of their women; and often the women helped them put on their armour, and when they left spoke some words that inflamed them and made them more than men. Then, in battle, they were aware that their women were watching them from the walls and the towers; and so they believed that they would win praise from them for every bold stroke and every proof of courage, and this to them was the greatest reward possible. There are many who consider that women were chiefly responsible for the victory of King Ferdinand and Queen Isabella of Spain against the King of Granada; for on most occasions when the Spanish army marched to confront the enemy, it was accompanied by Queen Isabella and all her maids of honour, and in its ranks there were many noble knights who were in love, and who, before they came in sight of the enemy, would always go along conversing with their ladies; and then each one would take his leave and, before his lady's eyes, go to challenge the enemy with the proud courage that sprang from love and the ambition to let the women see that they were served by men of valour. Thus very often a handful of Spanish noblemen proved able to put to flight and kill a great host of Moors, thanks to their gracious and much-loved women. So I do not understand, signor Gaspare, what perverse judgement has persuaded you to censure women.

'Do you not see that all those charming recreations which please everyone so much can be attributed solely to the influence of women? Who is there who studies how to dance gracefully for any other reason but to give pleasure to the ladies? Who studies to compose verses, at least in the vernacular, if not to express the emotions aroused by women? Consider how many noble poems we would be deprived of, both Latin and Greek, if our poets had thought little of women. Leaving all the others aside, would it not be a grievous loss if Francesco Petrarch, who wrote about his loves in this language of ours in such an inspired way, had turned his mind only to exercises in Latin, which he would have done if love for madonna Laura had not sometimes distracted him? I will not name the distinguished men of talent alive today (and some of them present here) who create something noble every day, and yet find their subject-matter solely in the beauty and virtue of women. Notice how Solomon, when he wanted to write mystically of very exalted and divine things, in order to veil them gracefully imagines an ardent and amorous dialogue between a lover and his lady, since he thought it was impossible to find in this world any more suitable and exact analogy for divine things than a man's love for a woman; and in this way he wished to give us some inkling of the divine reality that through learning and through grace he had come to know better than others. So it was unnecessary, signor Gaspare, to dispute about this, or at least to do so at such length; but in denying the truth you have prevented us hearing a thousand other beautiful and important things concerning the perfection of the Court lady.'

Signor Gaspare replied: 'I don't believe there is anything more to say to you. But if you think that the Magnifico has not sufficiently adorned her with good qualities, the fault has not been his but with the one who decided that there would not be more virtues in the world; for he has given her all there are.'

At this, the Duchess laughed and said: 'But now you will see that the Magnifico will find some more all the same.'

The Magnifico replied: 'Truly, madam, I think that I have said enough, and for myself I am well content with this lady of mine; and if these gentlemen do not want her the way she is made, they may leave her to me.'

EXPLANATORY NOTE

1. This means roughly: 'If you can't be chaste be careful.'

BALDESAR CASTIGLIONE

True Nobility

———

The Book of the Courtier *by Baldesar Castiglione ranks as one of the supreme expressions of the Italian Renaissance. First published in 1528 in the full glory of the High Renaissance, the book encapsulates more than a century of humanistic discussions concerning the ways to perfect human nature. Though formally confined to one particular way of life—the life of courtiers at princely courts—the dialogue in fact is a virtual compendium of themes central to Italian Renaissance thought: themes such as virtue and good manners, spiritual and sensual love, religion, the nature of beauty, true nobility, the correct use of language, the active and contemplative lives, the status of women, the ideal form of the polity, and the respective truths of arms, letters, and the arts. These subjects are laid out in the form of imaginary dialogues among the most distinguished Italian noblemen and noblewomen of the day, gathered together at the famous Renaissance court in the Duchy of Urbino.*

The author of the dialogues, Baldesar Castiglione (1478–1529), was a humanist, soldier, and diplomat who spent most of his career in the service of the dukes of Urbino. In 1524 he was appointed papal nuncio to Spain and died in Toledo of the plague in 1529. The Courtier *is his only important work, but it is one of surpassing literary artistry that represents the Urbino of his youth as a model of Renaissance ideals. In this selection from Book I, Castiglione presented two typical views about the nature of true nobility.*

———

The Count then continued: 'So, for myself, I would have our courtier of noble birth and good family, since it matters far less to a common man if he fails to perform virtuously and well than to a nobleman. For if a gentleman strays from the path of his forbears, he dishonours his family name and not only fails to achieve anything but loses what has already been achieved. Noble birth is like a bright lamp that makes clear and visible both good deeds and bad, and inspires and incites to high performance as much as fear of dishonour or hope of praise; and since their deeds do not possess such noble brilliance, ordinary people lack both this stimulus and the fear of dishonour; nor do they believe that they are bound to surpass what was achieved by their forbears. Whereas to people of noble birth it seems reprehensible not to attain at least the standard set them by their ancestors. Thus as a general rule, both in arms and in other worthy activities, those who are most distinguished are of noble birth, because Nature has implanted in everything a hidden seed which has a certain way of influencing and passing on its own essential characteristics to all that grows from it, making it similar to itself. We see this not only in breeds of horses and other animals but also in trees, whose off-shoots nearly always resemble the trunk; and if they sometimes degenerate, the fault lies with the man who tends them. So it happens with men, who, if they are well tended and properly brought up, nearly always resemble those from whom they spring, and are often even better; but if they have no one to give them proper attention, they grow wild and never reach maturity. It is true that, through the favour of the stars or of Nature, certain people come into the world endowed with such gifts that they seem not to have been born but to have been formed by some god with his own hands and blessed with every possible advantage of mind and body. Similarly, there are many to be found so uncouth and absurd that it can be believed simply that Nature was motivated by spite or mockery in bringing them into the world at all. Just as even with unceasing diligence and careful training the latter cannot usually be made to bear fruit, so with only the slightest effort the former reach the summit of excellence. And to give you an example, look at Don Ippolito d'Este, Cardinal of Ferrara, whose fortunate birth has influenced his person, his appearance, his words and all his actions. Because of this favour, despite his youth, even among the most venerable cardinals he carries such weighty authority that he seems more suited to teach than to be taught. Similarly, when conversing with men and women of every sort, when playing or laughing or joking, he has such charming ways and such a gracious manner that anyone who speaks to, or merely sets eyes on the Cardinal feels a lasting affection for him. However, to return to the subject, I say that between such supreme grace and such absurd folly can be found a middle way, and that those who are not perfectly endowed by Nature can, through care and effort, polish and to a great extent correct their natural defects. So in addition to noble birth, I would have the courtier favoured in this respect, too, and receive from Nature not only talent and beauty of countenance and person but also that certain air and grace that makes him immediately pleasing and attractive to all who meet him; and this grace should be an adornment informing and accompanying all his actions, so that he appears clearly worthy of the companionship and favour of the great.'

Then, refusing to wait any longer, signor Gaspare Pallavicino remarked:
'So that our game may proceed as it is meant to, and to show that we are not forgetting our privilege of contradicting, let me say that I do not believe that nobility of birth is necessary for the courtier. And if I thought I was saying something new to us, I would cite many people who, though of the most noble blood, have been wicked in the extreme, and, on the other hand, many of humble birth who, through their virtues, have won glory for their descendants. And if what you have just said is true, namely, that concealed in everything is the influence of its first seed, we should all be of the same character, since we all had the same beginning; nor would anyone be more noble than another. In fact, I hold that the various gradations of elevation and lowliness that exist among us have many other causes. The first and foremost is Fortune, who rules everything that happens in this world, and often appears to amuse herself by exalting whomever she pleases, regardless of merit, or hurling down those worthiest of being raised up. I fully concur with what you said about the happiness of those endowed at birth with all the perfections of mind and body; but this is seen among those of humble origins as well as those of noble birth, since Nature has no regard for these fine distinctions. On the contrary, as I have said, the finest gifts of Nature are often found in persons of very humble family. Therefore, since this nobility of birth is acquired neither through talent nor through force or skill, and is a matter for congratulating one's ancestors rather than oneself, it seems very odd to insist that, if the courtier's parents are of low birth, all his good qualities are spoilt and the other qualities you have mentioned are insufficient to bring him to the height of perfection: these being talent, good looks and disposition, and the grace which makes a person always pleasing at first sight.'

Count Lodovico answered: 'I do not deny that the same virtues can exist in men of low birth as in those of noble family. However, not to repeat what we have said already, let me give one more reason among many for praising nobility of birth, which, since it stands to reason that good should beget good, everyone always respects; and it is that (since we are to create a courtier without any defects, and endowed with every kind of merit) he must be a nobleman if only because of the immediate impression this makes on all concerned. For given two gentlemen of the Court, neither of whom as yet has shown what he is like by his actions, either good or bad, as soon as it is discovered that one of them was well born and the other not, the latter will be respected far less than the former, and only after a great deal of time and effort will he win the good opinion that the other acquires instantly, merely because of his nobility. It is well understood how important these impressions are, for, speaking of ourselves, we have seen men coming to this house who, although very stupid and dull, have been regarded throughout Italy as very great courtiers; and even though they were eventually found out, they still fooled us for a long time and sustained in our minds the opinion of themselves already formed before they arrived, despite the fact that their behaviour was in keeping with their lack of merit. We have seen others, who were regarded with very little favour to begin with, eventually meet with great success. Now there are various reasons for these mistakes, including the obstinacy of princes who, in the hope of achieving a miraculous transformation, sometimes deliberately favour someone who they know does not deserve it. Then again, sometimes they are themselves deceived; but, since princes always have countless imitators, their favour confers considerable fame which in turn influences the rest of us. And if people discover something that seems to contradict the prevailing opinion, they accept that they are mistaken and they always wait for some revelation. This is because it seems that what is universally believed must be based on true and reasonable grounds. Moreover, we are always most anxious to take sides either passionately for or against, as can be seen in public combats or games or any kind of contest, where the onlookers often for no clear reason favour one or other of the participants, desperately anxious that he should win and his opponent lose. Then as regards men's characters, their good or bad reputation, as soon as we hear of it, arouses in us either love or hatred, so that for the most part we judge on the basis of one of these emotions. So you see how important are first impressions, and how hard a man must strive to give a good impression at the beginning if he is ambitious to win the rank and name of a good courtier.

BALDESAR CASTIGLIONE

Serving the Prince with Honor

The Book of the Courtier *by Baldesar Castiglione ranks as one of the supreme expressions of the Italian Renaissance. First published in 1528 in the full glory of the High Renaissance, the book encapsulates more than a century of humanistic discussions concerning the ways to perfect human nature. Though formally confined to one particular way of life—the life of courtiers at princely courts—the dialogue in fact is a virtual compendium of themes central to Italian Renaissance thought: themes such as virtue and good manners, spiritual and sensual love, religion, the nature of beauty, true nobility, the correct use of language, the active and contemplative lives, the status of women, the ideal form of the polity, and the respective truths of arms, letters, and the arts. These subjects are laid out in the form of imaginary dialogues among the most distinguished Italian noblemen and noblewomen of the day, gathered together at the famous Renaissance court in the Duchy of Urbino.*

The author of the dialogues, Baldesar Castiglione (1478–1529), was a humanist, soldier, and diplomat who spent most of his career in the service of the dukes of Urbino. In 1524 he was appointed papal nuncio to Spain and died in Toledo of the plague in 1529. The Courtier *is his only important work, but it is one of surpassing literary artistry that represents the Urbino of his youth as a model of Renaissance ideals. In the present selection from Book II, Castiglione's interlocutors discuss how to faithfully serve a prince without engaging in flattery and losing one's self-respect, as well as the limits of the subject's obligation to his lord.*

'I consider that the dealings the courtier has with his prince are those which he should chiefly endeavour to make agreeable. I know that to talk of a courtier being conversant with his prince in this way implies a certain equality that can hardly exist between a ruler and his servant; but for the time being we shall let this go. Well then, I want the courtier not only to make it clear on all occasions and to all persons that he is of the quality we have already described but also to devote all his thought and strength to loving and almost adoring the prince he serves above all else, devoting all his ambitions, actions and behaviour to pleasing him.'

At this, without waiting further, Pietro da Napoli said:

'We would find plenty of courtiers like this nowadays, for it seems to me that in a few words you have sketched for us a first-class flatterer.'

'You are very much mistaken,' replied Federico. 'For flatterers love neither their prince nor their friends, and I am saying that this is, above all, what I want our courtier to do; and he can obey and further the wishes of the one he serves without adulation, since I am referring to those wishes that are reasonable and right, or that in themselves are neither good nor bad, as, for example, in sport, to devote oneself to one kind of recreation rather than another. And I would have our courtier try to act in this manner, even if it is against his nature, in such a way that whenever his prince sees him he believes that the courtier will have something agreeable to say. And this will be the case if he has the discretion to discern what pleases his prince, and the wit and judgement to know how to act accordingly, and the considered resolve to make himself like what he may instinctively dislike. Prepared in this way, he will never appear before his prince in a bad humour, or in a melancholy mood; nor will he be as taciturn as are so many who seem to bear a grudge against their masters, which is truly odious. He will not speak evil, and least of all of his lords: something that often happens, for in Courts there seems to be a tempest that drives those who are most favoured by their lords and are raised from the humblest condition to the most exalted always to complain and speak ill of them; and this is unseemly not only in their kind but also in those who may be treated badly. Our courtier will avoid foolish arrogance; he will not be the bearer of bad news; he will not be careless in sometimes saying things that may give offence, instead of striving to please; he will not be obstinate and contentious, as are some who seem to enjoy nothing more than being irritating and obnoxious like flies and make a habit of contradicting everyone spitefully without any misgivings; he will not be an idle or lying babbler, nor a stupid flatterer or boaster, but will be modest and reserved, observing always, and especially in public, the reverence and respect which should mark the attitude of a servant towards his master. And he will not behave in the way that so many do, who when they cross the path of a great prince, even if they have spoken to him only once before, go up to him with a certain smiling and friendly countenance, just as if they were going to embrace an equal or do a favour to someone of lower rank. Very rarely, or hardly ever, will he ask his master anything for himself, lest his prince, being reluctant to refuse, concedes it grudgingly, which is far worse. And when he asks for something on behalf of others he will take careful note of the time and place, and will request only what is right and reasonable; and he will present the request in such a way, leaving out the times he knows could be displeasing and cleverly smoothing over the difficulties, that his lord will always grant it or, if he wishes not to, will be able to refuse without worrying about giving offence to the petitioner. For very often when lords have refused to grant a favour to someone who has been seeking it importunately they imagine that the person who has been so insistent must be very anxious to get what he wants and therefore, when he is baulked, must be ill-disposed towards the one who has denied him; and this belief breeds in them a hatred of the person concerned, whom subsequently they can never see without distaste.

'The courtier will never attempt to make his way into the chamber or private quarters of his master uninvited, even though he possesses considerable authority himself; for often, when princes are by themselves, they enjoy the liberty of saying and doing just what they please, and so they do not want to be seen or overheard by anyone in a position to criticize, and this is quite proper. So it seems to me that those people are in error who condemn a ruler for keeping in his rooms persons of little worth except in the matter of knowing how to give good personal service, for I do not see why princes should not be free to relax just as we like to do. But if a courtier who is accustomed to dealing with important matters should find himself privately with his lord, he should then become another person, defer serious things for another time and place, and engage in conversation which will be pleasing and agreeable to his master, in order not to disturb his peace and quiet. However, in this as in everything else he will take care not to annoy his lord; and he should wait for favours to be offered freely rather than seek them, as do only too many who are so grasping that it seems they will die if they are refused, and who, if they happen to fall out of favour or if others are preferred instead, suffer such agonies that they find it impossible to conceal their envy. In this way, they win nothing but ridicule, and often they tempt their lord to bestow his favours indiscriminately, just to spite them. Then if they happen to be favoured out of the ordinary, they are so swept away that they seem almost drunk with joy, hardly know what to do with their hands or their feet, and can scarcely restrain themselves from calling the whole world to come and congratulate them, as if for something they have never experienced before. No, I do not wish our courtier to be like this. I wish him, on the contrary, to enjoy favours, but not to value them so highly as to appear unable to exist without them. And when they are granted to him, he should not let himself appear unaccustomed or alien to the experience, or amazed that such things should happen; nor should he decline them in the way some do, who out of pure ignorance refuse to accept and thereby show the bystanders that they are convinced of their own unworthiness. A man should, moreover, always be a little more humble than his rank requires, not accepting too easily the favours and honours offered him, but declining them modestly while showing that he values them highly, and yet in such a way that he inspires the person offering them to do so with still greater insistence. For the more resistance that is shown in accepting favours, the more the prince who is giving them will think that he is esteemed; and the favour he is granting will seem greater, the more the recipient shows his thanks and appreciation for the honour being done to him. These are the true and tangible favours which enhance the reputation of the one who is seen to be receiving them; for, since they are granted without being asked for, everyone realizes that they are the reward of true merit; and the more so if they are accepted modestly.'

Then Cesare Gonzaga remarked: 'It seems to me that you have plagiarized that passage in the Gospel where it says: "When you are invited to a wedding, go and sit down in the lowliest place, so that, when the one who has invited you comes, he may say: My friend, go higher; and thus you will be honoured in the presence of the other guests."'

Federico laughed and said: 'It would be too great a sacrilege to plagiarize the Gospel; but you are more learned in Holy Scripture than I thought.'

And then he continued: 'You see what great dangers those men sometimes run who rashly begin a conversation in the presence of a great prince without being asked. Often, in order to shame them, the lord will refuse to answer and look the other way; and if he does reply, everyone sees that he does so resentfully. So to receive a favour from one's lord, the best way is to deserve it. Nor when his prince is pleased with someone else, for whatever reason, must a man expect to achieve the same result simply by copying what the other person does; for the same things do not suit everybody alike. Sometimes one finds a man who is by nature so spontaneously witty that whatever he says provokes laughter, and he seems to have been born just for that; and then if someone who is more dignified tries to do the same, even if he is very clever, the result will be so flat and awkward that it will cause embarrassment; and he will be exactly like the ass that wanted to imitate the dog and play with its master. So it is necessary for everyone to know himself and his capabilities, and to accommodate himself accordingly, and decide what things he must imitate and what not.'

'Before you go on any further,' interrupted Vincenzo Calmeta, 'if I heard aright it seems to me that you said earlier that the best way to win favours is by deserving them, and that the courtier should rather wait for them to be offered than seek them presumptuously himself. But I fear that this precept is of little use, and I think that experience clearly teaches us the contrary. For nowadays very few people are favoured by lords, save only the arrogant; and I know that you yourself can testify that some who have found themselves little in favour with their princes have made themselves agreeable to them only through presumption. For myself, I know none who have risen through modesty; and I will even give you time to think about this, because I am confident that you will find very few of them yourself. Thus if you will consider the Court of France, which today is among the noblest of all Christendom, you will find that all those who there enjoy universal favour tend to be arrogant, not only among themselves but even towards the King.'

'Do not say so,' replied Federico. 'On the contrary, the gentlemen of France are very courteous and modest. It is true that they allow themselves a certain liberty as well as an unceremonious familiarity which is peculiar and natural to them and should not, therefore, be called presumption. For in the way they conduct themselves, whereas they laugh at and mock the arrogant, they greatly esteem those they believe to be worthy and modest.'

Calmeta replied: 'Look at the Spaniards, who appear to be the leaders in courtiership, and consider how many are to be found who are not extremely arrogant both with ladies and gentlemen. And they are worse than the French in so far as they first make a show of great modesty; and in this they are very shrewd because, as I said, the rulers of our day all keep their favours for those who behave in that way.'

Then Federico answered: 'I will certainly not allow you, Vincenzo, to slander our present-day rulers in this manner. For there are also many who love modesty, although I do not claim that this in itself is enough to make a man agreeable. However, I maintain that when it is accompanied by genuine valour, then it does great credit to the one who possesses it. And although modesty is silent, praiseworthy deeds speak for themselves and are far more admirable than if they were accompanied by arrogance and rashness. I will not deny that there are to be found many arrogant Spaniards; but I maintain that those who are highly esteemed are, for the most part, extremely modest. Then there are certain others who are so frigid that they go to absurd lengths to avoid the company of others and so unbalanced that they are judged to be either excessively timid or excessively proud. For these I have no praise at all, nor do I wish modesty to be so dry and arid as to degenerate into boorishness. So let the courtier be eloquent when it suits his purpose, and when discussing affairs of state, prudent and wise; and let him be judicious enough to know how to adapt himself to the customs of the people he may be living among. Then in lesser matters let him be entertaining, and in everything sensible. But above all else he should always hold to what is good; he should be neither envious nor slanderous, and he should never seek to gain grace or favour through wicked methods or by dishonest means.'

Calmeta then commented: 'I assure you that all other methods are far more uncertain and protracted than those you condemn. For nowadays, to repeat what I have already said, our rulers love only those who follow such paths.'

'Do not say so,' replied Federico, 'for that would be too plainly to argue that the rulers of our time are all wicked and evil; and this is not so, since we find some good princes among them. But if our courtier happens to find himself in the service of a lord who is wicked and malignant, he should leave as soon as he is aware of this, to avoid experiencing the bitter anguish of all those good men who serve bad masters.'

'We must pray God,' Calmeta replied, 'to grant us good ones, for once we have them we have to put up with them as they are. This is because there are countless considerations that prevent a gentleman from leaving his master once he has entered his service. The misfortune is in his ever having begun to do so, and in this matter courtiers are like caged birds.'

'It seems to me,' said Federico, 'that duty should come before all other considerations. Certainly, the courtier must not abandon his master when he is at war or in serious trouble, for then it could be believed that he did so to promote his own fortunes or because he thought that his chances of gainful advantage had disappeared. But at any other time he has the right and the duty to quit a service which is sure to bring him disgrace among honourable men. For everyone assumes that those who serve good masters are good and those who serve bad masters are bad.'

Then signor Lodovico Pio remarked: 'I should like you to clear up a doubt that exists in my mind: namely, whether a gentleman is obliged to obey the prince he is serving in everything that may be commanded, even if it is dishonourable or shameful.'

'In dishonourable things we are not bound to obey anyone,' answered Federico.

'But then,' went on signor Lodovico, 'if I were to be in the service of a prince who treated me well and was confident that I would do everything possible for him, and he were to command me to go and kill a certain person, or something of the sort, should I refuse?'

'What you must do,' answered Federico, 'is to obey your lord in everything that redounds to his profit and honour, but not as regards things that bring him loss and shame. Therefore, if he were to order you to commit some treacherous deed not only are you not obliged to do it but you are obliged not to do it, both for your own sake and to avoid ministering to your master's shame. It is true that many things which seem good at first sight are evil, and many things which seem evil are good. Thus it is sometimes allowable, in the service of one's masters, to kill not just one man but ten thousand, and to do many other things which on a superficial view would appear evil although they are not.'

Then signor Gaspare Pallavicino replied: 'Well, I beg you then, explain about this a little more, and teach us how to distinguish what is really good from what merely appears to be.'

'Allow me to refuse that,' answered Federico, 'for there would be too much to say. But let everything be decided by your discretion.'

'At least resolve another of my doubts,' said signor Gaspare.

'What is that?' asked Federico.

'It is as follows,' signor Gaspare continued. 'If I have been told precisely what I am to do in some project or affair of importance, what should I decide if during the course of it I become convinced that by departing more or less from his detailed instructions I can achieve a better or more profitable result for the master who gave me my orders? Should I obey his first command to the letter, or should I do what seems to me best?'

'Concerning this,' said Federico, 'I would base my opinion on the example of Manlius Torquatus, who in such circumstances killed his son because he was too dutiful, if I considered him at all praiseworthy which indeed I do not; none the less I would not venture to blame him, against the judgement of so many centuries, for without doubt it is highly dangerous to transgress the commands of one's superiors, and to trust one's own judgement more than that of those whom it is legitimate to obey. For if by chance one then fails in one's purpose, and the enterprise collapses, one is guilty of disobedience as well as failure, and no excuse or pardon is at all possible. On the other hand, if one achieves one's purpose, then one must give the credit to Fortune, and be satisfied with that. Then again, this kind of behaviour encourages people to slight the commands of their superiors; and following the example of one individual (who may have been successful but was perhaps a prudent man, making a considered departure and helped by Fortune) a thousand other ignorant and shallow men will trust themselves to follow their own inclinations in highly important matters and, to demonstrate their wisdom and powers of authority, will deviate from their lords' commands. This is a very heinous offence and often leads to countless other blunders. But in my opinion the person concerned should consider at length and, so to say, weigh in the balance the benefits and advantages accruing to him should he disobey, given that his purpose is achieved. On the other side, he should weigh the losses and the disadvantages that would ensue should it happen that, after he had disobeyed, his plan misfired. And if he realizes that, if he fails, the evil consequences will be greater and more serious than the advantages if he succeeds, he should check himself and obey meticulously the orders he has been given. On the other hand, if the advantages, in the case of success, would be greater than the harm resulting from failure, he can, I believe, reasonably set out to do what his judgement and common sense suggest, and depart a little from the letter of command, following the example of a merchant who will risk a little to gain a great deal, but not risk a great deal merely to gain a little. I would, above all, commend him for studying the nature of the lord whom he serves, and governing his own actions accordingly; for if his master were to be as strict as many rulers are, then if he were a friend of mine I would never advise him to modify his orders in the slightest. Then he would escape what is recorded to have happened to a military engineer of the Athenians to whom Publius Crassus Mucianus, when he was in Asia and intending to besiege a town, sent a request for one of two ships' masts that he had seen in Athens, in order to make a battering-ram, stipulating that he send the larger one. The engineer, being a highly skilled expert, knew that the larger mast was hardly suited for the purpose, and since the smaller was both easier to transport and more fitted for the machine that was to be constructed this was the one he sent to Mucianus. Hearing what had transpired, Mucianus sent for the wretched engineer and, after he had asked why he had disobeyed him, refusing to accept any of his explanations, he had him stripped naked and flogged and scourged with rods until he died; for he considered that rather than obey him the fellow had wanted to give him advice. When dealing with masters as strict as this, one should be on one's guard.

ERASMUS

Humanizing Religious Discipline

Born as an illegitimate child in Rotterdam, Desiderius Erasmus (c. 1466–
1536) eventually became known as the leading humanist of his day.
Although his natural inclination toward peace and conciliation eventually
put him at odds both with the great Protestant controversialist Martin
Luther as well as with more doctrinaire Catholics, his writings had a huge
influence on his contemporaries and continue to be actively studied today.
    At the age of nine Erasmus entered a school in Deventer run by the
Brethren of the Common Life, where he received a sound education in the
classics. After the death of his parents he joined a religious order, the Augustinian Canons of Steyn (1487), a move that he later regretted, finding himself
unsuited to the monastic life; in 1517 he finally obtained a papal dispensation
from his vows and returned officially to lay status. By that time, indeed, he
had left the monastery far behind, having become secretary to the bishop of
Cambrai in 1493 and having received permission to study theology in Paris
in 1495. The intellectual climate in Paris was nearly as distasteful to Erasmus
as that of the monastery—he cared neither for scholastic theology nor for
college food—and he left without a degree after less than four years. Erasmus's subsequent life involved a great deal of travel throughout Europe
where he came to know many of the rulers and intellectual leaders of his day.
In 1499 he traveled to England, where he made friends with Thomas More
and John Colet; in 1506 he went south to Italy, coming in contact with the
humanist circle of Aldus Manitius in the great printing center of Venice; in
1509 he returned to England, where he taught Greek for a time at the University of Cambridge. In 1514 he was back to the Continent, residing in
Louvain, where he had relationships with the university's faculty of theology,
but his application of philology to the Scriptures and reluctance to condemn
Luther bred hostility against him. Erasmus then moved to Basel (1521–29)
and, upon the city's becoming Protestant, to the nearby Catholic town of
Freiburg im Breisgau. He was back in Basel working on the publication of
one of his works when he died on July 12, 1536.
    Erasmus was a figure viewed with suspicion, during his lifetime and
afterward, both by Protestants and Catholics. His longing for a return to
the simplicity of the Gospel and his advocacy of an inner spiritual life, in

"Humanizing Religious Discipline," in Concerning the Eating of Fish, by Desiderius Erasmus, in The Essential Erasmus, translated by John P. Dolan, copyright © 1964 by John
P. Dolan, 305–318.

contrast with excessive dependence on outward rituals, placed him close in spirit to Luther and his followers. At the same time, he never parted ways with the Catholic church, differed with Luther fundamentally concerning the relationship between man and divine grace, and feared the social and political consequences of the Reformation. In particular, he feared (with unusual foresight) that Europe would be torn apart by war and religious controversy and hoped (rather naively) that the mild voice of reason would prevail over polemics. At the same time, Erasmus was viewed as the ideal type of the Christian humanist, one who combined great learning in the classics with sincere piety. Erasmus was a superb stylist and promoter of the classics and the ancient Church Fathers, and was among the first scholars to apply humanist philological methods to the study of the Bible. His critical edition of the New Testament, which included the Greek text and Erasmus's revised translation of the Latin Vulgate, appeared in 1516 and is considered one of his most significant accomplishments.

One of the works that best displays Erasmus's devastating wit was his Colloquies, *first published in 1526. Styled as dialogues, these pieces allowed Erasmus to treat a number of different topics of concern to the Europe of his day. One topic he repeatedly returned to was the religious discipline of the Catholic church, which Erasmus considered rigid and excessive. A typical example is the present selection, taken from the colloquy* Concerning the Eating of Fish, *in which a butcher and a fishmonger discuss dietary regulations such as the prohibition of eating meat on Fridays. In this selection, Erasmus made a distinction between human and divine laws, and inquired to what extent human laws should be obeyed when they are unjust. He mocked the absurdity of placing more emphasis on the observance of ceremonies than on honoring God. Erasmus then discussed the issue of Lenten observances in particular, pointing out that the original purpose of such traditions should always be borne in mind and interpreted in a spirit of Christian charity.*

Butcher. Divine laws are immutable, except those that were given only for a short time, that were used as prefigures or for coercion, that the prophets foretold should terminate, or that the Apostles taught should be omitted. In reference to human laws, sometimes unjust, foolish, and injurious ones are made, and therefore they are either abrogated by the authority of superiors or by the universal neglect of the people. But no such redress exists for divine law. Again, a human law ceases when the causes for its existence cease to exist. For instance, suppose a constitution required all persons yearly to contribute something toward the building of a Church; when the church is built, the requirement of the law ceases. In addition a human law is no law at all, unless it is approved by those who use it.

A divine law cannot be dispensed with or abrogated, although Moses, about to make a law, required the consent of the people. This was not done because it was necessary, however, but rather that it might render the violation of the law more criminal. It is indeed an imprudent thing to break a law to which you gave your approbation during its making. Finally, inasmuch as human laws commonly concern corporal matters and are the schoolmasters of piety, they seem to expire when people arrive at that strength of grace which allows them to stand with no need of any such restraints. They should merely endeavor to avoid giving offense to weak persons, who are conscientiously scrupulous.

For instance, suppose a father enjoins his daughter, who is under age, not to drink wine, so she may be better able to preserve her virginity until she is married. When she comes of age and is delivered to her husband, she is not bound by her father's injunction. There are many laws that are like a medicine, that are altered and give way according to the circumstances, and with the approval of the physicians themselves, who, if they should at all times use the remedies of the ancients, would kill more than they cure.

Fishmonger. You indeed group a great many things together, some of which I like, others I dislike, and some of which I don't understand.

Butcher. If a bishop's law aims manifestly at gain—that is, if he ordered every parish priest each year to purchase, at a gold ducat apiece, the right of absolution in episcopal cases, so that he might extort more money from those in his jurisdiction—do you think it ought to be obeyed?

Fishmonger. Yes, I think it should; but at the same time it should be exclaimed against as an unjust law, always avoiding sedition. How come you turn catechizer now, Butcher! Everyone should stick to his own trade.

Butcher. We are often perplexed by these questions in discussion at the table and sometimes the contest proceeds to blows and bloodshed.

Fishmonger. Let those who love fighting fight; I think we should accept with reverence the laws of our superiors and religiously observe them, as if they came from God. It is neither safe nor religious to conceive in the mind or sow among others any sinister suspicion concerning them. And if there is tyranny in any of the laws, as long as they do not compel impiety, it would be better to bear it than seditiously resist it.

Butcher. I admit this is a very good way to maintain the authority of persons in power. I pretty much agree with you, and as for those in authority, I do not envy them. I'd be quite happy to hear anything that aims at the liberty and advantage of the people.

Fishmonger. God will not forget His people.

Butcher. But where, all this while, is the liberty of the spirit that the Apostles promise in the Gospel, and that Paul so often inculcates, saying, "The Kingdom of God consists not in meat and drink"; and that "we are not children under a schoolmaster"; and that "we do no longer serve the elements of this world"; and an abundance of other expressions? Are Christians tied to the observance of so many more ceremonies than the Jews were; and are not the laws of man more binding than a great many commands of God?

Fishmonger. Well, Butcher, this much I tell you, the liberty of Christians does not consist of it being lawful for them to do what they will, being set free of human ordinances. But rather their liberty consists of doing those things they are enjoined to do with a fervor of spirit and readiness of mind, willingly and cheerfully, as if they were sons rather than servants.

Butcher. Very cleverly answered indeed! But there were sons under the Mosaic Law, and there are now servants under the Gospel. I am afraid the greatest part of mankind are servants who do their duty by compulsion. What difference is there then between the new dispensation and the old?

Fishmonger. In my opinion a great deal. Because the old taught under a veil and the new is laid open to the people. That which the old foretold by parables and riddles the new explains clearly; what the old promised obscurely the new exhibits for the most part manifestly. That which was given to one nation singly now equally teaches all the way to salvation. The old imparted that notable and spiritual grace to a few prophets and famous men, but the new sheds abroad every kind of gift, such as languages, the healing of diseases, prophecies, and miracles, to persons of every age, sex, and nation.

Butcher. Where are those gifts now?

Fishmonger. They have stopped, but are not lost, either because there is no longer any need of them now that the doctrine of Christ has spread abroad, or because many are Christians in name only and desire faith because it is a worker of miracles.

Butcher. If miracles are necessary because of unbelievers, I'm sure the world is full of them now.

Fishmonger. This is a disbelief of simple error, such as that of the Jews murmuring against Peter because he received Cornelius's family into the grace of the Gospel. The same situation prevailed among the Gentiles, who thought the religion they had received from their ancestors sufficient for salvation, and the doctrine of the Apostles a strange superstition. They were converted by seeing miracles. But now those who do not believe the Gospel when it shines so gloriously through the whole world do not just simply err, but being blinded by their evil affections, refuse to see that they should be good. These no miracle can improve.

Butcher. Indeed you have said many things that are probable; however, I am resolved not to depend upon the judgment of a salt-fishmonger. I will go to some theologian eminent in learning, and what he says concerning all these things, I'll believe.

Fishmonger. Who? Pharetrius?

Butcher. He is feeble before he is old and is fit to preach to nobody but doting old women.

Fishmonger. Well, then, who? Bliteus?

Butcher. Do you think I'd believe anything that prating sophist has to say?

Fishmonger. Well, then, Amphicholus?

Butcher. I'd never trust him to answer questions; he never paid his meat bill, when I trusted him. Can anyone who was always insolvent concerning his debts answer difficult questions?

Fishmonger. Who, then? Lemantius?

Butcher. I wouldn't choose a blind man to show me the way.

Fishmonger. Who, then?

Butcher. If you care to know, it is Cephalus, a man very well versed in three languages, and accomplished in good literature, familiarly acquainted with the sacred Scripture and the ancient Fathers.

Fishmonger. I'll give you better advice. Go to the Elysian Fields and there you'll find Rabin Druin—he'll cut all your knotty questions in two with a pair of shears.

Butcher. Will you go ahead of me and clear the way?

Fishmonger. All jesting aside, it is true that you told me of a dispensation for flesh-eating?

Butcher. No, I was just teasing you. And if the Pope ever had so much as a thought of doing it, you fishmongers would raise a stink about it. Besides, the world is full of this sort of Pharisee, who has no other way of appearing religious except by such superstitions, and who would neither be deprived of his ostentatious sanctity nor allow his successors to have more liberty than he had himself. Nor would it be in the interest of the butchers to allow people to eat everything, for then our trade would be very uncertain. Now our profit is more certain and we run less risks, as well as have less trouble.

Fishmonger. What you say is true, and we should be in the same condition.

Butcher. I am glad to find at last something upon which a fishmonger and a butcher can agree. But seriously, it would be better if Christians were not tied up in so many ceremonies, especially those that have little to do with true religion. In saying this I'm not against true religion and don't vindicate those people who reject and make light of all human ordinances, just because they are forbidden to do certain things. Yet I can't very well admire some of the absurd notions of mankind in many things.

Fishmonger. Nor can I help wondering about them.

Butcher. We would mix up heaven and earth if we suspected that there is grave danger unless priests abandon some of the weight they attach to their pronouncements. We are all asleep, under imminent danger of attributing so much to the authority of man that the authority of God will suffer. On the horns of a dilemma, we avoid one evil and fall into another even more pernicious. That honor is due bishops no one denies, especially if they act the way they talk. But it is a wicked thing to transfer the honor due to God alone to men; and in giving too much honor to men, to give too little to God. We should honor and revere God through our neighbor, but we should make sure at the same time that God is not robbed of His honor by this means.

Fishmonger. We see many men who put so much stress upon corporal ceremonies that, relying upon them, they neglect matters of real religion, arrogating to their own merits that which rightly should be attributed to the Divine, and there they rest, when they should begin to ascend to

greater perfection, reviling their neighbors for those things that are neither good nor bad in themselves.

Butcher. And when it comes to a choice between two things, one
being better than the other, we commonly choose the worse one. The
body, and those things that belong to the body, are everywhere preferred
to those of the mind. It is rightly considered a great crime to kill a man,
but to corrupt the minds of men with poisonous doctrine and pernicious
principles is a joke. If a priest lets his hair grow or wears lay clothes, he is
thrown into prison and severely punished; but if he sits drinking in a
brothel with whores, gambles or debauches the wives of other men and
never opens a Bible, he is still a pillar of the Church. Not that I excuse
the wearing of lay clothes, but I criticize the absurdity of men's ideas.

Fishmonger. No, if he neglects to say his prayers on the appointed
hours, he must be excommunicated; but if he is a usurer, or guilty of
simony, he goes scot-free.

Butcher. If anyone sees a Carthusian in other than his prescribed dress
or eating flesh, how does he not curse him, tremble before the sight, and
take flight, for fear the earth would open and swallow up the Carthusian
for his apparel and him for witnessing it. But let the same person see him
blind drunk, castigating his neighbor with lies, and openly defrauding
him, and he is not at all shocked.

Fishmonger. If a Franciscan is seen in a girdle without knots, or an
Augustinian gird in a woolen instead of a leather cord, or a Carmelite
without one, or a Rhodian with one, or a Franciscan with shoes on his
feet, or a Cruciferian with sandals on, would he not send the whole town
into an uproar?

Butcher. Recently in our neighborhood there were two women, both
of them considered level-headed; one of them miscarried and the other
one fell into a fit upon seeing a canon, who was president of the nuns in a
nearby cloister, appear in public without any underwear under his black
cloak. But these same women have frequently seen the same kind of
cattle out on the town, singing and dancing, not to say more; and their
stomachs never so much as heaved at it.

Fishmonger. Perhaps some allowance ought to be made for their sex.
But I suppose you know Polythrescus. He was dangerous ill with consumption. The physicians for a long time ordered him to eat eggs and
meat, but to no avail. The bishop exhorted him likewise to do so. But
being a man of learning and a bachelor in theology, he resolved to die

rather than take the advice of either of these physicians. Finally the doctors, in league with his friends, contrived to deceive him, giving him a potion of eggs and goat's milk and telling him it was the juice of almonds. He took it freely. For several days it improved his health, until a certain maid told him of the trick, whereupon he commenced to vomit it up again. But this very same man who was so superstitious in relation to milk had so little religion in him that he refused to pay a sum of money that he owed me. Having gotten an opportunity to destroy the note he had given me, he forswore his obligation and I had to take the loss. He took oaths with so little difficulty, that he seemed to wish he had such complaints made against him every day. Who can be more perverse than that? He sinned against the mind of the Church by not obeying the priest and doctors. But this man whose stomach was so weak in relation to milk had a conscience strong enough to commit perjury.

Butcher. This story brings to mind what I heard a Dominican say, while portraying the death of Christ on Easter Eve in an attempt to temper the sadness of the subject with the pleasantness of a story. A certain young man had gotten a nun pregnant, and the great size of her belly gave it away. A jury of nuns was impaneled, with the abbess sitting as judge of the court. Evidence was given against the nun; the facts were too plain for any denial; she was obliged to plead the unavoidableness of the crime and defended herself this way. She transferred the blame to another, having recourse to the "Status Qualitatis" or rather the "Status Translationis." "I was overcome by one who was too strong for me," she said. The abbess replied, "Then you should have cried out." "I would have," said the prisoner, "had it not been a crime to break silence in the dormitory." Whether this is fact or fiction I do not know, but there are a great many more foolish things than this done.

But now I will tell you what I have seen with my own eyes. The man's name and his place of residence I shall conceal. There was a cousin of mine, a prior next in degree to the abbot of the Benedictine order. He was the type who doesn't eat flesh, unless out of the place they call the great refectory. He was considered a learned man, and desired to be considered so. He was about fifty years of age. It was his daily practice to drink and live merrily, and once every twelve days he'd go to the public baths to sweat out the diseases of the kidneys.

Fishmonger. Had he the money to live like that?

Butcher. About six hundred florins a year.

Fishmonger. Such poverty I myself would wish for.

Butcher. In short, by drinking and whoring he came down with consumption. The doctors had given him up, the abbot ordered him to eat flesh, adding that terrible sentence, "Under pain of disobedience." But he, though at the point of death, could not be brought to taste flesh, even though for many years he had had no aversion to the flesh.

Fishmonger. A prior and an abbot well matched! I guessed who they are; I remember having heard the same story from their own mouths.

Butcher. Guess.

Fishmonger. Is not the abbot a lusty, fat man who has a stammer in his speech, and the prior a little man with a straight body and a long face?

Butcher. You've guessed correctly.

Fishmonger. Well, now I'll make amends to you. I'll tell you what I saw the other day with my own eyes; not only was I present, but was in a way the chief actor. Two nuns went to pay a visit to some of their relatives. When they arrived, they found that their manservant had left behind their prayer books, which were special ones according to the custom of the order and place in which they lived. Good God! What a horrible thing that was! They did not dare eat supper before they said their vespers, nor could they read from any book but their own. At the same time all the company was eager to go to supper. The servant ran back and brought back the book; and by the time they had said their prayers and gotten to supper, it was ten o'clock at night.

Butcher. There's nothing greatly wrong with that.

Fishmonger. You have heard only one part of the story. At the supper the nuns began to grow merry with wine; they laughed, joked, and kissed—not too modestly, either—until you could hardly hear what was said for the noise they made. Nobody acted with more freedom than those two virgins who would not go to supper before they had said their prayers. After supper there was dancing, singing of lewd songs, and activity that I dare not describe. I am afraid that night was not a very respectable one; if it was, the wanton plays, nods, and kisses deceived me.

Butcher. I don't blame the nuns for this as much as the priests who look after them. Come on, I'll match you story for story, or rather give you a history of that which I myself was an eyewitness. A little while ago a group of people were sent to prison for baking bread on Sunday, though they were fresh out of it. Indeed, I don't blame the deed, but I do blame the punishment. A little later, on Palm Sunday, I went over to the next street and, at about four o'clock in the afternoon, I saw a sight I don't know whether to call ridiculous or wretched. I don't believe any Bacchanal was ever so lewd. Some were so drunk they reeled to and fro, like a ship tossed on the waves without a rudder. Others, hardly able to stand themselves, were supporting one so drunk he couldn't move. Others fell down and could hardly get up. Some were crowned with leaves of oak.

Fishmonger. Vines and wands would have suited them better.

Butcher. The oldest of the group, acting the part of Silenus, was carried upon men's shoulders like a dead corpse, with his feet forward but his face downward, so that he would not be choked by his own vomiting, which ran down to the heels of those who carried him. There was not a sober man among the bearers; they went along laughing, as if they had all lost their senses. In short, they were all insane. In their pickled condition they made a procession into the city in the daytime.

Fishmonger. How did they all become insane?

Butcher. You know that in the next town wine was sold more cheaply than here. So a group of boon companions went there to obtain a greater amount of insanity for less money. Indeed, they did spend less money and got more insanity. If these men had but tasted an egg, they would have been hauled off to prison as if they had committed parricide. Besides their neglecting divine service and evening prayers on so sacred a day, they committed intemperance with impunity. Yet nobody seemed very displeased about it.

Fishmonger. Don't be too puzzled about it. In the center of the cities and in alehouses next to the churches on the most solemn holidays there was drinking, singing, dancing, fighting, and such noise and tumult that divine services could not be performed, nor could one word the priest said be heard. But if the same men had sown a stitch in a shoe or eaten pork on Friday, they would have been handled severely. Though the Lord's day was instituted chiefly to give people the leisure to concern themselves with the doctrine of the Gospel, it was therefore forbidden to mend shoes, so that there would be leisure to trim souls. But is not this a strange perversion of judgment?

Butcher. An amazing one. There are two elements in the precept of fasting, one abstinence from flesh, the other relating to the type of food. Almost everyone would agree that the first is either a divine command or very close to it. The latter is not only human in origin, but is in opposition to the doctrine really intended by the Apostles. However, we explain it by the preposterous idea that, although it is no crime to eat a meal, yet to taste a bit of meat that is prescribed by man though permitted by God and the Apostles, is a capital crime. Fasts, although they may not have been commanded by the Apostles, are recommended in their examples and epistles. But as to the prohibition against consuming meat, which God has created to be eaten with acts of thanksgiving, must we now defend this practice before the judgment seat of Paul? Yet almost the world over, men eat plentifully and nobody is offended by it. But if a sick man eats a piece of chicken, the whole of Christianity is in danger. In England the common people have a supper every other day during Lent, and no one is disturbed by it. But if a man at death's door with a fever should take a little chicken broth, it is considered a crime worse than sacrilege. There is nothing of greater antiquity nor more religiously observed among Christians than Lent. The same people who eat supper without penalty during Lent will not allow this to be done outside of Lent on a Friday. If you ask the reason, they say it is the custom of the country, and curse a man for not observing the customs of the land. Yet they forgive themselves for neglecting an ancient custom of the universal Church.

Fishmonger. One who without reason neglects the custom of the country in which he lives should not be praised.

Butcher. In the same way I blame those who divide Lent between God and their bellies, yet there is no reason for preposterous censuring in these matters.

Fishmonger. Although the Lord's day was instituted in order to have people meet together and hear the Gospel preached, one who does not hear the mass is looked upon as an abominable sinner, while one who neglects to hear the sermon and plays ball during that time is not considered a sinner.

Butcher. What a serious crime it is to receive the sacrament into an unwashed mouth! But at the same time many take it with an unpurified mind, defiled with perverse desires.

Fishmonger. How many priests would rather die than celebrate mass with a chalice and paten that have not been consecrated by a bishop, or do so in their everyday clothes? But among all of them, how many do we see not at all afraid to come to the Lord's table drunk after last night's debauchery? How fearful are they of touching the Host with that part of the hand which had not been dipped in consecrated oil? Why are they not as religious in making sure that a filthy mind does not offend the Lord himself?

Butcher. If we happen to so much as touch a consecrated vessel, we'd think ourselves guilty of a heinous offense; and yet how unconcerned are we when we violate the living temples of the Holy Spirit?

Fishmonger. Human constitutions require that no one illegitimate, lame, or one-eyed may be admitted to the priesthood; how strictly do we enforce this? But in the meantime the ignorant, gamblers, drunkards, soldiers, and murderers are admitted everywhere. We are told that the diseases of the mind cannot be seen. I don't speak of those things that are hidden, but of those that are more easily seen than the deformities of the body.

Butcher. There are bishops who have nothing to say for themselves but their sordid accomplishments. The gift of preaching, which is the chief dignity of a bishop, has given way to every sordid thing. This they would never do unless some set of false values hold them.

Fishmonger. Anyone profaning a holy day instituted by a bishop is quickly punished. But there are some great men who, disregarding the constitutions of popes and councils and all their thunderbolts, hinder canonical elections, ravage Church lands, not even sparing almshouses and hospitals, erected through the charity of pious persons for the care of the old, sick, and needy. These think themselves good enough Christians if they indulge their bad temper upon persons who have offended them in trivial matters.

Butcher. We'd better leave great men alone and talk about salt-fish and flesh.

Fishmonger. I agree with you. Let's get back to fasts and fish. I have heard that these papal laws explicitly excuse children, old men, sick and weak persons, those who work hard, pregnant women, breast-fed children, and the very poor.

Butcher. I have often heard this.

Fishmonger. I have also heard that a very excellent theologian, I think his name is Gerson, has said that if there are any other cases of equal weight with those excepted from the papal laws, the precept is mitigated for them also. There are some peculiarities of the body that are a greater excuse for not fasting than disease; and we find that some disorders that do not appear outwardly are more dangerous than those that do. Therefore, one knowing well his own constitution need not consult a priest, just as infants do not, because in both cases their circumstances exempt them from the law.

It follows that those who oblige children, very old men or physically weak people to fast or to eat fish commit a double sin: the first against brotherly charity, and the second against the Pope himself, who would not require those to observe the law when it would be injurious to them. Whatever Christ ordered he ordained for the health of both body and mind; and furthermore no pope claims for himself the power to endanger a person's life. For example, suppose a person by not eating in the evening is unable to rest well at night and as a result becomes delirious; whoever orders such a person to fast goes against the mind of the Church and the will of God.

Princes, often to suit their own convenience, publish edicts of this sort, threatening transgressors with capital punishment. How far their power extends I do not know, but this much I will say: they would be safer if they inflicted the death penalty for no other reasons than those expressed in the Holy Scriptures. Our Lord urges a pattern of conduct which avoids extremes in this matter. Instead of legislating against perjury he recommends that we avoid swearing of all kinds. If we follow His advice in never becoming angry we will avoid the extreme result of this, homicide. As often as we can we should reasonably follow the dictates of charity and exhort our neighbor, keeping in mind the weakness of human nature. If there is no other apparent reason, it is the role of Christian charity to assume that one's eating habits are done in good faith unless one eats with a manifest contempt of the ecclesiastical law. A civil magistrate justly punishes those who violate dietary laws in public; but what a person eats in his own house is the business of a physician rather than a magistrate. Those who are so wicked that they cause disorder of any kind are guilty of sedition, but hardly the person who consults his own health and breaks no law, neither of God nor man.

In cases like this the authority of the Pope is misapplied. It is absurd to pretend the authority of the Pope in such cases. They are themselves persons of great humanity, and would, if given good reasons on their own accord, protect the health of those who need it with dispensations against slanderous attacks. Besides, throughout Italy flesh is sold in certain markets, for the sake of people who need it for their health. In addition, I have heard theologians, differing little from the Pharisees, say not to be afraid to eat a piece of bread or drink a pint of wine or ale at suppertime to support the weakness of the body. If they take it upon themselves to allow a small supper to those who are in health, contrary to the ordinance of the Church, which requires fasting, may they not permit a much more hardy one for those people whose weakness require it—may not the Pope even approve it? If one treats his body with severity, it can be called zeal, for each person knows his own constitution best; but is there any piety and charity displayed by people who reduce a weak brother, wherein the spirit is willing but the flesh is weak, even to death's door, or cause him to contract a disease worse than death itself, against the law of nature, the law of God, and the sense of papal law?

Butcher. What you mention brings to mind what I myself saw about two years ago. I believe you know the old man, Eros, about sixty years of age, and a man of very weak constitution, who by a lingering illness, acute diseases, and study exhausting enough to fell even the great athlete Milo was brought to death's door. This man had, by a mystery of nature, from early childhood a great aversion to eating fish and an inability to endure fasting. Whenever he did fast, his life was endangered. He finally obtained a dispensation from the Pope to defend him against the tongues of some Pharisaical spirits.

Not long ago he accepted an invitation from friends to go to the city of Eleutheropolis, a city not at all like its name. It was during the Lenten season that he spent a few days devoted to the enjoyment of his friends. All during this time fish was the common diet; he, so as not to give offense to his friends, and even though he had the papal dispensation, ate fish. He felt the old disorder coming upon him, which was worse than death itself. So he prepared to leave his friends and go home, finding this necessary to avoid sickness. Some suspected that he was making a hasty departure because he could not eat fish and persuaded Glaucoplutus, a very learned man and chief magistrate in that province, to invite Eros to breakfast. Eros, quite tired of company that he could not avoid in a public inn, consented to go, but only on the condition that no preparation would be made for him, save a couple of eggs which he would eat standing up and immediately take to his horse and be gone. He was promised that his desires would be carried out, but when he arrived, there was fowl provided for him. Eros, taking it poorly, tasted only the eggs, rose from the table, and took to his horse with some learned men accompanying him part of the way.

But in some way or another the smell of the fowl was picked up by a number of parasites. Noise began to issue from the city, sounding as if ten men were being murdered; nor was the tumult only confined to that city, but was carried to places two days' journey from there, and as usual growing in volume as it extended. It was rumored that Eros had not gotten away but had been brought to justice. This was not true, but Glaucoplutus was obliged to give the magistrate satisfaction.

Now considering the circumstances of Eros, had he eaten flesh in public, who would have been justly offended by it? Yet in the same city all during Lent, but especially on holidays, many of these parasites drank until they were insane, howling, dancing, and shooting dice at the church door, so that the priest could not be heard when he was preaching. Yet this was not an offense against the law.

ERASMUS

Inner Faith Is Better than Mere Ritual

---

*Born as an illegitimate child in Rotterdam, Desiderius Erasmus (c. 1466–
1536) eventually became known as the leading humanist of his day.
Although his natural inclination toward peace and conciliation eventually
put him at odds both with the great Protestant controversialist Martin
Luther as well as with more doctrinaire Catholics, his writings had a huge
influence on his contemporaries and continue to be actively studied today.*

*At the age of nine Erasmus entered a school in Deventer run by the
Brethren of the Common Life, where he received a sound education in the
classics. After the death of his parents he joined a religious order, the Augustinian Canons of Steyn (1487), a move that he later regretted, finding himself
unsuited to the monastic life; in 1517 he finally obtained a papal dispensation
from his vows and returned officially to lay status. By that time, indeed, he
had left the monastery far behind, having become secretary to the bishop of
Cambrai in 1493 and having received permission to study theology in Paris
in 1495. The intellectual climate in Paris was nearly as distasteful to Erasmus
as that of the monastery—he cared neither for scholastic theology nor for college food – and he left without a degree after less than four years. Erasmus's
subsequent life involved a great deal of travel throughout Europe where he
came to know many of the rulers and intellectual leaders of his day. In 1499
he traveled to England, where he made friends with Thomas More and John
Colet; in 1506 he went south to Italy, coming in contact with the humanist
circle of Aldus Manitius in the great printing center of Venice; in 1509 he
returned to England, where he taught Greek for a time at the University of
Cambridge. In 1514 he was back on the Continent, residing in Louvain,
where he had relationships with the university's faculty of theology, but his
application of philology to the Scriptures and reluctance to condemn Luther
bred hostility against him. Erasmus then moved to Basel (1521–29) and,
upon the city's becoming Protestant, to the nearby Catholic town of Freiburg
im Breisgau. He was back in Basel working on the publication of one of his
works when he died on July 12, 1536.*

*Erasmus was a figure viewed with suspicion, during his lifetime and
afterward, both by Protestants and Catholics. His longing for a return to*

the simplicity of the Gospel and his advocacy of an inner spiritual life, in contrast with excessive dependence on outward rituals, placed him close in spirit to Luther and his followers. At the same time, he never parted ways with the Catholic church, differed with Luther fundamentally concerning the relationship between man and divine grace, and feared the social and political consequences of the Reformation. In particular, he feared (with unusual foresight) that Europe would be torn apart by war and religious controversy and hoped (rather naively) that the mild voice of reason would prevail over polemics. Erasmus was viewed as the ideal type of the Christian humanist, one who combined great learning in the classics with sincere piety. Erasmus was a superb stylist and promoter of the classics and the ancient Church Fathers, and was among the first scholars to apply humanist philological methods to the study of the Bible. His critical edition of the New Testament, which included the Greek text and Erasmus's revised translation of the Latin Vulgate, appeared in 1516 and is considered one of his most significant accomplishments.

One of the early works that established Erasmus's reputation through-out Europe was the Handbook of the Militant Christian (or Enchiridion Militis Christiani), *which appeared in Latin in 1503 and was soon trans-lated into many languages. The work originated in a pious woman's con-cern for the spiritual state of her wayward husband, but Erasmus provided much more than a call to repentance. The booklet is a handbook of spiritual devotion, which first encourages the reader to practice an inward piety, and then provides a set of practical rules for resisting temptation and sin. The present selection, taken from Part II, gives Erasmus's fifth rule for the spir-itual life. Erasmus here played on the contrasts between body and spirit, the literal and the true meaning, the visible and the invisible. After emphasiz-ing the value of allegorical interpretations, Erasmus applied this concept to the rituals of the Church: If they are not spiritualized but are only followed mechanically, they are of little worth. Although ceremonies and rituals are necessary, they should not become superstitions. Erasmus then considered what constitutes true worship and pointed to the need for inner cleansing, which went beyond outward piety and reliance on the visible.*

FIFTH RULE

I am now going to add a fifth, subsidiary rule. You will find that you can best maintain this piety if, turning away from visible things, which are for the most part either imperfect or of themselves indifferent, you seek the invisible. We will follow the divisions we mentioned previously in discussing the nature of man. I am going to stress the differences between the visible and invisible because I find so many Christians, either out of neglect or sheer ignorance, as superstitious as the pagans. Let us suppose that there are two worlds, the one intelligible, the other visible. The intelligible or angelic world is that in which God dwells with the blessed. The visible world embraces the circle of heaven, the planets, the stars, and all that is included in them.

Now let us imagine that man is a third world participating in both of the others, the visible referring to his corporeal part, the invisible to his soul. In the visible world, since we are, as it were, mere sojourners, we ought to consider all that we perceive through our senses in terms of its relationship to the intelligible world. The sun, for example, in the visible world might be compared to the divine mind. The moon might be thought of in terms of the whole assembly of the angelic hosts and of the elect whom we call the Church Triumphant. These celestial bodies operate in relation to the earth as God does in relation to our soul. It is the sun that quickens, produces, matures, purges, softens, illuminates, brightens, and gladdens. When you are delighted by the beauty of the rising sun, consider the joy of those in heaven upon whom the divine light shines eternally. Paul tells us, "For God, who commanded light to shine out of darkness, has shone in our hearts, to give enlightenment concerning the knowledge of the glory of God, shining on the face of Christ Jesus." I suggest that you repeat over and over those passages from Holy Scripture in which grace is compared to the rays of the sun. If the darkness of night is oppressive to you, then think of how destitute is the soul without the light of God. If you find any darkness within your soul, then pray that the Sun of righteousness may shine upon you.

The things that we can see with our physical eyes are mere shadows of reality. If they appear ugly and ill formed, then what must be the ugliness of the soul in sin, deprived of all light? The soul, like the body, can undergo transformation in appearance. In sin it appears as completely ugly to the beholder. In virtue it shines resplendently before God. Like the body the soul can be healthy, youthful, and so on. It can undergo pain, thirst, and hunger. In this physical life, that is, in the visible world, we avoid whatever would defile or deform the body; how much more, then, ought we to avoid that which would tarnish the soul? I feel that the entire spiritual life consists in this: That we gradually turn from those things whose appearance is deceptive to those things that are real . . . from the pleasures of the flesh, the honors of the world that are so transitory, to those things that are immutable and everlasting. Socrates had this in mind when he said that the soul will leave the body at the time of death with little fear if, during life, it has rehearsed death by despising material things.

Now the cross to which Christ calls us and the death in which St. Paul urges us to die with our Head are of this earth. Once we have tasted the sweetness of what is spiritual, the pleasures of the world will have no attraction for us. If we disregard the shadows of things, then we will penetrate their inner substance. Sickness, for example, can be a means of advancing in spirituality. In fact, a little less care for physical well-being will give us more time to devote to the mind. If you fear the death of the body, then certainly you should fear the death of the soul. If lightning terrifies you, then think of that invisible lightning that is the wrath of God saying, "Depart ye cursed persons into eternal fire." Are you attracted by what is beautiful in the human figure? Think rather of the beauty of the soul that it conceals. You worry whether the drought will end. It is far better that you pray that God may water your mind lest virtue wither away in it. You are greatly concerned with money that is lost or being wasted, or you worry about the advance of old age. I think it much to be desired that you provide first of all for the needs of your soul.

Now this distinction that we make of body and soul can be applied also to what we read in Holy Scripture. Everything that is written has both an external, or, as it were, corporeal, meaning as well as a mysterious, or spiritual, significance. The Old Testament is filled with the accounts of events that would in no way edify us if we did not understand them in an allegorical manner, that is, by searching out the spiritual meaning. St. Paul, following the example of our Lord Himself, has used allegory as a means of better understanding the Scriptures. Origen, of course, is also a great advocate of the allegorical approach. Yet I think you will have to admit that our modern theologians either despise this method of interpretation or are completely ignorant of it. As a matter of fact they surpass the pagans of antiquity in the subtlety of their distinctions.

I find that in comparison with the Fathers of the Church our present-day theologians are a pathetic group. Most of them lack the elegance, the charm of language, and the style of the Fathers. Content with Aristotle, they treat the mysteries of revelation in the tangled fashion of the logician. Excluding the Platonists from their commentaries, they strangle the beauty of revelation. Yet no less an authority than St. Augustine prefers to express himself in the flowing style that so enhanced the lovely writings of this Platonist school. He prefers them not only because they have so many ideas that are appropriate to our religion but also because the figurative language that they use, abounding in allegories, very closely approaches the language of Scripture itself. The great Christian writers of the past were able to treat even the most arid subjects with a beautiful prose. They enriched and colored their sermons and commentaries with the constant use of allegory. Almost all of them were at home with the writings of Plato and the poets, and they used this literary training to the very best advantage in interpreting the words of Scripture.

It is for this reason that I would recommend that you familiarize yourself with the Fathers. They will lead you to an inner penetration of the word of God, to an understanding of the spiritual worth it contains. This is certainly to be preferred to the scholastic method that invariably ends up in useless disputation. In getting closer to the inner spiritual meaning you will find what is really most important—a hope for the unknown. We have already referred to the Old Testament as abounding in this sort of figurative writing. It is also to be found in the Gospel. For the New Testament has its flesh and its spirit. Paul tells us that we see not the thing itself, but that we see in an obscure manner. We see as through a mirror. We see but an image or a representation of the real object. Christ Himself tells us, "The flesh profits nothing; it is the spirit that gives life." He actually goes beyond what I am saying. As Truth Itself, He says that the flesh profits nothing. St. Paul reiterates the same point when he says that the flesh is actually fatal if it does not lead to the spirit. We have already explained that the body cannot even exist without the spirit. Yet the spirit is completely independent of the body.

If, then, the spirit is that alone which gives life, then it is obvious enough that our every action should tend toward the spirit. Time and time again in his Epistles St. Paul exhorts us not to place our trust in the flesh but in the spirit. Here alone is life, liberty, adoption. Everywhere he belittles and condemns the flesh. This is even more evident in the case of our Lord. By giving sight to the blind, by allowing men to eat with unwashed hands and, on the Sabbath, to lift the ass from the pit and to pick grain from the fields, He shows His disdain for the flesh. The parable of the Pharisee and the publican, the boastings of the Jews, the bringing of gifts to the altar, are all examples of His condemning the flesh of the law and the superstition of those who preferred to be Jews in public rather than in their secret selves.

He makes this very plain in the case of the Samaritan woman: "Woman, believe me, the hour is coming when you shall neither on this mountain nor in Jerusalem adore the Father. But the hour is coming, and now is, when the true adorer shall adore the Father in spirit and truth. For the Father also seeks the spiritual to adore Him. God is spirit; and they that adore Him must adore His spirit and truth." He meant the same thing when at the marriage feast He turned the water of the cold and insipid letter into the wine of the spirit. And just in case you feel that this was the limit of His disdain for those who seek the flesh and not the spirit, recall to mind what contempt He had for those who eat His flesh and drink His blood in other than a spiritual manner. To whom do you suppose He directed those words? It was certainly to none other than those who think their salvation consists in wearing a blessed medal or carrying an indulgenced relic. If receiving the very sacrament of His Body is nothing unless done in a spiritual manner, then I think it is plain enough that all other material things are useless unless they are spiritualized.

Perhaps you celebrate Mass daily. Yet if you live as if this were only for your own welfare and have no concern for the difficulties and needs of your neighbor, you are still in the flesh of the sacrament. The sacrifice of the Mass in this spiritual sense really means that we are of one body with the Body of Christ, we are living members of the Church. If you love nothing except in Christ, if you hold that all of your possessions are the common property of all men, if you make the difficulties and privations of your neighbor your very own, then you may say Mass with great fruit because you do so in a spiritual manner. I think there are far too many who count up how many times they attend Mass and rely almost entirely upon this for their salvation. They are convinced that they owe nothing further to Christ. Leaving church, they immediately turn to their former habits. I certainly do not hesitate to praise them for getting to Mass but I am forced to condemn them for stopping at this point. They have failed to let what takes place at Mass also take place in their hearts; the death of our Head that is there represented does not take place in their souls. Examine yourself and see if attendance at divine services renders you dead to the world. If you are filled with ambition and envy, even though you offer the sacrifice yourself, you are far from the real significance of the Mass. Christ was slain for you. Sacrifice yourself, then, to Him who sacrificed Himself to the Father. If you believe in what takes place at the altar but fail to enter into the spiritual meaning of it, God will despise your flabby display of religion.

Let us consider a moment the matter of baptism. Do you really think that the ceremony of itself makes you a Christian? If your mind is preoccupied with the affairs of the world, you may be a Christian on the surface, but inwardly you are a Gentile of the Gentiles. Why is this? It is simply because you have grasped the body of the sacrament, not the spirit. The ceremony consists of washing the body with water, but for you this is not a cleansing of the soul. Salt is placed upon your tongue, but your mind remains uncured. The body is anointed with oil, but the soul remains unanointed. You have been sprinkled with holy water, but this accomplishes nothing unless you cleanse the inner filth of your mind.

Perhaps you are wont to venerate the relics of the saints, yet at the same time you condemn their greatest legacy, the example of their lives. No veneration of Mary is more beautiful than the imitation of her humility. No devotion to the saints is more acceptable to God than the imitation of their virtues. Say you have a great devotion to St. Peter and St. Paul. Then by all means imitate the faith of the former and the charity of the latter. This will certainly be more rewarding than a dozen trips to Rome. Do you really want to honor St. Francis? Then why not give away your wealth to the poor, restrain your evil inclinations, and see in everyone you meet the image of Christ? By avoiding contentions and overcoming evil with good, you will shine forth brighter in the sight of God than a hundred lighted candles. Do you value being buried in the Franciscan habit? The cowl of St. Francis will not benefit you after death if during your life you did not imitate his personal integrity. I have continually emphasized that the only complete example of perfect piety is to be found in the imitation of Christ. Yet I do not condemn the imitation of His saints; emulate them in such a way that each of them prompts you to eradicate one or another vice, and practice their particular virtues.

You may have a great veneration for the remains of St. Paul. If your religion conforms to this, then I cannot say that there is really anything wrong with it. But if you merely venerate the ashes of his remains and fail to imitate the resplendent image of him portrayed in his writings, you make your religion a ridiculous thing. You worship his bones hidden away and preserved in nooks and niches, but you fail to worship the great mind of Paul hidden in the Scriptures. A little fragment of his body seen through a glass covering evokes your admiration; why not marvel at his wonderful personality? The ashes you venerate are the very thing that vice will lead to. Let them evoke a feeling of sorrow. Our bodies will all one day be reduced to ashes. When you venerate the image of Christ in the paintings and other works of art that portray Him, think how much more you ought to revere that portrait of His mind that the inspiration of the Holy Spirit has placed in Holy Writ. No artist could possibly have reproduced those words and prayers of Christ that represent Him so exactly in the Gospel. If our Father in heaven finds His perfect reflection in His divine Son, so the words of His Son are the closest image of His divine personality. No relic of our Blessed Lord can possibly approach the strength and beauty of His very self. You may gaze in silent amazement at the tunic that reputedly belonged to Christ, yet you read the wonderful sayings of that same Christ half asleep. You are convinced that it is advantageous to have a small particle of the true Cross in your home, yet this is nothing compared with carrying the mystery of the Cross fixed in your mind. If these external things were the true source of holiness, then certainly there could never have been any people more religious than the Jews. They lived with Him, listened to His words, touched Him—yet most of them rejected Him. What could be more envied than what Judas did, to press the divine mouth with his own? Even our Blessed Lady would not have been the great beneficiary of what Christ did unless she had conceived Him in the Spirit.

Let us carry this idea a bit further. The Apostles are a fine example of this failure of spirit. Even after all the miracles of Christ, after having listened to His teachings for so many years, after so many proofs of His resurrection, what does He say to them? As He is about to leave them He reproves them for their unbelief. Why was this? Surely it was because the flesh of Christ stood in their way. He tells them, "If I go not, the Paraclete will not come to you; it is necessary that I go." If the very physical presence of Christ is useless to salvation, how can you put your trust in corporeal things? St. Paul actually saw Christ in the flesh. Yet he says, "And if we have known Christ according to the flesh, now we know Him no longer." He meant by this that, in the spirit, he had advanced beyond this kind of knowledge.

Perhaps I am arguing with more verbosity than He who taught the rules. I have a reason for doing so. The attitudes I am talking about are, in my opinion, the worst plague of Christianity. This false set of values brings more ruin than any other because in appearance it is very close to godliness. There are no vices that are more dangerous than those that have the veneer of virtue. And it is precisely because of this fact that so many good people easily fall into this deception and that the uneducated faithful are led astray. Violent objections are made to anyone who attempts to point out these things. I care very little about objections to my criticisms so long as they have been approved by ecclesiastical authority. They are signs, supports of piety. And they are quite necessary for children in Christ, at least until they have become a little more mature. Even those more advanced in perfection should not scorn them, lest their scorn work great harm among the simple and uninstructed. My approval rests on the assumption that they are steps, or gradations, that lead to more appropriate means of salvation.

But to place the whole of religion in external ceremonies is sublime stupidity. This amounts to revolt against the spirit of the Gospel and is a reversion to the superstitions of Judaism. St. Paul was incessant in his attempt to remove the Jews from their faith in external works. I feel that the vast majority of Christians have sunk once again into this unhealthy situation. . . .

Charity does not consist in many visits to churches, in many prostrations before the statues of saints, in the lighting of candles, or in the repetition of a number of designated prayers. Of all these things God has no need. Paul declares charity to be the edification of one's neighbor, the attempt to integrate all men into one body so that all men may become one in Christ, the loving of one's neighbor as one's self. Charity for Paul has many facets; he is charitable who rebukes the erring, who teaches the ignorant, who lifts up the fallen, who consoles the downhearted, who supports the needy. If a man is truly charitable, he will devote, if needs be, all his wealth, all his zeal, and all his care to the benefit of others.

Just as Christ gave Himself completely for us, so also should we give ourselves for our neighbor. If the attitude of the religious were comparable to the attitude of Christ, the life of the religious would be much easier and much happier than we now know it to be. No longer would the religious be sad, weary, superstitious, and prone to many temptations; no longer would he fall a victim to the vices of the laity. You who are religious claim to be followers of the rule of Augustine; were he now to return to this life, I wonder if he would recognize as disciples you who turn not to the rule of the Apostles as Augustine desired, but to the superstitions of the Jews. Some among you attempt to justify the emphasis you place on little things by claiming that unless you are faithful in the less important matters you are opening the door to greater vices. This view deserves some commendation, but there is also a danger that in emphasizing the less you may forget the more.

In short, you must avoid the horns of the dilemma. To observe these unimportant things is, of course, wholesome, but to make them the whole object of your devotions is extremely dangerous. St. Paul recommends ceremonies but he does not bind us to the law, since we are free in Christ. He is not opposed to good works (without them it would be impossible to be a good Christian), yet they do not make the Christian. Paul does not put great worth in the works of Abraham; why should you trust so in your works? Did not God chide the Jews of old for their empty sacrifices and fasts? He tells us that not every man who says "Lord, Lord" is saved and points out that the practice of charity is more important than empty ceremonies. Help him who is oppressed, aid the fatherless, the motherless, the friendless, defend the widow. He recommends that instead of fasting we cancel the debt of him who owes us, that we lighten the burden of him who labors, that we share our bread with the hungry, that we house the homeless and clothe the naked.

I am not advocating that you neglect the mandates of the Church or that you despise honorable traditions and godly customs. If, however, you consider yourselves to be good religious striving for perfection, let your acts be those of one who sincerely desires perfection. If there is a question as to what works should come first, there should be no doubt in your minds. I am not condemning manual works, but I am trying to impress upon you that such works are of little value unless they are accompanied by internal piety. God is a Spirit and is appeased by spiritual sacrifices. A little known poet once wrote, "If God is mind, in poems he's revealed; with a pure mind, then, you ought to worship him." Each one of us should meditate upon these words. While it is true that the author is a pagan and that he has no place of prominence in the world of letters, yet his message, which is read by few and understood by fewer, should not be despised. His advice is worthy of a great theologian. God is mind, the most pure and most simple mind of all; therefore, he must be worshipped with a pure mind.

You believe God to be greatly touched by such material things as a slain bull or the smell of incense; you think that burned wax is a sacrifice. Why, then, did David say, "An afflicted spirit is a sacrifice to God"? If God despised the blood of goats and bulls, he will not despise a contrite and humble heart. If you attend fervently to these things that men expect you to do, spend much more time on those things that God expects of you. Of what advantage to you is a body covered by a religious habit if that same body possesses a mind that is worldly? If your habit is white, should not your mind be white, too? If your tongue is at rest in public, should not your mind be also at rest? What does it profit you when you kneel to venerate the wood of the Cross and forget the mystery of the Cross? You fast and abstain from those things that do not pollute men, yet you do not refrain from obscene conversations, which are a cause of pollution not only to yourself but also to those to whom you speak.

Why do you feed the body and starve the soul? You keep the Sabbath outwardly, but in the secret recesses of your mind you permit all kinds of vices to run rampant. Your body does not commit adultery, but you make your soul to be an adulterer by your greediness. You sing psalms, but your thoughts do not keep pace with your tongue. You bless with the mouth and curse with the heart. You hear the word of God spoken to you, but you refuse it entrance to your heart. Listen closely to the words of the prophet: "Unless you hear within, your soul will weep." And again: "You hear, but you do not understand." Blessed are they who hear the word of God internally. Happy are they to whom the Lord speaks inwardly, for their salvation is assured. Do you wonder why the daughter of the king, she who was goodness itself, was ordered by David to listen within for the voice of God?

Finally, what does it mean if you do not do the evil things that your mind lusts after? What does it mean if you perform good deeds in public but allow evil deeds to dominate your mind? Where is the profit if you have the appearance of a Jerusalem but the character of a Sodom, an Egypt, or a Babylon? If it is to a man's credit that his body walks in Christ's footsteps, it is more to his credit that his mind has followed the way of Christ. If it is a wonderful thing to have touched the Lord's sepulcher, it is more wonderful to have learned the lesson of the mystery of the sepulcher. You who reproach yourselves when you confess your sins to a priest, how will you feel when God accuses you of the same sins? Perhaps you believe that by wax seals, by sums of money, or by pilgrimages your sins are washed away immediately. If you are confident that these are the ways of forgiveness, you are sadly mistaken. If you wish to be forgiven, you, who have loved what you should have hated and who have hated what you should have loved, must attack the enemy within.

Perhaps I am devoting too much time to discussing your external actions, but I will not be convinced of your sanctity until you begin to hate and to flee those things that you used to love. Mary Magdalene loved much, and many sins were forgiven her. The more you love Christ the more you will hate your vices, for just as the shadow follows the body, the hatred of sin follows the love of godliness. I would prefer that you really hate your evil deeds internally rather than enumerate them ten times before a priest.

Therefore, my brethren, put on Christ. Take as your rule that you no longer wish to crawl upon the ground with the beasts, but to rise upon those wings that sprout in the minds of those who love. Advance from the body to the spirit, from the visible world to the invisible, from things sensible to things intelligible, from things compound to things simple. If you come near to the Lord, He will come near to you; if you make a sincere effort to escape from the chains of blindness with which the love of sensible things has bound you, He will come to you, and you, no longer chained to the things of earth, will be enveloped in the silence of God.

MARTIN LUTHER

Christian Freedom

Martin Luther (1483–1546), the greatest of the Protestant reformers, was born in Thuringian Saxony, the son of a successful foundry owner and mine operator. He was sent to the University of Erfurt to study law, but joined the order of the Augustinian Hermits instead and embarked on a course of theological and Biblical studies. Eventually he succeeded his teacher, Johann von Staupitz, in the chair of Biblical studies at the University of Wittenberg, the town where he spent most of his later life. In his early thirties he underwent a religious crisis that caused him to question the theological bases of practices central to the life of the medieval Catholic church. Following the publication of the Ninety-five Thesis *in November 1517 (the traditional date for the beginning of the Protestant Reformation), Luther's critique of the Church and its authority became ever more radical and wide ranging. In 1520 he was finally condemned by the papal bull* Exsurge Domine. *Following this condemnation, Luther began to elaborate his own theological positions, most famously in three key treatises of 1520,* The Freedom of a Christian, The Pagan Servitude of the Church, *and* An Appeal to the Ruling Class of the German Nation. *These three treatises dealt, respectively, with Luther's theory of salvation (or soteriology), his theory of the Church (or ecclesiology), and his theory of the role of the secular power in the governance and reform of the Church. These three treatises, along with the enormous volume of tracts and broadsides that poured from the German presses, established Luther as the intellectual leader of the reform movement. After his heroic refusal to recant at the Diet of Worms, even under pressure from the emperor himself, Luther became the moral leader of the movement as well.*

MARTIN LUTHER'S TREATISE ON CHRISTIAN LIBERTY [THE FREEDOM OF A CHRISTIAN]

Many people have considered Christian faith an easy thing, and not a few have given it a place among the virtues. They do this because they have not experienced it and have never tasted the great strength there is in faith. It is impossible to write well about it or to understand what has been written about it unless one has at one time or another experienced the courage which faith gives a man when trials oppress him. But he who has had even a faint taste of it can never write, speak, meditate, or hear enough concerning it. It is a living "spring of water welling up to eternal life," as Christ calls it in John 4 [:14].

As for me, although I have no wealth of faith to boast of and know how scant my supply is, I nevertheless hope that I have attained to a little faith, even though I have been assailed by great and various temptations; and I hope that I can discuss it, if not more elegantly, certainly more to the point, than those literalists and subtile disputants have previously done, who have not even understood what they have written.

To make the way smoother for the unlearned—for only them do I serve—I shall set down the following two propositions concerning the freedom and the bondage of the spirit:

A Christian is a perfectly free lord of all, subject to none.

A Christian is a perfectly dutiful servant of all, subject to all.

These two theses seem to contradict each other. If, however, they should be found to fit together they would serve our purpose beautifully. Both are Paul's own statements, who says in I Cor. 9 [:19], "For though I am free from all men, I have made myself a slave to all," and in Rom. 13 [:8], "Owe no one anything, except to love one another." Love by its very nature is ready to serve and be subject to him who is loved. So Christ, although he was Lord of all, was "born of woman, born under the law" [Gal. 4:4], and therefore was at the same time a free man and a servant, "in the form of God" and "of a servant" [Phil. 2:6–7].

Let us start, however, with something more remote from our subject, but more obvious. Man has a twofold nature, a spiritual and a bodily one. According to the spiritual nature, which men refer to as the soul, he is called a spiritual, inner, or new man. According to the bodily nature, which men refer to as flesh, he is called a carnal, outward, or old man, of whom the Apostle writes in II Cor. 4 [:16], "Though our outer nature is wasting away, our inner nature is being renewed every day." Because of this diversity of nature the Scriptures assert contradictory things concerning the same man, since these two men in the same man contradict each other, "for the desires of the flesh are against the Spirit, and the desires of the Spirit are against the flesh," according to Gal. 5 [:17].

First, let us consider the inner man to see how a righteous, free, and pious Christian, that is, a spiritual, new, and inner man, becomes what he is. It is evident that no external thing has any influence in producing Christian righteousness or freedom, or in producing unrighteousness or servitude. A simple argument will furnish the proof of this statement. What can it profit the soul if the body is well, free, and active, and eats, drinks, and does as it pleases? For in these respects even the most godless slaves of vice may prosper. On the other hand, how will poor health or imprisonment or hunger or thirst or any other external misfortune harm the soul? Even the most godly men, and those who are free because of clear consciences, are afflicted with these things. None of these things touch either the freedom or the servitude of the soul. It does not help the soul if the body is adorned with the sacred robes of priests or dwells in sacred places or is occupied with sacred duties or prays, fasts, abstains from certain kinds of food, or does any work that can be done by the body and in the body. The righteousness and the freedom of the soul require something far different since the things which have been mentioned could be done by any wicked person. Such works produce nothing but hypocrites. On the other hand, it will not harm the soul if the body is clothed in secular dress, dwells in unconsecrated places, eats and drinks as others do, does not pray aloud, and neglects to do all the above-mentioned things which hypocrites can do.

Furthermore, to put aside all kinds of works, even contemplation, meditation, and all that the soul can do, does not help. One thing, and only one thing, is necessary for Christian life, righteousness, and freedom. That one thing is the most holy Word of God, the gospel of Christ, as Christ says, John 11 [:25], "I am the resurrection and the life; he who believes in me, though he die, yet shall he live"; and John 8 [36], "So if the Son makes you free, you will be free indeed"; and Matt. 4 [:4], "Man shall not live by bread alone, but by every word that proceeds from the mouth of God." Let us then consider it certain and firmly established that the soul can do without anything except the Word of God and that where the Word of God is missing there is no help at all for the soul. If it has the Word of God it is rich and lacks nothing since it is the Word of life, truth, light, peace, righteousness, salvation, joy, liberty, wisdom, power, grace, glory, and of every incalculable blessing. This is why the prophet in the entire Psalm [119] and in many other places yearns and sighs for the Word of God and uses so many names to describe it.

On the other hand, there is no more terrible disaster with which the wrath of God can afflict men than a famine of the hearing of his Word, as he says in Amos [8:11]. Likewise there is no greater mercy than when he sends forth his Word, as we read in Psalm 107 [:20]: "He sent forth his word, and healed them, and delivered them from destruction." Nor was Christ sent into the world for any other ministry except that of the Word. Moreover, the entire spiritual estate—all the apostles, bishops, and priests—has been called and instituted only for the ministry of the Word.

You may ask, "What then is the Word of God, and how shall it be used, since there are so many words of God?" I answer: The Apostle explains this in Romans 1. The Word is the gospel of God concerning his Son, who was made flesh, suffered, rose from the dead, and was glorified through the Spirit who sanctifies. To preach Christ means to feed the soul, make it righteous, set it free, and save it, provided it believes the preaching. Faith alone is the saving and efficacious use of the Word of God, according to Rom. 10 [:9]: "If you confess with your lips that Jesus is Lord and believe in your heart that God raised him from the dead, you will be saved." Furthermore, "Christ is the end of the law, that every one who has faith may be justified" [Rom. 10:4]. Again, in Rom. 1 [:17], "He who through faith is righteous shall live." The Word of God cannot be received and cherished by any works whatever but only by faith. Therefore it is clear that, as the soul needs only the Word of God for its life and righteousness, so it is justified by faith alone and not any works; for if it could be justified by anything else, it would not need the Word, and consequently it would not need faith.

This faith cannot exist in connection with works—that is to say, if you at the same time claim to be justified by works, whatever their character—for that would be the same as "limping with two different opinions" [I Kings 18:21], as worshiping Baal and kissing one's own hand [Job 31:27–28], which, as Job says, is a very great iniquity. Therefore the moment you begin to have faith you learn that all things in you are altogether blameworthy, sinful, and damnable, as the Apostle says in Rom. 3 [:23], "Since all have sinned and fall short of the glory of God," and, "None is righteous, no, not one; . . . all have turned aside, together they have gone wrong," Rom. 3 [:10–12]. When you have learned this you will know that you need Christ, who suffered and rose again for you so that, if you believe in him, you may through this faith become a new man in so far as your sins are forgiven and you are justified by the merits of another, namely, of Christ alone.

Since, therefore, this faith can rule only in the inner man, as Rom. 10 [:10] says, "For man believes with his heart and so is justified," and since faith alone justifies, it is clear that the inner man cannot be justified, freed, or saved by any outer work or action at all, and that these works, whatever their character, have nothing to do with this inner man. On the other hand, only ungodliness and unbelief of heart, and no outer work, make him guilty and a damnable servant of sin. Wherefore it ought to be the first concern of every Christian to lay aside all confidence in works and increasingly to strengthen faith alone and through faith to grow in the knowledge, not of works, but of Christ Jesus, who suffered and rose for him, as Peter teaches in the last chapter of his first Epistle, I Pet. [5:10]. No other work makes a Christian. Thus when the Jews asked Christ, as related in John 6 [:28], what they must do "to be doing the work of God," he brushed aside the multitude of works which he saw they did in great profusion and suggested one work, saying, "This is the work of God, that you believe in him whom he has sent" [John 6:29]; "for on him has God the Father set his seal" [John 6:27].

Therefore true faith in Christ is a treasure beyond comparison which brings with it complete salvation and saves man from every evil, as Christ says in the last chapter of Mark [16:16]: "He who believes and is baptized will be saved; but he who does not believe will be condemned." Isaiah contemplated this treasure and foretold it in chapter 10: "The Lord will make a small and consuming word upon the land, and it will overflow with righteousness" [Cf. Isa. 10:22]. This is as though he said, "Faith, which is a small and perfect fulfilment of the law, will fill believers with so great a righteousness that they will need nothing more to become righteous." So Paul says, Rom. 10 [:10], "For man believes with his heart and so is justified."

Should you ask how it happens that faith alone justifies and offers us such a treasure of great benefits without works in view of the fact that so many works, ceremonies, and laws are prescribed in the Scriptures, I answer: First of all, remember what has been said, namely, that faith alone, without works, justifies, frees, and saves; we shall make this clearer later on. Here we must point out that the entire Scripture of God is divided into two parts: commandments and promises. Although the commandments teach things that are good, the things taught are not done as soon as they are taught, for the commandments show us what we ought to do but do not give us the power to do it. They are intended to teach man to know himself, that through them he may recognize his inability to do good and may despair of his own ability. That is why they are called the Old Testament and constitute the Old Testament. For example, the commandment, "You shall not covet" [Exod. 20:17], is a command which proves us all to be sinners, for no one can avoid coveting no matter how much he may struggle against it. Therefore, in order not to covet and to fulfil the commandment, a man is compelled to despair of himself, to seek the help which he does not find in himself elsewhere and from someone else, as stated in Hosea [13:9]: "Destruction is your own, O Israel: your help is only in me." As we fare with respect to one commandment, so we fare with all, for it is equally impossible for us to keep any one of them.

. . .

Since these promises of God are holy, true, righteous, free, and peaceful words, full of goodness, the soul which clings to them with a firm faith will be so closely united with them and altogether absorbed by them that it not only will share in all their power but will be saturated and intoxicated by them. If a touch of Christ healed, how much more will this most tender spiritual touch, this absorbing of the Word, communicate to the soul all things that belong to the Word. This, then, is how through faith alone without works the soul is justified by the Word of God, sanctified, made true, peaceful, and free, filled with every blessing and truly made a child of God, as John 1 [:12] says: "But to all who . . . believed in his name, he gave power to become children of God."

From what has been said it is easy to see from what source faith derives such great power and why a good work or all good works together cannot equal it. No good work can rely upon the Word of God or live in the soul, for faith alone and the Word of God rule in the soul. Just as the heated iron glows like fire because of the union of fire with it, so the Word imparts its qualities to the soul. It is clear, then, that a Christian has all that he needs in faith and needs no works to justify him; and if he has no need of works, he has no need of the law; and if he has no need of the law, surely he is free from the law. It is true that "the law is not laid down for the just" [I Tim. 1:9]. This is that Christian liberty, our faith, which does not induce us to live in idleness or wickedness but makes the law and works unnecessary for any man's righteousness and salvation.

. . .

From this you once more see that much is ascribed to faith, namely, that it alone can fulfil the law and justify without works. You see that the First Commandment, which says, "You shall worship one God," is fulfilled by faith alone. Though you were nothing but good works from the soles of your feet to the crown of your head, you would still not be righteous or worship God or fulfil the First Commandment, since God cannot be worshiped unless you ascribe to him the glory of truthfulness and all goodness which is due him. This cannot be done by works but only by the faith of the heart. Not by the doing of works but by believing do we glorify God and acknowledge that he is truthful. Therefore faith alone is the righteousness of a Christian and the fulfilling of all the commandments, for he who fulfils the First Commandment has no difficulty in fulfilling all the rest.

But works, being inanimate things, cannot glorify God, although they can, if faith is present, be done to the glory of God. Here, however, we are not inquiring what works and what kind of works are done, but who it is that does them, who glorifies God and brings forth the works. This is done by faith which dwells in the heart and is the source and substance of all our righteousness. Therefore it is a blind and dangerous doctrine which teaches that the commandments must be fulfilled by works. The commandments must be fulfilled before any works can be done, and the works proceed from the fulfilment of the commandments [Rom. 13:10], as we shall hear.

That we may examine more profoundly that grace which our inner man has in Christ, we must realize that in the Old Testament God consecrated to himself all the first-born males. The birthright was highly prized for it involved a twofold honor, that of priesthood and that of kingship. The first-born brother was priest and lord over all the others and a type of Christ, the true and only first-born of God the Father and the Virgin Mary and true king and priest, but not after the fashion of the flesh and the world, for his kingdom is not of this world [John 18:36]. He reigns in heavenly and spiritual things and consecrates them—things such as righteousness, truth, wisdom, peace, salvation, etc. This does not mean that all things on earth and in hell are not also subject to him—otherwise how could he protect and save us from them?—but that his kingdom consists neither in them nor of them. Nor does his priesthood consist in the outer splendor of robes and postures like those of the human priesthood of Aaron and our present-day church; but it consists of spiritual things through which he by an invisible service intercedes for us in heaven before God, there offers himself as a sacrifice, and does all things a priest should do, as Paul describes him under the type of Melchizedek in the Epistle to the Hebrews [Heb. 6–7]. Nor does he only pray and intercede for us but he teaches us inwardly through the living instruction of his Spirit, thus performing the two real functions of a priest, of which the prayers and the preaching of human priests are visible types.

Now just as Christ by his birthright obtained these two prerogatives, so he imparts them to and shares them with everyone who believes in him according to the law of the above-mentioned marriage, according to which the wife owns whatever belongs to the husband. Hence all of us who believe in Christ are priests and kings in Christ, as I Pet. 2 [:9] says: "You are a chosen race, God's own people, a royal priesthood, a priestly kingdom, that you may declare the wonderful deeds of him who called you out of darkness into his marvelous light."

The nature of this priesthood and kingship is something like this: First, with respect to the kingship, every Christian is by faith so exalted above all things that, by virtue of a spiritual power, he is lord of all things without exception, so that nothing can do him any harm. As a matter of fact, all things are made subject to him and are compelled to serve him in obtaining salvation. Accordingly Paul says in Rom. 8 [:28], "All things work together for good for the elect," and in I Cor. 3 [:21–23], "All things are yours whether . . . life or death or the present or the future, all are yours; and you are Christ's. . . ." This is not to say that every Christian is placed over all things to have and control them by physical power—a madness with which some churchmen are afflicted—for such power belongs to kings, princes, and other men on earth. Our ordinary experience in life shows us that we are subjected to all, suffer many things, and even die. As a matter of fact, the more Christian a man is, the more evils, sufferings, and deaths he must endure, as we see in Christ the first-born prince himself, and in all his brethren, the saints. The power of which we speak is spiritual. It rules in the midst of enemies and is powerful in the midst of oppression. This means nothing else than that "power is made perfect in weakness" [II Cor. 12:9] and that in all things I can find profit toward salvation [Rom. 8:28], so that the cross and death itself are compelled to serve me and to work together with me for my salvation. This is a splendid privilege and hard to attain, a truly omnipotent power, a spiritual dominion in which there is nothing so good and nothing so evil but that it shall work together for good to me, if only I believe. Yes, since faith alone suffices for salvation, I need nothing except faith exercising the power and dominion of its own liberty. Lo, this is the inestimable power and liberty of Christians.

Not only are we the freest of kings, we are also priests forever, which is far more excellent than being kings, for as priests we are worthy to appear before God to pray for others and to teach one another divine things. These are the functions of priests, and they cannot be granted to any unbeliever. Thus Christ has made it possible for us, provided we believe in him, to be not only his brethren, co-heirs, and fellow-kings, but also his fellow-priests. Therefore we may boldly come into the presence of God in the spirit of faith [Heb. 10:19, 22] and cry "Abba, Father!" pray for one another, and do all things which we see done and foreshadowed in the outer and visible works of priests.

He, however, who does not believe is not served by anything. On the contrary, nothing works for his good, but he himself is a servant of all, and all things turn out badly for him because he wickedly uses them to his own advantage and not to the glory of God. So he is no priest but a wicked man whose prayer becomes sin and who never comes into the presence of God because God does not hear sinners [John 9:31]. Who then can comprehend the lofty dignity of the Christian? By virtue of his royal power he rules over all things, death, life, and sin, and through his priestly glory is omnipotent with God because he does the things which God asks and desires, as it is written, "He will fulfil the desire of those who fear him; he also will hear their cry and save them" [Cf. Phil. 4:13]. To this glory a man attains, certainly not by any works of his, but by faith alone.

From this anyone can clearly see how a Christian is free from all things and over all things so that he needs no works to make him righteous and save him, since faith alone abundantly confers all these things. Should he grow so foolish, however, as to presume to become righteous, free, saved, and a Christian by means of some good work, he would instantly lose faith and all its benefits, a foolishness aptly illustrated in the fable of the dog who runs along a stream with a piece of meat in his mouth and, deceived by the reflection of the meat in the water, opens his mouth to snap at it and so loses both the meat and the reflection.

You will ask, "If all who are in the church are priests, how do these whom we now call priests differ from laymen?" I answer: Injustice is done those words "priest," "cleric," "spiritual," "ecclesiastic," when they are transferred from all Christians to those few who are now by a mischievous usage called "ecclesiastics." Holy Scripture makes no distinction between them, although it gives the name "ministers," "servants," "stewards" to those who are now proudly called popes, bishops, and lords and who should according to the ministry of the Word serve others and teach them the faith of Christ and the freedom of believers. Although we are all equally priests, we cannot all publicly minister and teach. We ought not do so even if we could. Paul writes accordingly in I Cor. 4 [:1], "This is how one should regard us, as servants of Christ and stewards of the mysteries of God."

That stewardship, however, has now been developed into so great a display of power and so terrible a tyranny that no heathen empire or other earthly power can be compared with it, just as if laymen were not also Christians. Through this perversion the knowledge of Christian grace, faith, liberty, and of Christ himself has altogether perished, and its place has been taken by an unbearable bondage of human works and laws until we have become, as the Lamentations of Jeremiah [1] say, servants of the vilest men on earth who abuse our misfortune to serve only their base and shameless will.

To return to our purpose, I believe that it has now become clear that it is not enough or in any sense Christian to preach the works, life, and words of Christ as historical facts, as if the knowledge of these would suffice for the conduct of life; yet this is the fashion among those who must today be regarded as our best preachers. Far less is it sufficient or Christian to say nothing at all about Christ and to teach instead the laws of men and the decrees of the fathers. Now there are not a few who preach Christ and read about him that they may move men's affections to sympathy with Christ, to anger against the Jews, and such childish and effeminate nonsense. Rather ought Christ to be preached to the end that faith in him may be established that he may not only be Christ, but be Christ for you and me, and that what is said of him and is denoted in his name may be effectual in us. Such faith is produced and preserved in us by preaching why Christ came, what he brought and bestowed, what benefit it is to us to accept him. This is done when that Christian liberty which he bestows is rightly taught and we are told in what way we Christians are all kings and priests and therefore lords of all and may firmly believe that whatever we have done is pleasing and acceptable in the sight of God, as I have already said.

What man is there whose heart, upon hearing these things, will not rejoice to its depth, and when receiving such comfort will not grow tender so that he will love Christ as he never could by means of any laws or works? Who would have the power to harm or frighten such a heart? If the knowledge of sin or the fear of death should break in upon it, it is ready to hope in the Lord. It does not grow afraid when it hears tidings of evil. It is not disturbed when it sees its enemies. This is so because it believes that the righteousness of Christ is its own and that its sin is not its own, but Christ's, and that all sin is swallowed up by the righteousness of Christ. This, as has been said above, is a necessary consequence on account of faith in Christ. So the heart learns to scoff at death and sin and to say with the Apostle, "O death, where is thy victory? O death, where is thy sting? The sting of death is sin, and the power of sin is the law. But thanks be to God, who gives us the victory through our Lord Jesus Christ" [I Cor. 15:55–57]. Death is swallowed up not only in the victory of Christ but also by our victory, because through faith his victory has become ours and in that faith we also are conquerors.

Let this suffice concerning the inner man, his liberty, and the source of his liberty, the righteousness of faith. He needs neither laws nor good works but, on the contrary, is injured by them if he believes that he is justified by them.

. . .

For this reason, although we should boldly resist those teachers of traditions and sharply censure the laws of the popes by means of which they plunder the people of God, yet we must spare the timid multitude whom those impious tyrants hold captive by means of these laws until they are set free. Therefore fight strenuously against the wolves, but for the sheep and not also against the sheep. This you will do if you inveigh against the laws and the lawgivers and at the same time observe the laws with the weak so that they will not be offended, until they also recognize tyranny and understand their freedom. If you wish to use your freedom, do so in secret, as Paul says, Rom. 14 [:22], "The faith that you have, keep between yourself and God"; but take care not to use your freedom in the sight of the weak. On the other hand, use your freedom constantly and consistently in the sight of and despite the tyrants and the stubborn so that they also may learn that they are impious, that their laws are of no avail for righteousness, and that they had no right to set them up.

Since we cannot live our lives without ceremonies and works, and the perverse and untrained youth need to be restrained and saved from harm by such bonds; and since each one should keep his body under control by means of such works, there is need that the minister of Christ be far-seeing and faithful. He ought so to govern and teach Christians in all these matters that their conscience and faith will not be offended and that there will not spring up in them a suspicion and a root of bitterness and many will thereby be defiled, as Paul admonishes the Hebrews [Heb. 12:15]; that is, that they may not lose faith and become defiled by the false estimate of the value of works and think that they must be justified by works. Unless faith is at the same time constantly taught, this happens easily and defiles a great many, as has been done until now through the pestilent, impious, soul-destroying traditions of our popes and the opinions of our theologians. By these snares numberless souls have been dragged down to hell, so that you might see in this the work of Antichrist.

In brief, as wealth is the test of poverty, business the test of faithfulness, honors the test of humility, feasts the test of temperance, pleasures the test of chastity, so ceremonies are the test of the righteousness of faith. "Can a man," asks Solomon, "carry fire in his bosom and his clothes and not be burned?" [Prov. 6:27]. Yet as a man must live in the midst of wealth, business, honors, pleasures, and feasts, so also must he live in the midst of ceremonies, that is, in the midst of dangers. Indeed, as infant boys need beyond all else to be cherished in the bosoms and by the hands of maidens to keep them from perishing, yet when they are grown up their salvation is endangered if they associate with maidens, so the inexperienced and perverse youth need to be restrained and trained by the iron bars of ceremonies lest their unchecked ardor rush headlong into vice after vice. On the other hand, it would be death for them always to be held in bondage to ceremonies, thinking that these justify them. They are rather to be taught that they have been so imprisoned in ceremonies, not that they should be made righteous or gain great merit by them, but that they might thus be kept from doing evil and might more easily be instructed to the righteousness of faith. Such instruction they would not endure if the impulsiveness of their youth were not restrained.

Hence ceremonies are to be given the same place in the life of a Christian as models and plans have among builders and artisans. They are prepared, not as a permanent structure, but because without them nothing could be built or made. When the structure is complete the models and plans are laid aside. You see, they are not despised, rather they are greatly sought after; but what we despise is the false estimate of them since no one holds them to be the real and permanent structure.

If any man were so flagrantly foolish as to care for nothing all his life long except the most costly, careful, and persistent preparation of plans and models and never to think of the structure itself, and were satisfied with his work in producing such plans and mere aids to work, and boasted of it, would not all men pity his insanity and think that something great might have been built with what he has wasted? Thus we do not despise ceremonies and works, but we set great store by them; but we despise the false estimate placed upon works in order that no one may think that they are true righteousness, as those hypocrites believe who spend and lose their whole lives in zeal for works and never reach that goal for the sake of which the works are to be done, who, as the Apostle says, "will listen to anybody and can never arrive at a knowledge of the truth" [II Tim. 3:7]. They seem to wish to build, they make their preparations, and yet they never build. Thus they remain caught in the form of religion and do not attain unto its power [II Tim. 3:5]. Meanwhile they are pleased with their efforts and even dare to judge all others whom they do not see shining with a like show of works. Yet with the gifts of God which they have spent and abused in vain they might, if they had been filled with faith, have accomplished great things to their own salvation and that of others.

Since human nature and natural reason, as it is called, are by nature superstitious and ready to imagine, when laws and works are prescribed, that righteousness must be obtained through laws and works; and further, since they are trained and confirmed in this opinion by the practice of all earthly lawgivers, it is impossible that they should of themselves escape from the slavery of works and come to a knowledge of the freedom of faith. Therefore there is need of the prayer that the Lord may give us and make us *theodidacti*, that is, those taught by God [John 6:45], and himself, as he has promised, write his law in our hearts; otherwise there is no hope for us. If he himself does not teach our hearts this wisdom hidden in mystery [I Cor. 2:7], nature can only condemn it and judge it to be heretical because nature is offended by it and regards it as foolishness. So we see that it happened in the old days in the case of the apostles and prophets, and so godless and blind popes and their flatterers do to me and to those who are like me. May God at last be merciful to them and to us and cause his face to shine upon us that we may know his way upon earth [Ps. 67:1–2], his salvation among all nations, God, who is blessed forever [II Cor. 11:31]. Amen.

MARTIN LUTHER

Christian Marriage

***

Martin Luther (1483–1546), the greatest of the Protestant reformers, was born in Thuringian Saxony, the son of a successful foundry owner and mine operator. He was sent to the University of Erfurt to study law, but joined the order of the Augustinian Hermits instead and embarked on a course of theological and Biblical studies. Eventually he succeeded his teacher, Johann von Staupitz, in the chair of Biblical studies at the University of Wittenberg, the town where he spent most of his later life. In his early thirties he underwent a religious crisis that caused him to question the theological bases of practices central to the life of the medieval Catholic church. Following the publication of the Ninety-five Thesis *in November 1517 (the traditional date for the beginning of the Protestant Reformation), Luther's critique of the Church and its authority became ever more radical and wide ranging. In 1520 he was finally condemned by the papal bull* Exsurge Domine. *Following this condemnation, Luther began to elaborate his own theological positions, most famously in three key treatises of 1520,* The Freedom of a Christian, The Pagan Servitude of the Church, *and* An Appeal to the Ruling Class of the German Nation. *These three treatises dealt, respectively, with Luther's theory of salvation (or soteriology), his theory of the Church (or ecclesiology), and his theory of the role of the secular power in the governance and reform of the Church. These three treatises, along with the enormous volume of tracts and broadsides that poured from the German presses, established Luther as the intellectual leader of the reform movement. After his heroic refusal to recant at the Diet of Worms, even under pressure from the emperor himself, Luther became the moral leader of the movement as well.*

***

There is no Scriptural warrant whatsoever for regarding marriage as a sacrament; and indeed the Romanists have used the same traditions, both to extol it as a sacrament, and to make it naught but a mockery. Let us look into this matter.

We have maintained that a word of divine promise is associated with every sacrament, and anyone who receives the sacrament must also believe in that word of promise, for it is impossible that the sign should in itself be the sacrament. But nowhere in Scripture do we read that anyone would receive the grace of God by getting married; nor does the rite of matrimony contain any hint that that ceremony is of divine institution. Nowhere do we read that it was instituted by God in order to symbolize something, although we grant that all things done in the sight of men can be understood as metaphors and allegories of things invisible. Yet metaphors and allegories are not sacraments, and it is of sacraments that we are speaking.

There has been such a thing as marriage itself ever since the beginning of the world, and it also exists amongst unbelievers to the present day. Therefore no grounds exist on which the Romanists can validly call it a sacrament of the new law, and a function solely of the church. The marriages of our ancestors were no less sacred than our own, nor less real among unbelievers than believers. Yet no one calls marriage of unbelievers a sacrament. Also, there are irreligious marriages even amongst believers, worse than among any pagans. Why then should it be called a sacrament in such a case, and yet not among pagans? Or are we talking the same sort of nonsense about marriage as about baptism and the church, and saying it is only a sacrament within the church? Is it the case that some people speak as if they were demented, and declare that temporal power exists only in the church? Yet this is so childish and laughable as to expose our ignorance and foolhardiness to the ridicule of unbelievers.

The Romanists will reply that the apostle says in Ephesians 5 [:31f.], "The twain shall become one flesh; this is a great sacrament." Do you mean to contradict this plain statement of the apostle? My reply would be that to put forth this argument shows great negligence, and very careless and thoughtless reading. Nowhere in Holy Scripture does the noun, "sacrament", bear the meaning which is customary in the church, but rather the opposite. In every instance, it means, not "a sign of something sacred", but the sacred, secret, and recondite thing itself. Thus in I Corinthians 4 [:1], Paul says: "Let a man so account of us, as of ministers of Christ, and stewards of the mysteries of God", that is the sacraments. Where the Vulgate uses *sacramentum*, the Greek text reads *mysterion*, a word which the translator sometimes translates, and sometimes transliterates. Thus in the present case, the Greek says: "The twain shall become one flesh. This is a great mystery." That explains how it came about that they understood it as a sacrament of the new dispensation, and this they would have been far from doing if they had read *mysterion*, as it is in Greek.

So also in I Timothy 3 [:16], Paul calls Christ Himself a sacrament, when he says: He was evidently a great sacrament (i.e., *mysterion*), for He was manifested in the flesh, justified in the spirit, seen of angels, preached among the nations, believed on in the world, received up in glory. Why have the Romanists not made an eighth sacrament out of this, when Paul's authority is so plainly there? Although they restrained themselves in this instance, when they had abundant opportunity to contrive sacraments, why are they so extravagant in the others? Plainly, they have been betrayed by their ignorance both of the facts and of the vocabulary; going simply by the sound of the words, they have founded their own opinions on them. Once they had arbitrarily taken "sacrament" to mean "sign", they immediately, and without further criticism or closer examination, set down the word "sign" every time they read "sacrament" in Holy Scripture. In this manner also, they have brought verbal meanings, human customs and such like, into the sacred writings, transforming the proper meaning into what they themselves have fabricated, turning anything into anything else. Thus it comes about that they are always making a vague use of terms like "good works", "evil works", "sin", "grace", "justification", "virtue", and almost all the main terms and subjects. For they employ the whole of these arbitrarily, on the basis of writings which are merely human, to the detriment of God's truth and our salvation.

According to Paul, sacrament, or mystery, is the very wisdom of the Spirit, and this is hidden in the mystery, as he says in I Corinthians 2 [:7ff.]: "This wisdom is Christ, and, for the reason just given, He is unknown to the rulers of this world; and therefore they crucified Him. To them, He is still foolishness, a scandal, a stumbling-block, and a sign to be controverted." "Stewards of the mysteries" is the name given by Paul to those preachers who preach Christ and proclaim Him as the power and the wisdom of God, and this in such a way that, unless you believe, you will not understand [I Cor. 4:1]. Thus a sacrament is a *mysterion,* a secret thing described by words, but seized by faith in the heart. That is what is said in the passage under discussion: "The twain shall be one flesh, this is a great sacrament" (Greek—*mysterion*). The Romanists think this was said of matrimony, whereas Paul himself is using these words about Christ and the church, as he himself goes on to explain clearly when he says: "But I speak of Christ and of the church" [Eph. 5:32]. You see, then, the nature of the agreement between the Romanists and Paul? Paul says that he is speaking of the great sacrament in Christ and the church; they, however, preach it in terms of male and female. If it were permissible to handle Scripture in this unbridled fashion, there would be no room for surprise whatever sacrament they found in it, nor even if they found a hundred.

We conclude that Christ and the church are a "mystery", or something at once hidden and of great importance, a thing which can, and should, be spoken of metaphorically, and of which matrimony is a sort of material allegory; but matrimony ought not to be called a sacrament on this account. The heavens are meant to represent the apostles in Psalm 19 [:1ff.] and the sun is metaphorically Christ, and the seas the people; but this does not mean that they are sacraments. There is no mention of either a divine institution, or a promise, which together would constitute a sacrament. Therefore Paul, in Ephesians 5 [:23ff.], either quotes Genesis 2 [:24] for the words about marriage, and applies them on his own initiative to Christ; or else, according to prevailing opinion, he teaches that the spiritual marriage of Christ is contained here, when he says: "Even as Christ cherisheth the church, because we are members of His body, of His flesh, and of His bones. For this cause shall a man leave his father and mother, and shall cleave to his wife; and the twain shall become one flesh. This mystery is great, but I speak in regard of Christ and of the church [Eph. 5:29ff.]. You see that Paul means this whole passage to have been spoken by him about Christ, and he takes pains to warn the reader to understand that the sacrament is not in the marriage but in Christ and the Church.[1]

Granted, therefore, that matrimony is a figure for Christ and the church, yet it is not a sacrament of divine institution; it was introduced into the church by men who were misled by their ignorance both of the subject and the record. But, if this fact is not a hindrance to faith, it ought to be borne with in a charitable spirit, just as many other human devices due to weakness and ignorance in the church are to be tolerated so long as they do not stand in the way of faith and the Holy Scriptures. But at the present moment we are arguing on behalf of the certainty and purity of faith and the Scriptures. Our faith would be exposed to scoffing if we affirmed that something was contained in the Holy Scriptures or in the articles of our faith, which was later proved not to be there. Then we should be found unversed in our own special province, causing difficulties to our enemies and to the weak; but most of all we should detract from the authority of the Holy Scriptures. For there is a very great difference between what has been handed down about God in the Holy Scriptures, on the one hand; and, on the other, that which has been introduced into the church by men of no matter what sanctity or learning. Thus far about matrimony as a rite.

What then shall we say about those impious, man-made laws in which this divinely instituted way of life has become enmeshed, and which have sometimes exalted, and, at others, debased it? Merciful God! what a dreadful thing it is to examine the temerity of the Romanizing oppressors who divorce couples, or enforce marriages, just according to their own sweet will. I ask in all earnestness: Has the human race been handed over to the good pleasure of these men to be made sport of, to be subjected to any sort of misuse, and for the sake of whatever filthy lucre they can make out of it?

A greatly esteemed book entitled the *Summa Angelica*[2] enjoys a wide circulation, but it consists of a jumbled collection, a kind of bilge-water, of the offscourings of all that men have handed down. It would more appropriately be called the *Summa worse than Diabolical*. It contains numberless horrible things by which confessors think they receive instruction, whereas they are led into most pernicious confusion. It enumerates eighteen impediments to marriage; but, if you will examine them with the unbiased mind and the uncensored view given by faith, you will see that a number of them are foretold by the apostle when he said: "They shall give heed to the spirits of devils, who shall speak lies in hypocrisy, forbidding to marry" [I Tim. 4:1ff.] Is not the invention of so many impediments, and the setting of so many traps, the reason that people do not marry; or if they are married, the reason why the marriage is annulled? Who gave this power to man? It may be that they were religious men, zealous and devout, yet by what right does another man's saintliness put limits on my own liberty? Let any one who is so minded be a saint and a zealot to any extent he likes, but let him not harm any one else in doing it, or steal my freedom.

Yet I rejoice that these men have got their due in these disgraceful regulations. By their means the Romanists of today have become market-stall holders. What is it they sell? It is male and female pudenda, goods most worthy of these merchants whose avarice and irreligion are worse than the most sordid obscenity imaginable. For there is no impediment to marriage nowadays which they cannot legitimize for money. These man-made regulations seem to have come into existence for no other reason than raking in money and netting in souls, to serve these greedy and rapacious hunters. It is all done in order that the "Abomination" might stand in the church of God, and publicly sell to men the pudenda of both sexes; or, in Scriptural language, their "shame and nakedness" [Lev. 18:6ff.], of which they had already robbed them by the effect of these laws. O traffic worthy of our pontiffs who, being given up unto a reprobate mind, carry on that traffic with extreme baseness and utter lack of decency, instead of exercising the ministry of the gospel, which their greed and ambition make them despise!

You will probably ask me what I can say or do. If I were to enter into detail, I should go on without end. Everything is in such confusion that you do not know where to begin, in which direction to turn, or where to stop. But this I know, that the body politic cannot be felicitously governed merely by rules and regulations. If the administrator be sagacious, he will conduct the government more happily when guided by circumstances rather than by legal decrees. If he be not so wise, his legal methods will only result in harm, since he will not know how to use them, nor how to temper them to the case in hand. Hence, in public affairs, it is more important to make sure that good and wise men are in control than that certain laws are promulgated. Men of this kind will themselves be the best of laws, will be alert to every kind of problem, and will resolve them equitably. If knowledge of the divine laws accompanies native sagacity, it is obvious that written laws will be superfluous and noxious. Above all else, remember that Christian love has no need of any laws at all.

Similarly, with regard to those impediments to marriage in respect of which the pope claims power to grant dispensations, but which are not mentioned in Scripture, I would urge it upon every priest and friar with all the power I possess, to declare, without more ado, that all those marriages are valid, the only objection being that they have been contracted merely against one or other of the ecclesiastical or pontifical canons. Let them arm themselves with the divine law which says: "What God hath joined together, let no man put asunder" [Matt. 19:6]. The union of man and wife is in accordance with divine law, and this holds good no matter how it may contradict any regulations made by men; and these same regulations ought therefore to be disregarded without any hesitation. If a man ought to leave his father and mother, and cleave to his wife, so much the more ought he to trample upon frivolous and wicked human regulations, in order to cleave to his wife. And if the pope, or bishop, or official, should dissolve a marriage contracted contrary to one of these man-made laws, then he is an Antichrist; he does violence to nature, and is guilty of contempt of the divine Majesty; for the text still remains true that: "What God hath joined together let no man put asunder."

Remember, also, that no man has a right to promulgate such laws, that Christ has given Christians a freedom which rises above all human laws, especially when the divine law intervenes. Similarly, it says in Mark 2 [:28, 27], "The Son of Man is also lord of the Sabbath, for man was not made for the Sabbath, but the Sabbath for man." Further, Paul condemned such laws in advance when he foretold that there would be those who prohibited marriage [I Tim. 4:3]. Therefore, as far as the

Scriptures permit, there should be an end to the validity of those impediments which arise from spiritual or legal affinities, or from consanguinities. The Scriptures forbid only the second degree of consanguinity, as in Leviticus 18 [:6ff.]. Here twelve persons are within the prohibited degrees, viz.: mother, step-mother, full sister, half-sister by either parent, granddaughter, father's sister, mother's sister, daughter-in-law, brother's wife, wife's sister, step-daughter, uncle's wife. Thus only the first grade of affinity and the second of consanguinity are prohibited, and not even these in every respect, as is clear on close examination. The daughter and granddaughter of a brother or sister are not mentioned as prohibited, although they fall in the second grade. Therefore, if at any time a marriage has been contracted outside these grades, than which none other has at any time been prohibited by the divine laws, then it should never be dissolved on the ground that it is contrary to any laws of human origin. Marriage itself, as a divine institution, is incomparably superior to any laws, so that it ought not to be broken for the sake of laws, but laws for its sake.

In the same way, the nonsense about compaternity, commaternity, confraternity, consorority, and confiliety, ought to be completely blotted out, and the marriage contracted. These spiritual affinities are due purely to superstition. If neither the one who administers the baptism, nor the godparent at the baptism, is permitted to marry the one who has been baptized, then why is any Christian man permitted to marry any Christian woman? Does a fuller relationship arise from the rite or the sign of the sacrament, than from the sacrament itself? Is not a Christian man the brother of a Christian sister? Is not a baptized man spiritual brother to a baptized woman? What silly stuff they talk! If any husband teaches the gospel to his wife, and instructs her in faith in Christ, whereby he in very truth becomes her spiritual father—then ought she no longer to remain his wife? Would Paul not have been allowed to marry one of the Corinthian girls, all of whom he claims to have begotten in Christ? [I Cor. 4:15]. See how Christian liberty has been oppressed by the blindness of human superstition!

Even more trifling are the legal affinities, and yet the Romanists have made these superior to the divine right of marriage. Nor would I grant that there is any impediment in what they call "disparity of religion". This means that a Christian man is not permitted to marry an unbaptized woman, either as such, or only on condition that she be converted to the faith. Was it God or man who set up this prohibition? Who has given men the authority of prohibiting this kind of marriage? It was a spirit "speaking lies in hypocrisy", as Paul says [I Tim. 4:2]. It would be to the point to say of them; "The wicked have related fables to me, not according to thy law" [Ps. 119:85]. Patritius, a pagan, married the Christian Monica, the mother of St. Augustine; why should not a similar marriage be allowed nowadays? The same obstinate, if not sinful, harshness is seen in the "impediment of crime", e.g., if a man marries either a woman with whom he had previously committed adultery, or the widow of a man whose death he had contrived in order that he might marry her. I beg you, in all earnestness, to tell me whence comes this harshness of man towards men, such as God has nowhere demanded? Or do they pretend not to know that David, a man held in the highest reverence, married Bathsheba, Uriah's wife, after both the above crimes had been committed? I mean her previous adultery, and the murder of her husband. If the divine law operates in this way, why do men act despotically against their fellow servants?

What Romanists call the "impediment of a tie" is also recognized: whereby a man is engaged to one woman, but has sexual relations with another woman. In such a case their ruling is that his engagement to the first is ended. This I simply do not understand. My view is that a man who has betrothed himself to a woman is no longer his own, and though he has had sexual relations with the second, he belongs to the first by the divine commandment, even though he has had no sexual relations with her. He cannot give away the self he does not possess; rather, he has deceived the first, and in fact committed adultery with the second. The reason the Romanists see it differently is that they give more weight to the carnal union than to the divine command according to which the man has "plighted his troth" already, and ought to keep it for ever. For you can only give what is your own. God forbid that anyone should circumvent his brother in any matter that ought to be kept in good faith above and beyond all human traditions whatever. I do not believe that he could live with the second with a good conscience, and therefore I think that this impediment ought to be completely done away with. For if the vow of one of the religious orders takes away one's self-disposal, why not also a troth plighted and received? This is indeed one of the precepts and fruits of the spirit according to Galatians 5 [:22], whereas these vows derive from the human will. Moreover, if a married woman can claim her husband back, in spite of the fact that he has taken a monastic vow, why is it not allowed that an engaged woman should claim her betrothed back, even though he has had sexual connections with another woman? Rather, as I have already said, anyone who has plighted his troth to a woman cannot rightly take a monastic vow. His duty is to marry her, because it is his duty to keep faith. This precept comes from God, and therefore cannot be superseded by any human decree. In a case like this, he is under a far greater obligation to keep faith with the first woman, because he could only plight his faith with the second with a lie in his heart, and therefore it would not be plighted. What he has done, in God's sight, is to deceive her. For these reasons, the "impediment of error" operates here, and makes marriage with the second woman null and void.

The "impediment of ordination" is also a purely man-made regulation, especially when the Romanists blatantly say that it overrides a marriage which has already been solemnized; for they always exalt their own rules as superior to the divine ordinances. I am not criticizing ordination to the priesthood as known to-day, but I see that Paul commands that "the bishop be the husband of one wife" [I Tim. 3:2]. Therefore it is not possible to annul the marriage of a deacon, priest, bishop, or anyone who is ordained; although, of course, it must be admitted that Paul knew nothing of the kinds of priests and ordinations that pertain to-day. Perish then those accursed man-made regulations which seem only to have entered the church to multiply the dangers, the sins, and the evils there! Between a priest and his wife, therefore, there exists a valid and inseparable marriage, as is proved by the divine commands. What of it, then, if men who fear not God prohibit, and even annul, such a marriage entirely on their own authority? Nevertheless, what men have prohibited God permits, and His laws take precedence when at variance with human regulations.

The "impediment of public propriety", by which marriage contracts can be annulled, is a similar fiction. I am angered by the irreligious audacity which so speedily separates those whom God has joined, that you can recognize the Antichrist who attacks everything Christ said or taught. In the case of an engaged couple, if one of them should die before their marriage, what reason is there why the survivor should not marry one of the deceased's relatives who comes within the fourth degree of consanguinity? To forbid this is not a case of the vindication of public propriety, but ignorance of it. The people of Israel possessed the best laws, because they were divinely instituted, and yet there was none of this kind of vindication of public propriety. On the contrary, God commanded the next of kin to marry a woman left a widow. Otherwise, the question might be asked: Ought the people who possess the liberty of Christians to be burdened with more onerous laws than the people in bondage to the Mosaic law? To sum up my discussion of what should be called fictions rather than impediments: there appears to me at present to be no impediment which can annul a legal contract of marriage, except sexual impotence, ignorance of a marriage already existing, or a vow of chastity. Concerning such a vow, my uncertainty up to now is such that I do not know at what age it ought to be regarded as valid, as I have already said with reference to the sacrament of baptism. Matrimony, therefore, is an example sufficient in itself to show up the nature of the present unhappy and hopeless state of confusion. It also shows that any and all of the practices of the church are impeded, and entangled, and endangered, on account of the pestilential, unlearned, and irreligious, man-made ordinances. There is no hope of a cure unless the whole of the laws made by men, no matter what their standing, are repealed once for all. When we have recovered the freedom of the gospel, we should judge and rule in accordance with it in every respect. Amen.

Now it is needful to discuss sexual impotence, for, by so doing, it may be easier to give advice to those whose minds are labouring and in peril. But I would preface this with the remark that what I have said above about impediments applies to marriages already solemnized; and none of these should be annulled on account of such impediments as I have discussed. But in regard to a marriage which has yet to be solemnized, I will briefly repeat what I have already said. When if youthful passion makes the case urgent, or if there are other needs that the pope would meet by granting a dispensation, then any Christian can grant one to his brother, or he can grant one to himself. This opinion means that he is given permission to carry his wife off in the teeth of any oppressive laws whatsoever. Why should I be deprived of my freedom by someone else's ignorance or superstition? Or, if the pope would grant a dispensation for a fee, why should not I grant one to myself or my brother for the good of my salvation? Is it the pope who decrees laws? Let him decree them for himself, but leave my freedom to me, or I will take it without his knowing.

On the question of impotence:

Let us examine such a case as this. A woman is married to an impotent man, but cannot, or perhaps will not, prove in court her husband's impotence, because of the numerous items of evidence, and the notoriety, which would be occasioned by a legal process. Still she wishes to have a child, and is unable to remain continent. In addition, suppose I had advised her to seek a divorce in order to marry another, as she was content, in her conscience, to do, and after ample experience on the part of herself and her husband, that he was impotent; if, then, however, her husband would not agree to her proposal, I myself would give the further advice,[3] that, with her husband's consent (although now really he is not her husband, but only a man who lives in the same house) she should have coition with another man, say her husband's brother, but keeping this "marriage" secret, and ascribing the children to the putative father, as they call such a one. As to the question whether such a woman is "saved" or in a state of salvation, I would reply, Yes, because in this case a mistake due to ignorance of the man's impotence created a false situation which impedes the marriage proper; the harshness of the law does not allow divorce; yet by the divine law the woman is free, and so cannot be forced to remain continent. Therefore the husband ought to concede this right to her, allowing her coition with another, since she is his wife in a formal and unreal sense only.

Further, if the man will not consent, and if he does not wish to be separated, then, rather than let her burn or commit adultery, I would counsel her to contract matrimony with someone else, and flee to some distant and unknown region. What other counsel can be given to one constantly struggling with the dangers of her own natural emotions? I know, of course, that some will be disturbed because it would be unfair for the children of a secret marriage of this kind to be the heirs of the putative father. But, on the one hand, if it were done with the husband's consent, there would be no unfairness. If, on the other hand, he were ignorant of it, or had refused his consent, then let an unfettered, and therefore Christian, reasonableness, if not charity itself, judge the case and say which of the two was the more harmful to the other. The wife alienates her husband's estate, but the husband deceives the wife, and is defrauding her totally in body and life. Does not the man commit the greater sin by wasting the body and life of his wife, than the woman in alienating a quantity of temporal property? So either let him agree to a divorce, or else let him bear with children not his own. The fault is his in having deceived an innocent girl, and defrauded her of the full use of both her life and her body, besides giving her an almost unbearable cause for committing adultery. Let these two cases be weighed in a just balance. According to any legal code, forsooth, fraud ought to recoil on the fraudulent, and any one doing harm should make it good. In what respect does a husband, such as we are discussing, differ from a man who keeps another's wife in prison along with her husband? Would not such a bully be compelled to support the wife and children as well as the husband, or else set them free? And this should happen in the case under discussion. Hence, in my judgment, the man ought to be compelled either to accept divorce, or support his putative child as his own heir. Without doubt that is the judgment which charity calls for. In that case, the impotent man, because not really a husband, should support his wife's issue in the same spirit as if his wife were ill, or suffered some other indisposition, and he had to nurse her at great cost. For it is by his own fault, and not his wife's, that she labours under this wrong. I have set out my views to the best of my ability for the sake of giving instruction to those whose consciences are disquieted, for my desire is to bring what little comfort I can to my afflicted brethren who are in this kind of captivity.

In regard to divorce, it is still a subject for debate whether it should be allowed. For my part, I have such a hatred of divorce that I prefer bigamy to divorce, yet I do not venture an opinion whether bigamy should be allowed. Christ's own command, as chief pastor, is given in Matthew 5 [:32], "Every one that putteth away his wife, saving for the cause of fornication, maketh her an adulteress; and whosoever shall marry her when she is put away committeth adultery." Hence, Christ permitted divorce, but only in case of fornication. It follows that the pope is in error where he grants divorce for other causes. No one, therefore, should think his case sound if he has been granted a divorce by a papal dispensation, for that shows presumptuousness rather than authority. But I marvel even more that the Romanists do not allow the re-marriage of a man separated from his wife by divorce, but compel him to remain single. Christ permitted divorce in case of fornication, and compelled no one to remain single; and Paul preferred us to marry rather than to burn, and seemed quite prepared to grant that a man may marry another woman in place of the one he has repudiated [I Cor. 7:9]. But this is a subject that ought to be fully discussed, and a decision reached, so that it would be possible to give counsel to those who, though surrounded by an infinite number of dangers, are forced to remain unmarried to-day through no fault of their own; cases where wives or husbands have run away and deserted their partners, to return perhaps ten years later, or even never. This kind of thing distresses and depresses me, for there are instances day by day, whether due to some special piece of wickedness of Satan's, or to our neglect of God's word.

For my own part, and speaking entirely for myself in this matter, I cannot make any rules and regulations; yet I wish that passage in I Corinthians 7 [:15] were applied, which reads: "If the unbelieving departeth, let him depart; the brother or the sister is not in bondage in such cases." Here the apostle rules that the unbeliever who deserts his wife should be divorced, and he pronounces the believer free to marry another. Surely the same principle should hold good if a believer (i.e., nominally a believer, but in fact an unbeliever) deserts his wife, especially if he never intends to return. At least I can see no difference between the two cases. On the other hand, I believe that if, in the apostle's time, an unbeliever had returned, and had either become a believer, or promised to live together with his believing wife, he would not have been given that permission; rather, he would have been given permission to marry someone else. As I have said, however, in these matters I am not enunciating any principles, although there is nothing which I desire more to see settled; for there is nothing that disquiets me more to-day, and many others with me. Nevertheless, I would not have the matter settled by the mere fiat of the pope or the bishops. Rather, if two learned and good men were to agree, in Christ's name and in Christ's spirit, and issue a pronouncement, I myself would prefer their verdict even to that of a council. For the kinds of council which usually assemble nowadays are more notable for their numbers and power than for their learning and sanctity. So I hang up my harp, until I can discuss the subject with another and wiser man than myself.

EXPLANATORY NOTES

1. At this point, a passage from some other writing of Luther's has been interpolated. It clearly breaks the context, and is out of position here. A footnote in W., VI, p. 552, says it appears to have been introduced here by mistake. I have therefore followed the example of modern scholars in relegating the interpolation to a footnote as follows:

    "Of course, I agree that there was a sacrament of penance in the Old Law, and that it was so from the beginning of the world. But the new promise for penitence and the gift of the keys are peculiar to the New Law. Instead of circumcision, we now have baptism, and, similarly, instead of sacrifice, or other signs of repentance, we have the keys. I have already said that the same God gave different promises and different signs at different times, in regard to the forgiveness of sins and the salvation of men; yet all received the same grace. Thus, in II Cor. 4 Paul says: 'Having the same spirit of faith, we also believe, and therefore also we speak.' And in I Cor. 10: 'Our fathers did all eat the same spiritual meat and did all drink of the same spiritual drink; for they drank of a spiritual rock that followed them; and the rock was Christ.' Similarly, Heb. 11: 'And these all, being dead, received not the promise, God having provided some better thing concerning us, that apart from us they should not be made perfect. For Christ is yesterday, to-day, and forever, Himself the head of His Church from the beginning even to the end of the world.' Thus the signs vary, but the faith is the same in every case, because without faith it is impossible to please God, yet it is that by which Abel pleased Him. Heb. 11."—B.L.W.

2. The Summa Angelica of Angelus de Clavassio Chiavasso in Liguria (died 1495), published 1486, one of the favourite handbooks of casuistry, in which all possible cases of conscience were treated in alphabetical order. It was among the papal books burned by Luther.

3. In the confessional, was doubtless meant by Luther.

ANONYMOUS

Peasant Rebels State their Demands (1525)

*The most significant popular uprising in German history, known mislead-
ingly as "The Peasants' War," occurred during the period from May 1424 to
July 1526 and was closely associated with the social upheavals of the early
Protestant Reformation. The rebels included not only landowning peasants
but also poorer farmworkers, rural artisans, miners, and the lower social
strata of the towns. The discontents which led to the revolt were deeply
rooted in long-term economic and political conditions, but the anticlerical-
ism of the Reformation provided a trigger for these grievances to erupt in
open rebellion. Most of the complaints leading to the rebellion were economic in character. From 1450 on, local economies had become more and
more integrated into regional and supraregional markets, and the economic
boom resulting from this integration also led to an accentuation of existing
inequalities among classes. Landholding peasants, who provided the lead-
ership of the rebellion, resented attempts of large landowners to skim more
of their earnings and to deprive them of their traditional rights to use the
forests, waterways, and meadows. To the aggrieved peasants, government
officials, wealthy clerics, and noble landlords also appeared eager to reduce
them to servile status and take away their customary legal protections.*

*The protests of the peasants turned to open warfare in April of 1525,
when peasants attacked monastic landlords, often using slogans derived
from Reformation propaganda. The broadsides in which the peasants published their demands bristled with Biblical authorities and Protestant doc-
trines. The* Twelve Articles *given in this selection is the most famous of the
broadsides published by the rebels. Dressed in Lutheran language, it pro-
voked several responses from Martin Luther himself. Luther was at first
sympathetic. But soon, as the war become more violent and the peasant
demands more radical, Luther turned against the peasants and attacked
them.*

To the Christian Reader Peace and the Grace of God through Christ.

There are many Antichrists who on account of the assembling of the
peasants, cast scorn upon the gospel, and say: Is this the fruit of the new
teaching, that no one obeys but all everywhere rise in revolt, and band
together to reform, extinguish, indeed kill the temporal and spiritual

authorities. The following articles will answer these godless and blaspheming fault-finders. They will first of all remove the reproach from the word of God and secondly give a Christian excuse for the disobedience or even the revolt of the entire peasantry. . . . Therefore, Christian reader, read the following articles with care, and then judge. Here follow the articles:

The First Article. First, it is our humble petition and desire, indeed our will and resolution, that in the future we shall have power and authority so that the entire community should choose and appoint a minister, and that we should have the right to depose him should he conduct himself improperly. The minister thus chosen should teach us the holy gospel pure and simple, without any human addition, doctrine or ordinance. For to teach us continually the true faith will lead us to pray God that through His grace His faith may increase within us and be confirmed in us. For if His grace is not within us, we always remain flesh and blood, which avails nothing; since the Scripture clearly teaches that only through true faith can we come to God. Only through His mercy can we become holy. . . .

The Second Article. Since the right tithe is established in the Old Testament and fulfilled in the New, we are ready and willing to pay the fair tithe of grain. None the less it should be done properly. The word of God plainly provides that it should be given to God and passed on to His own. If it is to be given to a minister, we will in the future collect the tithe through our church elders, appointed by the congregation and distribute from it, to the sufficient livelihood of the minister and his family elected by the entire congregation, according to the judgment of the whole congregation. The remainder shall be given to the poor of the place, as the circumstances and the general opinion demand. . . .

The Third Article. It has been the custom hitherto for men to hold us as their own property, which is pitiable enough considering that Christ has redeemed and purchased us without exception, by the shedding of His precious blood, the lowly as well as the great. Accordingly, it is consistent with Scripture that we should be free and we wish to be so. Not that we want to be absolutely free and under no authority. God does not teach us that we should lead a disorderly life according to the lusts of the flesh, but that we should live by the commandments, love the Lord our God and our neighbor. . . .

The Fourth Article. In the fourth place it has been the custom heretofore that no poor man was allowed to catch venison or wild fowl, or fish in flowing water, which seems to us quite unseemly and unbrotherly, as well as selfish and not according to the word of God. . . . Accordingly, it is our desire if a man holds possession of waters that he should prove from satisfactory documents that his right has been wittingly acquired by purchase. We do not wish to take it from him by force, but his rights should be exercised in a Christian and brotherly fashion. . . .

The Fifth Article. In the fifth place we are aggrieved in the matter of woodcutting, for our noble folk have appropriated all the woods to themselves alone. . . . It should be free to every member of the community to help himself to such firewood as he needs in his home. Also, if a man requires wood for carpenter's purposes he should have it free, but with the approval of a person appointed by the community for that purpose. . . .

The Sixth Article. Our sixth complaint is in regard to the excessive services demanded of us, which increase from day to day. We ask that this matter be properly looked into, so that we shall not continue to be oppressed in this way, and that some gracious consideration be given us, since our forefathers served only according to the word of God.

The Seventh Article. Seventh, we will not hereafter allow ourselves to be further oppressed by our lords. What the lords possess is to be held according to the agreement between the lord and the peasant. . . .

The Eighth Article. In the eighth place, we are greatly burdened by holdings which cannot support the rent exacted from them. The peasants suffer loss in this way and are ruined. We ask that the lords may appoint persons of honor to inspect these holdings and fix a rent in accordance with justice, so that the peasant shall not work for nothing, since the laborer is worthy of his hire.

The Ninth Article. In the ninth place, we are burdened with the great evil in the constant making of new laws. We are not judged according to the offense, but sometimes with great ill will, and sometimes much too leniently. In our opinion we should be judged according to the old written law, so that the case shall be decided according to its merits, and not with favors.

The Tenth Article. In the tenth place we are aggrieved that certain individuals have appropriated meadows and fields which at one time belonged to the community. These we will take again into our own hands unless they were rightfully purchased.

The Eleventh Article. In the eleventh place we will entirely abolish the custom called *Todfall* [heriot], and will no longer endure it, nor allow widows and orphans to be thus shamefully robbed against God's will. . . .

Conclusion. In the twelfth place it is our conclusion and final resolution, that if any one or more of these articles should not be in agreement with the word of God, which we do not think, we will willingly recede from such article when it is proved to be against the word of God by a clear explanation of the Scripture. For this we shall pray God, since He can grant all this and He alone. The peace of Christ abide with us all.

MARTIN LUTHER

Luther Rebukes the Rebelling Peasants (May, 1525)

Martin Luther (1483–1546), the greatest of the Protestant reformers, was born in Thuringian Saxony, the son of a successful foundry owner and mine operator. He was sent to the University of Erfurt to study law, but joined the order of the Augustinian Hermits instead and embarked on a course of theological and Biblical studies. Eventually he succeeded his teacher, Johann von Staupitz, in the chair of Biblical studies at the University of Wittenberg, the town where he spent most of his later life. In his early thirties he underwent a religious crisis that caused him to question the theological bases of practices central to the life of the medieval Catholic Church. Following the publication of the 95 Theses in November 1517 (the traditional date for the beginning of the Protestant Reformation), Luther's critique of the Church and its authority became ever more radical and wide-ranging. In 1520 he was finally condemned by the papal bull Exsurge Domine. *Following this condemnation, Luther began to elaborate his own theological positions, most famously in three key treatises of 1520,* The Freedom of a Christian Man, The Pagan Servitude of the Church, *and* An Appeal to the Ruling Class of the German Nation. *These three treatises dealt, respectively, with Luther's theory of salvation (or soteriology), his theory of the Church (or ecclesiology), and his theory of the role of the secular power in the governance and reform of the Church. These three treatises, along with the enormous volume of tracts and broadsides that poured from the German presses, established Luther as the intellectual leader of the reform movement. After his heroic refusal to recant at the Diet of Worms, even under pressure from the Emperor himself, Luther became the moral leader of the movement as well.*

In 1525, inspired in part by Luther's attacks on the authority of the Roman Catholic Church, a great peasant revolt erupted in south and central Germany. Luther was at first sympathetic to the peasants's economic and social demands, though he rejected the idea that the Gospel could or should be adduced in support of them. His initial response was to urge a peaceful resolution of the conflict. Soon afterwards, however, as the war become more violent and the peasant demands more radical, Luther turned against the peasants and attacked them. The present selection illustrates Luther's later position on the revolt.

In the former book I did not venture to judge the peasants, since they had offered to be set right and to be instructed, and Christ's command, in Matthew 7[:1], says that we are not to judge. But before I look around they go on, and, forgetting their offer, they betake themselves to violence, and rob and rage and act like mad dogs. By this it is easy to see what they had in their false minds, and that the pretences which they made in their twelve articles,[1] under the name of the Gospel, were nothing but lies. It is the devil's work that they are at, and in particular it is the work of the archdevil who rules at Mühlhausen,[2] and does nothing else than stir up robbery, murder and bloodshed; as Christ says of him in John 8[:44], 'He was a murderer from the beginning.' Since, then, these peasants and wretched folk have let themselves be led astray, and do otherwise than they have promised, I too must write of them otherwise than I have written, and begin by setting their sin before them, as God commands Isaiah and Ezekiel, on the chance that some of them may learn to know themselves. Then I must instruct the rulers how they are to conduct themselves in these circumstances.

The peasants have taken on themselves the burden of three terrible sins against God and man, by which they have abundantly merited death in body and soul. In the first place they have sworn to be true and faithful, submissive and obedient, to their rulers, as Christ commands, when he says, 'Render unto Caesar the things that are Caesar's,' [Matthew 22:21] and in Romans 13[:1], 'Let everyone be subject unto the higher powers.' Because they are breaking this obedience, and are setting themselves against the higher powers, wilfully and with violence, they have forfeited body and soul, as faithless, perjured, lying, disobedient knaves and scoundrels are wont to do. St Paul passed this judgement on them in Romans 13[:2] when he said, that they who resist the power will bring a judgement upon themselves. This saying will smite the peasants sooner or later, for it is God's will that faith be kept and duty done.

In the second place, they are starting a rebellion, and violently robbing and plundering monasteries and castles which are not theirs, by which they have a second time deserved death in body and soul, if only as highwaymen and murderers. Besides, any man against whom it can be proved that he is a maker of sedition is outside the law of God and Empire, so that the first who can slay him is doing right and well. For if a man is an open rebel every man is his judge and executioner, just as when a fire starts, the first to put it out is the best man. For rebellion is not simple murder, but is like a great fire, which attacks and lays waste a whole land. Thus rebellion brings with it a land full of murder and bloodshed, makes widows and orphans, and turns everything upside down, like the greatest disaster. Therefore let everyone who can, smite, slay and stab, secretly or openly, remembering that nothing can be more poisonous, hurtful or devilish than a rebel. It is just as when one must kill a mad dog; if you do not strike him, he will strike you, and a whole land with you.

In the third place, they cloak this terrible and horrible sin with the Gospel, call themselves 'Christian brethren', receive oaths and homage, and compel people to hold with them to these abominations. Thus they become the greatest of all blasphemers of God and slanderers of his holy Name, serving the devil, under the outward appearance of the Gospel, thus earning death in body and soul ten times over. I have never heard of a more hideous sin. I suspect that the devil feels the Last Day coming and therefore undertakes such an unheard-of-act, as though saving to himself, 'This is the last, therefore it shall be the worst; I will stir up the dregs and knock out the bottom.' God will guard us against him! See what a mighty prince the devil is, how he has the world in his hands and can throw everything into confusion, when he can so quickly catch so many thousands of peasants, deceive them, blind them, harden them and throw them into revolt, and do with them whatever his raging fury undertakes.

It does not help the peasants, when they pretend that, according to Genesis 1 and 2, all things were created free and common, and that all of us alike have been baptized. For under the New Testament Moses does not Count; for there stands our Master, Christ, and subjects us, with our bodies and our property, to the emperor and the law of this world, when he says, 'Render to Caesar the things that are Caesar's.' Paul, too, says, in Romans 13[:1], to all baptized Christians, 'Let every man be subject to the power', and Peter says, 'Be subject to every ordinance of man' [1 Peter 2:13]. By this doctrine of Christ we are bound to live, as the Father commands from heaven, saying, 'This is My beloved Son; hear him.' For baptism does not make men free in body and property, but in soul; and the Gospel does not make goods common, except in the case of those who do of their own free will what the apostles and disciples did in Acts 4. They did not demand, as do our insane peasants in their raging, that the goods of others—of a Pilate and a Herod—should be common, but only their own goods. Our peasants, however, would have other men's goods common, and keep their own goods for themselves. Fine Christians these! I think there is not a devil left in hell; they have all gone into the peasants. Their raving has gone beyond all measure.

Since the peasants, then, have brought both God and man down upon them and are already so many times guilty of death in body and soul, since they submit to no court and wait for no verdict, but only rage on, I must instruct the worldly governors how they are to act in the matter with a clear conscience.

First, I will not oppose a ruler who, even though he does not tolerate the Gospel, will smite and punish these peasants without offering to submit the case to judgement. For he is within his rights, since the peasants are not contending any longer for the Gospel, but have become faithless, perjured, disobedient, rebellious murderers, robbers and blasphemers, whom even heathen rulers have the right and power to punish; nay, it is their duty to punish them, for it is just for this purpose that they bear the sword, and are 'the ministers of God upon him that doeth evil'.

But if the ruler is a Christian and tolerates the Gospel, so that the peasants have no appearance of a case against him, he should proceed with fear. First he must take the matter to God, confessing that we have deserved these things, and remembering that God may, perhaps, have thus aroused the devil as a punishment upon all Germany. Then he should humbly pray for help against the devil, for 'we are battling not only against flesh and blood, but against spiritual wickedness in the air', and this must be attacked with prayer. Then, when our hearts are so turned to God that we are ready to let his divine will be done, whether he will or will not have us to be princes and lords, we must go beyond our duty, and offer the mad peasants an opportunity to come to terms, even though they are not worthy of it. Finally, if that does not help, then swiftly grasp the sword.

For a prince and lord must remember in this case that he is God's minister and the servant of his wrath (Romans 13), to whom the sword is committed for use upon such fellows, and that he sins as greatly against God, if he does not punish and protect and does not fulfil the duties of his office, as does one to whom the sword has not been committed when he commits a murder. If he can punish and does not—even though the punishment consist in the taking of life and the shedding of blood—then he is guilty of all the murder and all the evil which these fellows commit, because, by wilful neglect of the divine command, he permits them to practise their wickedness, though he can prevent it, and is in duty bound to do so. Here, then, there is no time for sleeping; no place for patience or mercy. It is the time of the sword, not the day of grace.

The rulers, then, should go on unconcerned, and with a good conscience lay about them as long as their hearts still beat. It is to their advantage that the peasants have a bad conscience and an unjust cause, and that any peasant who is killed is lost in body and soul and is eternally the devil's. But the rulers have a good conscience and a just cause; and can, therefore, say to God with all assurance of heart, 'Behold, my God, thou hast appointed me prince or lord, of this I can have no doubt; and thou hast committed to me the sword over the evildoers (Romans 13). It is thy Word, and cannot lie. I must fulfil my office, or forfeit thy grace. It is also plain that these peasants have deserved death many times over, in thine eyes and the eyes of the world, and have been committed to me for punishment. If it be thy will that I be slain by them, and that my rulership be taken from me and destroyed, so be it: thy will be done. So shall I die and be destroyed fulfilling thy commandment and thy Word, and shall be found obedient to thy commandment and my office. Therefore will I punish and smite as long as my heart beats. Thou wilt judge and make things right.'

Thus it may be that one who is killed fighting on the ruler's side may be a true martyr in the eyes of God, if he fights with such a conscience as I have just described, for he is in God's Word and is obedient to him. On the other hand, one who perishes on the peasant's side is an eternal brand of hell, for he bears the sword against God's Word and is disobedient to him, and is a member of the devil. And even though it happens that the peasants gain the upper hand (which God forbid!)—for to God all things are possible, and we do not know whether it may be his will, through the devil, to destroy all order and rule and cast the world upon a desolate heap, as a prelude to the Last Day, which cannot be far off—nevertheless, they may die without worry and go to the scaffold with a good conscience, who are found exercising their office of the sword. They may leave to the devil the kingdom of the world, and take in exchange the everlasting kingdom. Strange times, these, when a prince can win heaven with bloodshed, better than other men with prayer!

Finally, there is another thing that ought to move the rulers. The peasants are not content to be themselves the devil's own, but they force and compel many good people against their wills to join their devilish league, and so make them partakers of all of their own wickedness and damnation. For anyone who consents to what they do, goes to the devil with them, and is guilty of all the evil deeds that they commit; though he has to do this because he is so weak in faith that he does not resist them. A pious Christian ought to suffer a hundred deaths, rather than give a hair's breadth of consent to the peasant's cause. O how many martyrs could now be made by the bloodthirsty peasants and the murdering prophets! Now the rulers ought to have mercy on these prisoners of the peasants, and if they had no other reason to use the sword, with a good conscience, against the peasants, and to risk their own lives and property in fighting them, there would be reason enough, and more than enough, in this—that thus they would be rescuing and helping these souls, whom the peasants have forced into their devilish league and who, without willing it, are sinning so horribly, and who must be damned. For truly these souls are in purgatory; nay, in the bonds of hell and the devil.

Therefore, dear lords, here is a place where you can release, rescue, help. Have mercy on these poor people [whom the peasants have compelled to join them]. Stab, smite, slay, whoever can. If you die in doing it, well for you! A more blessed death can never be yours, for you die in obeying the divine Word and commandment in Romans 13, and in loving service of your neighbour, whom you are rescuing from the bonds of hell and of the devil. And so I beg everyone who can to flee from the peasants as from the devil himself; those who do not flee, I pray that God will enlighten and convert. As for those who are not to be converted, God grant that they may have neither fortune nor success. To this let every pious Christian say Amen! For this prayer is right and good, and pleases God; this I know. If anyone think this too hard, let him remember that rebellion is intolerable and that the destruction of the world is to be expected every hour.

EXPLANATORY NOTES

1. The Twelve Articles of Memmingen, formal demands made by the Swabian peasants of their rulers, in March 1525.
2. Thomas Müntzer, c. 1489–1525, a university-educated priest with a living in Swabia, who originally followed Luther but broke with him in 1521 when he thought Luther had sold out to the powers that be. A genuine revolutionary, he was exiled for preaching inflammatory sermons. In 1525 he led the peasantry of Franconia against the princes, lost, was tortured and killed.

IGNATIUS LOYOLA

How to Become a Spiritual Soldier

Saint Ignatius Loyola (1491–1556) spent much of his youth as a soldier and courtier, swaggering, romancing, and fighting until roughly his thirtieth year, when a cannonball shattered his leg and confined him to his bed for many months. During his long and often excruciatingly painful convalescence, he resolved to reform his life according to the example of Jesus Christ and the saints. Thereafter he led a life of poverty and extreme spirituality, conducted with an almost military discipline. He made a pilgrimage to the Holy Land, studied in Spain and France, and founded a new order of Roman Catholic priests: the Society of Jesus, known as the Jesuits. Trained by his Spiritual Exercises, *the Jesuits acted as soldiers of Christ, making innumerable converts to Catholic Christianity in Europe and abroad, and founding hundreds of famous schools to educate Catholic youth. The new order grew with astounding rapidity. Ignatius was canonized in 1622 along with one of his followers, Francis Xavier, and Teresa of Ávila.*

The Spiritual Exercises *(1550) are not meant to be read, but rather "given" by a spiritual director over a period of four weeks to those who want to deepen their relationship with God in the Roman Catholic context. Directors use them to bring people into a state where they can pray fervently, acknowledge their own weaknesses, and resolve to live a more committed Christian life. The* Exercises *show an astonishing degree of psychological insight and have been used by Christians to deepen their spiritual life ever since Ignatius himself in the sixteenth century to Thomas Merton in the twentieth century. There is a remarkable literary portrayal of their character and effect in a key scene of James Joyce's* Portrait of the Artist as a Young Man.

ANNOTATIONS

JHS

[1] ANNOTATIONS (OR NOTES) TO PROVIDE SOME EXPLANATION OF THE SPIRITUAL EXERCISES THAT FOLLOW. THEY ARE INTENDED TO BE OF ASSISTANCE BOTH TO THE PERSON GIVING THEM AND TO THE PERSON WHO IS TO RECEIVE THEM.

ANNOTATION 1. The term 'spiritual exercises' denotes every way of examining one's conscience, of meditating, contemplating, praying vocally and mentally, and other spiritual activities, as will be said later. For just as strolling, walking and running are exercises for the body, so 'spiritual exercises' is the name given to every way of preparing and disposing one's soul to rid herself of all disordered attachments, so that once rid of them one might seek and find the divine will in regard to the disposition of one's life for the good of the soul.

[2] ANNOTATION 2. The person who gives to another a way and a plan for meditating or contemplating must provide a faithful account of the events to be meditated or contemplated, simply running over the salient points with brief or summary explanations. For if a person begins contemplating with a true historical foundation, and then goes over the historical narrative and reflects on it personally, one may by oneself come upon things that throw more light on the history or better bring home its meaning. Whether this results from one's own reasoning or from the enlightenment of divine grace, this is more gratifying and spiritually profitable than if the director had explained and developed at length the meaning of the history. For it is not so much knowledge that fills and satisfies the soul, but rather the intimate feeling and relishing of things.

[3] ANNOTATION 3. In all the spiritual exercises that follow we bring the intellect into action in order to think and the will in order to stir the deeper affections. We should therefore note that the activity of the will, when we are speaking vocally or mentally with God Our Lord or with His saints, requires greater reverence on our part than when we are using the intellect to understand.

[4] ANNOTATION 4. The exercises that follow are made up of four Weeks, corresponding to the four parts into which these Exercises are divided: namely, the First is the consideration and contemplation of sins; the Second is the life of Christ Our Lord up to, and including, Palm Sunday; the Third, the Passion of Christ Our Lord; the Fourth, the Resurrection and Ascension, with the three ways of praying. However this does not mean that each Week necessarily lasts for six or eight days, for in the First Week some may happen to be slower in finding what they are looking for,

namely contrition, sorrow, and tears over their sins. Then again, some may be more rapid than others, and some more stirred or tried by various spirits. Therefore it may be necessary sometimes to shorten the Week and at other times to lengthen it, and similarly in the subsequent Weeks one must always be seeking whatever is appropriate to the matter under consideration. But the Exercises should be completed in about thirty days.

[5] ANNOTATION 5. It is very profitable for the exercitant to begin the Exercises in a magnanimous spirit and with great liberality towards one's Creator and Lord, offering Him all one's power of desiring and one's liberty, so that the Divine Majesty may make use of one's person and of all that one has according to His most holy will.

[6] ANNOTATION 6. When the director giving the Exercises becomes aware that the exercitant is not affected by any spiritual movements, such as consolations or desolations, and is not being stirred by various spirits, the director should question the exercitant closely about the Exercises, whether they are being made at their appointed times, and in what way, and similarly whether the additions are being carefully followed. The director should inquire in detail about each of these points. There are remarks below on consolation and desolation [Exx. 316–24] and on the additions [Exx. 73–90].

[7] ANNOTATION 7. If the one giving the Exercises sees that the one receiving them is desolate and tempted, it is important not to be hard or curt with that person, but gentle and kind. Let the director give the exercitant courage and strength for the future, and lay open before that person the cunning tricks of the enemy of human nature, and encourage the person to prepare and make ready for the consolation that is to come.

[8] ANNOTATION 8. As the director giving the Exercises becomes aware of the particular needs of the receiver in the matter of desolations and cunning tricks of the enemy, as well as in the matter of consolations, the director will be able to instruct the exercitant about the rules of the First and Second Weeks for recognizing various spirits [Exx. 313–27, 328–36].

[9] ANNOTATION 9. The following should be noted when the exercitant is making the Exercises of the First Week. If it is a person with no previous experience of spiritual things, and who is tempted crudely and obviously, as for example by having obstacles suggested preventing advancement in the service of God Our Lord, such as fatigues, shame and fear inspired by worldly honour, etc, the director should not talk to that person about the Second Week rules for various spirits, because just as the First Week rules will be very profitable to such a person, so will those of the Second Week do harm, as they deal with questions too delicate and too elevated to be understood.

[10] ANNOTATION 10. When the giver of the Exercises sees that the receiver is being assailed and tempted under the appearance of good, that is the time to speak to such a person about the Second Week rules mentioned above. For normally the enemy of human nature tempts more under the appearance of good when a person exercises him- or herself in the illuminative life, which corresponds to the Exercises of the Second Week. Such temptations are less common in the purgative [way of] life, which corresponds to the Exercises of the First Week.

[11] ANNOTATION 11. Whilst the exercitant is in the First Week it is better for such a person to know nothing of what will have to be done in the Second Week. Rather, the exercitant should strive to obtain what is being looked for in the First Week as if there were nothing good to be hoped for in the Second.

[12] ANNOTATION 12. The giver of the Exercises should remind the receiver frequently that since an hour has to be spent in each of the five exercises or contemplations to be made each day, one should always try to find contentment in the thought that a full hour has indeed been spent in that exercise—and more, if anything, rather than less! For the enemy usually leaves nothing undone in his efforts to procure a shortening of the hour of contemplation, meditation or prayer.

[13] ANNOTATION 13. It should also be noted that whereas in time of consolation it is easy and undemanding to remain in contemplation for the full hour, in time of desolation it is very difficult to last out. Consequently, in order to go against desolation and overcome temptations the exercitant must always stay on a little more than the full hour, so that one gets used not only to standing up to the adversary, but even to overthrowing him.

[14] ANNOTATION 14. If the giver sees that the receiver is going along in consolation and full of fervour, the giver should forewarn the exercitant against making any unthinking or precipitate promise or vow, and the more unstable in temperament the person is known to be, the more should that person be warned and admonished. It is true that one person can legitimately move another to enter a religious order, with the intention of making vows of obedience, poverty and chastity, and it is also true that a good work done under vow is more meritorious than one done without a vow. Nevertheless careful consideration must be given to the individual temperament and capabilities of the exercitant, as well as to the helps or hindrances that may be met in fulfilling promises that such a person might want to make.

[15] ANNOTATION 15. The one giving the Exercises ought not to move the one receiving them more to poverty or to any particular promise

than to their contraries, nor to one state or way of life more than to another. Outside the Exercises it can indeed be lawful and meritorious for us to move all who seem suitable to choose continence, virginity, religious life and every form of evangelical perfection, but during these Spiritual Exercises it is more opportune and much better that the Creator and Lord communicate Himself to the faithful soul in search for the will of God, as He inflames her in His love and praise, disposing her towards the way in which she will be better able to serve Him in the future. Hence the giver of the Exercises should not be swayed or show a preference for one side rather than the other, but remaining in the middle like the pointer of a balance, should leave the Creator to work directly with the creature, and the creature with the Creator and Lord.

[16] ANNOTATION 16. For this, namely, that the Creator and Lord may work more surely in His creature, if the soul in question happens to be attached or inclined to something in an ill-ordered way, it is very useful for her to do all in her power to bring herself round to the contrary of that wrong attachment. This would be the case, for example, if a person were bent on seeking to obtain an appointment or benefice, not for the honour and glory of God Our Lord, nor for the spiritual good of souls, but for one's own advancement and temporal interests. One must then set one's heart on what is contrary to this, insisting upon it in prayers and other spiritual exercises, asking God Our Lord for the contrary, namely, not to want that appointment or benefice or anything else, unless the Divine Majesty gives a right direction to one's desires and changes the first attachment, so that the motive for desiring or keeping this or that thing be solely the service, honour and glory of the Divine Majesty.

[17] ANNOTATION 17. There is much to be gained if the giver of the Exercises, while not wanting to ask about or know the exercitant's self-chosen thoughts or sins, is given a faithful account of the different agitations and thoughts brought by the different spirits; because depending on the greater or lesser degree of progress, the director can give the exercitant some spiritual exercises that will be appropriate and suited to the needs of a soul agitated in a particular way.

[18] ANNOTATION 18. The Exercises are to be adapted to the capabilities of those who want to engage in them, i.e. age, education or intelligence are to be taken into consideration. Hence someone uneducated or of poor health should not be given things that cannot be undertaken without fatigue and from which no profit is to be derived. Similarly, in order that each may feel more at ease and derive the best benefit, what is given to each exercitant should be in accordance with his or her dispositions. Hence, one who is hoping to gain some instruction and to reach a certain

level of peace of soul can be given the particular examen [Exx. 24–31], then the general examen [Exx. 32–43]; also together with this, for half an hour in the morning, the way of praying about the commandments, capital sins, etc [Exx. 238–48]. Such persons can also be recommended to confess their sins each week, and if possible to receive communion every fortnight, and better still every week, if they are so inclined. This arrangement is more suited to unformed and uneducated people, to whom explanations can be given of each commandment, each of the capital sins, the precepts of the church, the five senses, and the works of mercy. Likewise, should the giver of the Exercises see that the receiver has poor health or little natural capacity, or that not much fruit is to be expected of such a person, it is more suitable to give some less demanding exercises until the person has been to confession. Afterwards some [topics for] examen of conscience can be given and the instruction to confess more frequently, so that such a person may maintain the progress made. One should not go on to the election material or to the other exercises that are outside the First Week, especially when the exercitant can gain greater profit from other exercises and there is no time for everything.

[19] ANNOTATION 19. When a person is taken up with public affairs or necessary business, and is someone who is educated or intelligent, such a person can set aside an hour and a half a day for the Exercises. Then one can talk with such a person about the end for which human beings are created, as well as giving a half-hour for the particular examen, then the general examen and method of confessing and receiving communion. On three days this exercitant can make for one hour each morning the meditation on the first, second and third sins [Exx. 45–53]; later for another three days at the same hour the meditation on the sequence of sins [Exx. 55–61]; later for another three days at the same hour the meditation on the punishments that correspond to sins [Exx. 65–71] should be made, and during these three sets of meditations the ten additions [Exx. 73–90] should be given. For the mysteries of Christ Our Lord the same procedure will be followed, as is explained in detail further on in these same Exercises.

[20] ANNOTATION 20. To one who is more at liberty and desires to benefit as much as possible, all the Spiritual Exercises should be given in the exact order in which they are set down. As a general rule in making the Exercises, the more one disengages oneself from all friends and acquaintances, and from all worldly preoccupations, the more profit will there be. For example, one can change residence and go to a house or room so as to live there in the most complete privacy possible, with the opportunity to attend mass and vespers each day without fear of acquaintances getting in the way.

This withdrawal will have three principal advantages, among many others. The first is that when one separates oneself from many friends and acquaintances as well as from distracting business in order to serve and praise God Our Lord, one gains no small merit before the Divine Majesty. The second is that in this state of withdrawal, with one's mind not divided amongst many things but entirely taken up with one thing alone, namely, serving one's Creator and doing good to one's soul, one is able to use one's natural powers all the more freely in the diligent search for what one's heart desires. The third, the more we are alone and by ourselves, the more capable we become of drawing near to and reaching our Creator and Lord, and the more we reach Him, the more we make ourselves ready to receive graces and gifts from His divine and supreme Goodness.

FIRST WEEK

[21] SPIRITUAL EXERCISES HAVING AS THEIR PURPOSE THE OVERCOMING OF SELF AND THE ORDERING OF ONE'S LIFE ON THE BASIS OF A DECISION MADE IN FREEDOM FROM ANY ILL-ORDERED ATTACHMENT.

[22]   PRESUPPOSITION

So that the director and the exercitant may collaborate better and with greater profit, it must be presupposed that any good Christian has to be more ready to justify than to condemn a neighbour's statement. If no justification can be found, one should ask the neighbour in what sense it is to be taken, and if that sense is wrong he or she should be corrected lovingly. Should this not be sufficient, one should seek all suitable means to justify it by understanding it in a good sense.

[23]   PRINCIPLE AND FOUNDATION

The human person is created to praise, reverence and serve God Our Lord, and by so doing to save his or her soul. The other things on the face of the earth are created for human beings in order to help them pursue the end for which they are created. It follows from this that one must use other created things in so far as they help towards one's end, and free oneself from them in so far as they are obstacles to one's end. To do this we need to make ourselves indifferent to all created things, provided the matter is subject to our free choice and there is no prohibition. Thus as far as we are concerned, we should not want health more than illness, wealth more than poverty, fame more than disgrace, a long life more than a short one, and similarly for all the rest, but we should desire and choose only what helps us more towards the end for which we are created.

[24]   PARTICULAR DAILY EXAMEN
            containing three times and two examens

The FIRST TIME is in the morning immediately on rising: the exercitant makes a firm resolve to take great care to avoid the particular sin or defect that he or she wants to correct and reform.

[25] The SECOND TIME comes after the mid-day meal, when one asks God Our Lord for what one wants, i.e. grace to remember how often one has fallen into that particular sin or defect, and to reform in the future. Then the exercitant makes the FIRST EXAMEN: it consists of demanding of oneself an account of the particular point proposed for correction and reform, running over each hour or each period of time, beginning from the hour of rising, up to the hour and moment of the present examen. On the first line of the diagram as many marks should be made as times one has fallen into the particular sin or defect. Then one should resolve again to do better up to the next examen to be made.

[26] The THIRD TIME is after supper, when the SECOND EXAMEN will be made in the same way, going from hour to hour from the first examen to this second one. On the second line of the same diagram as many marks should be made as the times one has fallen into the particular sin or defect.

[27]   FOUR ADDITIONS
        for getting rid of the particular sin or defect more quickly

ADDITION 1 Each time one falls into the particular sin or defect, one should put a hand to the breast in sorrow for having fallen. This can be done even in the presence of many people without their noticing.

[28] ADDITION 2 Since the first line of the diagram represents the first examen, and the second line the second examen, the exercitant can see at night if there is an improvement from the first line to the second, i.e. from the first examen to the second.

[29] ADDITION 3 The second day should be compared with the first, i.e. today's two examens with yesterday's two examens, to see if there is an improvement from one day to another.

[30] ADDITION 4 One week should be compared with another to see if there is an improvement between the present week and the preceding.

[31] NOTE The first two long lines in the following diagram stand for Sunday, the second shorter ones for Monday, the third for Tuesday, and so on.

[32]   GENERAL EXAMEN OF CONSCIENCE
in order to purify the soul and to make a better confession

I presuppose that there are three sorts of thought processes in me, one sort which are properly mine and arise simply from my free will and choice, and two other sorts which come from outside, one from the good spirit and the other from the bad.

[33]   *Thoughts*

There are two ways of gaining merit when an evil thought comes from outside: the first—for example, if the thought of committing a mortal sin comes, I resist it promptly and it is overcome; [34] the second way of meriting is when the same bad thought comes to me and I resist it, it recurs again and again and I keep on resisting until the thought goes away defeated. This second way is more meritorious than the first.
[35] One sins venially when the same thought of committing a mortal sin comes and one gives ear to it, dwelling on it a little or taking some sensual enjoyment from it, or when there is some negligence in rejecting this thought.
[36] There are two ways of sinning mortally. The first is when one consents to a sinful thought in order to put one's consent into immediate action, or to act on it if one could [37]. The second way of sinning mortally is when that sin is actually committed, and this is more serious for three reasons—(i) because more time is spent, (ii) because there is more intensity, (iii) because greater harm is done both to others and to oneself.

[38]   *Words*

One should not swear either by the Creator or the creature except with truth, necessity and reverence. By 'necessity' I mean not when one swears to any kind of truth using an oath, but when the matter is one of importance, concerning the welfare of the soul or body, or involving temporal goods. By 'reverence' I mean that when invoking the name of one's Creator and Lord one consciously pays to Him the honour and reverence that are His due.

[39] It is to be noted that although in a vain oath we sin more seriously when we swear by the Creator than when we swear by the creature, it is more difficult to swear as we ought—with truth, necessity and reverence—by the creature than by the Creator for the following reasons: FIRST. When we want to swear by some creature, the choice of invoking the creature does not make us as careful and alert about telling the truth, or affirming it with necessity, as would the choice of invoking the name of the Lord and Creator of all things. SECOND. In swearing by the creature it is not as easy to pay reverence and submission to the Creator as when swearing by and invoking the name of the Creator and Lord Himself, because the intention of invoking God Our Lord brings with it more submission and reverence than is aroused by the intention of invoking created things. Therefore it is more permissible for the perfect to swear by the creature than it is for the imperfect, because the perfect, thanks to constant contemplation and to an enlightened understanding, are more in the habit of considering, meditating and contemplating how God Our Lord is in every creature according to His own essence, presence and power, and so when swearing by the creature are better prepared and predisposed to pay homage and reverence to their Creator and Lord than are the imperfect. THIRD. With persistent swearing by the creature, the imperfect are in more danger than the perfect of falling into idolatry.

[40] One should not speak 'idle words', by which I understand those of no profit to either myself or to others, and those not directed to that end. Consequently to speak about anything that benefits or seeks to benefit my own soul or my neighbour's, or that is for the good of the body or for temporal welfare, is never idle. Nor is it idle even to speak of things that do not belong to one's state of life, e.g. if a religious speaks about wars or trade. Rather in all these cases there is merit in speaking to a well-ordered purpose, and sin in ill-directed or aimless talk.

[41] One should say nothing to defame another or to spread gossip, because if I make known a mortal sin which is not public knowledge, I sin mortally, and if the sin is venial, I sin venially, while if it is a defect, I show my own defect. But when there is a right intention there are two possible ways of speaking of the sin or fault of another: WAY 1. When the sin is public, as in the case of a public prostitute, and where a sentence has been passed in court, or a public error poisons the minds of those with whom

one deals. WAY 2. When a hidden sin is revealed to someone so that such a person can help the sinner to rise from sin; however there should be some expectation or probable likelihood that help can be given.

[42]   *Deeds*

One should take as subject-matter the Ten Commandments, the precepts of the Church and the recommendations of superiors; any action done against any of these three is a greater or smaller sin depending on the greater or lesser importance of the matter. By 'recommendations of superiors' I mean e.g. fasting dispensations and other indulgences, such as those granted for peace treaties, which can be obtained by confession and reception of the Blessed Sacrament, as there can be no little sin in inciting others to act or acting oneself against the religious exhortations and recommendations of those in authority.

[43]   WAY OF MAKING THE GENERAL EXAMEN
                   containing five points

POINT 1: to give thanks to God for the benefits received.
POINT 2: to ask for grace to know one's sins and reject them.
POINT 3: to ask an account of one's soul from the hour of rising to the present examen, hour by hour, or from one period to another, first about thoughts, then about words and finally about deeds, following the order given in the particular examen [Exx. 25].
POINT 4: to ask God Our Lord for pardon for sins.
POINT 5: to determine to do better with His grace, ending with an Our Father.

[44]   GENERAL CONFESSION AND COMMUNION

Anybody wanting of one's own accord to make a General Confession will find in it three particular benefits amongst many others: (i) while granting that a person who goes to confession every year is not obliged to make a general confession, yet if such a person does make one, there is greater profit and merit because of the greater present sorrow being felt for all the sins and wrongs of one's whole life; (ii) during the Spiritual Exercises one gains a greater interior knowledge of sins and of their malice than when one is not engaged in the same way with matters of the inner life; with the greater knowledge and grief for sins, one will have greater profit and merit than would previously have been had; (iii) as a consequence of making a better confession and being better disposed, the person is better prepared and readier to receive the Blessed Sacrament (the reception of which helps us not only to avoid falling into sin, but also to keep on increasing in grace). It is better to make this General Confession immediately after the exercises of the First Week.

[45]   *THE FIRST EXERCISE*

A MEDITATION WITH THE THREE POWERS ON THE FIRST, SECOND
AND THIRD SINS
*containing—after a preparatory prayer and two preambles—
three principal points and a colloquy*

[46] PRAYER The preparatory prayer is to ask God Our Lord for grace that all my intentions, actions and operations may be directed purely to the service and praise of His Divine Majesty.

[47] PREAMBLE 1 This is the composition, seeing the place.

It should be noted here that for contemplation or meditation about visible things, e.g. a contemplation about Christ Our Lord who is visible, the 'composition' consists in seeing through the gaze of the imagination the material place where the object I want to contemplate is situated. By 'material place' I mean e.g. a temple or a mountain where Jesus Christ or Our Lady is to be found, according to what I want to contemplate. Where the object is invisible, as is the case in the present instance dealing with sins, the composition will be to see with the gaze of the imagination and to consider that my soul is imprisoned in this body which will one day disintegrate, and my whole composite self as if exiled in this valley among brute beasts. When I say 'my whole composite self', I mean body and soul together.

[48] PREAMBLE 2 This is to ask God for what I want and desire.

The request must be adapted to the matter under consideration, so e.g. in contemplating the Resurrection one asks for joy with Christ joyful, but in contemplating the Passion one asks for grief, tears and suffering with the suffering Christ. Here I will ask for personal shame and confusion as I see how many have been damned on account of a single mortal sin, and how many times I deserved to be damned for ever on account of my numerous sins.

[49] NOTE Before any of the contemplations or meditations the preparatory prayer should always be made without any change, and also the two preambles mentioned, the latter being adapted at times to suit the matter under consideration.

[50] POINT 1 Bring the memory to bear on the first sin, which was that of the angels, then apply the intellect to the same event, in order to reason over it, and then the will, so that by seeking to recall and to comprehend all this, I may feel all the more shame and confusion, comparing the one sin of the angels with my many sins, for while they went to hell for one sin, how many times have I deserved hell for my many sins! When I say 'bring to memory the sin of the angels', I mean how they were created in grace, but as they did not want to avail themselves of their liberty in order to give reverence and obedience to their Creator and Lord, and fell into pride, they became changed over from grace to malice and were cast out of heaven into hell. Similarly afterwards one should go over the subject more in detail with the understanding, and then stir up the heart's affections with the will.

[51] POINT 2 In the same way bring the three powers to bear on the case of the sin of Adam and Eve, calling to mind the long penance they did on account of that sin, and the corruption that came upon the human race, with so many people going their way toward hell. When I talk about recalling the second sin, that of our [first] parents, I mean how after Adam had been created in the plain of Damascus and placed in the earthly Paradise, and Eve had been created from his rib, they were forbidden to eat of the tree of knowledge. But they ate and by doing so sinned. Afterwards, dressed in tunics of skins and cast out of Paradise, they lived all their life without their original justice, which they had lost, in great labours and much penance. Then go over the subject in greater detail with the understanding, and use the will as has been explained above.

[52] POINT 3 Do the same for the third sin, the particular one of any individual who has gone to hell for a single mortal sin, and also the numberless other people who have gone to hell for fewer sins than I have committed. Do the same, I say, with regard to such a third sin, a particular one, calling to memory the gravity and malice of sin against one's Creator and Lord, reflecting with the understanding how someone who has sinned and acted against the infinite goodness has justly been damned for ever, then end with the will as has been said.

[53] COLLOQUY Imagining Christ Our Lord before me on the cross, make a colloquy asking how it came about that the Creator made Himself man, and from eternal life came to temporal death, and thus to die for my sins. Then, turning to myself I shall ask, what have I done for Christ? what am I doing for Christ? what ought I to do for Christ? Finally, seeing Him in that state hanging on the cross, talk over whatever comes to mind.

[54] A colloquy, properly so-called, means speaking as one friend speaks with another, or a servant with a master, at times asking for some favour, at other times accusing oneself of something badly done, or telling the other about one's concerns and asking for advice about them. And then say an Our Father.

IGNATIUS LOYOLA

Thinking with the Church

---

*Saint Ignatius Loyola (1491–1556) spent much of his youth as a soldier and
courtier, swaggering, romancing, and fighting until roughly his thirtieth
year, when a cannonball shattered his leg and confined him to his bed for
many months. During his long and often excruciatingly painful convalescence, he resolved to reform his life according to the example of Jesus Christ
and the saints. Thereafter he led a life of poverty and deep spirituality, conducted with an almost military discipline. He made a pilgrimage to the
Holy Land, studied in Spain and France, and founded a new order of
Roman Catholic priests: the Society of Jesus, known as the Jesuits. Trained
by his* Spiritual Exercises, *the Jesuits acted as soldiers of Christ, making
innumerable converts to Catholic Christianity in Europe and abroad, and
founding hundreds of famous schools to educate Catholic youth. The new
order grew with astounding rapidity. Ignatius was canonized in 1622 along
with one of his followers, Francis Xavier, and Teresa of Ávila.*

The Spiritual Exercises *(1550) are not meant to be read, but rather
"given" by a spiritual director over a period of four weeks to those who
want to deepen their relationship with God in the Roman Catholic context.
Directors use them to bring people into a state where they can pray fervently,
acknowledge their own weaknesses, and resolve to live a more committed
Christian life. The* Exercises *show an astonishing degree of psychological
insight and have been used by Christians to deepen their spiritual life from
Ignatius himself in the sixteenth century to Thomas Merton in the twentieth
century. There is a remarkable literary portrayal of their character and
effect in a key scene of James Joyce's* Portrait of the Artist as a Young Man.

RULES TO FOLLOW IN VIEW OF THE TRUE
ATTITUDE OF MIND THAT WE OUGHT TO MAINTAIN
[AS MEMBERS] WITHIN THE CHURCH MILITANT

[353] RULE 1 Laying aside all our own judgements, we ought to keep our minds open and ready to obey in everything the true bride of Christ Our Lord, our holy mother, the hierarchical Church.

[354] RULE 2 We should praise confession made to a priest, and the reception of the Blessed Sacrament once a year, much more its reception once a month, and very much more its reception once a week, given the duly required dispositions.

[355] RULE 3 We should praise frequent attendance at mass; also hymns, psalms and long prayers, whether in or out of church; and likewise, appointed hours at the appropriate times for all the divine services, prayers and the canonical Hours.

[356] RULE 4 We should praise greatly religious life, virginity and continence, and we should not praise matrimony to the same extent as any of these.

[357] RULE 5 We should praise the vows of religion—obedience, poverty and chastity—and other vows of perfection made voluntarily; it should be noted however that vows should not be made about matters that withdraw from evangelical perfection, e.g. to be a merchant, to marry, etc., as a vow has to do with things that lead to that perfection.

[358] RULE 6 We should praise the cult of the saints, venerating their relics and praying to the saints themselves, praising also the stations, pilgrimages, indulgences, jubilees, dispensations and the lighting of candles in churches.

[359] RULE 7 We should praise the decrees about fasting and abstinence, e.g. in Lent, on the ember days, vigils, Fridays and Saturdays; similarly penances, not only interior but also exterior.

[360] RULE 8 We should praise the decoration and architecture of churches, also statues, which should be venerated according to what they represent.

[361] RULE 9 Finally we should praise all the precepts of the Church, being ready to seek arguments in their defence and never in any way to attack them.

[362] RULE 10 We should be more inclined to approve and praise the decrees and regulations of those in authority, and their conduct as well; for although some of these things do not or did not in the past deserve approval, more grumbling and scandal than profit would be aroused by speaking against them, either in public sermons or in conversations in front of simple people. In that way people would become hostile towards

authority, either temporal or spiritual. But just as harm can be done by speaking ill to simple people about those in authority in their absence, so it can do good to speak of their unworthy behaviour to the actual people who can bring about a remedy.

[363] RULE 11 We should praise both positive theology and scholastic theology, for as it is more characteristic of the positive doctors, such as St Jerome, St Augustine and St Gregory, to move the heart to love and serve God Our Lord in all things, so it is more characteristic of the scholastics like St Thomas, St Bonaventure, the Master of the Sentences, etc, to define or explain for our times what is necessary for eternal salvation and for more effectively combating and exposing all errors and fallacies. This is because the scholastic doctors, being more recent, not only have the benefit both of the true understanding of Sacred Scripture and of the holy positive Doctors, but while being themselves enlightened and illuminated by divine grace, they can avail themselves of the councils, canons and decrees of our holy mother Church.

[364] RULE 12 We must avoid making comparisons between those of our own day and the blessed of former times, for there is no small error in doing this, i.e. in saying of someone, 'He knows more than St Augustine,' or 'He is another St Francis or greater', or 'He is another St Paul for virtue, sanctity, etc'.

[365] RULE 13 To maintain a right mind in all things we must always maintain that the white I see, I shall believe to be black, if the hierarchical Church so stipulates; for we believe that between Christ Our Lord, the bridegroom, and the Church, His bride, there is the same Spirit who governs and directs us of the good of our souls because it is by that same Spirit and Lord of us all who gave the Ten Commandments that our holy mother Church is directed and governed.

[366] RULE 14 Even granting as perfectly true that no one can be saved without being predestined, and without having faith and grace, nevertheless much caution is needed in the way in which we discuss and propagate these matters.

[367] RULE 15 We must not make a habit of talking much about predestination, but if sometimes mention is made of it one way or another, our language should be such that simple people are not led into error, as sometimes happens with them saying, 'It is already decided whether I am to be saved or damned, so whether I do good or evil can change nothing'; paralysed by this notion, they neglect the works that lead to the salvation and spiritual progress of their souls.

[368] RULE 16 In the same way we must be careful lest by speaking about faith at great length and with much emphasis, without distinctions and

THINKING WITH THE CHURCH

explanations, we give people occasion to be dilatory and lazy in works, either before they have a faith informed by charity, or even afterwards. [369] RULE 17 Similarly we must not talk of grace at such length and with such insistence as to poison people's attitude to free will. Thus our way of talking about faith and grace should result, as far as we can with God's help, in the greater praise of His Divine Majesty, but not in such a way and with such expressions (especially in times as dangerous as ours) that there is any prejudice against, or contempt for, good works and free will. [370] RULE 18 Given that the motive of pure love in the constant service of God Our Lord is to be valued above all, yet we ought also greatly to praise fear of the Divine Majesty. The reason is that not only filial fear is a good and holy thing, but where someone is not capable of attaining anything better or more useful, even servile fear can be a great help to escape from mortal sin, and once free a person can easily reach the filial fear, which is wholly acceptable and pleasing to God Our Lord, as it is all one with divine love.

SAINT TERESA OF ÁVILA

Saint Teresa's Spiritual Ecstasies

Saint Teresa (1515–1582) was the most celebrated female religious figure in Counter-Reformation Europe. She was born into a prosperous family, became a Carmelite nun at the age of twenty-one, and suffered from severe bouts of illness. It was not until her middle age that she decided to take the lead in reforming her religious order. Her followers were known as the "Discalced," or barefoot, Carmelites. Despite many obstacles she traveled all over Spain and managed to found seventeen new houses throughout the country. Her writings on her extraordinary mystical experiences made her famous; her autobiography became the most popular work of prose literature in Spain after Cervantes's Don Quixote. *She died in 1582 and was canonized scarcely forty years after her death, in 1622.*

Her Life *(c. 1565) is one of the best examples of Spanish Counter-Reformation mysticism. The language is simple, direct, and almost conversational. She made no claims to be a great intellectual; one of the few books that she said she knew well was Saint Augustine's* Confessions. *Her confessors pressured her into writing the* Life. *The work describes her often overpowering religious raptures and demonstrates that in her belief she was orthodox and obedient to the Catholic Church.*

One night when I was so ill that I intended to excuse myself from mental prayer, I took up a rosary, so as at least to occupy myself with vocal recitation. At the same time I tried not to be recollected in mind, though I was so outwardly since I was in an oratory. But such precautions are of no avail when the Lord wills otherwise. I had been there only a few moments when I was seized by a rapture so violent that I could offer no resistance. I seemed to be raised to Heaven, and the first persons I saw there were my father an my mother. Such mighty things happened in so short a time—it can have been no longer than it would take to recite an *Ave Maria*—that I was quite lifted out of myself, finding it altogether too great a favour. As to the question of time, it may have been longer than I say, but it all passed in a very short space.

I was afraid that this might be an illusion, though it did not seem like one. I could not think what to do, since I felt ashamed to go to my confessor about it—not, I think, out of humility, but because I was afraid he might laugh at me and say: 'What a St Paul she is with her heavenly visions, or another St Jerome!' The fact that these glorious saints had similar visions made me the more afraid, and all I could do was to weep copious tears, for I did not think I could possibly have seen what they saw. In the end, though feeling even more upset, I went to my confessor. I never dared keep such things to myself, however much it pained me to speak of them; I was too much afraid of being deceived. When he saw me in this distressed state, he comforted me a great deal, and gave me plenty of sound reasons why I need not worry.

In the course of time, the Lord showed me other great secrets, and He sometimes does so still. The soul may wish to see more than is put before it, but this is impossible; there is no way in which it may do so. I never saw more on any occasion, therefore, than the Lord was pleased to show me. But what I saw was so great that the least part of it was enough to leave the soul amazed, and so to benefit it that it considers all the things of this life as of small account. I wish that I could describe at least some small part of what I learnt, but when I consider how to do so I find that it is impossible. The mere difference between the light we see here and the light of vision is inexpressible. Both are alike light, but the brightness of the sun seems dull in comparison with that other. In fact, however skilful the imagination may be, it will not succeed in describing or indicating the nature of this light, or any of the other things that the Lord revealed to me. This revelation is accompanied by a joy so sublime as to be indescribable. All the sense are filled with such a profound bliss and sweetness that no description is possible. It is better, therefore, to say no more about this.

On one occasion, when I had been in this state for more than an hour and the Lord had been showing me the most wonderful things, just as He seemed on the point of leaving me, He said: 'Daughter, see what they lose who are against me. Do not fail to tell them of it.' Ah, Lord, how little good will my words do to people blinded by their own actions, unless Your Majesty gives them light! There are some to whom You have given it who have profited by the knowledge of Your wonders. But when they see them, Lord, revealed to such a poor and base creature as myself, I think it is remarkable if anyone believes me. Blessed be Your name and Your mercy, for at least I have seen a notable improvement in my soul.

After that vision I wished it had stayed in that state for ever, and never returned to life, for I was left with a great contempt for all earthly things. They seemed to me like so much dross, and I see the meanness of our occupations, while we are detained here below.

When I was staying with the lady of whom I have spoken, I happened on one occasion to have pains in my heart—as I have said, I used to suffer severely from these, though I do so less now. Being a very kind person, she had some precious golden jewels and stones brought out for me, one set of diamonds in particular which she valued most highly. She thought that these would cheer me. But I only laughed to myself, and felt sorry that people should value such things, when I remembered what the Lord has in store for us. I thought how impossible it would be for me to attach any value to such objects, even if I tried, unless the Lord were to expunge other things from my memory.

A soul in this state has so great a dominion over itself that I do not think anyone can understand it who does not possess it. It is a real, natural detachment, achieved without any labour of our own, and it is all of God's doing. For when His Majesty reveals these truths to us, the very deep impression that they make upon our souls clearly shows us that we could not possibly acquire them for ourselves in this very short time. With that experience, I lost almost all my fear of death, which had always terrified me. Now it seems to me a very easy thing for a servant of God that in a single moment the soul should find itself freed from this prison and at rest. This moment in which God raises and transports the soul to show it things of such a sublime excellence seems to me very like that in which the soul leaves the body. In just such a single instant it finds itself in possession of all its blessings. Let us, therefore, leave out of account the agonies at the moment of parting, to which no great importance need be attached, because to those who really love God and have put aside the things of this world death must come very gently.

I think that this experience also helped me greatly to recognize my true home and to realize that here we are but pilgrims. It is a great thing to see what awaits us there, and to know where we shall live hereafter. For if someone has to go and settle in another country, it makes the hardships of the journey much lighter for him if he has evidence that he is going to a place where he will live in great comfort. It also makes death easier if we turn our minds to heavenly things and try to hold conversation with heaven. This is a great gain; merely to glance up to heaven makes the soul recollected, for as the Lord has graciously revealed some part of what is there, the thoughts turn to it. It sometimes happens that my companions and those who give me the greatest comfort are amongst those whom I know to dwell there; they are, as I see it, the people who are truly alive, whilst those who are on earth are so dead that I seem unable to find a companion in the whole world, especially when these raptures come upon me.

Everything seems to me like a dream. That which I see with the eyes of the body is a mockery, and that which I have seen with the eyes of the soul is what the soul desires. Finding itself so far from all such things is for it death. In brief it is a very great favour that the Lord is granting when He gives people such visions. He is helping them greatly, while at the same time he gives them a heavy cross to bear, for then nothing on earth is pleasing, everything is an impediment. I do not know how one could live if the Lord did not sometimes allow His high mysteries to be forgotten— though they are soon remembered again. Blessed and praised be He for ever and ever! May His Majesty grant, by the blood which His Son spilt for me, that since He has been pleased to give me some understanding of these great blessings and since I have now begun in some degree to enjoy them, I may not share the fate of Lucifer, who lost everything through his own fault. May He not permit this, for His own sake. Sometimes I am afraid that He will, although at other times, and more generally, I am comforted by the thought of God's mercy. Since He has rescued me from so many sins, He will not let me slip from His hand and be lost. I implore you, your Reverence, always to beg this of Him for me.

The favours of which I have spoken so far are less great, in my opinion, than the one that I shall now describe. There are many reasons for this, including the great benefits with which it left me, and the great strengthening that it brought to my soul. But each favour, considered by itself, is so great as to be beyond comparison. One day—it was on the eve of Pentecost—I went after Mass to a very lonely spot where I used often to pray, and began to read about this festival in the Carthusian book.[1] I read about the signs by which beginners, improvers, and the perfect may know if the Holy Spirit is with them; and when I had read of these three states, it seemed to me, in so far as I could understand it, that God, of His goodness, was certainly with me. I praised Him for this, and remembered another occasion when I had read this passage, and when I had lacked much that I have now. I saw the difference very clearly and, as I grew aware of how radically I had altered, I realized what a great favour God had done me. Then I began to meditate on the place in hell that I had earned by my sins, and gave great praise to God, for I did not seem to recognize my own soul, so great was the change that had come over it. While I was meditating in this way, a great impulse swept over me, without my seeing the manner of it; my soul seemed to be on the point of leaving my body, because it could no longer contain itself and was incapable of waiting for its great blessing. The impulse was so strong that I could do nothing against it; it did not seem the same as on other occasions, and my soul was so changed that I did not understand what happened to it, or what it desired. I leaned for support, because even seated I could not stay upright; my natural strength entirely failed me.

While in this condition, I saw above my head a dove very different from the doves of this world. It was not feathered like them, but its wings were made of little shells which shone with a great brilliance. It was bigger than a dove, and I seemed to hear the rustling of its wings. It must have been hovering like this for the space of an *Ave Maria*. But my soul was in such a state that, as it became lost to itself, so it lost sight of the dove. My spirit was calmed by the goodness of its guest, though I think that this marvellous favour disturbed and alarmed it. But once it began to rejoice in the vision, all fear left it and, as this rapture continued, with joy came tranquillity.

The glory of this rapture was very great; for the remaining days of the feast I was so bewildered and foolish that I did not know what to do, or how I could have received this great favour and grace. Such was my inward rejoicing that, as you might say, I could neither hear nor see. From that day I realized the very great progress that I had made in the highest love of God, and the great increase in the strength of my virtues. May He be blessed and praised for ever. Amen.

On another occasion I saw this same dove above the head of a Father of the Order of St Dominic. But the rays and the brightness of the wings seemed to extend much further. I understood by this that he was to bring souls to God.

On yet another occasion I saw Our Lady putting a pure white cope on a Licentiate of this same Order, of whom I have spoken several times. She told me that she was giving him that vestment as a reward for the services he had rendered her in helping toward the foundation of this house. She meant it as a sign that his soul would remain pure from that time onwards, and that he would not fall into mortal sin. I am quite sure that he never did. He passed the remainder of his life in penitence and sanctity, and a few years later died so holy and contrite a death that, so far as anything can be known, there can be no doubt about his freedom from sin. A friar who had been present at this deathbed told me that before he breathed his last he said that St Thomas was beside him. He then died with great joy, fervently desiring to depart from this exile. He has appeared to me several times since his death in very great glory, and has informed me of certain things. He was so given to prayer that when, on the point of death, he was so weak that he would have liked to cease praying, he was too continuously enraptured to be able to do so. Some time before he died, he had written to ask me what he ought to do, for as soon as he finished saying Mass he would go into a long rapture and could not avoid doing so. At the last, God gave him the reward for the many services he had rendered Him throughout his life.

As for the Rector of the Society of Jesus, whom I have mentioned many times, I had several visions of the great favours that the Lord was granting him, but for fear of being too long I will say nothing of them here. There was an occasion when he was in great trouble, being very sorely persecuted and suffering great distress. One day when I was hearing Mass, at the elevation of the Host I saw Christ on the Cross, and He gave me a message of comfort for the Rector, together with a warning of what was to come. He wished him to remember what He had suffered on his behalf and to prepare himself to suffer also. This gave the Rector great consolation and courage, and everything has since fallen out as the Lord told me it would.

I have seen great things concerning other members of the Society of Jesus to which this Father belonged, and concerning the Order as a whole. I have several times seen them in Heaven with white banners in their hands and, as I say, I have seen other visions of them that are truly wonderful. I have a great veneration, therefore, for the Order, with which I have had many dealings. I see too that their lives conform to what the Lord has told me about them.

One night when I was at prayer, the Lord began to speak to me. He reminded me of the wickedness of my past life, and filled me with shame and distress. Although He did not speak severely, He roused a consuming grief and sorrow within me. But a single word of this kind makes one more conscious of one's progress in self-knowledge than many days spent in the contemplation of one's wretchedness, since it bears the undeniable stamp of truth. He set before me the former bent of my will towards vanities, and told me that I must set great store by my present desire to fix my will, which had hitherto been so ill-employed, upon Him. He promised to accept this desire, and He told me to remember how I had once thought it honourable to oppose His honour. At other times, He said, I must remember my debt to Him, for when I was dealing Him the harshest blows He was all the time bestowing favours on me. Now, when I am doing anything wrong—and my wrong-doings are many—His Majesty makes me so conscious of it that I become entirely dissolved with shame—and as my faults are frequent the occasions for this are numerous. Sometimes I have been rebuked by my confessor, and when I have tried to find consolation in prayer, I have received a real reprimand there.

To return to what I was saying, when the Lord began to remind me of the wickedness of my past life, I wept to think that until then I had achieved nothing. But in the midst of my tears, I would wonder if He was not just about to grant me some favour. For quite often when I receive some particular favour from the Lord, it follows after a moment of complete humiliation. I think that His purpose in treating me like this is to show me how little I deserve His favours.

Soon after this my spirit was so transported that I felt it to be almost entirely out of the body, or at least I had no realization that it was still in it. I saw the most sacred Humanity in far greater glory than ever before. I saw Him with amazing clarity in the bosom of the Father. I cannot possibly say how it was, but without seeing, I seemed to see myself in the presence of that Divine Being. I was so amazed that I think it must have been several days before I came to myself again. All the time I seemed to have that majesty of the Son of God present with me, although not in the same way as in the original vision. I understood this well enough, but it remained so impressed on my imagination that, quickly though it passed, for some time I could not be rid of it. It has been a great comfort to me, and also a great blessing.

I have seen this same vision on three subsequent occasions. I think it is the most sublime vision that the Lord has ever given me the grace to see. It brings great benefits with it, and seems to have a most purifying effect upon the soul, almost entirely taking the strength out of our sensual nature. It is a great flame that seems to burn up and annihilate all worldly desires. For though—glory be to God!—I had no desires for the usual vanities, it was plainly shown to me here how all things are vain, and how absolutely vain are the dignities of this world. This is a great incentive towards raising the desires to pure truth. It impresses on the soul a sense of reverence of which I can say little except that it is very different from anything that we can acquire on earth. The soul is overwhelmed with amazement to think that it has dared offend His Supreme Majesty, or indeed that anyone should have the temerity to do so.

I must have spoken several times of the effects left by visions and other such experiences. As I have already said, they may bring greater or lesser benefits; this kind of vision brings the greatest benefits of all. When I came up to take Communion, and remembered that tremendous majesty that I had seen, and reflected that it was He that was in the most holy Sacrament, and that the Lord often graciously appeared to me in the Host, my hair would stand on end and I would seem to be utterly annihilated. O my Lord, if You did not veil Your greatness, who would dare, being so foul and wretched, to bring himself into such frequent contact with Your great majesty? May You be blessed, O Lord, and may the angels and all creatures praise You, who measure all things by our weakness. Otherwise, when we are receiving Your sovereign favours, we might be so alarmed by Your great power as not to dare enjoy them, because we are weak and miserable creatures. The same thing might happen to us as happened, to my positive knowledge, to a certain peasant, who found a treasure far more precious than his poor mind could grasp. The mere possession of it made him so sad that little by little he wasted away to death out of pure grief and perturbation, because he did not know what to do with it. If he had not found it all at once, but had been given it bit by bit, so that he could have lived on it, he would have been happier than when he was poor and it would not have cost him his life.

O Treasure of the poor, how wonderfully You can nourish souls, by revealing Your great riches to them gradually, and not allowing them to be seen all at once! Since that vision I have never seen so great a majesty hidden in anything so small as the Host without marvelling at Your great wisdom. I do not know how the Lord gives me the courage and strength to approach Him. I only know that they were—and still are—bestowed on me by Him who grants me these great favours, and that I could not possibly conceal this, or refrain from proclaiming it aloud. What must be the feelings of a wretch like myself, weighed down by abominations, who has spent her life with so little fear of God, when she finds herself approaching that majestic Lord? It is His will that my soul shall see Him. But how can I open my mouth, that has spoken so many words against this same Lord, to receive that most glorious Body, which is all purity and compassion? For the soul, conscious that it has not served Him, is far more pained and grieved by the love that shines in that most beautiful, kind, and tender face than frightened by the majesty that it sees there.

Think then what my feelings must have been on the two occasions when I saw what I shall now describe. I feel impelled to say, O my Lord and my Glory, that my soul has performed some sort of service for You by suffering the great afflictions that it did. But I do not know what I am saying. I am writing this as if it were not myself that speaks. I find myself confused and almost beside myself when I recall these things to my memory. If my feelings really emanated from me, I should have a right to say that I have done something for You, my Lord. But since there can be no good thought unless You give it, I have nothing to thank myself for. I am the debtor, Lord, and it is You who have been offended.

Once when I was about to take Communion, I saw with the eyes of my soul, more clearly than ever I could with my bodily eyes, two most hideous devils. Their horns seemed to be about the poor priest's throat; and when I saw my Lord, in all His majesty, held in those hands, in the form of the Host that he was about to present to me, I knew for certain that they had offended against Him, and that here was a man in mortal sin. How terrible, O my Lord, to see that beauty of Yours between two such hideous shapes! They seemed so cowed and alarmed in Your presence that I think they would gladly have fled if You had let them go. I was so upset, Lord, that I do not know how I was able to receive the Host; and afterwards I was afraid, for I thought that if the visions had been of God, His Majesty would not have allowed me to see the evil that was in that soul. Then the Lord Himself told me to pray for him, and said that he had allowed this in order that I might realize what power there was in the words of consecration, and that God never fails to be present however wicked the priest who pronounces them. He also wanted me to realize His great goodness in placing Himself in the hands of His enemy, only for the good of myself and of all men. This clearly showed me that priests are under an even greater obligation to be good than other men, and what a terrible thing it is to receive this Most Holy Sacrament when one is unworthy, also how completely the devil is master of a soul that is in mortal sin. This vision was a very great help to me, and made me fully understand what I owe to God. Blessed be He for ever and ever.

On another occasion I saw something else of a similar kind, which greatly alarmed me. I was in a certain place where someone had died who, as I knew, had lived a very evil life for many years. But for the last two he had been ill and seemed in some respects to have improved his ways. He died without confessing, but I did not think, all the same, that he would be damned. While his body was being laid in its shroud, I saw a number of devils lay hold of it. They seemed to be playing with it and tearing at it, tossing it from one to another with great hooks. I was utterly horrified. But when I saw it carried to the grave with all the honour and ceremony that is paid to the dead, I kept thinking of God's great goodness in not allowing that soul to be dishonoured, or the fact that it had been His enemy to be revealed.

What I had seen drove me half out of my mind. But during the funeral service I saw no more devils. Afterwards, however, when they laid the body in the grave, there was such a multitude of them waiting there to seize it that I was beside myself at the sight, and needed no small presence of mind to conceal the fact. I thought of what they would do to his soul, if they could take possession of his body in this manner. Would to God that everyone who is in an evil state could see that hideous spectacle that I saw. I think it would be a great incentive towards the reformation of their lives. All this makes me more conscious of what I owe to God and of what He has delivered me from. Until I had talked to my confessor, I was in a state of great fear, for although this man had no great reputation for piety I wondered whether this was not a trick of the devil's intended simply to discredit him. The truth is that, illusion or no, every time I remember it I am afraid.

Now that I have begun to speak of visions of the dead, I will refer to some matters which Our Lord has been pleased to reveal to me concerning certain souls. For the sake of brevity, and because such tales are unnecessary—for our profit, I mean—I will relate only a few. I was told that a former Provincial of ours had died—at the time of his death he was Provincial of another province—a man with whom I had dealings and to whom I was grateful for various kindnesses, and a person of many virtues. I was very much upset when I heard that he had died, because I feared for his salvation. He had been a superior for twenty years, and this always makes me afraid, for I think it is a most dangerous thing to have charge of souls. I went in some distress to an oratory and offered on his behalf all the good that I had done in my whole life, which must have been very little. Then I begged the Lord to make up the deficiency from His own merits, so as to deliver that soul from purgatory.

Whilst I was offering the Lord the best prayers that I could on his behalf, he seemed to rise out of the depths of the earth on my right, and I saw him ascend into Heaven with the greatest joy. He had been very old, but as I saw him he appeared to be thirty or even less, and his face was bright. This vision was quickly over, but I was so comforted that I could never grieve for his death again, although I found people much distressed by it, for he was very well liked. My soul felt so much comfort that nothing disturbed it and I could have no doubt that this was a genuine vision—I mean, that it was no illusion. He had not been dead more than a fortnight at the time. Nevertheless I was tireless in getting people to commend him to God and in doing so myself, though I could not pray with as much earnestness as if I had not seen that vision. For once the Lord gives me a demonstration like that, I cannot help thinking that attempts to commend a soul to His Majesty are like gifts of alms to the rich. He died a long way away. So it was not till afterwards that I learnt what kind of death the Lord gave him. It was one of great edification; everyone was astounded by the consciousness, the tears, and the humility with which he died.

It was about a day and a half after the death, in our house, of a nun who had been a great servant of God, that the following incident occurred. The service for the dead was being recited for her in the choir. A sister was reading the lesson, and I was standing there to assist her with the response. Half way through, I seemed to see the dead woman's soul rising on my right, as in my earlier vision, and ascending to Heaven. This was not an imaginary vision, like the last, but was similar to the others of which I have spoken. But there was no more doubt about it than about those visions that are seen.

Another nun died in this same house, at the age of eighteen or twenty. She had always been in poor health, but was a great servant of God, dutiful in the choir and extremely virtuous. I certainly thought she would be excused purgatory, for not only had she suffered from severe illness but she had a superfluity of merits. About four hours after her death, while the Office was being said preparatory to her burial, I saw her rise on the same side and ascend into Heaven.

Once I was in a College of the Company of Jesus, suffering severely both in my body and soul as I have said I sometimes used to and still do, I was in such a state that I do not think I was capable of thinking a single good thought. A member of the Company, who belonged to that house, had died that night and I was endeavouring to commend his soul to God, while listening to a Mass said for him by another Father of the Company. Suddenly I became deeply recollected and saw him ascend to Heaven in great glory; and the Lord ascended with him. I understood that it was by a special favour that His Majesty rose with him.

Another friar of our Order, a very good man, was extremely ill. I was at Mass and became recollected. Then I saw that he was dead and was ascending into Heaven without passing through purgatory. He had died, as I afterwards learnt, at the hour when I had seen him. It amazed me that he had not gone to purgatory. But I realized that as he had been a friar who had carefully kept the Rule, the Bulls of the Order had been efficacious in saving him from a sojourn there. I do not know why this was revealed to me. I think it must have been to teach me that a habit—I mean the wearing of a habit—is not enough to make a man a friar, and does not imply that state of great perfection which is proper to a friar.

I will say no more on this subject, although the Lord has graciously allowed me to see many such things. For, as I have said, it is unnecessary. But from all the visions I have seen I have never learnt that any soul escaped purgatory, except those of this father, of the saintly friar, Peter of Alcántara, and of the Dominican father whom I have mentioned. It has pleased the Lord to show me the degrees of glory to which some souls have been raised, and He has shown them to me in the places assigned to them. There is a great difference between some of these places and others.

EXPLANATORY NOTE

1. *The Life of Christ,* by Ludolf of Saxony, translated into Spanish by Ambrosio de Montesinos at the beginning of the sixteenth century.

BALDESAR CASTIGLIONE

Monarchy or Republic?

The Book of the Courtier *by Baldesar Castiglione ranks as one of the supreme expressions of the Italian Renaissance. First published in 1528 in the full glory of the High Renaissance, the book encapsulates more than a century of humanistic discussions concerning the ways to perfect human nature. Though formally confined to one particular way of life—the life of courtiers at princely courts—the dialogue in fact is a virtual compendium of themes central to Italian Renaissance thought: themes such as virtue and good manners, spiritual and sensual love, religion, the nature of beauty, true nobility, the correct use of language, the active and contemplative lives, the status of women, the ideal form of the polity, and the respective truths of arms, letters, and the arts. These subjects are laid out in the form of imaginary dialogues among the most distinguished Italian noblemen and noblewomen of the day, gathered together at the famous Renaissance court in the Duchy of Urbino.*

The author of the dialogues, Baldesar Castiglione (1478–1529), was a humanist, soldier, and diplomat who spent most of his career in the service of the dukes of Urbino. In 1524 he was appointed papal nuncio to Spain and died in Toledo of the plague in 1529. The Courtier *is his only important work, but it is one of surpassing literary artistry that represents the Urbino of his youth as a model of Renaissance ideals. In the present selection from Book IV, Castiglione's interlocutors debate the relative merits of monarchical and republican constitutions; the palm is awarded to monarchy, which is distinguished from tyranny.*

'What you do think, signor Ottaviano, is the happier form of government and the more likely to restore the golden age that you mentioned: the single rule of a good prince, or the government of a good republic?'

Signor Ottaviano replied: 'I should always prefer the rule of a good prince, since this kind of dominion is more in accord with Nature and (if it is permissible to compare such small things with the infinite) more similar to that of God, who governs the universe by Himself alone. But leaving this aside, you notice that in all human creations, such as armies, armadas, buildings and so forth, the whole is referred to one man who governs as he wishes; similarly, in our bodies all the members perform and carry out their functions according to the decisions taken by the mind. Moreover, it seems fitting that people should be ruled in this way by one head, as are many of the animals, to whom Nature teaches this obedience as a most salutary thing. Notice how deer, like cranes and many other birds, when they migrate always choose a single leader to follow and obey; and the bees, almost as if they could reason, obey their royal leader as respectfully as the most law-abiding people on earth. And all this goes to prove conclusively that government by a prince is more in accord with Nature than that of a republic.'

At this, Pietro Bembo remarked: 'But it seems to me that, since God has given us the supreme gift of freedom, it is wrong that it should be taken from us or that one man's share should be greater than another's. Yet this is what happens when there is government by princes, who for the most part keep their subjects under the strictest surveillance, whereas in well-constituted republics this freedom is always conserved. Moreover, in judgements and deliberations, it more often happens that the opinion of a single man is false than that of many; for, because of anger or indignation or lust, a single man is more prone to lose his equanimity than a multitude, which is like a vast expanse of water and therefore less subject to contamination than a small quantity. I must add that I am not convinced that the examples you give from the animal world are applicable: for the deer and the cranes and all the others do not always prefer to follow and obey a single leader. On the contrary, they change and vary their behaviour, giving full authority now to one from among them and now to another; and in this way they are organized more in the style of a republic than of a monarchy. Indeed this can be called freedom among true equals, when those who sometimes command, sometimes obey as well. Likewise, the example of the bees does not seem relevant to me, for their royal leader is not of the same species; and therefore whoever wished to give men a truly worthy lord would have to choose him from another species, endowed with a nature superior to ours, if they are reasonably bound to obey him, like the herd which obeys not an animal of its own but a herdsman who is human and therefore of a superior species. Because of what I have said, signor Ottaviano, I think that a republic is a more desirable form of government than a monarchy.'

'In contradiction,' answered signor Ottaviano, 'I will deploy just one argument, namely, that there are only three forms of sound government:

monarchy, the rule of the good (in the ancient world called the *opti-mates*) and government by the citizens. And the degenerate and lawless forms taken by these systems when they are ruined and corrupted are, in place of monarchy, tyranny, in place of the best, government by a few powerful men, and in place of the citizens, government by the common people, which wrecks the constitution and surrenders complete power to the control of the multitude. Of these three bad forms of government, there is no doubt that tyranny is the worst, as could be proved by many arguments; and so it follows that of the three good forms of government, monarchy is best, being the opposite of the worst. (For as you know, contrary causes produce contrary effects.) Now, in regard to what you said concerning freedom, I reply that it should not be said that true freedom consists in living as one wishes but rather in living under good laws. Nor is it any less natural and useful and necessary to obey than to command; and some things are born and devised and ordained by Nature to obey, just as others are to command. It is true that there are two ways of exercising rule: one is arbitrary and violent, like that of masters over their slaves, or the way the soul commands the body; the other way is milder and gentler, like that of good princes ruling their citizens through the laws, or the way reason commands our desires. Both of these ways are useful, for the body is naturally so constituted as to obey the soul, and likewise man's desires to obey his reason. There are also many men concerned solely with physical activities, and these differ from men versed in the things of the mind as much as the soul differs from the body. As rational creatures, however, they share in reason to the extent of being able to recognize it; but they do not possess it themselves or profit from it. These, then, are essentially slaves, and it is more advantageous for them to obey than to command.'

Then signor Gaspare said: 'Then in what way are men to be ruled who are judicious and intelligent in the way you said, and not essentially slaves?'

Replied signor Ottaviano: 'By the gentle government of a constitutional monarch. And it is advisable sometimes to let men of this kind take part in the local administration of government as far as their capabilities allow, so that they themselves may also be able to command and to govern those who are less wise than they, though in such a way that the authority of the ruler remains supreme. Then, since you have claimed that a single person is corrupted more easily than many, I also claim that it is easier to find one good and wise man than to find many who are such. And it is to be supposed that a monarch of noble stock can be good and wise, inclined towards virtuous things by his natural instincts and by the example of his illustrious forbears, and trained to excellence in his conduct. And even if he is not of a species superior to ours (as you said with regard to the bees), being assisted by the instructions and teachings and skill of the courtier, whom these gentlemen have made so prudent and good, he will be very just, continent, temperate, strong and wise, full of liberality, munificence, religion and clemency; in short, he will earn glory and favour among men and God, through whose grace he will acquire that heroic virtue that will raise him above human limitations, and be capable of being regarded as a demigod rather than a mortal man. For God rejoices in and protects, not those princes who wish to imitate Him by displaying their great power and making themselves adored by men, but those who, apart from the power they wield, strive also to resemble Him in goodness and wisdom, by means of which they strive successfully to work as His good servants and distribute for the benefit of mankind the benefits and gifts He has given them. Thus just as in the heavens the sun, the moon and the stars exhibit to the world, as if in a mirror, a certain likeness of God, so on earth a far truer image of God is provided by those good rulers who love and reverence Him and display to their people the resplendent light of His justice accompanied by a semblance of the divine reason and intellect. With men such as these, God shares His righteousness, fairness, justice and goodness with other indefinable blessings, which are a far clearer proof of divinity than the light of the sun or the perpetual motion of the heavens and the various courses of the stars.

'Thus, men have been entrusted by God to the protection of their rulers, who should therefore take diligent care to render Him a good account of them, like good stewards to their master, to love them and to regard their every blessing or misfortune as their own, and to strive for their happiness above all else. So the prince must not only be good but make others good as well, like the set-square used by architects that is true and straight itself and also makes true and straight everything to which it is applied. And it is convincing proof that the ruler is good when his people are good, because the way the prince lives acts as a model and guide for the citizens, and the way he behaves necessarily governs the behaviour of all the others. Nor is it fitting for an ignorant man to teach, or a lawless man to order the affairs of others, or one who falls to help raise others up. So if the prince is to perform these duties well, he must put every care and effort into acquiring knowledge; then he must establish within himself and never once deviate from the rule of reason, inscribed not on paper or metal but graven on his very soul, so that it will be not only familiar to him but inherent in his nature and he will live with it as part of himself. In this way, day in and day out, in every place and time, it may admonish and speak to him within his mind, ridding him of the disturbances experienced by those intemperate souls which because they are afflicted on the one hand by, as it were, the stupor of ignorance, and on the other, by the turmoil caused by their blind and perverse desires, are shaken by a frenzy that leaves them no peace, like the strange nightmares that sometimes come in sleep.

'Moreover, the greater the power that evil enjoys, the more harm it is able to do; and when the ruler can do whatever he wants, then there is a great danger that he will not want what he should. So Bias was right to say that the test is how a man performs in office. For just as a cracked vase cannot be detected so long as it is empty but at once shows where it is flawed when filled with water, so corrupt and depraved souls rarely reveal their defects except when they are filled with authority. For then they prove unable to sustain the heavy weight of power, and so they collapse and spill forth on every side their cupidity, pride, rage, insolence and all the tyrannical urges they have within themselves. Without restraint they persecute those who are good and wise, and exalt the wicked; in their cities they do not tolerate friendships or societies or common interests among the citizens; instead they foster spies, informers and murderers, to create terror and turn men into cowards; and they sow dissension in order to keep men disunited and weak. These methods cause the wretched people endless loss and ruin, and often enough ensure the cruel death of the tyrant himself or at least cause him to live in a state of perpetual fear. For whereas good rulers fear not for themselves but for their people, tyrants go in fear of the very people they rule. And so the more people they rule, and the more power they possess, the more they live in fear and the more enemies they have. Consider how frightened and uneasy was Clearchus, the tyrant of Pontus, whenever he went to the public square or the theatre, or to some banquet or other public place; for, so it is recorded, he used to sleep shut up in a chest. Or remember that other tyrant, Aristodemus the Argive, who turned his own bed into a kind of prison; for in his palace he had a little room suspended in mid-air, and so high that it could be reached only by a ladder; and here he slept with his mistress, whose mother used to take the steps away at night and put them back in the morning. In all things, the life of a good prince should be the contrary to this, free and safe, as dear to the citizens as their own lives, and so arranged as to be both active and contemplative, insofar as is convenient for the welfare of his people.'

JAMES I

The Divine Right of Kings

James Stuart was born in 1566, the product of the tumultuous and short-lived marriage of Mary Queen of Scots and Henry Stewart, Lord Darnley. His father was killed in a palace coup and his mother was long imprisoned in England before she was beheaded in 1587. James was nominal ruler of Scotland from his first year, but assumed power under the protection of a regent in 1581. He was an effective king of Scotland, able to balance the complex factions of highland and lowland nobles and to resist the demands of an increasingly radical Presbyterian Church. He had a traditional humanist education and proved to be a surprisingly able writer. From his youth he composed poetry and wrote both religious and secular tracts on a wide variety of subjects that ultimately included the nature of witchcraft and the evils of tobacco. He penned an instructional work for the edification of his eldest son Henry, the Basilikon Doron, *and in 1598 he responded to French resistance theorists with* The True Law of a Free Monarchy, *the classic statement of the divine right of kings. In 1603 he inherited the thrones of England and Ireland from his distant cousin, Elizabeth I, and moved his royal court to London. The English resented James's Scottish habits, background, and friends, though he proved an able ruler. His chief characteristics were an attraction to luxury and an aversion to war. He commissioned the famous version of the Bible that still bears his name. James died in 1625 and was succeeded by his surviving son, Charles I.*

The True Law of a Free Monarchy was a contribution to a debate, begun during the French wars of religion, between those who argued that lawful rulers must be obeyed and those who advocated resistance to tyrants. The crux of the issue was the divine foundation of monarchy and God's commandments about obedience. James I asserted the divine right of kings on the basis of natural, civil, and divine law and claimed that only God could judge a king.

. . . The king towards his people is rightly compared to a father of children, and to a head of a body composed of divers members, for as fathers

Reprinted from *Divine Right and Democracy: An Anthology of Political Writing in Stuart England*, edited by David Wooton (2003), by permission of Hackett Publishing Company, Inc.

the good princes and magistrates of the people of God acknowledged themselves to their subjects. And for all other well-ruled commonwealths, the style of *pater patriae* was ever, and is, commonly used to kings. And the proper office of a king towards his subjects agrees very well with the office of the head towards the body and all members thereof, for from the head, being the seat of judgement, proceeds the care and foresight of guiding, and preventing all evil that may come to the body or any part thereof. The head cares for the body: so the king for his people. As the discourse and direction flows from the head, and the execution according thereunto belongs to the rest of the members, every one according to their office, so it is betwixt a wise prince and his people. As the judgement coming from the head may not only employ the members, every one in their own office, as long as they are able for it, but likewise, in case any of them be affected with any infirmity, must care and provide for their remedy, in case it be curable, and, if otherwise, gar cut them off for fear of infecting of the rest, even so is it betwixt the prince and his people. And as there is ever hope of curing any diseased member by the direction of the head, as long as it is whole; but by the contrary, if it be troubled all the members are partakers of that pain: so is it betwixt the prince and his people.

And now first for the father's part (whose natural love to his children I described in the first part of this my discourse, speaking of the duty that kings owe to their subjects) consider, I pray you, what duty his children owe to him, and whether, upon any pretext whatsoever, it will not be thought monstrous and unnatural to his sons to rise up against him, to control him at their appetite, and when they think good to slay him, or to cut him off and adopt to themselves any other they please in his room. Or can any pretence of wickedness or rigour on his part be a just excuse for his children to put hand into him? And although we see by the course of nature that love useth to descend more than to ascend, in case it were true that the father hated and wronged the children never so much, will any man endowed with the least spunk of reason think it lawful for them to meet him with the line? Yea, suppose the father were furiously following his sons with a drawn sword, is it lawful for them to turn and strike again, or make any resistance but by flight? I think, surely if there were no more but the example of brute beasts and unreasonable creatures, it may serve well enough to qualify and prove this my argument. We read often [of] the piety that the storks have to their old and decayed parents; and generally we know that there are many sorts of beasts and fowls that, with violence and many bloody strokes, will beat and banish their young ones from them, how soon they perceive them to be able to fend for themselves. But we never read or heard of any resistance on their part, except among the vipers: which proves such persons as ought to be reasonable creatures, and yet unnaturally follow this example, to be endued with their viperous nature.

And for the similitude of the head and the body, it may very well fall out that the head will be forced to gar cut off some rotten members (as I have already said) to keep the rest of the body in integrity. But what state the body can be in if the head, for any infirmity that can fall to it, be cut off, I leave it to the reader's judgement.

So as (to conclude this part) if the children may, upon any pretext that can be imagined, lawfully rise up against their father, cut him off, and choose any other whom they please in his room, and if the body for the weal of it may, for any infirmity that can be in the head, strike it off, then I cannot deny that the people may rebel, control, and displace or cut off their king at their own pleasure, and upon respects moving them. And whether these similitudes represent better the office of a king, or the offices of masters or deacons of crafts, or doctors in physic (which jolly comparisons are used by such writers as maintain the contrary proposition), I leave it also to the reader's discretion.

And in case any doubts might arise in any part of this treatise, I will (according to my promise) with the solution of four principal and most weighty doubts that the adversaries may object conclude this discourse. And first it is cast up by divers that employ their pens upon apologies for rebellions and treasons that every man is born to carry such a natural zeal and duty to his commonwealth as to his mother, that, seeing it so rent and deadly wounded as whiles it will be by wicked and tyrannous kings, good citizens will be forced, for the natural zeal and duty they owe to their own native country, to put their hand to work for freeing their commonwealth from such a pest.

Whereunto I give two answers. First, it is a sure axiom in theology that evil should not be done that good may come of it. The wickedness, therefore, of the king can never make them that are ordained to be judged by him to become his judges. And if it be not lawful to a private man to revenge his private injury upon his private adversary (since God has only given the sword to the magistrate) how much less it is lawful to the people, or any part of them (who all are but private men, the authority being always with the magistrate, as I have already proved), to take upon them the use of the sword, whom to it belongs not, against the public magistrate, whom to only it belongs.

Next, in place of relieving the commonwealth out of distress (which is their only excuse and colour) they shall heap double distress and desolation upon it, and so their rebellion shall procure the contrary effects that they pretend it for. For a king cannot be imagined to be so unruly and tyrannous, but the commonwealth will be kept in better order, notwithstanding thereof, by him than it can be by his way-taking. For first, all sudden mutations are perilous in commonwealths, hope being thereby given to all bare men to set up themselves, and fly with other men's feathers, the reins being loosed to all the insolencies that disordered people can commit by hope of impunity, because of the looseness of all things.

And next, it is certain that a king can never be so monstrously vicious, but he will generally favour justice and maintain some order, except in the particulars wherein his inordinate lusts and passions carry him away; where, by the contrary, no king being, nothing is unlawful to none. And so the old opinion of the philosophers proves true, that better it is to live in a commonwealth where nothing is lawful, than [one] where all things are lawful to all men: the commonwealth at that time resembling an undaunted young horse that has cast his rider. For, as the divine poet Du Bartas says, 'Better it were to suffer some disorder in the state, and some spots in the commonwealth, than in pretending to reform utterly to overthrow the republic.'

The second objection they ground upon the curse that hangs over else every man may be both party and judge in his own case—which is absurd once to be thought. Now in this contract (I say) betwixt the king and his people, God is doubtless the only judge, both because to him only the king must make count of his administration (as is oft said before), as likewise, by the oath in the coronation, God is made judge and revenger of the breakers. For in his presence, as only judge of oaths, all oaths ought to be made. Then since God is the only judge betwixt the two parties contractors, the cognition and revenge must only appertain to him. It follows therefore of necessity that God must first give sentence upon the king that breaks, before the people can think themselves freed of their oath. What justice then is it that the party shall be both judge and party, usurping upon himself the office of God, may by this argument easily appear. And shall it lie in the hands of [the] headless multitude, when they please to weary of subjection, to cast off the yoke of government that God has laid upon them, to judge and punish him, whom-by they should be judged and punished, and in that case wherein by their violence they kythe themselves to be most passionate parties to use the office of an ungracious judge or arbiter? Nay, to speak truly of that case, as it stands betwixt the king and his people, none of them ought to judge of the other's break. For, considering rightly the two parties at the time of their mutual promise, the king is the one party and the whole people in one body are the other party. And therefore, since it is certain that a king, in case so it should fall out that his people in one body had rebelled against him, he should not in that case, as thinking himself free of his promise and oath, become an utter enemy and practise the wreck of his whole people and native country (although he ought justly to punish the principal authors and bellows of that universal rebellion), how much less then ought the people (that are always subject unto him and naked of all authority on their part) press to judge and overthrow him? Otherwise the people, as the one party contractors, shall no sooner challenge the king as breaker, but he as soon shall judge them as breakers; so as the victors making the tyners the traitors (as our proverb is) the party shall aye become both judge and party in his own particular, as I have already said.

And it is here likewise to be noted that the duty and allegiance which the people swears to their prince is not only bound to themselves, but likewise to their lawful heirs and posterity, the lineal succession of crowns being begun among the people of God and happily continued in divers Christian commonwealths. So as no objection either of heresy, or whatsoever private statute or law may free the people from their oath-giving to their king and his succession [as] established by the old fundamental laws of the kingdom. For, as he is their heritable overlord, and so by birth, not by any right in the coronation, comes to his crown, it is alike unlawful (the crown ever standing full) to displace him that succeeds thereto as to eject the former. For at the very moment of the expiring of the king reigning the nearest and lawful heir enters in his place. And so to refuse him, or intrude another, is not to hold out one coming in, but to expel and put out their righteous king. And I trust at this time whole France acknowledges the superstitious rebellion of the liguers, who, upon pretence of heresy, by force of arms held so long out, to the great desolation of their whole country, their native and righteous king from possessing of his own crown and natural kingdom.

Not that by all this former discourse of mine, and apology for kings, I mean that whatsoever errors and intolerable abominations of sovereign prince commit, he ought to escape all punishment, as if thereby the world were only ordained for kings, and they without controlment to turn it upside down at their pleasure. But by the contrary, by remitting them to God (who is their only ordinary judge) I remit them to the sorest and sharpest schoolmaster that can be devised for them, for the further a king is preferred by God above all other ranks and degrees of men, and the higher that his seat is above theirs, the greater is his obligation to his maker. And therefore in case he forgot himself (his unthankfulness being in the same measure of height) the sadder and sharper will his correction be; and according to the greatness of the height he is in, the weight of his fall will recompense the same. For the further that any person is obliged to God, his offence becomes and grows so much the greater than it would be in any other. Jove's thunderclaps light oftener and sorer upon the high and stately oaks than on the low and supple willow trees, and the highest bench is slipperiest to sit upon. Neither is it ever heard that any king forgets himself towards God, or in his vocation, but God with the greatness of the plague revenges the greatness of his ingratitude. Neither think I by the force and argument of this my discourse so to persuade the people, that none will hereafter be raised up and rebel against wicked princes. But remitting to the justice and providence of God to stir up such scourges as pleases him for punishment of wicked kings (who made the very vermin and filthy dust of the earth to bridle the insolency of proud Pharaoh), my only purpose and intention in this treatise is to persuade, as far as lies in me, by these sure and infallible grounds, all such good Christian readers as bear not only the naked name of a Christian but kythe the fruits thereof in their daily form of life to keep their hearts and hands free from such monstrous and unnatural rebellions whensoever the wickedness of a prince shall procure the same at God's hands; that, when it shall please God to case such scourges of princes and instruments of his fury in the fire, ye may stand up with clean hands and unspotted consciences, having proved yourselves in all your actions true Christians toward God, and dutiful subjects towards your king, having remitted the judgement and punishment of all his wrongs to Him, whom to only of right it appertains.

But craving at God, and hoping that God shall continue his blessing with us in not sending such fearful desolation, I heartily wish our king's behaviour so to be, and continue among us, as our God in earth and loving father, endued with such properties as I described a king in the first part of this treatise. And that ye (my dear countrymen and charitable readers) may press by all means to procure the prosperity and welfare of your king, that as he must on the one part think all his earthly felicity and happiness grounded upon your weal, caring more for himself for your sake than for his own, thinking himself only ordained for your weal, such holy and happy emulation may arise betwixt him and you as his care for your quietness and your care for his honour and preservation may in all your actions daily strive together, that the land may think themselves blessed with such a king, and the king may think himself most happy in ruling over so loving and obedient subjects.

THOMAS MORE

Imagining the Ideal Community

Thomas More (1477/8–1535) had the unusual distinction of combining the roles of humanist, lawyer, statesman, knight, and Catholic saint. He was the son of Sir John More, a successful London lawyer, and received a humanist education in London and Oxford; he also served as a page in the household of John Morton, archbishop of Canterbury (who is mentioned favorably in the Utopia). About 1494 he began to study law, after which he embarked on a career as a politician and royal servant. He served as a member of Parliament in 1504 and 1523 (when he was elected speaker of the house); as under-sheriff of London (1510–19); as royal counselor (after 1517); as well as in a number of other important offices, culminating in his appointment in 1529 as Lord Chancellor. In the early 1530s King Henry VIII's policy of bringing the Church of England under royal control alienated More, a pious Roman Catholic, from government service, and he resigned as Lord Chancellor in 1532. He refused to subscribe to a new oath required by the Act of Succession in 1534, and was named in a bill of attainder. After being examined by the King's Council, More was imprisoned in the Tower of London and eventually found guilty of treason on the basis of perjured testimony. He was beheaded on July 6, 1535, after pronouncing the famous last words, "I am the king's good servant, but God's first."

More's career as a humanist was influenced decisively by his friendship with the great Dutch humanist Erasmus of Rotterdam as well as by his Greek studies with William Grocyn and Thomas Linacre. More wrote a number of humanistic literary works, including a history of Richard III, an English translation of the life of Giovanni Pico della Mirandola, and a small body of Latin poetry, but his most famous and enduring work by far was the Utopia. Begun while on an embassy to Flanders in 1515, the work captures the atmosphere of hope and new possibilities that pervaded humanist circles in the early years of Henry VIII's reign. It also documents brilliantly the impact on the European imagination of the exploration of the New World. The Utopia (from the Greek ou-topos, no place) is inspired in part by Plato's Republic and other ancient writings, but gave rise to an entirely new genre of Utopian literature that flourished in western countries down to the twentieth century. In the present selection,

More's main interlocutor, Raphael Nonsenso, describes the geography, physical layout, economy, social customs, and political system of Utopia.

BOOK TWO

RAPHAEL: Well, the island is broadest in the middle, where it measures about two hundred miles across. It's never much narrower than that, except towards the very ends, which gradually taper away and curve right round, just as if they'd been drawn with a pair of compasses, until they almost form a circle five hundred miles in circumference. So you can picture the island as a sort of crescent, with its tips divided by a strait approximately eleven miles wide. Through this the sea flows in, and then spreads out into an enormous lake—though it really looks more like a vast standing pool, for, as it's completely protected from the wind by the surrounding land, the water never gets rough. Thus practically the whole interior of the island serves as a harbour, and boats can sail across it in all directions, which is very useful for everyone.

The harbour mouth is alarmingly full of rocks and shoals. One of these rocks presents no danger to shipping, for it rises high out of the water, almost in the middle of the gap, and has a tower built on it, which is permanently garrisoned. But the other rocks are deadly, because you can't see them. Only the Utopians know where the safe channels are, so without a Utopian pilot it's practically impossible for a foreign ship to enter the harbour. It would be risky enough even for the local inhabitants, if it weren't for certain landmarks erected on the shore—and by simply shifting these landmarks they could lure any number of enemy warships to destruction. Of course, there are plenty of harbours on the other side of the island, but they're all so well fortified, either naturally or artificially, that a handful of men could easily prevent a huge invading force from landing at any of them.

They say, though, and one can actually see for oneself, that Utopia was originally not an island but a peninsula. However, it was conquered by somebody called Utopos, who gave it its present name—it used to be called Sansculottia—and was also responsible for transforming a pack of ignorant savages into what is now, perhaps, the most civilized nation in the world. The moment he landed and got control of the country, he immediately had a channel cut through the fifteen-mile isthmus connecting Utopia with the mainland, so that the sea could flow all round it. Fearing it might cause resentment if he made the local inhabitants do all the work, he put his whole army on the job as well. With this colossal labour force, he got it done incredibly quickly, to the great surprise and terror of the people on the mainland, who'd begun by making fun of the whole idea.

There are fifty-four splendid big towns on the island, all with the same language, laws, customs, and institutions. They're all built on the same plan, and, so far as the sites will allow, they all look exactly alike. The minimum distance between towns is twenty-four miles, and the maximum, no more than a day's walk.

Each town sends three of its older and more experienced citizens to an annual meeting at Aircastle, to discuss the general affairs of the island. Aircastle is regarded as the capital, because of its central position, which makes it easy to get at from every part of the country. The distribution of land is so arranged that the territory of each town stretches for at least twenty miles in every direction, and in one direction much farther—that is, where the distance between towns reaches its maximum. No town has the slightest wish to extend its boundaries, for they don't regard their land as property but as soil that they've got to cultivate.

At regular intervals all over the countryside there are houses supplied with agricultural equipment, and town dwellers take it in turns to go and live in them. Each house accommodates at least forty adults, plus two slaves who are permanently attached to it, and is run by a reliable, elderly married couple, under the supervision of a District Controller, who's responsible for thirty such houses. Each year twenty people from each house go back to town, having done two years in the country, and are replaced by twenty others. These new recruits are then taught farming by the ones who've had a year on the land already, and so know more about the job. Twelve months later the trainees become the instructors, and so on. This system reduces the risk of food shortages, which might occur if the whole agricultural population were equally inexperienced.

Two years is the normal period of work on the land, so that no one's forced to rough it for too long, but those who enjoy country life—and many people do—can get special permission to stay there longer. Land-workers are responsible for cultivating the soil, raising livestock, felling timber, and transporting it to the towns, either by land or sea, whichever is more convenient. They breed vast numbers of chickens by a most extraordinary method. Instead of leaving the hens to sit on the eggs, they hatch out dozens at a time by applying a steady heat to them—with the result that, when the chicks come out of the shells, they regard the poultryman as their mother, and follow him everywhere!

They keep very few horses, and no really tame ones, as they only use them for riding practice. Ploughing and pulling carts is done by oxen.

Admittedly they can't go as fast as horses, but the Utopians say they're tougher and subject to fewer diseases. They're also less trouble and less expensive to feed, and, when they're finally past work, they're still useful as meat.

Corn is used solely for making bread, for they drink no beer, only wine, cider, perry, or water—sometimes by itself, but often flavoured with honey or liquorice, which are both very plentiful. The authorities of each town work out very accurately the annual food consumption of their whole area, but they always grow corn and breed livestock far in excess of their own requirements, so that they've plenty to spare for their neighbours.

Any necessary equipment which is not available in the country is got from one's home town—for there's a holiday once a month, when most people go there. You simply ask an official for what you want, and he hands it over, without any sort of payment.

Just before harvest-time District Controllers notify the urban authorities how much extra labour they'll need. So exactly that number of harvesters turns up punctually on the right day, and, if the weather's good, gets the whole job done in something like twenty-four hours.

But I must tell you some more about the towns. Well, when you've seen one of them, you've seen them all, for they're as nearly identical as local conditions will permit. So I'll just give you one example—it doesn't much matter which. However, the obvious choice is Aircastle, for the fact that Parliament meets there gives it a special importance, and it's the one I know best, having lived there for five years.

Aircastle is built on a gently sloping hill-side, and its groundplan is practically square. It stretches from just below the top of the hill to the River Nowater, two miles away, and extends for two miles and a bit along the river-bank.

The source of the Nowater is quite a small spring eighty miles further inland, but it's joined by several tributaries, two of them pretty big ones, so by the time it gets to Aircastle it's already more than fifty yards wide. It then keeps on growing wider, until it reaches the sea sixty miles away. Right up to the town, and for several miles beyond it, there are strong tidal currents which change direction every six hours. At high tide the sea comes thirty miles inland, filling the whole river-bed and forcing the river back. The water turns brackish for some distance further upstream, but after that the taste of salt gradually disappears, and the water which flows past Aircastle is absolutely fresh. At low tide the river chases the sea back, and continues pure and uncontaminated practically all the way to the coast.

The town is connected with the other bank of the river by a splendid arched bridge, with stone piers—not just wooden ones. That's at the landward end, so that ships can have unobstructed access to one whole side of the town. There's also another river, not very big, but delightfully calm and peaceful. It gushes out of the hill on which Aircastle is built, and flows down through the middle of it to join the Nowater. The fountain-head is just outside the town, but they've brought it within the circuit of the city wall, so that in case of invasion the enemy couldn't either cut off, divert, or poison their water supply. From that point water is run off to the lower districts of the town through a system of brickwork pipes. Where this method won't work, they have huge cisterns to collect rainwater—which serves the purpose equally well.

The town is surrounded by a thick, high wall, with towers and blockhouses at frequent intervals. On three sides of it there's also a moat, which contains no water, but is very broad and deep, and obstructed by a thorn-bush entanglement. On the fourth side the river serves as a moat. The streets are well designed, both for traffic and for protection against the wind. The buildings are far from unimpressive, for they take the form of terraces, facing one another and running the whole length of the street. The fronts of the houses are separated by a twenty-foot carriageway. Behind them is a large garden, also as long as the street itself, and completely enclosed by the backs of other streets. Each house has a front door leading into the street, and a back door into the garden. In both cases they're double swing-doors, which open at a touch, and close automatically behind you. So anyone can go in and out—for there's no such thing as private property. The houses themselves are allocated by lot, and changed round every ten years.

They're extremely fond of these gardens, in which they grow fruit, including grapes, as well as grass and flowers. They keep them in wonderful condition—in fact, I've never seen anything to beat them for beauty or fertility. The people of Aircastle are keen gardeners not only because they enjoy it, but because there are inter-street competitions for the best-kept garden. Certainly it would be hard to find any feature of the town more calculated to give pleasure and profit to the community—which makes me think that gardening must have been one of the founder's special interests.

By the founder I mean Utopos himself, who is said to have designed the whole layout of the town right from the start. However, he left posterity to embellish it and add the finishing touches, which he realized would take more than a single lifetime. According to their historical records, which cover a period of 1,760 years from the Conquest, and have always been most carefully written up, the original houses were merely small huts or cottages, built hurriedly with the first timber that came to hand. The walls were plastered with mud, the roofs ridged and thatched. But nowadays every house is an imposing three-storey structure. The walls are faced with flint or some other hard stone, or else with bricks, and lined with roughcast. The sloping roofs have been raised to the horizontal, and covered with a special sort of concrete which costs next to nothing, but is better than lead for resisting bad weather conditions, and is also fireproof. They keep out draughts by glazing the windows—oh yes, they use a great deal of glass there—or sometimes by fitting screens of fine linen treated with clear oil or amber, which has the effect of making it more transparent and also more airtight.

Now for their system of local government. The population is divided into groups of thirty households, each of which elects an official called a Styward every year. Styward is the Old Utopian title—the modern one is District Controller. For every ten Stywards and the households they represent there is a Bencheater, or Senior District Controller.

Each town has two hundred Stywards, who are responsible for electing the Mayor. They do it by secret ballot, after solemnly swearing to vote for the man that they consider best qualified, He has to be one of four candidates nominated by the whole electorate—for each quarter of the town chooses its own candidate and submits his name to the Council of Bencheaters. The Mayor remains in office for life, unless he's suspected of wanting to establish a dictatorship. Bencheaters are elected annually, but they're not normally changed. All other municipal appointments are for one year only.

Every three days, or more often if necessary, the Bencheaters have a meeting with the Mayor, at which they discuss public affairs, and promptly settle any private disputes—though these are very rare. They always invite two Stywards, a different pair each day, to attend their meetings, and there's a rule that no question affecting the general public may be finally decided until it has been debated for three days. It's a capital crime to discuss such questions anywhere except in the Council or the Assembly. Apparently this is to discourage the Mayor and Bencheaters from plotting to override the people's wishes and change the constitution. For the same reason any major issue is referred to the Assembly of Stywards, who explain it to all their households, talk it over among themselves, and then report their views to the Council. Occasionally the matter is referred to Parliament.

There's also a rule in the Council that no resolution can be debated on the day that it's first proposed. All discussion is postponed until the next well-attended meeting. Otherwise someone's liable to say the first thing that comes into his head, and then start thinking up arguments to justify what he has said, instead of trying to decide what's best for the community. That type of person is quite prepared to sacrifice the public to his own prestige, just because, absurd as it may sound, he's ashamed to admit that his first idea might have been wrong—when his first idea *should* have been to think before he spoke.

And now for their working conditions. Well, there's one job they all do, irrespective of sex, and that's farming. It's part of every child's education. They learn the principles of agriculture at school, and they're taken for regular outings into the fields near the town, where they not only watch farm-work being done, but also do some themselves, as a form of exercise.

Besides farming which, as I say, is everybody's job, each person is taught a special trade of his own. He may be trained to process wool or flax, or he may become a stonemason, a blacksmith, or a carpenter. Those are the only trades that employ any considerable quantity of labour. They have no tailors or dressmakers, since everyone on the island wears the same sort of clothes—except that they vary slightly according to sex and marital status—and the fashion never changes. These clothes are quite pleasant to look at, they allow free movement of the limbs, they're equally suitable for hot and cold weather—and the great thing is, they're all home-made. So everybody learns one of the other trades I mentioned, and by everybody I mean the women as well as the men— though the weaker sex are given the lighter job, like spinning and weaving, while the men do the heavier ones.

Most children are brought up to do the same work as their parents, since they tend to have a natural feeling for it. But if a child fancies some other trade, he's adopted into a family that practises it. Of course, great care is taken, not only by the father, but also by the local authorities, to see that the foster-father is a decent, respectable type. When you've learned one trade properly, you can, if you like, get permission to learn another—and when you're an expert in both, you can practise whichever you prefer, unless the other one is more essential to the public.

The chief business of the Stywards—in fact, practically their only business—is to see that nobody sits around doing nothing, but that everyone gets on with his job. They don't wear people out, though, by keeping them hard at work from early morning till late at night, like cart-horses. That's just slavery—and yet that's what life is like for the working classes nearly everywhere else in the world. In Utopia they have a six-hour working day—three hours in the morning, then lunch— then a two-hour break—then three more hours in the afternoon, followed by supper. They go to bed at 8 P.M., and sleep for eight hours. All the rest of the twenty-four they're free to do what they like—not to waste their time in idleness or self-indulgence, but to make good use of if in some congenial activity. Most people spend these free periods on further education, for there are public lectures first thing every morning. Attendance is quite voluntary, except for those picked out for academic training, but men and women of all classes go crowding in to hear them—I mean, different people go to different lectures, just as the spirit moves them. However, there's nothing to stop you from spending this extra time on your trade, if you want to. Lots of people do, if they haven't the capacity for intellectual work, and are much admired for such public-spirited behaviour.

After supper they have an hour's recreation, either in the gardens or in the communal dining-halls, according to the time of year. Some people practise music, others just talk. They've never heard of anything so silly and demoralizing as dice, but they have two games rather like chess. The first is a sort of arithmetical contest, in which certain numbers 'take' others. The second is a pitched battle between virtues and vices, which illustrates most ingeniously how vices tend to conflict with one another, but to combine against virtues. It also shows which vices are opposed to which virtues, how much strength vices can muster for a direct assault, what indirect tactics they employ, what help virtues need to overcome vices, what are the best methods of evading their attacks, and what ultimately determines the victory of one side or the other.

But here's a point that requires special attention, or you're liable to get the wrong idea. Since they only work a six-hour day, you may think there must be a shortage of essential goods. On the contrary, those six hours are enough, and more than enough to produce plenty of everything that's needed for a comfortable life. And you'll understand why it is, if you reckon up how large a proportion of the population in other countries is totally unemployed. First you have practically all the women—that gives you nearly fifty per cent for a start. And in countries where the women *do* work, the men tend to lounge about instead. Then there are all the priests, and members of so-called religious orders—how much work do they do? Add all the rich, especially the landowners, popularly known as nobles and gentlemen. Include their domestic staffs—I mean those gangs of armed ruffians that I mentioned before. Finally, throw in all the beggars who are perfectly hale and hearty, but pretend to be ill as an excuse for being lazy. When you've counted them up, you'll be surprised to find how few people actually produce what the human race consumes.

And now just think how few of these few people are doing essential work—for where money is the only standard of value, there are bound to be dozens of unnecessary trades carried on, which merely supply luxury goods or entertainment. Why, even if the existing labour force were distributed among the few trades really needed to make life reasonably comfortable, there'd be so much over-production that prices would fall too low for the workers to earn a living. Whereas, if you took all those engaged in non-essential trades, and all who are too lazy to work—each of whom consumes twice as much of the products of other people's labour as any of the producers themselves—if you put the whole lot of them on to something useful, you'd soon see how few hours' work a day would be amply sufficient to supply all the necessities and comforts of life—to which you might add all real and natural forms of pleasure.

But in Utopia the facts speak for themselves. There, out of all the able-bodied men and women who live in a town, or in the country round it, five hundred at the most are exempted from ordinary work. This includes the Stywards, who, though legally exempt, go on working voluntarily to set a good example. It also includes those who are permanently relieved of other duties so that they can concentrate on their studies. This privilege is only granted on the recommendation of the priests, confirmed by the Stywards in a secret ballot—and, if such a student produces disappointing results, he's sent back to the working class. On the other hand, it's not at all unusual for a manual worker to study so hard in his spare time, and make such good progress, that he's excused from practising his trade, and promoted to the intelligentsia.

This is the class from which the diplomats, priests, Bencheaters, and of course mayors are recruited. The old-fashioned word for a mayor, by the way, is *Barzanes,* though nowadays he's usually called a Nopeople. As hardly any other member of the population is either unemployed or non-productively employed, you can guess how much good work they get done in a few hours. Their labour problem is also reduced by the fact that they tackle essential jobs with more economy of effort than we do. For instance, the reason why the building trade usually absorbs so much labour is that people put up houses which their improvident heirs allow to tumble down. So the next generation has to start building all over again, which costs infinitely more than it would have cost to keep the original houses standing. In fact, what often happens is this: A builds a very expensive house, which then fails to satisfy B's fastidious taste. B therefore neglects it so badly that it's soon in ruins, and builds himself an equally expensive house elsewhere. But in Utopia, where everything's under state control, houses are very seldom built on entirely new sites, and repairs are carried out immediately they become necessary, if not before. Thus they achieve maximum durability with the minimum of labour, which means that builders sometimes have practically nothing to do. On such occasions they're sent home to saw up planks and get stones ready squared, so that if they do have to build anything it can go up all the faster.

Then think how much labour they save on clothes. Their working clothes are just loose-fitting leather overalls, which last for at least seven years. When they go about in public, they cover these rough garments with a sort of cloak, which is always the same colour—the natural colour of wool. Thus not only is their consumption of woollen fabric the lowest in the world, but so are their production costs for this material. Linen is even easier to produce, and therefore more often used—but, as long as the linen is white and the wool is clean, they don't care how fine or coarse the thread is. So whereas in other countries you won't find anyone satisfied with less than five or six suits and as many silk shirts, while dressy types want over ten of each, your Utopian is content with a single piece of clothing every two years. For why should he want more? They wouldn't make him any warmer—or any better looking.

With everybody doing useful work, and with such work reduced to a minimum, they build up such large reserves of everything that from time to time they can release a huge labour force to mend any roads which are in bad condition. And quite often, if there's nothing of that sort to be done, the authorities announce a shorter working day. They never force people to work unnecessarily, for the main purpose of their whole economy is to give each person as much time free from physical drudgery as the needs of the community will allow, so that he can cultivate his mind—which they regard as the secret of a happy life.

Now I'd better explain their social arrangements—how society is organized, how they behave towards one another, how goods are distributed, and so on. Well, the smallest social unit is the household, which is virtually synonymous with the family. When a girl grows up and gets married, she joins her husband's household, but the boys of each generation stay at home, under the control of their oldest male relative—unless he becomes senile, in which case the next oldest takes over.

Each town consists of six thousand households, not counting the country ones, and to keep the population fairly steady there's a law that no household shall contain less than ten or more than sixteen adults—as they can't very well fix a figure for children. This law is observed by simply moving supernumerary adults to smaller households. If the town as a whole gets too full, the surplus population is transferred to a town that's comparatively empty. If the whole island becomes overpopulated, they tell off a certain number of people from each town to go and start a colony at the nearest point on the mainland where there's a large area that hasn't been cultivated by the local inhabitants. Such colonies are governed by the Utopians, but the natives are allowed to join in if they want to. When this happens, natives and colonists soon combine to form a single community with a single way of life, to the great advantage of both parties—for, under Utopian management, land which used to be thought incapable of producing anything for one lot of people produces plenty for two.

If the natives won't do what they're told, they're expelled from the area marked out for annexation. If they try to resist, the Utopians declare war—for they consider war perfectly justifiable, when one country denies another its natural right to derive nourishment from any soil which the original owners are not using themselves, but are merely holding on to as a worthless piece of property.

Should any town become so depopulated that it can't be brought up to strength by transfers from elsewhere on the island, without reducing the population of some other town below the prescribed minimum—a thing which is said to have happened only twice in their history, each time as the result of a violent epidemic—they recall colonists to fill the gap, on the principle that it's better to lose a colony than to weaken any part of Utopia itself.

But let's get back to their social organization. Each household, as I said, comes under the authority of the oldest male. Wives are subordinate to their husbands, children to their parents, and younger people generally to their elders. Every town is divided into four districts of equal size, each with its own shopping centre in the middle of it. There the products of every household are collected in warehouses, and then distributed according to type among various shops. When the head of a household needs anything for himself or his family, he just goes to one of these shops and asks for it. And whatever he asks for, he's allowed to take away without any sort of payment, either in money or in kind. After all, why shouldn't he? There's more than enough of everything to go round, so there's no risk of his asking for more than he needs—for why should anyone want to start hoarding, when he knows he'll never have to go short of anything? No living creature is naturally greedy, except from fear of want—or in the case of human beings, from vanity, the notion that you're better than people if you can display more superfluous property than they can. But there's no scope for that sort of thing in Utopia.

THOMAS MORE

The Root of All Evil

Thomas More (1477/8–1535) had the unusual distinction of combining the roles of humanist, lawyer, statesman, knight, and Catholic saint. He was the son of Sir John More, a successful London lawyer, and received a humanist education in London and Oxford; he also served as a page in the household of John Morton, archbishop of Canterbury (who is mentioned favorably in the Utopia*). About 1494 he began to study law, after which he embarked on a career as a politician and royal servant. He served as a member of Parliament in 1504 and 1523 (when he was elected speaker of the house); as under-sheriff of London (1510–19); as royal counselor (after 1517); as well as in a number of other important offices, culminating in his appointment in 1529 as Lord Chancellor. In the early 1530s King Henry VIII's policy of bringing the Church of England under royal control alienated More, a pious Roman Catholic, from government service, and he resigned as Lord Chancellor in 1532. He refused to subscribe to a new oath required by the Act of Succession in 1534, and was named in a bill of attainder. After being examined by the King's Council, More was imprisoned in the Tower of London and eventually found guilty of treason on the basis of perjured testimony. He was beheaded on July 6, 1535, after pronouncing the famous last words, "I am the king's good servant, but God's first."*

More's career as a humanist was influenced decisively by his friendship with the great Dutch humanist Erasmus of Rotterdam as well as by his Greek studies with William Grocyn and Thomas Linacre. More wrote a number of humanistic literary works, including a history of Richard III, an English translation of the life of Giovanni Pico della Mirandola, and a small body of Latin poetry, but his most famous and enduring work by far was the Utopia. *Begun while on an embassy to Flanders in 1515, the work captures the atmosphere of hope and new possibilities that pervaded humanist circles in the early years of Henry VIII's reign. It also documents brilliantly the impact on the European imagination of the exploration of the New World. The* Utopia *(from the Greek* ou-topos, *no place) is inspired in part by Plato's* Republic *and other ancient writings, but gave rise to an entirely new genre of Utopian literature that flourished in western*

THE ROOT OF ALL EVIL

countries down to the twentieth century. In the present selection from the end of the Utopia, *More's main interlocutor, Raphael Nonsenso, reflects on the deeper moral roots of societal misery.*

Well, that's the most accurate account I can give you of the Utopian Republic. To my mind, it's not only the best country in the world, but the only one that has any right to call itself a republic. Elsewhere, people are always talking about the public interest, but all they really care about is private property. In Utopia, where there's no private property, people take their duty to the public seriously. And both attitudes are perfectly reasonable. In other 'republics' practically everyone knows that, if he doesn't look out for himself, he'll starve to death, however prosperous his country may be. He's therefore compelled to give his own interests priority over those of the public; that is, of other people. But in Utopia, where everything's under public ownership, no one has any fear of going short, as long as the public storehouses are full. Everyone gets a fair share, so there are never any poor men or beggars. Nobody owns anything, but everyone is rich—for what greater wealth can there be than cheerfulness, peace of mind, and freedom from anxiety? Instead of being worried about his food supply, upset by the plaintive demands of his wife, afraid of poverty for his son, and baffled by the problem of finding a dowry for his daughter, the Utopian can feel absolutely sure that he, his wife, his children, his grandchildren, his great-grandchildren, his great-great-grandchildren, and as long a line of descendants as the proudest peer could wish to look forward to, will always have enough to eat and enough to make them happy. There's also the further point that those who are too old to work are just as well provided for as those who are still working.

Now, will anyone venture to compare these fair arrangements in Utopia with the so-called justice of other countries?—in which I'm damned if I can see the slightest trace of justice or fairness. For what sort of justice do you call this? People like aristocrats, goldsmiths, or money-lenders, who either do no work at all, or do work that's really not essential, are rewarded for their laziness or their unnecessary activities by a splendid life of luxury. But labourers, coachmen, carpenters, and farmhands, who never stop working like cart-horses, at jobs so essential that, if they *did* stop working, they'd bring any country to a standstill within twelve months—what happens to them? They get so little to eat, and have such a wretched time, that they'd be almost better off if they

157

were cart-horses. Then at least, they wouldn't work quite such long hours, their food wouldn't be very much worse, they'd enjoy it more, and they'd have no fears for the future. As it is, they're not only ground down by unrewarding toil in the present, but also worried to death by the prospect of a poverty-stricken old age—since their daily wages aren't enough to support them for one day, let alone leave anything over to be saved up when they're old.

Can you see any fairness or gratitude in a social system which lavishes such great rewards on so-called noblemen, goldsmiths, and people like that, who are either totally unproductive or merely employed in producing luxury goods or entertainment, but makes no such kind provision for farm-hands, coal-heavers, labourers, carters, or carpenters, without whom society couldn't exist at all? And the climax of ingratitude comes when they're old and ill and completely destitute. Having taken advantage of them throughout the best years of their lives, society now forgets all the sleepless hours they've spent in its service, and repays them for all the vital work they've done, by letting them die in misery. What's more, the wretched earnings of the poor are daily whittled away by the rich, not only through private dishonesty, but through public legislation. As if it weren't unjust enough already that the man who contributes most to society should get the least in return, they make it even worse, and then arrange for injustice to be legally described as justice.

In fact, when I consider any social system that prevails in the modern world, I can't, so help me God, see it as anything but a conspiracy of the rich to advance their own interests under the pretext of organizing society. They think up all sorts of tricks and dodges, first for keeping safe their ill-gotten gains, and then for exploiting the poor by buying their labour as cheaply as possible. Once the rich have decided that these tricks and dodges shall be officially recognized by society—which includes the poor as well as the rich—they acquire the force of law. Thus an unscrupulous minority is led by its insatiable greed to monopolize what would have been enough to supply the needs of the whole population. And yet how much happier even these people would be in Utopia! There, with the simultaneous abolition of money and the passion for money, how many other social problems have been solved, how many crimes eradicated! For obviously the end of money means the end of all those types of criminal behaviour which daily punishments are powerless to check: fraud, theft, burglary, brawls, riots, disputes, rebellion, murder, treason, and black magic. And the moment money goes, you can also say good-bye to fear, tension, anxiety, overwork, and sleepless nights. Why, even poverty itself, the one problem that has always seemed to need money for its solution, would promptly disappear if money ceased to exist.

Let me try to make this point clearer. Just think back to one of the years when the harvest was bad, and thousands of people died of starvation. Well, I bet if you'd inspected every rich man's barn at the end of that lean period you'd have found enough corn to have saved all the lives that were lost through malnutrition and disease, and prevented anyone from suffering any ill effects whatever from the meanness of the weather and the soil. Everyone could so easily get enough to eat, if it weren't for that blessed nuisance, money. There you have a brilliant invention which was designed to make food more readily available. Actually it's the only thing that makes it unobtainable.

I'm sure that even the rich are well aware of all this, and realize how much better it would be to have everything one needed, than lots of things one didn't need—to be evacuated altogether from the danger area, than to dig oneself in behind a barricade of enormous wealth. And I've no doubt that either self-interest, or the authority of our Saviour Christ—Who was far too wise not to know what was best for us, and far too kind to recommend anything else—would have led the whole world to adopt the Utopian system long ago, if it weren't for that beastly root of all evils, pride. For pride's criterion of prosperity is not what you've got yourself, but what other people haven't got. Pride would refuse to set foot in paradise, if she thought there'd be no under-privileged classes there to gloat over and order about—nobody whose misery could serve as a foil to her own happiness, or whose poverty she could make harder to bear, by flaunting her own riches. Pride, like a hellish serpent gliding through human hearts—or shall we say, like a sucking-fish that clings to the ship of state?—is always dragging us back, and obstructing our progress towards a better way of life.

But as this fault is too deeply ingrained in human nature to be easily eradicated, I'm glad that at least one country has managed to develop a system which I'd like to see universally adopted. The Utopian way of life provides not only the happiest basis for a civilized community, but also one which, in all human probability, will last for ever. They've eliminated the root causes of ambition, political conflict, and everything like that. There's therefore no danger of internal dissension, the one thing that has destroyed so many impregnable towns. And as long as there's unity and sound administration at home, no matter how envious neighbouring kings may feel, they'll never be able to shake, let alone to shatter, the power of Utopia. They've tried to do so often enough in the past, but have always been beaten back.

* * *

While Raphael was telling us all this, I kept thinking of various objections. The laws and customs of that country seemed to me in many cases perfectly ridiculous. Quite apart from such things as their military tactics, religions, and forms of worship, there was the grand absurdity on which their whole society was based, communism minus money. Now this in itself would mean the end of the aristocracy, and consequently of all dignity, splendour, and majesty, which are generally supposed to be the real glories of any nation.

However, I could see that he was tired after talking so much, and I was not quite sure how tolerant he would be of any opinion that contradicted his own—especially when I remembered his sarcastic reference to the sort of person who is afraid of looking a fool if he cannot pick holes in other people's ideas. So I just made some polite remarks about the Utopian system, and thanked him for his interesting talk—after which I took his arm and led him in to supper, saying:

'Well, I must think it over. Then perhaps we can meet again and discuss it at greater length.'

I certainly hope we shall, some day. In the meantime I cannot agree with everything that he said, for all his undoubted learning and experience. But I freely admit that there are many features of the Utopian Republic which I should like—though I hardly expect—to see adopted in Europe.

NICCOLÒ MACHIAVELLI

Whether It Is Better to Be Loved than Feared

Niccolò Machiavelli (1469–1527), the most famous of all Renaissance polit-
ical writers, is also the most controversial. He has been called the founder
of the social sciences, the originator of the theory of "power politics" in
international relations, the greatest Renaissance representative of "civic
humanism," a great theorist of republican liberty, as well as many less com-
plimentary names. He was born into an old but declining Florentine family
and received a standard humanistic education in the Greek and Latin clas-
sics. In his twenties he witnessed the expulsion of the Medici from Florence
and the ascendency of Fra Girolamo Savonarola, who temporarily turned
Florence into a kind of theocracy. From 1498 to 1512 he was employed as
the Second Chancellor (or under-secretary of state) to Florence's republican
regime, and became a close confidant ("lapdog," said his enemies) of Piero
Soderini, the Florentine head of state. In this period Machiavelli also served
as secretary to the emergency war commission, and secretary of the civic
board governing the militia. He was an ambassador and envoy on some
thirty-five diplomatic missions, including several to important leaders such
as King Louis XII of France, Cesare Borgia, Pope Julius II, and the
emperor Maximilian I. He had a much more extensive acquaintance with
men and affairs than most political theorists.

In 1512 the Soderini regime fell and the Medici returned to power.
Machiavelli was removed from office, and briefly imprisoned and tortured.
Yet he was still eager to serve the new regime and wrote The Prince *(1513,*
printed in 1531) in part to give the new Medici rulers proof of his political
acumen. Eventually he was commissioned by Cardinal Giulio de'Medici to
write a history of Florence. After his initial rejection by the Medici, Machi-
avelli sought to curry favor with leading oligarchs of the old republic, spec-
ulating on the possibility of their return to power. With this end in view he
composed The Discourses on the First Ten Books of Titus Livy *(1513–17,*
printed 1531). The dialogues on The Art of War, *written around 1520 and*
printed in 1521, display Machiavelli's credentials as an expert on military
matters. All of Machiavelli's works were on the papal Index of Prohibited
Books from 1557 until 1850.

In this selection from chapters XVII and XVIII of The Prince, *Machi-avelli explained that the prince's power and success must always trump lesser considerations such as his reputation for compassion, the love of the people, and his personal honor.*

XVII. CRUELTY AND COMPASSION; AND WHETHER IT IS BETTER TO BE LOVED THAN FEARED, OR THE REVERSE

Taking others of the qualities I enumerated above, I say that a prince must want to have a reputation for compassion rather than for cruelty: none the less, he must be careful that he does not make bad use of compassion. Cesare Borgia was accounted cruel; nevertheless, this cruelty of his reformed the Romagna, brought it unity, and restored order and obedience. On reflection, it will be seen that there was more compassion in Cesare than in the Florentine people, who, to escape being called cruel, allowed Pistoia to be devastated.[1] So a prince must not worry if he incurs reproach for his cruelty so long as he keeps his subjects united and loyal. By making an example or two he will prove more compassionate than those who, being too compassionate, allow disorders which lead to murder and rapine. These nearly always harm the whole community, whereas executions ordered by a prince only affect individuals. A new prince, of all rulers, finds it impossible to avoid a reputation for cruelty, because of the abundant dangers inherent in a newly won state. Vergil, through the mouth of Dido, says:

> Res dura, et regni novitas me talia cogunt
> Moliri, et late fines custode tueri.[2]

None the less, a prince must be slow to believe allegations and to take action, and must watch that he does not come to be afraid of his own shadow; his behaviour must be tempered by humanity and prudence so that over-confidence does not make him rash or excessive distrust make him unbearable.

From this arises the following question: whether it is better to be loved than feared, or the reverse. The answer is that one would like to be both the one and the other; but because it is difficult to combine them, it is far better to be feared than loved if you cannot be both. One can make this generalization about men: they are ungrateful, fickle, liars, and deceivers, they shun danger and are greedy for profit; while you treat them well, they are yours. They would shed their blood for you, risk their property, their lives, their sons, so long, as I said above, as danger is remote; but when you are in danger they turn away. Any prince who has come to depend entirely on promises and has taken no other precautions ensures his own ruin; friendship which is bought with money and not with greatness and nobility of mind is paid for, but it does not last and it yields nothing. Men worry less about doing an injury to one who makes himself loved than to one who makes himself feared. For love is secured by a bond of gratitude which men, wretched creatures that they are, break when it is to their advantage to do so; but fear is strengthened by a dread of punishment which is always effective.

The prince must none the less make himself feared in such a way that, if he is not loved, at least he escapes being hated. For fear is quite compatible with an absence of hatred; and the prince can always avoid hatred if he abstains from the property of his subjects and citizens and from their women. If, even so, it proves necessary to execute someone, this is to be done only when there is proper justification and manifest reason for it. But above all a prince must abstain from the property of others; because men sooner forget the death of their father than the loss of their patrimony. It is always possible to find pretexts for confiscating someone's property; and a prince who starts to live by rapine always finds pretexts for seizing what belongs to others. On the other hand, pretexts for executing someone are harder to find and they are sooner gone.

However, when a prince is campaigning with his soldiers and is in command of a large army then he need not worry about having a reputation for cruelty; because, without such a reputation, no army was ever kept united and disciplined. Among the admirable achievements of Hannibal is included this: that although he led a huge army, made up of countless different races, on foreign campaigns, there was never any dissension, either among the troops themselves or against their leader, whether things were going well or badly. For this, his inhuman cruelty was wholly responsible. It was this, along with his countless other qualities, which made him feared and respected by his soldiers. If it had not been for his cruelty, his other qualities would not have been enough. The historians, having given little thought to this, on the one hand admire what Hannibal achieved, and on the other condemn what made his achievements possible.

That his other qualities would not have been enough by themselves can be proved by looking at Scipio, a man unique in his own time and through all recorded history. His armies mutinied against him in Spain, and the only reason for this was his excessive leniency, which allowed his soldiers more licence than was good for military discipline. Fabius

Maximus reproached him for this in the Senate and called him a corrupter of the Roman legions. Again, when the Locrians were plundered by one of Scipio's officers, he neither gave them satisfaction nor punished his officer's insubordination; and this was all because of his being too lenient by nature.[3] By way of excuse for him some senators argued that many men were better at not making mistakes themselves than at correcting them in others. But in time Scipio's lenient nature would have spoilt his fame and glory had he continued to indulge it during his command; when he lived under orders from the Senate, however, this fatal characteristic of his was not only concealed but even brought him glory.

So, on this question of being loved or feared, I conclude that since some men love as they please but fear when the prince pleases, a wise prince should rely on what he controls, not on what he cannot control. He must only endeavour, as I said, to escape being hated.

XVIII. HOW PRINCES SHOULD HONOUR THEIR WORD

Everyone realizes how praiseworthy it is for a prince to honour his word and to be straightforward rather than crafty in his dealings; none the less contemporary experience shows that princes who have achieved great things have been those who have given their word lightly, who have known how to trick men with their cunning, and who, in the end, have overcome those abiding by honest principles.

You must understand, therefore, that there are two ways of fighting: by law or by force. The first way is natural to men, and the second to beasts. But as the first way often proves inadequate one must needs have recourse to the second. So a prince must understand how to make a nice use of the beast and the man. The ancient writers taught princes about this by an allegory, when they described how Achilles and many other princes of the ancient world were sent to be brought up by Chiron, the centaur, so that he might train them his way. All the allegory means, in making the teacher half beast and half man, is that a prince must know how to act according to the nature of both, and that he cannot survive otherwise.

So, as a prince is forced to know how to act like a beast, he must learn from the fox and the lion; because the lion is defenceless against traps and a fox is defenceless against wolves. Therefore one must be a fox in order to recognize traps, and a lion to frighten off wolves. Those who simply act like lions are stupid. So it follows that a prudent ruler cannot, and must not, honour his word when it places him at a disadvantage and when the reasons for which he made his promise no longer exist. If all men were good, this precept would not be good; but because men are wretched creatures who would not keep their word to you, you need not keep your word to them. And no prince ever lacked good excuses to colour his bad faith. One could give innumerable modern instances of this, showing how many pacts and promises have been made null and void by the bad faith of princes: those who have known best how to imitate the fox have come off best. But one must know how to colour one's actions and to be a great liar and deceiver. Men are so simple, and so much creatures of circumstance, that the deceiver will always find someone ready to be deceived.

There is one fresh example I do not want to omit. Alexander VI never did anything, or thought of anything, other than deceiving men; and he always found victims for his deceptions. There never was a man capable of such convincing asseverations, or so ready to swear to the truth of something, who would honour his word less. None the less his deceptions always had the result he intended, because he was a past master in the art.

A prince, therefore, need not necessarily have all the good qualities I mentioned above, but he should certainly appear to have them. I would even go so far as to say that if he has these qualities and always behaves accordingly he will find them harmful; if he only appears to have them they will render him service. He should appear to be compassionate, faithful to his word, kind, guileless, and devout. And indeed he should be so. But his disposition should be such that, if he needs to be the opposite, he knows how. You must realize this: that a prince, and especially a new prince, cannot observe all those things which give men a reputation for virtue, because in order to maintain his state he is often forced to act in defiance of good faith, of charity, of kindness, of religion. And so he should have a flexible disposition, varying as fortune and circumstances dictate. As I said above, he should not deviate from what is good, if that is possible, but he should know how to do evil, if that is necessary.

A prince, then, must be very careful not to say a word which does not seem inspired by the five qualities I mentioned earlier. To those seeing and hearing him, he should appear a man of compassion, a man of good faith, a man of integrity, a kind and a religious man. And there is nothing so important as to seem to have this last quality. Men in general judge by their eyes rather than by their hands; because everyone is in a position to watch, few are in a position to come in close touch with you. Everyone sees what you appear to be, few experience what you really are. And those few dare not gainsay the many who are backed by the majesty of the state. In the actions of all men, and especially of princes, where there is no court of appeal, one judges by the result. So let a prince set about the task of conquering, and maintaining his state; his methods will always be judged honourable and will be universally praised. The common people are always impressed by appearances and results. In this context, there are only common people, and there is no leeway for the few when the many are firmly sustained. A certain contemporary ruler, whom it is better not to name, never preaches anything except peace and good faith;[4] and he is an enemy of both one and the other, and if he had ever honoured either of them he would have lost either his standing or his state many times over.

EXPLANATORY NOTES

1. Pistoia was a subject-city of Florence, which forcibly restored order there when conflict broke out between two rival factions in 1501–2. Machiavelli was concerned with this business at first hand.
2. 'Harsh necessity, and the newness of my kingdom, force me to do such things and to guard my frontiers everywhere.' *Aeneid* i, 563.
3. Locri Epizephyrii was in Calabria. Machiavelli liked to make comparisons—elaborated in the *Discorsi*—between Hannibal and Publius Cornelius Scipio, called Scipio Africanus Major (326–182 B.C.), who defeated Hannibal during the Punic wars at Zama in 202 B.C.
4. Ferdinand of Aragon.

CHRISTOPHER COLUMBUS

Letter on the Discovery of the New World

Christopher Columbus was born in Genoa, Italy, in 1451. His father was a weaver and wool merchant and the Genoese were a seafaring people who lived by trade. By his early twenties, Christopher had become a sailor in the Portuguese merchant marine, as well as an amateur cartographer. He became involved in the West African gold trade and made a number of voyages along the African coast under the Portuguese flag. It was during these years that he conceived his idea of reaching the spice-rich Indies by sailing directly west across the Atlantic rather than east around Africa to Asia. By 1486 he was in Spain attempting to interest Queen Isabella of Castille in his project, and bargaining hard for a portion of the riches he was sure would be the result of his voyage. In 1492, with royal backing, he set out with three small ships to test his plan. Columbus had grossly underestimated the size of the globe and when he reached land on October 12, 1492, it was in the Caribbean near Cuba rather than in the Pacific near Japan. Columbus made four voyages to the New World, proving his outstanding navigational abilities even if he never could be persuaded that he had found a new continent rather than a passage to the Indies. He was rewarded with the title of Admiral of the Ocean Seas and his family reaped the benefits of his fame. He died in 1506.

On the return voyage from his initial discovery, Columbus wrote a letter to the heads of European states announcing his success and claiming the lands he had reached for the Spanish monarchy. He described the exotic flora and fauna, the customs of some of the natives he encountered, and the riches to be found on the islands.

LETTER OF COLUMBUS TO VARIOUS PERSONS DESCRIBING THE RESULTS OF HIS FIRST VOYAGE AND WRITTEN ON THE RETURN JOURNEY

Since I know that you will be pleased at the great success with which the Lord has crowned my voyage, I write to inform you how in thirty-three days I crossed from the Canary Islands to the Indies, with the fleet which our most illustrious sovereigns gave me. I found very many islands with large populations and took possession of them all for their Highnesses; this I did by proclamation and unfurled the royal standard. No opposition was offered.

I named the first island that I found 'San Salvador', in honour of our Lord and Saviour who has granted me this miracle. The Indians call it 'Guanahani'. The second island I named 'Santa Maria de Concepción', the third 'Fernandina', the fourth 'Isabela' and the fifth 'Juana'; thus I renamed them all.

When I reached Cuba, I followed its north coast westwards, and found it so extensive that I thought this must be the mainland, the province of Cathay.[1] Since there were no towns or villages on the coast, but only small groups of houses whose inhabitants fled as soon as we approached, I continued on my course, thinking that I should undoubtedly come to some great towns or cities. We continued for many leagues but found no change, except that the coast was bearing me northwards. This I wished to avoid, since winter was approaching and my plan was to journey south. As the wind was carrying me on I decided not to wait for a change of weather but to turn back to a remarkable harbour which I had observed. From here I sent two men inland to discover whether there was a king or any great cities. They travelled for three days, finding only a large number of small villages and great numbers of people, but nothing more substantial. Therefore they returned.

I understood from some Indians whom I had captured elsewhere that this was an island, and so I followed its coast for 107 leagues to its eastward point. From there I saw another island eighteen leagues eastwards which I then named 'Hispaniola'.[2] I crossed to this island and followed its northern coast eastwards for 188 leagues continuously, as I had followed the coast of Cuba. All these islands are extremely fertile and this one is particularly so. It has many large harbours finer than any I know in Christian lands, and many large rivers. All this is marvellous. The land is high and has many ranges of hills, and mountains incomparably finer than Tenerife. All are most beautiful and various in shape, and all are accessible. They are covered with tall trees of different kinds which seem to reach the sky. I have heard that they never lose their leaves, which I can well believe, for I saw them as green and lovely as they are in Spain in May; some were flowering, some bore fruit and others were at different stages according to their nature. It was November but everywhere I went the nightingale[3] and many other birds were singing. There are palms of six or eight different kinds—a marvellous sight because of their great variety—and the other trees, fruit and plants are equally marvellous. There are splendid pine woods and broad fertile plains, and there is honey. There are many kinds of birds and varieties of fruit. In the interior are mines and a very large population.

Hispaniola is a wonder. The mountains and hills, the plains and meadow lands are both fertile and beautiful. They are most suitable for planting crops and for raising cattle of all kinds, and there are good sites for building towns and villages. The harbours are incredibly fine and there are many great rivers with broad channels and the majority contain gold.[4] The trees, fruits and plants are very different from those of Cuba. In Hispaniola there are many spices and large mines of gold and other metals. . . .[5]

The inhabitants of this island, and all the rest that I discovered or heard of, go naked, as their mothers bore them, men and women alike. A few of the women, however, cover a single place with a leaf of a plant or piece of cotton which they weave for the purpose. They have no iron or steel or arms and are not capable of using them, not because they are not strong and well built but because they are amazingly timid. All the weapons they have are canes cut at seeding time, at the end of which they fix a sharpened stick, but they have not the courage to make use of these, for very often when I have sent two or three men to a village to have a conversation with them a great number of them have come out. But as soon as they saw my men all fled immediately, a father not even waiting for his son. And this is not because we have harmed any of them; on the contrary, wherever I have gone and been able to have conversation with them, I have given them some of the various things I had, a cloth and other articles, and received nothing in exchange. But they have still remained incurably timid. True, when they have been reassured and lost their fear, they are so ingenuous and so liberal with all their possessions that no one who has not seen them would believe it. If one asks for anything they have they never say no. On the contrary, they offer a share to anyone with demonstrations of heartfelt affection, and they are immediately content with any small thing, valuable or valueless, that is given them. I forbade the men to give them bits of broken crockery, fragments of glass or tags of laces, though if they could get them they fancied them the finest jewels in the world. One sailor was known to have received gold to the weight of two and a half *castellanos* for the tag of a breeches lace, and others received much more for things of even less value. For newly minted *blancas* they would give everything they possessed, even two or three *castellanos* of gold or an arroba or two of spun cotton. They even took bits of broken hoops from the wine barrels and, as simple as animals, gave what they had. This seemed to me to be wrong and I forbade it.

I gave them a thousand pretty things that I had brought, in order to gain their love and incline them to become Christians. I hoped to win them to the love and service of their Highnesses and of the whole Spanish nation and to persuade them to collect and give us of the things which they possessed in abundance and which we needed. They have no religion and are not idolaters; but all believe that power and goodness dwell in the sky and they are firmly convinced that I have come from the sky with these ships and people. In this belief they gave me a good reception everywhere, once they had overcome their fear; and this is not because they are stupid—far from it, they are men of great intelligence, for they navigate all those seas, and give a marvellously good account of everything—but because they have never before seen men clothed or ships like these.

As soon as I came to the Indies, at the first island I discovered I seized some natives, intending them to inquire and inform me about things in these parts. These men soon understood us, and we them, either by speech or signs and they were very useful to us. I still have them with me and despite all the conversation they have had with me they are still of the opinion that I come from the sky and have been the first to proclaim this wherever I have gone. Then others have gone running from house to house and to the neighbouring villages shouting: 'Come, come and see the people from the sky,' so, once they were reassured about us, all have come, men and women alike, and not one, old or young, has remained behind. All have brought us something to eat and drink which they have given with a great show of love. In all the islands they have very many canoes like oared *fustas*.

They are of various sizes, some as large as a *fusta* of eighteen benches. But they are not as broad, since they are hollowed out of a single tree. A *fusta* would not be able to keep up with them, however, for they are rowed at an incredible speed. In these they travel and transport their goods between the islands, which are innumerable. I have seen some of these canoes with eighty men in them, all rowing.

In all these islands I saw no great difference in the looks of the people, their customs or their language. On the other hand, all understand one another, which will be of singular assistance in the work of their conversion to our holy faith, on which I hope your Highness will decide, since they are very well disposed towards it.

I have already told of my voyage of 107 leagues in a straight line from west to east along the coast of Cuba, according to which I reckon that the island is larger than England and Scotland put together.[6]

One of these provinces is called Avan[7] and there the people are born with tails, and these provinces cannot have a length of less than fifty or sixty leagues, according to the information I received from those Indians whom I have with me and who know all the islands.

The other island, Hispaniola, is greater in circumference than the whole of Spain[8] from Collioure to Fuenterabia in the Basque province, since I travelled along one side for 188 great leagues[9] in a straight line from west to east.

These islands are richer than I yet know or can say and I have taken possession of them in their Majesties' name and hold them all on their behalf and as completely at their disposition as the Kingdom of Castile. In this island of Hispaniola I have taken possession of a large town which is most conveniently situated for the goldfields and for communications with the mainland both here,[10] and there in the territories of the Grand Khan, with which there will be very profitable trade. I have named this town Villa de Navidad and have built a fort there. Its fortifications will by now be finished and I have left sufficient men to complete them. They have arms, artillery and provisions for more than a year, and a *fusta;* also a skilled shipwright who can build more.

I have established warm friendship with the king of that land, so much so, indeed, that he was proud to call me and treat me as a brother. But even should he change his attitude and attack the men of La Navidad, he and his people know nothing about arms and go naked, as I have already said; they are the most timorous people in the world. In fact, the men I have left there would be enough to destroy the whole land, and the island holds no dangers for them so long as they maintain discipline.

In all these islands the men are seemingly content with one woman, but their chief or king is allowed more than twenty. The women appear to work more than the men and I have not been able to find out if they have private property. As far as I could see whatever a man had was shared among all the rest and this particularly applies to food.

I have not found the human monsters which many people expected. On the contrary, the whole population is very well made. They are not Negroes as in Guinea, and their hair is straight, for where they live the sun's rays do not strike too harshly, but they are strong nevertheless, despite the fact that Hispaniola is 20 to 21 degrees from the Equator.

There are high mountains in these islands and it was very cold this winter but the natives are used to this and withstand the weather, thanks to their food, which they eat heavily seasoned with very hot spices. Not only have I found no monsters but I have had no reports of any except at the island called 'Quaris',[11] which is the second as you approach the Indies from the east, and which is inhabited by a people who are regarded in these islands as extremely fierce and who eat human flesh. They have many canoes in which they travel throughout the islands of the Indies, robbing and taking all they can. They are no more ill-shaped than any other natives of the Indies, though they are in the habit of wearing their hair long like women. They have bows and arrows with the same canes as the others, tipped with splinters of wood, for lack of iron which they do not possess. They behave most savagely to the other peoples but I take no more account of them than the rest. It is these men who have relations with the women of Matinino,[12] where there are no men and which is the first island you come to on the way from Spain to the Indies. These women do not follow feminine occupations but use cane bows and arrows like those of the men and arm and protect themselves with plates of copper, of which they have much.

In another island, which I am told is larger than Hispaniola, the people have no hair. Here there is a vast quantity of gold, and from here and the other islands I bring Indians as evidence.

In conclusion, to speak only of the results of this very hasty voyage, their Highnesses can see that I will give them as much gold as they require, if they will render me some very slight assistance; also I will give them all the spices and cotton they want, and as for mastic, which has so far been found only in Greece and the island of Chios and which the Genoese authorities have sold at their own price, I will bring back as large a cargo as their Highnesses may command. I will also bring them as much aloes as they ask and as many slaves, who will be taken from the idolaters. I believe also that I have found rhubarb and cinnamon and there will be countless other things in addition, which the people I have left there will discover. For I did not stay anywhere unless delayed by lack of wind except at the town of La Navidad, which I had to leave secure and well established. In fact I should have done much more if the ships had been reasonably serviceable, but this is enough.

Thus the eternal God, Our Lord, grants to all those who walk in his way victory over apparent impossibilities, and this voyage was preeminently a victory of this kind. For although there was much talk and writing of these lands, all was conjectural, without ocular evidence. In fact, those who accepted the stories judged rather by hearsay than on any tangible information. So all Christendom will be delighted that our Redeemer has given victory to our most illustrious King and Queen and their renowned kingdoms, in this great matter. They should hold great celebrations and render solemn thanks to the Holy Trinity with many solemn prayers, for the great triumph which they will have, by the conversion of so many people to our holy faith and for the temporal benefits which will follow, for not only Spain, but all Christendom will receive encouragement and profit.

This is a brief account of the facts.

Written in the caravel off the Canary Islands.[13]

15 February 1493

At your orders

THE ADMIRAL

EXPLANATORY NOTES

1. In the log-book and later in this letter Columbus accepts the native story that Cuba is an island which they can circumnavigate in something more than twenty-one days, yet he insists here and later, during the second voyage, that it is in fact part of the Asiatic mainland.
2. This is referred to in the log-book as Bohio or Bofio.
3. Columbus was mistaken; he probably heard the mocking-bird.
4. This did not prove to be true.
5. These statements are also inaccurate.
6. Cuba is actually considerably smaller than England without Scotland.
7. From which the Spaniards took the name La Habana, which they gave first to a town that they built on the southern coast of the island and afterwards to the present city of that name.
8. This also is an exaggeration.
9. Reckoned to be four (Roman) miles.
10. Columbus is apparently assuming now that Cuba is part of the mainland, but that a further part of the mainland of Asia is still to be discovered.
11. Either Dominica or Maria Galante. Reports of monsters seem generally to refer to the Carabis.
12. Martinique.
13. Actually Columbus was off Santa Maria in the Azores.

BARTOLOMÉ DE LAS CASAS

The Destruction of the Amerindians

Bartolomé de las Casas (1474–1566) was born in Seville and traveled to the New World at the age of eighteen. He entered the order of the Dominicans, ultimately rising to the office of Bishop in the New World. Las Casas witnessed firsthand the destruction of native American peoples and their enslavement, and was himself a holder of Indian slaves. Yet from the beginning Las Casas was appalled by what he saw and attempted both through his actions and his writings to ease the plight of the conquered native peoples. He made several return trips to Spain, pleading with successive Spanish monarchs to prohibit the eradication of the indigenous peoples of the West Indies and Central America. His most effective tool was the publication of highly sympathetic accounts of the plight of native Americans including A Short Account of the Destruction of the Indies *and the* Apologetic History of the Indies, *both of which went through many editions and became the basis for the condemnation of Spanish imperialism in the New World and of the so-called "Black Legend" of Spanish cruelty.*

A Short Account of the Destruction of the Indies (1542) was dedicated to Philip II and was an attempt to persuade him to regulate the nature of Spanish rule in South America after its conquest. It was a best seller in its time, translated into all major European languages and reprinted constantly. Las Casas described the brutality of the subjugation of the Indians in graphic detail and many editions were illustrated with woodcuts of torture and executions.

The Americas were discovered in 1492, and the first Christian settlements established by the Spanish the following year. It is accordingly forty-nine years now since Spaniards began arriving in numbers in this part of the world.[1] They first settled the large and fertile island of Hispaniola, which boasts six hundred leagues of coastline and is surrounded by a great many other large islands, all of them, as I saw for myself, with as high a native population as anywhere on earth.[2] Of the coast of the mainland, which, at its nearest point, is a little over two hundred and fifty leagues from Hispaniola, more than ten thousand leagues had been explored by 1541, and more are being discovered every day. This coastline, too, was swarming with people and it would seem, if we are to judge by those areas so far explored, that the Almighty selected this part of the world as home to the greater part of the human race.

God made all the peoples of this area, many and varied as they are, as open and as innocent as can be imagined. The simplest people in the world—unassuming, long-suffering, unassertive, and submissive—they are without malice or guile, and are utterly faithful and obedient both to their own native lords and to the Spaniards in whose service they now find themselves. Never quarrelsome or belligerent or boisterous, they harbour no grudges and do not seek to settle old scores; indeed, the notions of revenge, rancour, and hatred are quite foreign to them. At the same time, they are among the least robust of human beings: their delicate constitutions make them unable to withstand hard work or suffering and render them liable to succumb to almost any illness, no matter how mild. Even the common people are no tougher than princes or than other Europeans born with a silver spoon in their mouths and who spend their lives shielded from the rigours of the outside world. They are also among the poorest people on the face of the earth; they own next to nothing and have no urge to acquire material possessions. As a result they are neither ambitious nor greedy, and are totally uninterested in worldly power. Their diet is every bit as poor and as monotonous, in quantity and in kind, as that enjoyed by the Desert Fathers. Most of them go naked, save for a loincloth to cover their modesty; at best they may wrap themselves in a piece of cotton material a yard or two square. Most sleep on matting, although a few possess a kind of hanging net, known in the language of Hispaniola as a hammock.[3] They are innocent and pure in mind and have a lively intelligence, all of which makes them particularly receptive to learning and understanding the truths of our Catholic faith and to being instructed in virtue; indeed, God has invested them with fewer impediments in this regard than any other people on earth. Once they begin to learn of the Christian faith they become so keen to know more, to receive the Sacraments, and to worship God, that the missionaries who instruct them do truly have to be men of exceptional patience and forbearance; and over the years I have time and again met Spanish laymen who have been so struck by the natural goodness that shines through these people that they frequently can be heard to exclaim: 'These would be the most blessed people on earth if only they were given the chance to convert to Christianity.'

It was upon these gentle lambs, imbued by the Creator with all the qualities we have mentioned, that from the very first day they clapped eyes on them the Spanish fell like ravening wolves upon the fold, or like tigers and savage lions who have not eaten meat for days. The pattern established at the outset has remained unchanged to this day, and the Spaniards still do nothing save tear the natives to shreds, murder them and inflict upon them untold misery, suffering and distress, tormenting, harrying and persecuting them mercilessly. We shall in due course describe some of the many ingenious methods of torture they have invented and refined for this purpose, but one can get some idea of the effectiveness of their methods from the figures alone. When the Spanish first journeyed there, the indigenous population of the island of Hispaniola stood at some three million; today only two hundred survive. The island of Cuba, which extends for a distance almost as great as that separating Valladolid from Rome, is now to all intents and purposes uninhabited;[4] and two other large, beautiful and fertile islands, Puerto Rico and Jamaica, have been similarly devastated. Not a living soul remains today on any of the islands of the Bahamas, which lie to the north of Hispaniola and Cuba, even though every single one of the sixty or so islands in the group, as well as those known as the Isles of Giants and others in the area, both large and small, is more fertile and more beautiful than the Royal Gardens in Seville and the climate is as healthy as anywhere on earth.[5] The native population, which once numbered some five hundred thousand, was wiped out by forcible expatriation to the island of Hispaniola, a policy adopted by the Spaniards in an endeavour to make up losses among the indigenous population of that island. One God-fearing individual was moved to mount an expedition to seek out those who had escaped the Spanish trawl and were still living in the Bahamas and to save their souls by converting them to Christianity, but, by the end of a search lasting three whole years, they had found only the eleven survivors I saw with my own eyes.[6] A further thirty or so islands in the region of Puerto Rico are also now uninhabited and left to go to rack and ruin as a direct result of the same practices. All these islands, which together must run to over two thousand leagues, are now abandoned and desolate.

On the mainland, we know for sure that our fellow-countrymen have, through their cruelty and wickedness, depopulated and laid waste an area which once boasted more than ten kingdoms, each of them larger in area than the whole of the Iberian Peninsula. The whole region, once teeming with human beings, is now deserted over a distance of more than two thousand leagues: a distance, that is, greater than the journey from Seville to Jerusalem and back again.

. . .

As we have said, the islands of Hispaniola was the first to witness the arrival of Europeans and the first to suffer the wholesale slaughter of its people and the devastation and depopulation of the land. It all began with the Europeans taking native women and children both as servants and to satisfy their own base appetites; then, not content with what the local people offered them of their own free will (and all offered as much as they could spare), they started taking for themselves the food the natives contrived to produce by the sweat of their brows, which was in all honesty little enough. Since what a European will consume in a single day normally supports three native households of ten persons each for a whole month, and since the newcomers began to subject the locals to other vexations, assaults, and iniquities, the people began to realize that these men could not, in truth, have descended from the heavens. Some of them started to conceal what food they had, others decided to send their women and children into hiding, and yet others took to the hills to get away from the brutal and ruthless cruelty that was being inflicted on them. The Christians punched them, boxed their ears and flogged them in order to track down the local leaders, and the whole shameful process came to a head when one of the European commanders raped the wife of the paramount chief of the entire island.[7] It was then that the locals began to think up ways of driving the Europeans out of their lands and to take up arms against them. Their weapons, however, were flimsy and ineffective both in attack and in defence (and, indeed, war in the Americas is no more deadly than our jousting, or than many European children's games) and, with their horses and swords and lances, the Spaniards easily fended them off, killing them and committing all kind of atrocities against them.

They forced their way into native settlements, slaughtering everyone they found there, including small children, old men, pregnant women, and even women who had just given birth. They hacked them to pieces, slicing open their bellies with their swords as though they were so many sheep herded into a pen. They even laid wagers on whether they could manage to slice a man in two at a stroke, or cut an individual's head from his body, or disembowel him with a single blow of their axes. They grabbed suckling infants by the feet and, ripping them from their mothers' breasts, dashed them headlong against the rocks. Others, laughing and joking all the while, threw them over their shoulders into a river, shouting: 'Wriggle, you little perisher.' They slaughtered anyone and everyone in their path, on occasion running through a mother and her baby with a single thrust of their swords. They spared no one, erecting especially wide gibbets on which they could string their victims up with their feet just off the ground and then burn them alive thirteen at a time, in honour of our Saviour and the twelve Apostles, or tie dry straw to their bodies and set fire to it. Some they chose to keep alive and simply cut their wrists, leaving their hands dangling, saying to them: 'Take this letter'—meaning that their sorry condition would act as a warning to those hiding in the hills. The way they normally dealt with the native leaders and nobles was to tie them to a kind of griddle consisting of sticks resting on pitchforks driven into the ground and then grill them over a slow fire, with the result that they howled in agony and despair as they died a lingering death.

It once happened that I myself witnessed their grilling of four or five local leaders in this fashion (and I believe they had set up two or three other pairs of grills alongside so that they might process other victims at the same time) when the poor creatures' howls came between the Spanish commander and his sleep. He gave orders that the prisoners were to be throttled, but the man in charge of the execution detail, who was more bloodthirsty than the average common hangman (I know his identity and even met some relatives of his in Seville), was loath to cut short his private entertainment by throttling them and so he personally went round ramming wooden bungs into their mouths to stop them making such a racket and deliberately stoked the fire so that they would take just as long to die as he himself chose. I saw all these things for myself and many others besides. And, since all those who could do so took to the hills and mountains in order to escape the clutches of these merciless and inhuman butchers, these mortal enemies of human kind trained hunting dogs to track them down—wild dogs who would savage a native to death as soon as look at him, tearing him to shreds and devouring his flesh as though he were a pig. These dogs wrought havoc among the natives and were responsible for much carnage. And when, as happened on the odd occasion, the locals did kill a European, as, given the enormity of the crimes committed against them, they were in all justice fully entitled to, the Spanish came to an unofficial agreement among themselves that for every European killed one hundred natives would be executed.

. . .

After the fighting was over and all the men had been killed, the surviving natives—usually, that is, the young boys, the women, and the children—were shared out between the victors. One got thirty, another forty, a third as many as a hundred or even twice that number; everything depended on how far one was in the good books of the despot who went by the title of governor. The pretext under which the victims were parcelled out in this way was that their new masters would then be in a position to teach them the truths of the Christian faith; and thus it came about that a host of cruel, grasping and wicked men, almost all of them pig-ignorant, were put in charge of these poor souls. And they discharged this duty by sending the men down the mines, where working conditions were appalling, to dig for gold, and putting the women to labour in the fields and on their master's estates, to till the soil and raise the crops, properly a task only for the toughest and strongest of men. Both women and men were given only wild grasses to eat and other unnutritious foodstuffs. The mothers of young children promptly saw their milk dry up and their babies die; and, with the women and the men separated and never seeing each other, no new children were born. The men died down the mines from overwork and starvation, and the same was true of the women who perished out on the estates. The islanders, previously so numerous, began to die out as would any nation subjected to such appalling treatment.[8] For example, they were made to carry burdens of three and four *arrobas*[9] for distances of up to a hundred or even two hundred leagues, and were forced to carry their Christian masters in hammocks, which are like nets slung from the shoulders of the bearers. In short, they were treated as beasts of burden and developed huge sores on their shoulders and backs as happens with animals made to carry excessive loads. And this is not to mention the floggings, beatings, thrashings, punches, curses and countless other vexations and cruelties to which they were routinely subjected and to which no chronicle could ever do justice nor any reader respond save with horror and disbelief.

It is of note that all these island territories began to go to the dogs once news arrived of the death of our most gracious Queen Isabella, who departed this life in 1504.[10] Up to then, only a small number of provinces had been destroyed through unjust military action, not the whole area, and news of even this partial destruction had by and large been kept from the Queen, because, she—may her soul rest in peace—took a close personal interest in the physical and spiritual welfare of the native peoples, as those of us who lived through those years and saw examples of it with our own eyes can attest. There is one other general rule in all this, and it is that, wherever the Spaniards set foot, right throughout the Americas, they subjected the native inhabitants to the cruelties of which we have spoken, killing these poor and innocent people, tyrannizing them, and

oppressing them in the most abominable fashion. The longer they spent
in the region the more ingenious were the torments, each crueller than
the last, that they inflicted on their victims, as God finally abandoned
them and left them to plummet headlong into a life of full-time crime
and wickedness.

. . .

This same tyrant[11] set out in 1522 or 1523—a black date for the inhabitants of the area—to add to his fiefdom the very fertile province of
Nicaragua. It would be impossible to express in words the beauty and
fertility of this region, its healthy climate and the prosperity of its many
people. The sheer number and size of the towns in the area was truly
astonishing: it was often three and four leagues from one end of a town
to the other, and the quality and abundance of the local produce was sufficient to support a huge population. The terrain here is flat and level and
there are no mountains for the locals to hide in; it is also quite delightful
and the people were extremely reluctant to leave. So they stayed and put
up as best they might with persecution by the soldiers, with the atrocities they committed, and the slavery they inflicted upon them. These
people are also naturally gentle and unaggressive. The despot himself and
his tyrannical companions proceeded to wreck this region just as they had
wrecked others: they indulged in the same outrages, the same wanton
destruction, the same wholesale slaughter, the same atrocities as they had
elsewhere; indeed, it is beyond human capacity to compile an accurate log
of the murder, cruelty, false imprisonment and other crimes they committed. He sent fifty men on horseback who proceeded to annihilate the
entire population of an area greater than the county of Roussillon,[12] sparing not a single man or woman, old man or child, and this they did on
the flimsiest of pretexts, accusing their victims of not coming quickly
enough when they were summoned, or of not having brought enough
cargas[13] of maize (which is to the region what wheat is to Europe), or of
not surrendering sufficient of their kinsmen as slaves either to the governor himself or to one or another of his henchmen. These men were
driven by the Devil and not a single native managed to escape, what with
the land being as flat as it was and the Spaniards having horses.

He sent expeditionary forces (that is, raiding parties) to other
provinces and permitted his accomplices to take off as slaves as many of
these harmless and peace-loving natives as they chose. They would chain
their prisoners together so that none could slip the load of three *arrobas*
which he or she was forced to carry. On one of these occasions—
and there were many such—of the four thousand natives who began the

journey loaded down in this fashion not even six ever saw their homeland again, all the others being left by the roadside where they fell. And when a native bearer flagged and became utterly debilitated and wearied by the enormous burden he was expected to carry and the shortage of food and lack of rest, they cut his head from his shoulders so they would not have to break the chains that held the line of prisoners together, and his head would fall to one side of the baggage train and his trunk to the other. You can imagine what effect this had upon his companions in misery. And, in time, as they came to realize that none of their people ever returned from pilgrimages of this kind, the impressed natives would set out on such a trip with tears running down their cheeks, sighing and bemoaning their fate, saying: 'These are the roads we travelled to go and offer to work for the Christians, and, however hard the work, we thought to return in time to our homes and to our wives and children. That expectation is now a thing of the past, and we know that this trip will be our last.'

On one occasion the governor decided on a re-allocation of slaves, either on a whim or (as some say) because he wanted to remove them from a number of his companions with whom he was no longer on good terms and share them out among his latest cronies. As a result of this upheaval, the natives did not get a chance to sow some of the fields, and consequently there was not enough grain to go round. The Christians seized all the maize the locals had grown for themselves and their own families and, as a consequence, some twenty or thirty thousand natives died of hunger, some mothers even killing their own children and eating them.

As we have said, all the towns of the region stood amid fertile lands of their own. Each of the settlers took up residence in the town allotted to him (or *encommended* to him as the legal phrase has it), put the inhabitants to work for him, stole their already scarce foodstuffs for himself and took over the lands owned and worked by the natives and on which they traditionally grew their own produce. The settler would treat the whole of the native population—dignitaries, old men, women and children—as members of his household and, as such, make them labour night and day in his own interests, without any rest whatever; even the small children, as soon as they could stand, were made to do as much as they could, and more. Thus have the settlers exterminated the few indigenous people who have survived, stripping them of their houses and all their possessions and leaving them nothing for themselves (and these abuses continue to this day). In this regard, their treatment of the locals here has been even worse than on Hispaniola.

They have oppressed the many people of the province, worn them to a shadow and hastened their demise, forcing them to carry over distances of thirty leagues, from the interior of the country to the port, all the blocks of wood and planking needed to make ships and sending them to search for honey and wax up in the hills where jaguars tear them to pieces. And they have used and still use even pregnant women and the mothers of newborn babes as beasts of burden.

The most insidious pestilence dreamed up by this governor was the system whereby he granted licences to Spaniards to demand slaves from native caciques and nobles. This development has done more to ravage that country than anything else. Demands for fifty slaves at a time were made every four or five months or whenever an individual obtained permission and a licence from the governor to make such a demand. The demand was always accompanied by the threat that, if the requisite number of slaves was not produced, the noble concerned would be burned alive or thrown to the wild dogs. Since slavery is practically unknown among the local population, even their caciques having at most two or three or four of them, the lords would themselves have to find the slaves. At first they might round up all the orphans they could find; then they might ask any family with two children to surrender one, and a family with three to produce two, thereby fulfilling the demand made of them by the tyrant in their midst. But they did so against a background of wailing and gnashing of teeth, for these people appear to entertain a love for their children which surpasses that of any other people in the world. Since demands of this nature were so frequent, the whole region was devastated within the space of a few years, for during six or seven of the years between 1523 and 1533 five or six slaving vessels patrolled the coast and carted off vast numbers of these innocents to be sold in Panama and Peru, where they all perished. Indeed, experience shows time and time again that these people die very quickly once you remove them from their native lands, especially as they often are forced to go without food while still being made to do a full day's work, those who buy and sell them having no other thought in their heads but the work these slaves can be forced to undertake. In this fashion, more than five hundred thousand poor souls, each of them as free as you or me,[14] have been taken from their homelands. On top of that, a further five or six hundred thousand have so far been killed, either during the course of the hellish fighting initiated by the Spanish or as a direct result of the horrendous conditions in which they have been imprisoned. And the carnage continues to this day. All this devastation has taken place over the past fourteen years, and in the whole of the province of Nicaragua today, once (as I have said) among the most densely populated places on the face of the earth, there remain only four to five thousand people and every day sees

even some of these succumb to the work they are made to do, and the personal abuses to which they are subjected every day of their lives.
. . .

From Cholula they made their way to Mexico City.[15] On their journey, they were showered with thousands of gifts from the great king Montezuma who also sent some of his men to stage entertainments and banquets for them on the way. When they reached the Great Causeway which runs for some two leagues right up to the city itself, they were greeted by Montezuma's own brother and many local dignitaries bearing valuable gifts of gold, silver and apparel from the great lord.[16] At the city gates, Montezuma himself came out to meet them, carried on a litter of gold and was surrounded by the entire court. He escorted them into the city to the great houses where he had directed they should be lodged. Yet that same day, or so I am reliably informed by a number of eye-witnesses, the Spaniards seized the great king unawares by means of a trick and held him under armed guard of eighty soldiers, eventually putting him in irons.[17] But, leaving aside all of this, although much passed of consequence and one could dwell upon it at length, I should like to relate just one incident contrived by these tyrants. It happened that the Spanish commander had occasion to go to the sea-port to deal with one of his captains who was planning an attack on him,[18] and he left another of his henchmen, with a hundred or so men at his command, to guard King Montezuma while he was away.[19] The garrison decided to stage a show of strength and thereby boost the fear they inspired in the people of this kingdom, a classic Spanish tactic in these campaigns, as we have had occasion to remark before. All the local citizens, great and small, as well as all the members of the court, were wholly taken up with entertaining their imprisoned lord. To this end, they organized fiestas, some of which involved staging traditional dances every afternoon and evening in squares and residential quarters throughout the city. These dances are called in the local language *mitotes* (those typical of the islands being known as *arreitos*);[20] and since these dances are the principal form of public entertainment and enjoyment among the people, they deck themselves out in all their best finery. And the entertainments were organized with close attention to rank and station, the noblest of the citizens dancing nearest the building where their lord was being held. Close by this building, then, danced over two thousand youths of quality, the flower of the nobility of Montezuma's whole empire. Thither the Spanish captain made his way, accompanied by a platoon of his men, under pretence of wanting to watch the spectacle but in fact carrying orders to attack the revellers at a prearranged time, further platoons with identical orders having been despatched to the other squares where entertainments were being staged. The nobles were totally absorbed in what they were doing and had no thought for their own safety when the soldiers drew their swords and shouting: 'For Saint James, and at 'em, men!'[21] proceeded to slice open the lithe and naked bodies of the dancers and to spill their noble blood. Not one dancer was left alive, and the same story was repeated in the other squares throughout the city. This series of events caused horror, anguish and bitterness throughout the land; the whole nation was plunged into mourning and, until the end of time, or at least as long as a few of these people survive, they will not cease to tell and re-tell, in their *areitos* and dances, just as we do at home in Spain with bal-lads, this sad story of a massacre which wiped out their entire nobility, beloved and respected by them for generations and generations.

Once the native population learned of this barbaric and unprece-dented outrage, perpetrated against innocent individuals who had done nothing whatever to deserve such cruelty, the whole city, which had up to then tolerated the equally unmerited imprisonment of its lord and master simply because he himself had issued orders that no one was to fight the Christians nor to offer any resistance to them, took up arms and attacked them. Many Spaniards were wounded and only narrowly man-aged to make good their escape. They ordered Montezuma out on to the terrace at dagger point and forced him to order his men not to attack the house and to cease their insurrection. But the people ceased altogether at that juncture to obey such orders and there was a feeling that they should elect another lord in Montezuma's place who would be able and willing to lead them in battle. At this point, it became known that the Spanish commander was on his way back from the coast after his vic-tory over the rebel forces and that he was not far off and was bringing reinforcements. There followed a lull in the fighting which lasted until he arrived some three or four days later; meanwhile, the number of protesters had swollen with the influx of people from all over the terri-tory. Once the commander arrived, the natives attacked with such unrelenting ferocity that it seemed to the garrison that not one of them would be left alive, and they decided to abandon the city in secret and at night. The locals got wind of this, catching up with many as they fled across the causeways that span the lake and killing them in great num-bers,[22] as, indeed, they had every right to, given the attacks we have described that had been made on them: a reasonable and fair-minded man will see that theirs was a defensive action and a just one. The Spaniards then regrouped and there followed a battle for the city in which terrible and bizarre outrages were committed against the indigenous population, vast numbers of whom were killed and many others, several leaders among them, burned alive.[23]

After the vile outrages and abominations perpetrated by the Spaniards, both in Mexico City itself and throughout the whole region (an area of ten or fifteen or twenty leagues all round the city saw countless natives perish at their hands), they transferred their pestilential attentions to the densely populated Pánuco province, where once again they swept through the territory, pillaging and murdering on the grand scale as they went. They then moved on to the provinces of Tuxtepec,[24] Impilcingo,[25] and finally Colima,[26] each one of them greater in extent than the kingdoms of Castile and León, and in each they wrought the same destruction as they had in Mexico City and its province. It would be impracticable to compile a complete dossier of all the atrocities, foul murders and other barbarities they committed, and any such account would be so lengthy it would prove impossible for the reader to take in.

It should be recalled that the pretext upon which the Spanish invaded each of these provinces and proceeded to massacre the people and destroy their lands—lands which teemed with people and should surely have been a joy and a delight to any true Christian—was purely and simply that they were making good the claim of the Spanish Crown to the territories in question. At no stage had any order been issued entitling them to massacre the people or to enslave them. Yet, whenever the natives did not drop everything and rush to recognize publicly the truth of the irrational and illogical claims that were made, and whenever they did not immediately place themselves completely at the mercy of the iniquitous and cruel and bestial individuals who were making such claims, they were dubbed outlaws and held to be in rebellion against His Majesty. This, indeed, was the tenor of the letters that were sent back to the Spanish court, and everybody involved in the administration of the New World was blind to the simple truth enshrined in the first principles of law and government that nobody who is not a subject of a civil power in the first place can be deemed in law to be in rebellion against that power. Any reasonable person who knows anything of God, of rights and of civil law can imagine for himself what the likely reaction would be of any people living peaceably within their own frontiers, unaware that they owe allegiance to anyone save their natural lords, were a stranger suddenly to issue a demand along the following lines: 'You shall henceforth obey a foreign king, whom you have never seen nor ever heard of and, if you do not, we will cut you to pieces'—especially when they discover that these strangers are indeed quite prepared to carry out this threat to the letter. Even more shocking is the fact that when the local people do obey such commands they are harshly treated as common slaves, put to hard labour and subjected to all manner of abuse and to agonizing torments that ensure a slower and more painful death than would summary execution. Indeed, for them, the end result is the same: they, their wives and their children all perish and the whole of their nation is wiped from the face of the earth. And so blinded by ambition and driven by greed are the devils who advocate such treatment of these people that they cannot see that, when their victims come to obey under duress this foreign overlord and publicly recognize his authority over them, simply because of their fear of what will happen to them if they do not, such a recognition of suzerainty has no standing in law whatever, any such prerogative obtained by menaces from any people anywhere in the world being invalid. In practice, the only rights these perfidious crusaders have earned which can be upheld in human, divine, or natural law are the right to eternal damnation and the right to answer for the offences and the harm they have done the Spanish Crown by utterly ruining every one of these kingdoms and (as far as it is within their power) invalidating all claims the Spanish Crown may have to the territories of the New World. These, then, are the true services they have performed and continue to perform for their sovereign in this part of the world.

EXPLANATORY NOTES

1. The *Short Account* was written in 1542 . . .
2. The island of Hispaniola, comprising today Haiti and the Dominican Republic, is, at its most extensive, some 400 miles from west to east and covers an area of nearly 30,000 square miles. The Spanish league (*legua*) was calculated as one twenty-fifth of a degree of latitude measured on the earth's surface, or about 2.6 miles (compare the 'maritime' or 'mariners'' league equal to three minutes or one twentieth of a degree of latitude). In the absence of reliable means of measuring distances accurately, a day's journey on horseback was often calculated, whatever the terrain, at seven *leguas* (Hernán Cortés, *Letters from Mexico,* translated by Anthony Pagden (London: OUP, 1972, 2nd ed., New Haven and London: Yale U.P., 1986, p. 529).
3. 'Hammock' (*hamaca* in Spanish) is one of a dozen or so words common to a great number of European languages—among them potato, tomato, hurricane—which derive from the Taino language of Santo Domingo.
4. The maximum east-west extent of Cuba is approximately 700 miles; the distance from Valladolid to Rome some 750.
5. The Royal Gardens (*Huerta del Rey*) were an extensive pleasure ground lying outside the Seville city walls.

6. On this expedition, mounted by Pedro de Isla, who would latter become a Franciscan friar, see Las Casas, *History of the Indies,* book II, chapter 45.
7. Guarionex.
8. Figures for the pre-contact population of the Antilles are necessarily wildly approximate. The highest is about eight million; the lowest—and, because it is based on the potential agricultural yield of the land, the most reliable—is around half a million. The total population of the islands when the *Short Account* was written did not exceed three hundred thousand. By the middle of the seventeenth century, the Arawak were virtually extinct.
9. The *arroba,* in origin an Arabic term, was widely used throughout the Spanish empire as a measure, both of weight (roughly 25 pounds) and of dry capacity (roughly 15 litres), though its precise value varied regionally.
10. This is a pious exaggeration. Yet it was Queen Isabella (died Medina del Campo, Old Castle, 26 November 1504) who, in 1495, had prevented Columbus from selling Amerindians as slaves and who, in 1501, instructed Ovando that she wished the inhabitants of Hispaniola 'to be well treated as our subjects and our vassals'; see Anthony Pagden, *The Fall of Natural Man: The American Indians and the Origins of Comparative Ethnology,* second edition (Cambridge: Cambridge University Press, 1986), pp. 41–2.
11. Pedrarias Dávila.
12. The county of Roussillon, astride the Eastern Pyrenees with its capital at Perpignan.
13. The Spanish term *carga,* generally denoting the maximum quantity a single man could carry at any one time, was also used more narrowly in Castile as a measure of cereals, equal to four *fanegas* or just over six bushels.
14. Legally, all Amerindians were subjects of the Crown of Castile and enjoyed equal rights with all other subjects of the Crown. Making war on Amerindians, said the great theologian Francisco de Vitoria, was like making war on the inhabitants of Seville; see Introduction, p. xx, and Pagden, *The Fall of Natural Man,* pp. 29–33.
15. The proper name for the city which Las Casas calls 'Mexico' was Temixtitán or Tenochtitlán.
16. Montezuma's brother Cuitlahuac (Cuetravicin) was lord of Yztapalapa, a city through which Cortés had passed on his journey from Cholula. See Cortés's account of this episode in *Letters from Mexico,* pp. 83–4.
17. By Cortés's own account, Montezuma was not seized until more than a week later (*Letters from Mexico,* pp. 88–90).
18. The commander was Cortés, the captain Pánfilo de Narváez. On this expedition and the reasons behind the Narváez expedition, see the essay by J.H. Elliott, 'Cortés, Velázquez, and Charles V', in *Letters from Mexico,* pp. xi–xxxvii (xxiii–xxvi).
19. The captain left in charge was Pedro de Alvarado, a veteran of Juan de Grijalva's expedition and effectively second-in-command to Cortés; see J.E. Kelly, *Pedro de Alvarado, conquistador* (Princeton: Princeton University Press, 1932; reissue Washington, etc.: Kennikat Press, 1971). Cortés's claim

that he left Mexico City garrisoned by 'five hundred men' (*Letters from Mexico*, p. 119) is at odds with eye-witness accounts which put the number at about one hundred and twenty, many of them sick and wounded.

20. For a previous reference to *arteitos*, see above p. 28.

21. Santiago, the name of Saint James of Compostela, was traditionally used by the Spanish as a battle-cry, the legend being that he appeared in person, mounted on a white charger, at the battle of Clavijo against the Moors which supposedly took place in the year 822.

22. On the site of Tenochtitlán and Cortés's retreat on what became known as the 'Black Night' *(noche triste)*, see his *Letters from Mexico*, pp. 131–8.

23. Las Casas is here conflating two events: the retreat which took place in 1520 and the siege of the city by Cortés the following year.

24. Variously 'Tatutepeque', 'Tuchitebeque', 'Tututepec', or 'Tuxtepeque'.

25. Or 'Ipilcingo'.

26. Also known as 'Colimán' or 'Alimán'.

ST. FRANCIS XAVIER

A Jesuit Missionary Gives His First Impressions of Japan

St. Francis Xavier (1506–52) was perhaps the most extraordinary mission-ary in the history of the Christian religion. A Basque of noble family, he was one of the original six companions of Ignatius of Loyola who formed the nucleus of the Jesuit Order, founded in 1540. In 1541, at the invitation of King John III of Portugal, he sailed for the East on a mission to convert the whole of Asia to Christianity. Landing at first in Goa, where he tried to reform the Portuguese traders and soldiers who had lapsed from their vows, he then proceeded to Ceylon (Sri Lanka), Mylapore (near Madras), and Malacca in India, and went as far as the Moluccas (or Spice Islands) in Indonesia.

In 1549 he traveled to Japan, the "Cipangu" of travelers' legends, and so was among the very first Westerners to visit that land. He worked as a missionary for over two years, and made nearly 800 converts to Christian-ity. His success was in large part due to the cooperation of the local lords who may have allowed him freedom of action in the desire to get access to Portuguese trade and firearms. Eventually some 300,000 Japanese con-verted to Christianity before the religion was suppressed by the emperor in 1614.

The selection given here is from a letter written in 1549 by Francis to the Jesuits in Goa, which conveys his (extremely positive) first impressions of Japan and his hopes of converting the land to Christianity. Later letters were more appreciative of the obstacles presented by the entrenched Bud-dhist beliefs of most of Japan's rulers and people.

By the experience which we have of this land of Japan, I can inform you thereof as follows. Firstly, the people whom we have met so far, are the best who have yet been discovered, and it seems to me that we shall never find among heathens another race to equal the Japanese. It is a people of very good manners, good in general, and not malicious; they are men of honor to a marvel, and prize honor above all else in the world. They are a poor people in general; but their poverty, whether among the gen-try or those who are not so, is not considered as a shame. They have one

quality which I cannot recall in any people of Christendom; this is that
their gentry howsoever poor they may be, and the commoners howsoever rich they may be, render as much honor to a poor gentleman as if he
were passing rich. On no account would a poverty-stricken gentleman
marry with someone outside the gentry, even if he were given great sums
to do so; and this they do because they consider that they would lose
their honor by marrying into a lower class. Whence it can clearly be seen
that they esteem honor more than riches. They are very courteous in
their dealings with another; they highly regard arms and trust much in
them; always carrying sword and dagger, both high and low alike, from
the age of fourteen onwards. They are a people who will not submit to
any insults or contemptuous words. Those who are not of gentle birth
give much honor to the gentry, who in their turn pride themselves on
faithfully serving their feudal lord, to whom they are very obedient. It
seems to me that they act thus rather because they think that they would
lose their honor if they acted contrarily, than for fear of the punishment
they would receive if disobedient. They are small eaters albeit somewhat
heavy drinkers, and they drink rice wine since there are no ordinary
wines in these parts. They are men who never gamble, because they consider it a great dishonor, since those who gamble desire what is not theirs
and hence tend to become thieves. They swear but little, and when they
do it is by the Sun. There are many persons who can read and write,
which is a great help to their learning quickly prayers and religious matters. It is a land where there are but few thieves in some kingdoms, and
this by the strict justice which is executed against those that are, for their
lives are never spared. They abhor beyond measure this vice of theft.
They are a people of very good will, very sociable and very desirous of
knowledge; they are very fond of hearing about things of God, chiefly
when they understand them. Of all the lands which I have seen in my
life, whether those of Christians or of heathens, never yet did I see a people
so honest in not thieving. Most of them believe in the men of old, who
were (so far as I understand) persons who lived like philosophers; many
of them adore the Sun and others the Moon. They like to hear things
propounded according to reason; and granted that there are sins and
vices among them, when one reasons with them pointing out that what
they do is evil, they are convinced by this reasoning. I discerned fewer
sins in the laity and found them more obedient to reason, than those
whom they regard as fathers and priests, whom they call Bonzes.

Two things have astonished me greatly about this country. The first, to
see how lightly they regard great sins; and the reason is because their fore-
bears were accustomed to live in them, from whom those of the present

generation take their example; see how continuation in vices which are against nature corrupts the people, in the same manner as continual disregard of imperfections undermines and destroys perfection. The second point is to see that the laity live better in their state than the Bonzes in theirs; and withal this is so manifest, it is astonishing in what esteem the former hold the latter. There are many other errors and evils among these Bonzes, and the more learned are the worst sinners. I spoke many times with some of the wiser, chiefly with one who is highly regarded by all in these parts, both for his letters, life, and dignity, as for his great age, he being eighty years old, and called Ningit [Ninjitsu], which is to say in Japanese "truthful heart"; he is as a bishop amongst them, and if the term could be applied to him, might well be called "blessed." In many talks which I had with him, I found him doubtful, and unable to decide whether our soul is immortal, or whether it dies with the body; sometimes he told me yes, at others no, and I fear that the other learned are alike. This Ningit is so great a friend of mine, that it is a marvel to see. All, both laity and Bonzes like us very much, and are greatly astonished to see how we have come from such distant lands as from Portugal to Japan, which is more than six thousand leagues, only to speak of the things of God, and how people can save their souls by belief in Jesus Christ; saying that our coming to these lands is the work of God. One thing I tell you, for which you may give many thanks to God Our Lord, that this land of Japan is very fit for our holy faith greatly to increase therein; and if we knew how to speak the language, I have no doubt whatsoever that we would make many Christians. May it please Our Lord that we may learn it soon, for already we begin to appreciate it, and we learned to repeat the ten commandments in the space of forty days which we applied ourselves thereto.

In the place of Paulo de Santa Fé,[1] our good and true friend, we were received by the local Captain and by the Alcayde, with much benignity and love, and likewise by all the people; everyone marveling to see Fathers from the land of the Portuguese. They were not in the least surprised at Paul having become a Christian, but rather are pleased and delighted thereat, both his relatives as those who are not so, since he has been in India and seen things which they here have never seen. And the Duke [Daimyo] of this land is well affected to him, and renders him much honor, and asked many questions concerning the customs, worth, and authority of the Portuguese and of their Empire in India; and Paulo gave him a very full account of everything, whereat the Duke was greatly contented.

Here they are not now surprised at people becoming Christians, and as a great part of them can read and write, they very soon learn the prayers; may it please God to give us tongue whereby we can speak to them of the things of God, for then we would reap much more fruit with His aid, grace, and favor. Now we are like so many statues among them, for they speak and talk to us about many things, whilst we, not understanding the language, hold our peace. And now we have to be like little children learning the language; God grant that we may likewise imitate them in true simplicity and purity of soul, striving by all means to become like them, both as regards learning the language as in showing the simplicity of children devoid of malice. And in this did God grant us great and notable favors in bringing us to these infidel lands, so that we should not neglect ourselves, since this land is wholly of idolators and enemies of Christ, and we have none in whom we can confide or trust, save only in God, for here we have neither relatives nor friends nor acquaintances, nor even some Christian piety, but only foes of Him who made the heaven and earth; and for this cause are we forced to place all our faith, hope, and trust in Christ Our Lord, and not in any living creature, since, through unbelief, all are enemies of God.

Likewise it is necessary that we should give you an account of other favors which God hath granted us, teaching us through His mercy, so that you may help us in rendering thanks to God always for them. This is, that elsewhere the abundance of bodily provisions is often the reason whereby disordered appetites are given free rein, frequently despising the virtue of abstinence, which leads to the no little detriment of men's souls and bodies. This is the origin of the majority of corporal ills, and even spiritual, and men have much difficulty in finding a means of relief, and many find that the days of their life are shortened before obtaining it, suffering all kinds of bodily pains and torments, taking physic to cure themselves which gives them more distaste to swallow than enjoyment they received from the dainties which they ate and drank. God granted us a signal favor in bringing us to these lands which lack such abundancies, so that even if we wished to minister to our bodies with these superfluities, the country does not allow of it. They neither kill nor eat anything which they rear. Sometimes they eat fish; there is rice and corn, albeit little; there are numerous herbs, on which they live, and some fruit but not much. This people live wonderfully healthy lives and there are many aged. The Japanese are a convincing proof of how our nature can subsist on little, even if it is not a pleasing sustenance. We live in this land very healthy in body, God grant that we may be likewise in our souls. A great part of the Japanese are Bonzes, and these are strictly obeyed in the places where they are, even if their sins are manifest to all; and it seems to me that the reason why they are held in such esteem is because of their rigorous abstinence, for they never eat meat, nor fish, but only herbs, fruit, and rice, and this once a day and very strictly, and they are never given wine. There are many Bonzes and their temples are of but little revenue. By reason of their continual abstinence and because they have no intercourse with women (especially those who go dressed in black like clergy) on pain of death, and because they know how to relate some histories or rather fables of the things in which they believe, it seems to me they are held in great veneration. And it may well happen that since they and we feel so differently about God and the method of salvation, that we may be persecuted by them with something stronger than words. What we in these parts endeavor to do, is to bring people to the knowledge of their Creator and Saviour, Jesus Christ Our Lord. We live with great hope and trust in Him to give us strength, grace, help, and favor to prosecute this work. It does not seem to me that the laity will oppose or persecute us of their own volition, but only if they ere importuned by the Bonzes. We do not seek to quarrel with them, neither for fear of them will we cease to speak of the glory of God, and of the salvation of souls. They cannot do us more harm than God permits, and what harm comes to us through them is a mercy of God; if through them for His love, service, and zeal for souls, He sees good to shorten the days of our life, in order to end this continual death in which we live, our desires will be speedily fulfilled and we will go to reign forever with Christ. Our intentions are to proclaim and maintain the truth, however much they may contradict us, since God compels us to seek rather the salvation of our future than the safety of our present lives; we endeavoring with the grace and favor of Our Lord to fulfil this precept, He giving us internal strength to manifest the same before the innumerable idolatries which there are in Japan.

It is well that we should give you an account of our stay in Cangoxima [Kagoshima]. We arrived here at a season when the winds were contrary for going to Miaco, [Kyoto] which is the chief city of Japan, where the King and the greatest lords of the Kingdom reside. And there is no wind that will serve us to go thither, save only five months from now, and then we will go with the help of Our Lord. It is three hundred leagues from here to Miaco, according to what they tell us, and we are likewise told great things of that city, which is said to contain more than ninety thousand houses; there is also a great university frequented by students therein, which has six principal colleges and more than two hundred houses of Bonzes, and of others like friars who are called Ieguixu [Zenshu], and of nuns who are called Hamacata [Amakata]. Besides this university of Miaco, there are five other chief universities whose names are these, Coya [Koya], Nenguru [Negoro], Feizan [Hieizen], Taninomine [Tamu no mine]. These are in the neighborhood of Miaco, and it is said that there are more than 3,500 students in each one of them. There is another university, a great way off, which is called Bandou [Bando, the Ashikaga Gakko] which is the best and biggest in Japan, and more frequented by students than any other. Bandou is a great lordship where there are six dukes, and a chief one among them, whom the others obey. This chief owes allegiance to the King of Japan who is the great King of Miaco. They tell us such things of the greatness of these lands and universities, that we would prefer to see them before affirming and writing them; and if things be as they tell us, then we will write of our experiences in detail. In addition to these principal universities, they say that there are many other smaller ones throughout the kingdom. During the year 1551, we hope to write you at length concerning the disposition that there is in Miaco and its universities for the knowledge of Jesus Christ Our Lord to be spread therein. This year two Bonzes are going to India who have studied in the universities of Bandou and Miaco, and with them many other Japanese to learn the things of our law.

On St. Michael's day we spoke with the duke of this land, who gave us great honor, saying that we should keep well the books in which was written the law of the Christians, and that if it was the true and good law of Jesus Christ, it would be troublesome to the Devil. A few days afterwards he gave leave to all his vassals that those who might wish to become Christians could do so. This good news I write at the end of the letter for your consolation, and that you may give thanks unto God our Lord. It seems to me that this winter we must occupy ourselves in making a declaration concerning the Articles of Faith in Japanese, somewhat copiously, for it to be printed (because all the principal persons here know how to read and write) so that our holy faith may be understood and spread throughout many parts, since we cannot go to all. Our dearest brother Paulo will translate faithfully into his own tongue everything which is necessary for the salvation of souls.

From Cangoxima, fifth of November of the year 1549.

Your most loving brother wholly in Christ,

EXPLANATORY NOTES

1. Yajiro.

194

GALILEO GALILEI

An Exciting Scientific Discovery

Born in Florence and educated in Pisa, Galileo Galilei (1564–1642) was one of the greatest of the seventeenth century scientists. His early studies of motion led him to accept the basic theories of Copernicus, the Polish astronomer who postulated that the Earth was a planet that revolved around the sun. Galileo perfected the first telescope, and with it he was able to identify the moons of Jupiter and describe the lunar surface. His work did much to confirm the theories of astronomers before him such as Copernicus and Kepler, whose work relied upon mathematical calculation. Galileo's telescope allowed for actual observation of the movements of heavenly bodies. His studies of motion were an important contribution to the development of a new scientific worldview. After 1616 Galileo was prohibited by the Church from teaching Copernicanism, but in 1632 he received a license for the publication of A Dialogue Between the Two Great Systems of the World, *a tract that took the form of a debate between an adherent of the old Aristotelian system and a convert to the new Copernican one. Galileo was subsequently arrested by the Inquisition, tried, condemned, and forced to recant his Copernican views.*

Galileo wrote The Starry Messenger *in 1610 to announce the exciting new discoveries he had made by turning a recent invention, the telescope, upon the heavens. The evidence of his senses proved, Galileo claimed, that the old physical and cosmological theories of Aristotle were wrong and those of Copernicus were correct.*

ASTRONOMICAL MESSAGE

Which contains and explains recent observations
made with the aid of a new spyglass[1]
concerning the surface of the moon,
the Milky Way, nebulous stars, and
innumerable fixed stars,

"An Exciting Scientific Discovery," excerpted from "Astronomical Message," by Galileo Galilei, reprinted from *The Discoveries and Opinions of Galileo*, 1957, 27–29, 31–38, 45–48, 50–53, 56–58.

as well as four planets never before seen, and
now named
THE MEDICEAN STARS

Great indeed are the things which in this brief treatise I propose for observation and consideration by all students of nature. I say great, because of the excellence of the subject itself, the entirely unexpected and novel character of these things, and finally because of the instrument by means of which they have been revealed to our senses.

Surely it is a great thing to increase the numerous host of fixed stars previously visible to the unaided vision, adding countless more which have never before been seen, exposing these plainly to the eye in numbers ten times exceeding the old and familiar stars.

It is a very beautiful thing, and most gratifying to the sight, to behold the body of the moon, distant from us almost sixty earthly radii,[2] as if it were no farther away than two such measures—so that its diameter appears almost thirty times larger, its surface nearly nine hundred times, and its volume twenty-seven thousand times as large as when viewed with the naked eye. In this way one may learn with all the certainty of sense evidence that the moon is not robed in a smooth and polished surface but is in fact rough and uneven, covered everywhere, just like the earth's surface, with huge prominences, deep valleys, and chasms.

Again, it seems to me a matter of no small importance to have ended the dispute about the Milky Way by making its nature manifest to the very senses as well as to the intellect. Similarly it will be a pleasant and elegant thing to demonstrate that the nature of those stars which astronomers have previously called "nebulous" is far different from what has been believed hitherto. But what surpasses all wonders by far, and what particularly moves us to seek the attention of all astronomers and philosophers, is the discovery of four wandering stars not known or observed by any man before us. Like Venus and Mercury, which have their own periods about the sun, these have theirs about a certain star that is conspicuous among those already known, which they sometimes precede and sometimes follow, without ever departing from it beyond certain limits. All these facts were discovered and observed by me not many days ago with the aid of a spyglass which I devised, after first being illuminated by divine grace. Perhaps other things, still more remarkable, will in time be discovered by me or by other observers with the aid of such an instrument, the form and construction of which I shall first briefly explain, as well as the occasion of its having been devised. Afterwards I shall relate the story of the observations I have made.

About ten months ago a report reached my ears that a certain Fleming[3] had constructed a spyglass by means of which visible objects, though very distant from the eye of the observer, were distinctly seen as if nearby. Of this truly remarkable effect several experiences were related, to which some persons gave credence while others denied them. A few days later the report was confirmed to me in a letter from a noble Frenchman at Paris, Jacques Badovere,[4] which caused me to apply myself wholeheartedly to inquire into the means by which I might arrive at the invention of a similar instrument. This I did shortly afterwards, my basis being the theory of refraction. First I prepared a tube of lead, at the ends of which I fitted two glass lenses, both plane on one side while on the other side one was spherically convex and the other concave. Then placing my eye near the concave lens I perceived objects satisfactorily large and near, for they appeared three times closer and nine times larger than when seen with the naked eye alone. Next I constructed another one, more accurate, which represented objects as enlarged more than sixty times. Finally, sparing neither labor nor expense, I succeeded in constructing for myself so excellent an instrument that objects seen by means of it appeared nearly one thousand times larger and over thirty times closer than when regarded with our natural vision.

It would be superfluous to enumerate the number and importance of the advantages of such an instrument at sea as well as on land, But forsaking terrestrial observations, I turned to celestial ones, and first I saw the moon from as near at hand as if it were scarcely two terrestrial radii away. After that I observed often with wondering delight both the planets and the fixed stars, and since I saw these latter to be very crowded, I began to seek (and eventually found) a method by which I might measure their distances apart.

[...]

Now let us review the observations made during the past two months, once more inviting the attention of all who are eager for true philosophy to the first steps of such important contemplations. Let us speak first of that surface of the moon which faces us. For greater clarity I distinguish two parts of this surface, a lighter and a darker; the lighter part seems to surround and to pervade the whole hemisphere, while the darker part discolors the moon's surface like a kind of cloud, and makes it appear covered with spots. Now those spots which are fairly dark and rather large are plain to everyone and have been seen throughout the ages; these I shall call the "large" or "ancient" spots, distinguishing them from others that are smaller in size but so numerous as to occur all over the lunar surface, and especially the lighter part. The latter spots had never been seen by anyone before me. From observations of these spots repeated many times I have been led to the opinion and conviction that the surface of the moon is not smooth, uniform, and precisely spherical as a great number of philosophers believe it (and the other heavenly bodies) to be, but is uneven, rough, and full of cavities and prominences, being not unlike the face of the earth, relieved by chains of mountains and deep valleys. The things I have seen by which I was enabled to draw this conclusion are as follows.

On the fourth or fifth day after new moon, when the moon is seen with brilliant horns, the boundary which divides the dark part from the light does not extend uniformly in an oval line as would happen on a perfectly spherical solid, but traces out an uneven, rough, and very wavy line as shown in the figure below. Indeed, many luminous excrescences extend beyond the boundary into the darker portion, while on the other hand some dark patches invade the illuminated part. Moreover a great quantity of small blackish spots, entirely separated from the dark region, are scattered almost all over the area illuminated by the sun with the exception only of that part which is occupied by the large and ancient spots. Let us note, however, that the said small spots always agree in having their blackened parts directed toward the sun, while on the side opposite the sun they are crowned with bright contours, like shining summits. There is a similar sight on earth about sunrise, when we behold the valleys not yet flooded with light though the mountains surrounding them are already ablaze with glowing splendor on the side opposite the sun. And just as the shadows in the hollows on earth diminish in size as the sun rises higher, so these spots on the moon lose their blackness as the illuminated region grows larger and larger.

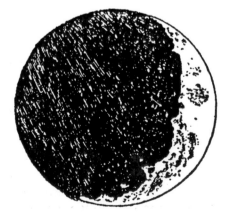

Again, not only are the boundaries of shadow and light in the moon seen to be uneven and wavy, but still more astonishingly many bright points appear within the darkened portion of the moon, completely divided and separated from the illuminated part and at a considerable distance from it. After a time these gradually increase in size and brightness, and an hour or two later they become joined with the rest of the lighted part which has now increased in size. Meanwhile more and more peaks shoot up as if sprouting now here, now there, lighting up within the shadowed portion; these become larger, and finally they too are united with that same luminous surface which extends ever further. An illustration of this is to be seen in the figure above. And on the earth, before the rising of the sun, are not the highest peaks of the mountains illuminated by the sun's rays while the plains remain in shadow? Does not the light go on spreading while the larger central parts of those mountains are becoming illuminated? And when the sun has finally risen, does not the illumination of plains and hills finally become one? But on the moon the variety of elevations and depressions appears to surpass in every way the roughness of the terrestrial surface, as we shall demonstrate further on.

At present I cannot pass over in silence something worthy of consideration which I observed when the moon was approaching first quarter, as shown in the previous figure. Into the luminous part there extended a great dark gulf in the neighborhood of the lower cusp. When I had observed it for a long time and had seen it completely dark, a bright peak began to emerge, a little below its center, after about two hours. Gradually growing, this presented itself in a triangular shape, remaining completely detached and separated from the lighted surface. Around it three other small points soon began to shine, and finally, when the moon was about to set, this triangular shape (which had meanwhile become more widely extended) joined with the rest of the illuminated region and suddenly burst into the gulf of shadow like a vast promontory of light, surrounded still by the three bright peaks already mentioned. Beyond the ends of the cusps, both above and below, certain bright points emerged which were quite detached from the remaining lighted part, as may be seen depicted in the same figure. There were also a great number of dark spots in both the horns, especially in the lower one; those nearest the boundary of light and shadow appeared larger and darker, while those more distant from the boundary were not so dark and distinct. But in all cases, as we have mentioned earlier, the blackish portion of each spot is turned toward the source of the sun's radiance, while a bright rim surrounds the spot on the side away from the sun in the direction of the shadowy region of the moon. This part of the moon's surface, where it is spotted as the tail of a peacock is sprinkled with azure eyes, resembles those glass vases which have been plunged while still hot into cold water and have thus acquired a crackled and wavy surface, from which they receive their common name of "ice-cups."

As to the large lunar spots, these are not seen to be broken in the above manner and full of cavities and prominences; rather, they are even and uniform, and brighter patches crop up only here and there. Hence if anyone wished to revive the old Pythagorean[5] opinion that the moon is like another earth, its brighter part might very fitly represent the surface of the land and its darker region that of the water. I have never doubted that if our globe were seen from afar when flooded with sunlight, the land regions would appear brighter and the watery regions darker.[6] The large spots in the moon are also seen to be less elevated than the brighter tracts, for whether the moon is waxing or waning there are always seen, here and there along its boundary of light and shadow, certain ridges of brighter hue around the large spots (and we have attended to this in preparing the diagrams); the edges of these spots are not only lower, but also more uniform, being uninterrupted by peaks or ruggedness.

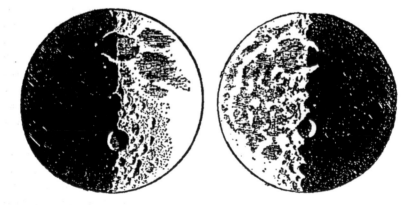

Near the large spots the brighter part stands out particularly in such a way that before first quarter and toward last quarter, in the vicinity of a certain spot in the upper (or northern) region of the moon, some vast prominences arise both above and below as shown in the figures reproduced below. Before last quarter this same spot is seen to be walled about with certain blacker contours which, like the loftiest mountaintops, appear darker on the side away from the sun and brighter on that which faces the sun. (This is the opposite of what happens in the cavities, for there the part away from the sun appears brilliant, while that which is turned toward the sun is dark and in shadow.) After a time, when the lighted portion of the moon's surface has diminished in size and when all (or nearly all) the said spot is covered with shadow, the brighter ridges of the mountains gradually emerge from the shade. This double aspect of the spot is illustrated in the ensuing figures.

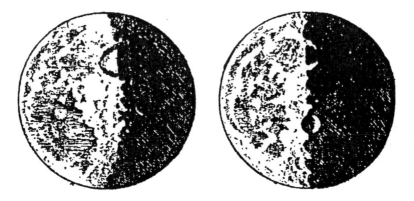

There is another thing which I must not omit, for I beheld it not without a certain wonder; this is that almost in the center of the moon there is a cavity larger than all the rest, and perfectly round in shape. I have observed it near both first and last quarters, and have tried to represent it as correctly as possible in the second of the above figures. As to light and shade, it offers the same appearance as would a region like Bohemia[7] if that were enclosed on all sides by very lofty mountains arranged exactly in a circle. Indeed, this area on the moon is surrounded by such enormous peaks that the bounding edge adjacent to the dark portion of the moon is seen to be bathed in sunlight before the boundary of light and shadow reaches halfway across the same space. As in other spots, its shaded portion faces the sun while its lighted part is toward the dark side of the moon; and for a third time I draw attention to this as a very cogent proof of the ruggedness and unevenness that pervades all the bright region of the moon. Of these spots, moreover, those are always darkest which touch the boundary line between light and shadow, while those farther off appear both smaller and less dark, so that when the moon ultimately becomes full (at opposition[8] to the sun), the shade of the cavities is distinguished from the light of the places in relief by a subdued and very tenuous separation.

The things we have reviewed are to be seen in the brighter region of the moon. In the large spots, no such contrast of depressions and prominences is perceived as that which we are compelled to recognize in the brighter parts by the changes of aspect that occur under varying illumination by the sun's rays throughout the multiplicity of positions from which the latter reach the moon. In the large spots there exist some holes rather darker than the rest, as we have shown in the illustrations. Yet these present always the same appearance, and their darkness is neither intensified nor diminished, although with some minute difference they appear sometimes a little more shaded and sometimes a little lighter according as the rays of the sun fall on them more or less obliquely. Moreover, they join with the neighboring regions of the spots in a gentle linkage, the boundaries mixing and mingling. It is quite different with the spots which occupy the brighter surface of the moon; these, like precipitous crags having rough and jagged peaks, stand out starkly in sharp contrasts of light and shade. And inside the large spots there are observed certain other zones that are brighter, some of them very bright indeed. Still, both these and the darker parts present always the same appearance; there is no change either of shape or of light and shadow; hence one may affirm beyond any doubt that they owe their appearance to some real dissimilarity of parts. They cannot be attributed merely to irregularity of shape, wherein shadows move in consequence of varied illuminations from the sun, as indeed is the case with the other, smaller, spots which occupy the brighter part of the moon and which change, grow, shrink, or disappear from one day to the next, as owing their origin only to shadows of prominences.

[...]

Thus far we have spoken of our observations concerning the body of the moon. Let us now set forth briefly what has thus far been observed regarding the fixed stars. And first of all, the following fact deserves consideration: The stars, whether fixed or wandering,[9] appear not to be enlarged by the telescope in the same proportion as that in which it magnifies other objects, and even the moon itself. In the stars this enlargement seems to be so much less that a telescope which is sufficiently powerful to magnify other objects a hundredfold is scarcely able to enlarge the stars four or five times. The reason for this is as follows.

When stars are viewed by means of unaided natural vision, they present themselves to us not as of their simple (and, so to speak, their physical) size, but as irradiated by a certain fulgor and as fringed with sparkling rays, especially when the night is far advanced. From this they appear larger than they would if stripped of those adventitious hairs of light, for the angle at the eye is determined not by the primary body of the star but by the brightness which extends so widely about it. This appears quite clearly from the fact that when stars first emerge from twilight at sunset they look very small, even if they are of the first magnitude; Venus itself, when visible in broad daylight, is so small as scarcely to appear equal to a star of the sixth magnitude. Things fall out differently with other objects, and even with the moon itself; these, whether seen in daylight or the deepest night, appear always of the same bulk. Therefore the stars are seen crowned among shadows, while daylight is able to remove their headgear; and not daylight alone, but any thin cloud that interposes itself between a star and the eye of the observer. The same effect is produced by black veils or colored glasses, through the interposition of which obstacles the stars are abandoned by their surrounding brilliance. A telescope similarly accomplishes the same result. It removes from the stars their adventitious and accidental rays, and then it enlarges their simple globes (if indeed the stars are naturally globular) so that they seem to be magnified in a lesser ratio than other objects. In fact a star of the fifth or sixth magnitude when seen through a telescope presents itself as one of the first magnitude.

Deserving of notice also is the difference between the appearances of the planets and of the fixed stars.[10] The planets show their globes perfectly round and definitely bounded, looking like little moons, spherical and flooded all over with light; the fixed stars are never seen to be bounded by a circular periphery, but have rather the aspect of blazes whose rays vibrate about them and scintillate a great deal. Viewed with a telescope they appear of a shape similar to that which they present to the naked eye, but sufficiently enlarged so that a star of the fifth or sixth magnitude seems to equal the Dog Star, largest of all the fixed stars. Now, in addition to stars of the sixth magnitude, a host of other stars are perceived through the telescope which escape the naked eye; these are so numerous as almost to surpass belief. One may, in fact, see more of them than all the stars included among the first six magnitudes. The largest of these, which we may call stars of the seventh magnitude, or the first magnitude of invisible stars, appear through the telescope as larger and brighter than stars of the second magnitude when the latter are viewed with the naked eye. In order to give one or two proofs of their almost inconceivable number, I have adjoined pictures of two constellations. With these as samples, you may judge of all the others.

In the first I had intended to depict the entire constellation of Orion, but I was overwhelmed by the vast quantity of stars and by limitations of time, so I have deferred this to another occasion. There are more than five hundred new stars distributed among the old ones within limits of one or two degrees of arc. Hence to the three stars in the Belt of Orion and the six in the Sword which were previously known, I have added eighty adjacent stars discovered recently, preserving the intervals between them as exactly as I could. To distinguish the known or ancient stars, I have depicted them larger and have outlined them doubly; the other (invisible) stars I have drawn smaller and without the extra line. I have also preserved differences of magnitude as well as possible.

[...]

We have now briefly recounted the observations made thus far with regard to the moon, the fixed stars, and the Milky Way. There remains the matter which in my opinion deserves to be considered the most important of all—the disclosure of four PLANETS never seen from the creation of the world up to our own time, together with the occasion of my having discovered and studied them, their arrangements, and the observations made of their movements and alterations during the past two months. I invite all astronomers to apply themselves to examine them and determine their periodic times, something which has so far been quite impossible to complete, owing to the shortness of the time. Once more, however, warning is given that it will be necessary to have a very accurate telescope such as we have described at the beginning of this discourse.

On the seventh day of January in this present year 1610, at the first hour of night, when I was viewing the heavenly bodies with a telescope, Jupiter presented itself to me; and because I had prepared a very excellent instrument for myself, I perceived (as I had not before, on account of the weakness of my previous instrument) that beside the planet there were three starlets, small indeed, but very bright. Though I believed them to be among the host of fixed stars, they aroused my curiosity somewhat by appearing to lie in an exact straight line parallel to the ecliptic, and by their being more splendid than others of their size. Their arrangement with respect to Jupiter and each other was the following:

East   *   *   O   *   West

that is, there were two stars on the eastern side and one to the west. The most easterly star and the western one appeared larger than the other. I paid no attention to the distances between them and Jupiter, for at the outset I thought them to be fixed stars, as I have said.[11] But returning to the same investigation on January eighth—led by what, I do not know— I found a very different arrangement. The three starlets were now all to the west of Jupiter, closer together, and at equal intervals from one another as shown in the following sketch:

East   O   *   *   *   West

At this time, though I did not yet turn my attention to the way the stars had come together, I began to concern myself with the question how Jupiter could be east of all these stars when on the previous day it had been west of two of them. I commenced to wonder whether Jupiter was not moving eastward at that time, contrary to the computations of the astronomers, and had got in front of them by that motion.[12] Hence it was with great interest that I awaited the night. But I was disappointed in my hopes, for the sky was then covered with clouds everywhere.

On the tenth of January, however, the stars appeared in this position with respect to Jupiter:

East   *   *   O   West

that is, there were but two of them, both easterly, the third (as I supposed) being hidden behind Jupiter. As at first, they were in the same straight line with Jupiter and were arranged precisely in the line of the zodiac. Noticing this, and knowing that there was no way in which such alterations could be attributed to Jupiter's motion, yet being certain that these were still the same stars I had observed (in fact no other was to be found along the line of the zodiac for a long way on either side of Jupiter), my perplexity was now transformed into amazement. I was sure that the apparent changes belonged not to Jupiter but to the observed stars, and I resolved to pursue this investigation with greater care and attention.

And thus, on the eleventh of January, I saw the following disposition:

East   ✳   ✳   ◯   *West*

There were two stars, both to the east, the central one being three times as far from Jupiter as from the one farther east. The latter star was nearly double the size of the former, whereas on the night before they had appeared approximately equal.

I had now decided beyond all question that there existed in the heavens three stars wandering about Jupiter as do Venus and Mercury about the sun, and this became plainer than daylight from observations on similar occasions which followed. Nor were there just three such stars; four wanderers complete their revolutions about Jupiter, and of their alterations as observed more precisely later on we shall give a description here. Also I measured the distances between them by means of the telescope, using the method explained before. Moreover I recorded the times of the observations, especially when more than one was made during the same night—for the revolutions of these planets are so speedily completed that it is usually possible to take even their hourly variations.

[. . .]

I have reported these relations of Jupiter and its companions with the fixed star so that anyone may comprehend that the progress of those planets, both in longitude and latitude, agrees exactly with the movements derived from planetary tables.

Such are the observations concerning the four Medicean planets recently first discovered by me, and although from these data their periods have not yet been reconstructed in numerical form, it is legitimate at least to put in evidence some facts worthy of note. Above all, since they sometimes follow and sometimes precede Jupiter by the same intervals, and they remain within very limited distances either to east or west of Jupiter, accompanying that planet in both its retrograde and direct movements in a constant manner, no one can doubt that they complete their revolutions about Jupiter and at the same time effect all together a twelve-year period about the center of the universe. That they also revolve in unequal circles is manifestly deduced from the fact that at the greatest elongation[13] from Jupiter it is never possible to see two of these planets in conjunction, whereas in the vicinity of Jupiter they are found united two, three, and sometimes all four together. It is also observed that the revolutions are swifter in those planets which describe smaller circles about Jupiter, since the stars closest to Jupiter are usually seen to the east when on the previous day they appeared to the west, and vice versa, while the planet which traces the largest orbit appears upon accurate observation of its returns to have a semimonthly period.

Here we have a fine and elegant argument for quieting the doubts of those who, while accepting with tranquil mind the revolutions of the planets about the sun in the Copernican system, are mightily disturbed to have the moon alone revolve about the earth and accompany it in an annual rotation about the sun. Some have believed that this structure of the universe should be rejected as impossible. But now we have not just one planet rotating about another while both run through a great orbit around the sun; our own eyes show us four stars which wander around Jupiter as does the moon around the earth, while all together trace out a grand revolution about the sun in the space of twelve years.

And finally we should not omit the reason for which the Medicean stars appear sometimes to be twice as large as at other times, though their orbits about Jupiter are very restricted. We certainly cannot seek the cause in terrestrial vapors, as Jupiter and its neighboring fixed stars are not seen to change size in the least while this increase and diminution are taking place. It is quite unthinkable that the cause of variation should be their change of distance from the earth at perigee and apogee, since a small circular rotation could by no means produce this effect, and an oval motion (which in this case would have to be nearly straight) seems unthinkable and quite inconsistent with the appearances.[14] But I shall gladly explain what occurs to me on this matter, offering it freely to the judgment and criticism of thoughtful men. It is known that the interposition of terrestrial vapors makes the sun and moon appear large, while the fixed stars and planets are made to appear smaller. Thus the two great luminaries are seen larger when close to the horizon, while the stars appear smaller and for the most part hardly visible. Hence the stars appear very feeble by day and in twilight, though the moon does not, as we have said. Now from what has been said above, and even more from what we shall say at greater length in our *System,* it follows that not only the earth but also the moon is surrounded by an envelope of vapors, and we may apply precisely the same judgment to the rest of the planets. Hence it does not appear entirely impossible to assume that around

Jupiter also there exists an envelope denser than the rest of the aether, about which the Medicean planets revolve as does the moon about the elemental sphere. Through the interposition of this envelope they appear larger when they are in perigee by the removal, or at least the attenuation, of this envelope.

Time prevents my proceeding further, but the gentle reader may expect more soon.

FINIS

EXPLANATORY NOTES

1. The word "telescope" was not coined until 1611. A detailed account of its origin is given by Edward Rosen in *The Naming of the Telescope* (New York, 1947). In the present translation the modern term has been introduced for the sake of dignity and ease of reading, but only after the passage in which Galileo describes the circumstances which led him to construct the instrument (pp. 28–29).

2. The original text reads "diameters" here and in another place. That this error was Galileo's and not the printer's has been convincingly shown by Edward Rosen (*Isis*, 1952, pp. 344 ff.). The slip was a curious one, as astronomers of all schools had long agreed that the maximum distance of the moon was approximately sixty terrestrial radii. Still more curious is the fact that neither Kepler nor any other correspondent appears to have called Galileo's attention to this error; not even a friend who ventured to criticize the calculations in this very passage.

3. Credit for the original invention is generally assigned to Hans Lipperhey, a lens grinder in Holland who chanced upon this property of combined lenses and applied for a patent on it in 1608.

4. Badovere studied in Italy toward the close of the sixteenth century and is said to have been a pupil of Galileo's about 1598. When he wrote concerning the new instrument in 1609 he was in the French diplomatic service at Paris, where he died in 1620.

5. Pythagoras was a mathematician and philosopher of the sixth century B.C., a semilegendary figure whose followers were credited at Galileo's time with having anticipated the Copernican system. This tradition was based upon a misunderstanding. The Pythagoreans made the earth revolve about a "central fire" whose light and heat were reflected to the earth by the sun.

6. Leonardo da Vinci had previously suggested that the dark and light regions of the moon were bodies of land and water, though Galileo probably did not know this. Da Vinci, however, had mistakenly supposed that the water would appear brighter than the land.

7. This casual comparison between a part of the moon and a specific region on earth was later the basis of much trouble for Galileo; see the letter of G. Ciampoli, p. 158. Even in antiquity the idea that the moon (or any other heavenly body) was of the same nature as the earth had been dangerous to hold. The Athenians banished the philosopher Anaxagoras for teaching such notions, and charged Socrates with blasphemy for repeating them.

8. Opposition of the sun and moon occurs when they are in line with the earth between them (full moon, or lunar eclipse); conjunction, when they are in line on the same side of the earth (new moon, or eclipse of the sun).

9. That is, planets. Among these bodies Galileo counted his newly discovered satellites of Jupiter. The term "satellites" was introduced somewhat later by Kepler.

10. Fixed stars are so distant that their light reaches the earth as from dimensionless points. Hence their images are not enlarged by even the best telescopes, which serve only to gather more of their light and in that way increase their visibility. Galileo was never entirely clear about this distinction. Nevertheless, by applying his knowledge of the effects described here, he greatly reduced the prevailing overestimation of visual dimensions of stars and planets.

11. The reader should remember that the telescope was nightly revealing to Galileo hundreds of fixed stars never previously observed. His unusual gifts for astronomical observation are illustrated by his having noticed and remembered these three merely by reason of their alignment, and recalling them so well that when by chance he happened to see them the following night he was certain that they had changed their positions. No such plausible and candid account of the discovery was given by the rival astronomer Simon Mayr, who four years later claimed priority. See pp. 233 ff. and note 4, pp. 233–34.

12. See note 4, p. 12. Jupiter was at this time in "retrograde" motion; that is, the earth's motion made the planet appear to be moving westward among the fixed stars.

13. By this is meant the greatest angular separation from Jupiter attained by any of the satellites.

14. The marked variation in brightness of the satellites which Galileo observed may be attributed mainly to markings upon their surfaces, though this was not determined until two centuries later. The mention here of a possible oval shape of the orbits is the closest Galileo ever came to accepting Kepler's great discovery of the previous year (cf. p. 17). Even here, however, he was probably not thinking of Kepler's work but of an idea proposed by earlier astronomers for the moon and the planet Venus.

GALILEO GALILEI

Science and Scripture

Born in Florence and educated in Pisa, Galileo Galilei (1564–1642) was one of the greatest of the seventeenth century scientists. His early studies of motion led him to accept the basic theories of Copernicus, the Polish astronomer who postulated that the Earth was a planet that revolved around the sun. Galileo perfected the first telescope, and with it he was able to identify the moons of Jupiter and describe the lunar surface. His work did much to confirm the theories of astronomers before him such as Copernicus and Kepler whose work relied upon mathematical calculation. Galileo's telescope allowed for actual observation of the movements of heavenly bodies. His studies of motion were an important contribution to the development of a new scientific worldview. After 1616 Galileo was prohibited by the Church from teaching Copernicanism, but in 1632 he received a license for the publication of A Dialogue Between the Two Great Systems of the World, *a tract that took the form of a debate between an adherent of the old Aristotelian system and a convert to the new Copernican one. Galileo was subsequently arrested by the Inquisition, tried, condemned, and forced to recant his Copernican views.*

Galileo wrote this letter in 1615 to the Christina of Lorraine, Grand Duchess of Tuscany, the mother of his patron, Cosimo II de' Medici, Grand Duke of Tuscany. The Medici court was well known as a sponsor of learning and culture, and the duchess was a generous patron, but also a devout Roman Catholic. In his letter Galileo explains how his theories could be reconciled with Scripture. It is his most important statement on the relationship of religion and science.

I declare (and my sincerity will make itself manifest) not only that I mean to submit myself freely and renounce any errors into which I may fall in this discourse through ignorance of matters pertaining to religion, but that I do not desire in these matters to engage in disputes with anyone, even on points that are disputable. My goal is this alone; that if, among errors that may abound in these considerations of a subject remote from my profession, there is anything that may be serviceable to the holy Church in making a decision concerning the Copernican system, it may be taken and utilized as seems best to the superiors. And if not, let my book be torn and burnt, as I neither intend nor pretend to gain from it any fruit that is not pious and Catholic. And though many of the things I shall reprove have been heard by my own ears, I shall freely grant to those who have spoken them that they never said them, if that is what they wish, and I shall confess myself to have been mistaken. Hence let whatever I reply be addressed not to them, but to whoever may have held such opinions.

The reason produced for condemning the opinion that the earth moves and the sun stands still is that in many places in the Bible one may read that the sun moves and the earth stands still. Since the Bible cannot err, it follows as a necessary consequence that anyone takes an erroneous and heretical position who maintains that the sun is inherently motionless and the earth movable.

With regard to this argument, I think in the first place that it is very pious to say and prudent to affirm that the holy Bible can never speak untruth—whenever its true meaning is understood. But I believe nobody will deny that it is often very abstruse, and may say things which are quite different from what its bare words signify. Hence in expounding the Bible if one were always to confine oneself to the unadorned grammatical meaning, one might fall into error. Not only contradictions and propositions far from true might thus be made to appear in the Bible, but even grace heresies and follies. Thus it would be necessary to assign to God feet, hands, and eyes, as well as corporeal and human affections, such as anger, repentance, hatred, and sometimes even the forgetting of things past and ignorance of those to come. These propositions uttered by the Holy Ghost were set down in that manner by the sacred scribes in order to accommodate them to the capacities of the common people, who are rude and unlearned. For the sake of those who deserve to be separated from the herd, it is necessary that wise expositors should produce the true senses of such passages, together with the special reasons for which they were set down in these words. This doctrine is so widespread and so definite with all theologians that it would be superfluous to adduce evidence for it.

Hence I think that I may reasonably conclude that whenever the Bible has occasion to speak of any physical conclusion (especially those which are very abstruse and hard to understand), the rule has been observed of avoiding confusion in the minds of the common people which would render them contumacious toward the higher mysteries. Now the Bible, merely to condescend to popular capacity, has not hesitated to obscure some very important pronouncements, attributing to God himself some qualities extremely remote from (and even contrary to) His essence. Who then, would positively declare that this principle has been set aside, and the Bible has confined itself rigorously to the bare and restricted sense of its words, when speaking but casually of the earth, of water, of the sun, or of any other created thing? Especially in view of the fact that these things in no way concern the primary purpose of the sacred writings, which is the service of God and the salvation of souls—matters infinitely beyond the comprehension of the common people.

This being granted, I think that in discussions of physical problems we ought to begin not from the authority of scriptural passages, but from sense-experiences and necessary demonstrations; for the holy Bible and the phenomena of nature proceed alike from the divine Word, the former as the dictate of the Holy Ghost and the latter as the observant executrix of God's commands. It is necessary for the Bible, in order to be accommodated to the understanding of every man, to speak many things which appear to differ from the absolute truth so far as the bare meaning of the words is concerned. But Nature, on the other hand, is inexorable and immutable; she never transgresses the laws imposed upon her, or cares a whit whether her abstruse reasons and methods of operation are understandable to men. For that reason it appears that nothing physical which sense-experience sets before our eyes, or which necessary demonstrations prove to us, ought to be called in question (much less condemned) upon the testimony of biblical passages which may have some different meaning beneath their words. For the Bible is not chained in every expression to conditions as strict as those which govern all physical effects; nor is God any less excellently revealed in Nature's actions than in the sacred statements of the Bible. Perhaps this is what Tertullian meant by these words.

"We conclude that God is known first through Nature, and then again, more particularly, by doctrine; by Nature in His works, and by doctrine in His revealed word."

From this I do not mean to infer that we need not have an extraordinary esteem for the passages of holy Scripture. On the contrary, having arrived at any certainties in physics, we ought to utilize these as the most appropriate aids in the true exposition of the Bible and in the investigation of those meanings which are necessarily contained therein, for these must be concordant with demonstrated truths. I should judge that the authority of the Bible was designed to persuade men of those articles and propositions which, surpassing all human reasoning, could not be made credible by science, or by any other means than through the very month of the Holy Spirit.

Yet even in those propositions which are not matters of faith, this authority ought to be preferred over that of all human writings which are supported only by bare assertions or probable arguments, and not set forth in a demonstrative way. This I hold to be necessary and proper to the same extent that divine wisdom surpasses all human judgment and conjecture.

But I do not feel obliged to believe that that same God who has endowed us with senses, reason, and intellect has intended to forgo their use and by some other means to give us knowledge which we can attain by them. He would not require us to deny sense and reason in physical matters which are set before our eyes and minds by direct experience or necessary demonstrations. This must be especially true in those sciences of which but the faintest trace (and that consisting of conclusions) is to be found in the Bible. Of astronomy, for instance, so little is found that none of the planets except Venus are so much as mentioned, and this only once or twice under the name of "Lucifer." If the sacred scribes had had any intention of teaching people certain arrangements and motions of the heavenly bodies, or had they wished us to derive such knowledge from the Bible, then in my opinion they would not have spoken of these matters so sparingly in comparison with the infinite number of admirable conclusions which are demonstrated in that science. Far from pretending to teach us the constitution and motions of the heavens and the stars, with their shapes, magnitudes, and distances, the authors of the Bible intentionally forbore to speak of these things, though all were quite well known to them. . . .

From these things it follows as a necessary consequence that, since the Holy Ghost did not intend to teach us whether heaven moves or stands still, whether its shape is spherical or like a discus or extended in a plane, not whether the earth is located at its center or off to one side, then so much the less was it intended to settle for us any other conclusion of the same kind. And the motion or rest of the earth and the sun is so closely linked with the things just named, that without a determination of the one, neither side can be taken in the other matters. Now if the Holy Spirit has purposely neglected to teach us propositions of this sort as irrelevant to the highest goal (that is, to our salvation), how can anyone affirm that it is obligatory to take sides on them, and that one belief is required by faith, while the other side is erroneous? Can an opinion be heretical and yet have no concern with the salvation of souls? Can the Holy Ghost be asserted not to have intended teaching us something that does concern our salvation? I would say here something that was heard from an ecclesiastic of the most eminent degree: "That the intention of the Holy Ghost is to teach us how one goes to heaven, not how heaven goes."

But let us again consider the degree to which necessary demonstrations and sense experiences ought to be respected in physical conclusions, and the authority they have enjoyed at the hands of holy and learned theologians. From among a hundred attestations I have selected the following:

"We must also take heed, in handling the doctrine of Moses, that we altogether avoid saying positively and confidently anything which contradicts manifest experiences and the reasoning of philosophy or the other sciences. For since every truth is in agreement with all other truth, the truth of Holy Writ cannot be contrary to the solid reasons and experiences of human knowledge."

And in St. Augustine we read: "If anyone shall set the authority of Holy Writ against clear and manifest reason, he who does this knows not what he has undertaken; for he opposes to the truth not the meaning of the Bible, which is beyond his comprehension, but rather his own interpretation; not what is in the Bible, but what he has found in himself and imagines to be there."

This granted, and it being true that two truths cannot contradict one another, it is the function of wise expositors to seek out the true senses of scriptural texts. These will unquestionably accord with the physical conclusions which manifest sense and necessary demonstrations have previously made certain to us. Now the Bible, as has been remarked, admits in many places expositions that are remote from the signification of the words for reasons we have already given. Moreover, we are unable to affirm that all interpreters of the Bible speak by divine inspiration, for if that were so there would exist no differences between them about the sense of a given passage. Hence I should think it would be the part of prudence not to permit anyone to usurp scriptural texts and force them in some way to maintain any physical conclusion to be true, when at some future time the senses and demonstrative or necessary reasons may show the contrary. Who indeed will set bounds to human ingenuity? Who will assert that everything in the universe capable of being perceived is already discovered and known? Let us rather confess quite truly that "Those truths which we know are very few in comparison with those which we do not know."

We have it from the very mouth of the Holy Ghost that God delivered up the world to disputations, *so that man cannot find out the work that God hath done from the beginning even to the end.* In my opinion no one, in contradiction to that dictum, should close the road to free philosophizing about mundane and physical things, as if everything had already been discovered and revealed with certainty. Nor should it be considered rash not to be satisfied with those opinions which have become common. No one should be scorned in physical disputes for not holding to the opinions which happen to please other people best, especially concerning problems which have been debated among the greatest philosophers for thousands of years.

MARY ASTELL

Proposal for a Women's College and Its Advanced Curriculum

Mary Astell (1668–1731) is considered the most important English feminist theorist of the late seventeenth century. She came from Newcastle-upon-Tyne, where her family were merchants and her grandfather was the under sheriff. Her family was generally important in local royalist politics among the commercial classes there. She gained a superior education mostly through the efforts of her uncle, and later from her brother and his friends. She was particularly influenced by Cartesian epistemology and consistently stressed the importance of women's pursuit of advanced training that would test their mental faculties and lead them to read complex philosophical, theological, and literary works. Her writings fall under three categories: feminist arguments concerning women's inadequate education and the oppressive nature of marriage; Anglican defenses and polemics; and arguments supporting the royalist position on the nature of and justification for Charles I's execution. Astell's Serious Proposal to the Ladies *proposed the establishment of a religious college for women that would allow them to pursue an advanced education so they could defend their faith with sophisticated arguments and understand the abstract arguments of philosophy and political theory. Both in secular and religious matters, Astell argued that women were responsible for themselves; they should thus know scriptures and theology thoroughly and not rely on simple memorization of the catechism, a regimen that was often pressed on them. Finally, she strongly doubted the motives of those who led parliamentary and military forces against Charles I, and she was especially angry at their omission of women from their views of a commonwealth. In her words, "Not even Milton would cry up freedom to poor female slaves." Her conservative political views blended with her negative views of marriage, in which she claimed that women were treated as "upper servants." Her educational proposal was quite popular — Queen Anne even offered to help fund it, until Bishop Burnet convinced her that it would be too like a Catholic nunnery.*

Astell's writings were reproduced in periodicals and collections directed to women during the first half of the 1700s; but her fame had lessened by the end of the century, and it is only with the recent emergence of feminist scholarship that her works have returned to print. In this selection, Astell delineated the ways in which the limited education of even well-off women undercut their self-esteem, and she proposed to overcome this reality with

216

*religiously based but intellectually rigorous education offered through a
residential women's college.*

A SERIOUS PROPOSAL TO THE LADIES FOR THE
ADVANCEMENT OF THEIR TRUE AND GREATEST INTEREST

BY A LOVER OF HER SEX

Part I (2ND ED., 1695)
Ladies,

   Since the Profitable Adventures that have gone abroad in the World
have met with so great Encouragement, . . . I therefore persuade my self,
you will not be less kind to a Proposition that comes attended with more
certain and substantial Gain; whose only design is to improve your
Charms and heighten your Value, by suffering you no longer to be cheap
and contemptible. Its aim is to fix that Beauty, to make it lasting and permanent, which Nature with all the helps of Art cannot secure, and to
place it out of the reach of Sickness and Old Age, by transferring it from
a corruptible Body to an immortal Mind. An obliging Design, which
wou'd procure them *inward* Beauty, to whom Nature has unkindly
denied the *outward,* and not permit those Ladies who have comely Bodies, to tarnish their Glory with deformed Souls. Wou'd have you all be
wits, or what is better, Wise. Raise you above the Vulgar by something
more truly illustrious, than a sounding Title or a great Estate. Wou'd
excite in you a generous Emulation to excel in the best things, and not in
such Trifles as every mean person who has but Money enough may purchase as well as you. Not suffer you to take up with the low thought of
distinguishing your selves by any thing that is not truly valuable, and
procure you such Ornaments as all the Treasures of the *Indies* are not
able to purchase. Wou'd help you to surpass the Men as much in Vertue
and Ingenuity, as you do in Beauty, that you may not only be as lovely,
but as wise as Angels. Exalt and Establish your Fame, more than the best
wrought *Poems* and loudest *Panegyricks,* by ennobling your Minds with
such Graces as really deserve it. And instead of the Fustian Comple-
ments and Fulsome Flatteries of your Admirers, obtain for you the Plau-
dit of Good Men and Angels, and the approbation of Him who cannot
err. In a word, render you the Glory and Blessing of the present Age, and
the Admiration and Pattern of the next. . . .

   Remember, I pray you, the famous Women of former Ages, the
Orinda's of late [seventeenth-century poet Katherine Philips], and the

more Modern Heroins, and blush to think how much is now, and will hereafter be said of them, when you your selves (as great a Figure as you make) must be buried in silence and forgetfulness! Shall your Emulation fail *there only* where 'tis commendable? Why are you so preposterously humble, as not to contend for one of the highest Mansions in the Court of Heav'n? Believe me, Ladies, this is the only *Place* worth contending for, you are neither better nor worse in your selves for going before, or coming after *now*, but you are really so much the better, by how much the higher your station is in an Orb of Glory. How can you be content to be in the World like Tulips in a Garden, to make a fine *shew* and be good for nothing; have all your Glories set in the Grave, or perhaps much sooner! What your own sentiments are I know not, but I can't without pity and resentment reflect, that those Glorious Temples on which your kind Creator has bestow'd such exquisite workmanship, shou'd enshrine no better than *Aegyptian* Deities; be like a garnish'd Sepulchre, which for all its glittering, has nothing within but emptiness or putrefaction! . . .

For shame let's abandon that *Old,* and therefore one wou'd think, unfashionable employment of pursuing Butterflies and Trifles! No longer drudge on in the dull beaten road of Vanity and Folly, which so many have gone before us, but dare to break the enchanted Circle that custom has plac'd us in, and scorn the vulgar way of imitating all the Impertinencies of our Neighbours. Let us learn to pride our selves in something more excellent than the invention of a Fashion, and not entertain such a degrading thought of our own *worth,* as to imagine that our Souls were given us only for the service of our Bodies, and that the best improvement we can make of these, is to attract the Eyes of Men. We value *them* too much, and our *selves* too little, if we place any part of our desert in their Opinion, and don't think our selves capable of Nobler Things than the pitiful Conquest of some worthless heart. She who has opportunities of making an interest in Heaven, of obtaining the love and admiration of GOD and Angels, is too prodigal of her Time, and injurious to her Charms, to throw them away on vain insignificant men. . . .

Pardon me the seeming rudeness of this Proposal, which goes upon a supposition that there's something amiss in you, which it is intended to amend. My design is not to expose, but to rectifie your Failures. To be exempt from mistake, is a priviledge few can pretend to, the greatest is to be past Conviction and too obstinate to reform. Even the *Men,* as exact as they wou'd seem, and as much as they divert themselves with our Miscarriages, are very often guilty of greater faults, and such, as considering the advantages they enjoy, are much more inexcusable. But I will not pretend to correct their Errors, who either are, or at least *think* themselves too wise to receive Instruction from a Womans Pen.

My earnest desire is, That you Ladies, would be as perfect and happy as 'tis possible to be in this imperfect state; for I love you too well to endure a spot upon your Beauties, if I can by any means remove and wipe it off. I would have you live up to the dignity of your Nature, and express your thankfulness to GOD for the benefits you enjoy by a due improvement of them: As I know very many of you do, who countenance that Piety which the men decry, and are the brightest Patterns of Religion that the Age affords, 'tis my grief that all the rest of our Sex do not imitate such Illustrious Examples, and therefore I would have them encreas'd and render'd more conspicuous, that Vice being put out of countenance, (because Vertue is the only thing in fashion) may sneak out of the World, and its darkness be dispell'd by the confluence of so many shining Graces.

The Men perhaps will cry out that I teach you false Doctrin, for because by their deductions some amongst us are become very mean and contemptible, they would fain persuade the rest to be as despicable and forlorn as they. We're indeed oblig'd to them for their management, in endeavouring to make us so, who use all the artifice they can to spoil, and deny us the means of improvement. So that instead of inquiring why all Women are not wise and good, we have reason to wonder that there are any so. Were the Men as much neglected, and as little care taken to cultivate and improve them, perhaps they wou'd be so far from surpassing those whom they now despise, that they themselves wou'd sink into the greatest stupidity and brutality. . . . Hither, Ladies, I desire you wou'd aspire, 'tis a noble and becoming Ambition, and to remove such Obstacles as lie in your way is the design of this Paper. We will therefore enquire what it is that stops your flight, that keeps you groveling here below, like *Domitian* catching Flies when you should be busied in obtaining Empires.

Altho' it has been said by Men of more Wit than Wisdom, and perhaps of more malice than either, that Women are naturally incapable of acting Prudently, or that they are necessarily determined to folly, I must by no meanes grant it; that Hypothesis would render my endeavours impertinent, for then it would be in vain to advise the one, or endeavour the Reformation of the other. Besides, there are Examples in all Ages, which sufficiently confute the Ignorance and Malice of this assertion.

The Incapacity, if there be any, is acquired not natural, and none of their Follies are so necessary, but that they might avoid them if they pleas'd themselves. Some disadvantages indeed they labour under, and what these are we shall see by and by and endeavour to surmount; but Women need not take up with mean things, since (if they are not wanting to themselves) they are capable of the best. Neither God nor Nature have excluded them from being Ornaments to their Families and useful in their Generation; there is therefore no reason they should be content to be Cyphers in the World, useless at the best, and in a little time a burden and nuisance to all about them. And 'tis very great pity that they who are so apt to overrate themselves in smaller Matters, shou'd, where it most concerns them to know and stand upon their Value, be so insensible of their own worth. The Cause therefore of the defects we labour under is, if not wholly, yet at least in the first place, to be ascribed to the mistakes of our Education, which like an Error in the first Concoction, spreads its ill Influence through all our Lives.

The Soil is rich and would if well cultivated produce a noble Harvest. . . . Women are from their very Infancy debar'd those Advantages, with the want of which they are afterwards reproached, and nursed up in those Vices which will hereafter be upbraided to them. So partial are Men as to expect Brick where they afford no Straw; and so abundantly civil as to take care we shou'd make good that obliging Epithet of *Ignorant,* which out of an excess of good Manners, they are pleas'd to bestow on us!

One would be apt to think indeed, that Parents shou'd take all possible care of their Childrens Education, not only for *their* sakes, but even for their *own.* And tho' the Son convey the Name to Posterity, yet certainly a great Part of the Honour of their Families depends on their Daughters. . . . To introduce poor Children into the World and neglect to fence them against the temptations of it, and so leave them expos'd to temporal and eternal Miseries, is a wickedness for which I want a Name; 'tis beneath Brutality; the Beasts are better natur'd for they take care of their offspring, till they are capable of caring for themselves. And if Mothers had a due regard to their Posterity, how *Great* soever they are, they wou'd not think themselves too Good to perform what Nature requires, nor through Pride and Delicacy remit the poor little one to the care of a Foster Parent. Or if necessity inforce them to depute another to perform *their* Duty, they wou'd be as choice at least, in the Manners and Inclinations, as they are in the complections of their Nurses, lest with their Milk they transfuse their Vices, and form in the Child such evil habits as will not easily be eradicated. . . .

. . . She who rightly understands wherein the perfection of her Nature consists, will lay out her Thoughts and Industry in the acquisition of such Perfections: But she who is kept ignorant of the matter, will take up with such Objects as first offer themselves, and bear any plausible resemblance to what she desires; a shew of advantage being sufficient to render them agreeable baits to her who wants Judgment and Skill to discern between reality and pretence. From whence it easily follows, that she who has nothing else to value her self upon, will be proud of her Beauty, or Money and what that can purchase, and think her self mightily oblig'd to him, who tells her she has those Perfections which she naturally longs for. Her inbred self-esteem and desire of good, which are degenerated into Pride and mistaken Self-love, will easily open her Ears to whatever goes about to nourish and delight them; and when a cunning designing Enemy from without, has drawn over to his Party these Traitors within, he has the Poor unhappy Person, at his Mercy, who now very glibly swallows down his Poison, because 'tis presented in a Golden Cup, and credulously hearkens to the most disadvantageous Proposals, because they come attended with a seeming esteem. She whose Vanity makes her swallow praises by the wholesale, without examining whether she deserves them, or from what hand they come, will reckon it but gratitude to think well of him who values her so much, and think she must needs be merciful to the poor despairing Lover whom her Charms have reduc'd to die at her feet.

Love and Honour are what every one of us naturally esteem, they are excellent things in themselves and very worthy our regard, and by how much the readier we are to embrace what ever resembles them, by so much the more dangerous it is that these venerable Names should be wretchedly abus'd and affixt to their direct contraries, yet this is the Custom of the World: And how can she possibly detect the fallacy, who has no better Notion of either than what she derives from Plays and Romances? How can she be furnished with any solid Principles whose very Instructors are Froth and emptiness? Whereas Women were they rightly Educated, had they obtain'd a well inform'd and discerning Mind, they would be proof against all those Batteries, see through and scorn those little silly Artifices which are us'd to ensnare and deceive them. . . .

Whence is it but from ignorance, from a want of Understanding to compare and judge of things, to chuse a right End, to proportion the Means to the End, and to rate ev'ry thing according to its proper value, that we quit the Substance for the Shadow, Reality for Appearance, and embrace those very things which if we understood we shou'd hate and fly, but now are reconcil'd to, merely because they usurp the Name, tho' they have nothing of the Nature of those venerable Objects we desire and seek? Were it not for this delusion, is it probable a Lady who passionately desires to be admir'd, shou'd ever consent to such Actions as render her base and contemptible? . . . In sum, did not ignorance impose on us, we would never lavish out the greatest part of our Time and Care, on the decoration of a Tenement, in which our Lease is so very short, and which for all our industry, may loose it's Beauty e'er that Lease be out, and in the mean while neglect a more glorious and durable Mansion! We would never be so curious of the House and so careless of the Inhabitant, whose beauty is capable of great improvement and will endure for ever without diminution or decay!

Thus Ignorance and a narrow Education lay the Foundation of Vice, and Imitation and Custom rear it up. Custom, that merciless torrent that carries all before it, and which indeed can be stem'd by none but such as have a great deal of Prudence and a rooted Vertue. For 'tis but Decorous that she who is not capable of giving better Rules, shou'd follow those she sees before her, least she only change the instance and retain the absurdity. 'Twou'd puzzle a considerate Person to account for all that Sin and Folly that is in the World (which certainly has nothing in it self to recommend it) did not Custom help to solve the difficulty. For Vertue without question has on all accounts the preeminence of Vice, 'tis abundantly more pleasant in the *Act,* as well as more advantageous in the *Consequences,* as any one who will but rightly use her reason, in a serious reflection on her self and the nature of things, may easily perceive. 'Tis Custom therefore, that Tyrant Custom, which is the grand motive to all those irrational choices which we daily see made in the World, so very contrary to our *present* interest and pleasure, as well as to our Future. We think it an unpardonable mistake not to do as our neighbours do, and part with our Peace and Pleasure as well as our Innocence and Vertue, meerly in complyance with an unreasonable Fashion. And having inur'd ourselves to Folly, we know not how to quit it; we go on in Vice, not because we find satisfaction in it, but because we are unacquainted with the Joys of Vertue. . . .

. . . She is it may be, taught the Principles and Duties of Religion, but not Acquainted with the Reasons and Grounds of them; being told 'tis enough for her to believe, to examine why, and wherefore, belongs not to her. And therefore, though her Piety may be tall and spreading, yet because it wants foundation and Root, the first rude Temptation overthrows and blasts it, or perhaps the short liv'd Gourd decays and withers of its own accord. But why should she be blamed for setting no great value on her Soul, whose noblest Faculty her Understanding is render'd useless to her? Or censur'd for relinquishing a course of Life, whose Prerogatives she was never acquainted with, and tho' highly reasonable in it self, was put upon the embracing it with as little reason as she now forsakes it? For if her Religion it self be taken up as the Mode of the Country, 'tis no strange thing that she lays it down again in conformity to the Fashion. Whereas she whose Reason is suffer'd to display it self, to inquire into the grounds and Motives of Religion, to make a disquisition of its Graces and search out its hidden Beauties; who is a Christian out of Choice, not in conformity to those among whom she lives; and cleaves to Piety, because 'tis her Wisdom, her Interest, her Joy, not because she has been accustomed to it; she who is not only eminently and unmoveably good, but able to give a Reason *why* she is so, is too firm and stable to be mov'd by the pitiful Allurements of sin, too wise and too well bottom'd to be undermin'd and supplanted by the strongest Efforts of Temptation. Doubtless a truly Christian Life requires a clear Understanding as well as regular Affections, that both together may move the Will to a direct choice of Good and a stedfast adherence to it. For tho' the heart may be honest, it is but by chance that the Will is right if the Understanding be ignorant and Cloudy. . . .

And now having discovered the Disease and its cause, 'tis proper to apply a Remedy; single Medicines are too weak to cure such complicated Distempers, they require a full Dispensatory; and what wou'd a good Woman refuse to do, could she hope by that to advantage the greatest part of the World, and to improve her Sex in Knowledge and true Religion? . . . I have therefore no more to do but to make the Proposal, to prove that it will answer these great and good Ends, and then 'twill be easy to obviate the Objections that Persons of more Wit than Vertue may happen to raise against it.

Now as to the Proposal, it is to erect a *Monastery,* or if you will (to avoid giving offence to the scrupulous and injudicious, by names which tho' innocent in themselves, have been abus'd by superstitious Practices,) we will call it a *Religious Retirement,* and such as shall have a double aspect, being not only a Retreat from the World for those who desire that advantage, but likewise, an Institution and previous discipline, to fit us to do the greatest good in it; such an Institution as this (if I do not mightily deceive my self,) would be the most probable method to amend the present, and improve the future Age. . . .

You are therefore Ladies, invited into a place, where you shall suffer no other confinement, but to be kept out of the road of sin: You shall not be depriv'd of your Grandeur but only exchange the vain Pomps and Pageantry of the world, empty Titles and Forms of State, for the true and solid Greatness of being able to despise them. You will only quit the Chat of insignificant people for an ingenious Conversation; the froth of flashy Wit for real Wisdom; idle tales for instructive discourses. . . . Happy Retreat! which will be the introducing you into such a *Paradise* as your Mother *Eve* forfeited, where you shall feast on Pleasures, that do not like those of the World, disappoint your expectations, pall your Appetites, and by the which when obtain'd are as empty as the former; but such as will make you *truly* happy now, and prepare you to be *perfectly* so hereafter. . . .

But because we were not made for our selves, nor can by any means so effectually glorify GOD, and do good to our own Souls, as by doing Offices of Charity and Beneficence to others; and to the intent that every Vertue, and the highest degrees of every Vertue may be exercis'd and promoted the most that may be; your Retreat shall be so manag'd as not to exclude the good works of an *Active,* from the pleasure and serenity of a *Contemplative* Life, but by a due mixture of both retain all the advantages and avoid the inconveniencies that attend either. It shall not so cut you off from the world as to hinder you from bettering and improving it, but rather qualify you to do it the greatest Good, and be a Seminary to stock the Kingdom with pious and prudent Ladies, whose good Example it is to be hop'd, will so influence the rest of their Sex, that Women may no longer pass for those little useless and impertinent Animals, which the ill conduct of too many has caus'd 'em to be mistaken for.

. . . Therefore, one great end of this Institution shall be, to expel that cloud of Ignorance which Custom has involv'd us in, to furnish our minds with a stock of solid and useful Knowledge, that the souls of Women may no longer be the only unadorn'd and neglected things. . . . Such a course of Study will neither be too troublesome nor out of the reach of a Female Virtuoso; for it is not intended that she shou'd spend her hours in learning *words* but *things,* and therefore no more Languages than are necessary to acquaint her with useful Authors. Nor need she trouble her self in turning over a great number of Books, but take care to understand and digest a few well chosen and good ones. Let her but obtain right Ideas, and be truly acquainted with the nature of those Objects that present themselves to her mind, and then no matter whether or no she be able to tell what fanciful people have said about them: And thoroughly to understand Christianity as profess'd by the *Church of England,* will be sufficient to confirm her in the truth, tho' she have not a Catalogue of those particular errors which oppose it. . . .

For since GOD has given Women and Men intelligent Souls, why should they be forbidden to improve them? Since he has not denied us the faculty of Thinking, why shou'd we not (at least in gratitude to him) employ our Thoughts on himself their noblest Object, and not unworthily bestow them on Trifles and Gaities and secular Affairs? Being the Soul was created for the contemplation of Truth as well as for the fruition of Good, is it not as cruel and unjust to exclude Women from the knowledge of the one as from the enjoyment of the other? Especially since the Will is blind, and cannot chuse but by the direction of the Understanding; or to speak more properly, since the Soul always *Wills* according as she *Understands,* so that if she Understands amiss, she Wills amiss. . . .

Let such therefore as deny us the improvement of our Intellectuals, either take up *his* Paradox, who said that *Women have no Souls,* (which at this time a day, when they are allow'd to Brutes, wou'd be as unphilosophical as it is unmannerly,) or else let them permit us to cultivate and improve them. There is a sort of Learning indeed which is worse than the greatest Ignorance: A Woman may study Plays and Romances all her days, and be a great deal more knowing but never a jot wiser. Such a knowledge as this serves only to instruct and put her forward in the practice of the greatest Follies, yet how can they justly blame her who forbid, or at least won't afford opportunity of better? A rational mind *will* be employ'd, it will never be satisfy'd in doing nothing, and if you neglect to furnish it with good materials, 'tis like to take up with such as come to hand.

We pretend not that Women shou'd teach in the Church, or usurp Authority where it is not allow'd them; permit us only to understand our *own* duty, and not be forc'd to take it upon trust from others; to be at least so far learned, as to be able to form in our minds a true Idea of Christianity, it being so very necessary to fence us against the danger of these *last* and *perilous days,* in which Deceivers a part of whose Character is to *lead captive silly Women,* need not *creep into Houses* since they have Authority to proclaim their Errors on the *House top.* And let us also acquire a true Practical knowledge, such as will convince us of the absolute necessity of *Holy Living* as well as of *Right Believing,* and that no Heresy is more dangerous than that of an ungodly and wicked Life. And since the *French Tongue* is understood by most Ladies, methinks they may much better improve it by the study of Philosophy (as I hear the *French Ladies* do) *Des Cartes, Malebranche* and others, than by reading idle *Novels* and *Romances.* 'Tis strange that we shou'd be so forward to imitate their Fashions and Fopperies, and have no regard to what really deserves our Imitation. And why shall it not be thought as genteel to understand *French Philosophy,* as to be accoutred in a *French mode?* Let therefore the famous Madam *D'acier, Scudery, &c,* and our own incomparable *Orinda,* excite the Emulation of the English Ladies.

The Ladies, I'm sure, have no reason to dislike this Proposal, but I know not how the Men will resent it to have their enclosure broke down, and Women invited to taste of that Tree of knowledge they have so long unjustly *Monopoliz'd.* But they must excuse me, if I be as partial to my own Sex as they are to theirs, and think Women as capable of Learning as Men are, and that it becomes them as well. . . .

To enter into the detail of the particulars concerning the Government of the *Religious,* their Offices of Devotion, Employments, Work &c. is not now necessary. Suffice it at present to signify, that they will be more than ordinarily careful to redeem their Time. . . . For a stated portion of it being daily paid to GOD in Prayers and Praises, the rest shall be imploy'd in innocent, charitable, and useful Business; either in study in learning themselves or instructing others, for it is design'd that part of their Employment be the Education of those of their own Sex; or else in spiritual and corporal Works of Mercy, relieving the Poor, healing the Sick, mingling Charity to the Soul with that they express to the Body, instructing the Ignorant, counselling the Doubtful, comforting the Afflicted, and correcting those that err and do amiss. . . .

And as this institution will strictly enjoyn all pious and profitable Employments, so does it not only permit but recommend harmless and ingenious Diversions, Musick particularly, and such as may refresh the Body without enervating the Mind. They do a disservice to Religion who make it an enemy to innocent Nature, and injure the almighty when they represent him as imposing burdens that are not to be born. . . .

As to *Lodging, Habit,* and *Diet,* they may be quickly resolv'd on by the Ladies who shall subscribe; who I doubt not will make choice of what is most plain and decent, what Nature not Luxury requires. . . . She who considers to how much better account that Money will turn which is bestow'd on the Poor, than that which is laid out in unnecessary Expences on her self, needs no Admonitions against superfluities. . . .

In a word, this happy Society will be but one Body, whose Soul is love—animating and informing us; and perpetually breathing forth it self in flames of holy desires after GOD and acts of Benevolence to each other. . . .

In the last place, by reason of this loss of time and the continual hurry we are in, we can find no opportunities for thoughtfulness and recollection; we are so busied with what passes abroad, that we have no leisure to look at home, nor to rectifie the disorders there. And such an unthinking mechanical way of living, when like Machines we are condemn'd every day to repeat the impertinencies of the day before, shortens our Views, contracts our Minds, exposes to a thousand practical Errors, and renders Improvement impossible, because it will not permit us to consider and recollect, which is the only means to attain it. So much for the inconveniences of living in the World; if we enquire concerning Retirement, we shall find it does not only remove all these, but brings considerable advantages of its own.

For first, it helps us to mate Custom and delivers us from its Tyranny, which is the most considerable thing we have to do, it being nothing else but the habituating our selves to Folly that can reconcile us to it. . . .

And by that Learning which will be here afforded, and that leisure we have to enquire after it, and to know and reflect on our own minds, we shall rescue our selves out of that woeful incogitancy we have slept into, awaken our sleeping Powers and make use of that reason which GOD has given us. . . .

Farther yet, besides that holy emulation which a continual view of the brightest and most exemplary Lives will excite in us, we shall have opportunity of contracting the purest and noblest Friendship; a Blessing, the purchase of which were richly worth all the World besides! For she who possesses a worthy Person, has certainly obtain'd the richest Treasure. A Blessing that Monarchs may envy, and she who enjoys is happier than she who fills a Throne! A Blessing, which next to the love of GOD, is the choicest Jewel in our Celestial Diadem; which, were it duly practis'd wou'd both fit us for Heav'n and bring it down into our hearts whilst we tarry here. For Friendship is a Vertue which comprehends all the rest; none being fit for this, who is not adorn'd with every other Vertue. Probably one considerable cause of the degeneracy of the present Age, is the little true Friendship that is to be found in it; or perhaps you will rather say that this is the effect of our corruption. The cause and the effect are indeed reciprocal; for were the World better there wou'd be more Friendship, and were there more Friendship we shou'd have a better World. But because *Iniquity abounds,* therefore the *love of many* is not only *waxen cold,* but quite benumb'd and perish'd. But if we have such narrow hearts, be so full of mistaken Self-love, so unreasonably fond of our selves, that we cannot spare a hearty Goodwill to one or two choice Persons, how can it ever be thought, that we shou'd well acquit our selves of that Charity which is due to all Mankind? For Friendship is nothing else but Charity contracted; it is (in the words of an admired Author) a kind of revenging our selves on the narrowness of our Faculties, by exemplifying that extraordinary Charity on one or two, which we are willing, but not able to exercise towards all. . . .

. . . [I]t were well if we could look into the very Soul of the beloved Person, to discover what resemblance it bears to our own, and in this Society we shall have the best opportunities of doing so. There are no Interests here to serve, no contrivances for another to be a stale to; the

Souls of all the *Religious* will be open and free, and those particular Friendships must be no prejudice to the general Amity. But yet, as in Heav'n that region of perfect Love, the happy Souls (as some are of opinion) now and then step aside from more general Conversations, to entertain themselves with a peculiar Friend; so, in this little emblem of that blessed place, what shou'd hinder, but that two Persons of a sympathizing disposition, the *make* and *frame* of whose Souls bears an exact conformity to each other, and therefore one wou'd think were purposely design'd by Heaven to unite and mix; what shou'd hinder them from entering into an holy combination to watch over each other for Good, to advise, encourage and direct, and to observe the minutest fault in order to its amendment. The truest effect of love being to endeavour the bettering the beloved Person. And therefore nothing is more likely to improve us in Vertue, and advance us to the very highest pitch of Goodness than unfeigned Friendship, which is the most beneficial, as well as the most pleasant thing in the world. . . .

If any object against a Learned Education, that it will make Women vain and assuming, and instead of correcting encrease their Pride: I grant that a smattering in Learning may, for it has this effect on the Men, none so Dogmatical and so forward to shew their Parts as your little *Pretenders* to Science. But I wou'd not have the Ladies content themselves with the *shew,* my desire is, that they shou'd not rest till they obtain the *Substance.* And then, she who is most knowing will be forward to own with the wise *Socrates* that she knows nothing: nothing that is matter of Pride and Ostentation; nothing but what is attended with so much ignorance and imperfection, that it cannot reasonably elate and puff her up. The more she knows, she will be the less subject to talkativeness and its sister Vices, because she discerns, that the most difficult piece of Learning is to know when to use and when to hold ones Tongue, and never to speak but to the purpose.

But the men if they rightly understand their own interest, have no reason to oppose the ingenious Education of the Women, since 'twou'd go a great way towards reclaiming the men. Great is the influence we have over them in their Childhood, in which time if a Mother be discreet and knowing as well as devout, she has many opportunities of giving such a *Form* and *Season* to the tender Mind of the Child, as will shew its good effects thro' all the stages of his Life. But tho' you should not allow her capable of doing *good,* 'tis certain she may do *hurt;* If she do not *make* the Child, she has the power to *marr* him, by suffering her fondness to get the better of discreet affection. But besides this, a good and prudent wife wou'd wonderfully work on an ill man; he must be a Brute indeed, who cou'd hold out against all those innocent Arts, those gentle persuasives and obliging methods she wou'd use to reclaim him. Piety is often offensive when it is accompanied with indiscretion; but she who is as Wise as Good, possesses such Charms as can hardly fail of prevailing. Doubtless her Husband is a much happier Man and more likely to abandon all his ill Courses than he who has none to come home to, and an ignorant, froward and fantastick Creature. An ingenious Conversation will make his life comfortable, and he who can be so well entertain'd at home, needs not run into Temptations in search of diversions abroad. The only danger is that the Wife be more knowing than the Husband; but if she be 'tis his own fault, since he wants no opportunities of improvement; unless he be a natural *Blockhead,* and then such an one will need a wise Woman to govern him, whose prudence will conceal it from publick Observation, and at once both cover and supply his defects. Give me leave therefore to hope, that no Gentleman who has honourable designs, will henceforward decry Knowledge and Ingenuity in her he would pretend to Honour; If he does, it may serve for a Test to distinguish the feigned and unworthy from the real Lover.

Now who that has a spark of Piety will go about to oppose so Religious a design? What generous Spirit that has a due regard to the good of Mankind, will not be forward to advance and perfect it? Who will think 500 pounds too much to lay out for the purchase of so much Wisdom and Happiness? Certainly we shou'd not think them too dearly paid for by a much greater Sum did not our pitiful and sordid Spirits set a much higher value on Money than it deserves. But granting so much of that dear Idol were given away, a person thus bred, will easily make it up by her Frugality & other Vertues; if she bring less, she will not waste so much as others do in superflous and vain Expences. Nor can I think of any expedient so useful as this to Persons of Quality who are over-stock'd with Children, for thus they may honourably dispose of them without impairing their Estates. Five or six hundred pounds may be easily spar'd with a Daughter, when so many thousands would go deep; and yet as the world goes be a very inconsiderable Fortune for Ladies of their Birth, neither maintain them in that *Port* which Custom makes almost necessary, nor procure them an equal Match, those of their own Rank (contrary to the generous custom of the *Germans*) chusing rather to fill their Coffers than to preserve the purity of their Blood, and therefore think a weighty Bag the best Gentility, preferring a wealthy Upstart before the best Descended and best Qualified Lady; their own Extravagances perhaps having made it necessary, that they may keep up an empty shadow of Greatness, which is all that remains to shew what their Ancestors have been. . . .

Part II (1697): *WHEREIN A METHOD IS OFFER'D FOR THE IMPROVEMENT OF THEIR MINDS*

Chap. III. *Concerning the Improvement of the Understanding. I. Of the Capacity of the Humane Mind in General. II. Of Particular Capacities. . . . IV. A Natural Logic. . . .*

The perfection of the Understanding consisting in the Clearness and Largeness of its view, it improves proportionably as its Ideas become Clearer and more Extensive. But this is not so to be understood as if all sorts of Notices contributed to our Improvement, there are some things which make us no wiser when we know 'em, others which 'tis best to be ignorant of. But that Understanding seems to me the most exalted, which has the Clearest and most Extensive view of such Truths as are suitable to its Capacity, and Necessary or Convenient to be Known in this Present State. For being that we are but Creatures, our Understanding in its greatest Perfection has only a limited excellency. It has indeed a vast extent, and it were not amiss if we tarried a little in the Contemplation of its Powers and Capacities, provided that the Prospect did not make us giddy, that we remember from whom we have receiv'd them, and ballance those lofty Thoughts which a view of our Intellectuals may occasion, with the depressing ones which the irregularity of our Morals will suggest, and that we learn from this inspection, how indecorous it is to busy this bright side of us in mean things, seeing it is capable of such noble ones.

Human Nature is indeed a wonderful Composure admirable in its outward structure, but much more excellent in the Beauties of its Inward, and she who considers in whose Image her Soul was Created, and whose Blood was shed to Redeem it, cannot prize it too much, nor forget to pay it her utmost regard. There's nothing in this Material World to be compar'd to't, all the gay things we dote on, and for which we many times expose our Souls to ruin, are of no consideration in respect of it. They are not the good of the Soul, it's happiness depends not on 'em, but they often deceive and withdraw it from its true Good. It was made for the Contemplation and Enjoyment of its GOD, and all Souls are capable of this tho in a different degree and by measures somewhat different, as we hope will appear from that which follows.

I. Truth in general is the Object of the Understanding, but all Truths are not equally Evident, because of the Limitation of the Humane Mind, which tho' it can gradually take in many Truths, yet cannot any more than our sight attend to many things at once: And likewise, because GOD has not thought fit to communicate such Ideas to us as are necessary to the disquisition of some particular Truths. For knowing nothing without us but by the Idea we have of it, and Judging only according to the Relation we find between two or more Ideas, when we cannot discover the Truth we search after by Intuition or the immediate comparison of two Ideas, 'tis necessary that we shou'd have a third by which to compare them. But if this middle Idea be wanting, though we have sufficient Evidence of those two which we wou'd compare, because we have a Clear and Distinct Conception of them, yet we are Ignorant of those Truths which wou'd arise from their Comparison, because we want a third by which to compare them. . . .

Tho the Human Intellect has a large extent, yet being limited as we have already said, this Limitation is the Cause of those different Modes of Thinking, which for distinction sake we call Faith, Science and Opinion. For in this present and imperfect State in which we know not any thing by Intuition, or immediate View, except a few first Principles which we call Self-evident, the most of our Knowledge is acquir'd by Reasoning and Deduction: And these three Modes of Understanding, Faith, Science and Opinion are no otherwise distinguish'd than by the different degrees of Clearness and Evidence in the Premises from whence the Conclusion is drawn. . . .

In this enumeration of the several ways of Knowing, I have not reckon'd the Senses, in regard that we're more properly said to be *Conscious* of than to *Know* such things as we perceive by Sensation. And also because that Light which we suppose to be let into our Ideas by our Senses is indeed very dim and fallacious, and not to be relied on till it has past the Test of Reason; neither do I think there's any Mode of Knowledge which mayn't be reduc'd to those already mentioned.

Now tho there's a great difference between Opinion and Science, true Science being immutable but Opinion variable and uncertain, yet there is not such a difference between Faith and Science as is usually suppos'd. The difference consists not in the Certainty but in the way of Proof; the Objects of Faith are as Rationally and as Firmly Prov'd as the Objects of Science, tho by another way. As Science Demonstrates things that are *Seen*, so Faith is the Evidence of such as are *Not Seen*. And he who rejects the Evidence of Faith in such things as belong to its Cognizance, is as unreasonable as he who denies Propositions in Geometry that are prov'd with Mathematical exactness.

There's nothing true which is not in it self demonstrable, or which we should not pronounce to be true had we a Clear and Intuitive View of it. But as was said above we see very few things by Intuition, neither are we furnish'd with Mediums to make the Process our selves in Demonstrating all Truths, and therefore there are some Truths which we must either be totally ignorant of, or else receive them on the Testimony of another Person, to whose Understanding they are clear and manifest tho not to ours. And if this Person be one who can neither be Deceiv'd nor Deceive, we're as sertain of those Conclusions which we prove by his Authority, as we're of those we demonstrate by our own Reason: nay more Certain, by how much his Reason is more Comprehensive and Infallible than our own.

Science is following the Process our Selves upon Clear and Evident principles; Faith is a Dependance on the Credit of another, in such matters as are out of our View. And when we have very good Reason to submit to the Testimony of the Person we Believe, Faith is as Firm, and those Truths it discovers to us as truly Intelligible and as strongly Prov'd in their kind as Science.

In a word, as every Sense so every Capacity of the Understanding has its proper Object. The Objects of Science are things within our View, of which we may have Clear and Distinct Ideas, and nothing shou'd be determin'd here without Clearness and Evidence. To be able to repeat any Persons *Dogma* without forming a Distinct Idea of it our selves, is not to Know but to Remember; and to have a Confused Indeterminate Idea is to Conjecture not to Understand.

The Objects of Faith are as Certain and as truly, Intelligible in themselves as those of Science, as has been said already, only we become persuaded of the Truth of them by another Method, we do not *See* them so clearly and distinctly as to be unable to disbelieve them. Faith has a mixture of the Will that it may be rewardable, for who will thank us for giving our Assent where it was impossible to withold it? Faith then may be said to be a sort of Knowledge capable of Reward, and Men are Infidels not for want of Conviction, but thro an *Unwillingness* to Believe. . . .

II. It is therefore very fit that after we have consider'd the Capacity of the Understanding in general, we shou'd descend to the view of our own particular, observing the bent and turn of our own Minds, which way our Genius lies and to what it is most inclin'd. I see no reason why there may not be as great a variety in Minds as there is in Faces, that the Soul as well as the Body may not have something in it to distinguish it, not only from all other Intelligent Natures but even from those of its own kind. There are different proportions in Faces which recommend them to some Eyes sooner than to others, and tho *All* Truth is amiable to a Reasonable Mind, and proper to employ it, yet why may there not be some particular Truths, more agreeable to each individual Understanding than others are? Variety gives Beauty to the Material World and why not to the Intellectual? We can discern the different Abilities which the Wise Author of all things has endow'd us with, the different Circumstances in which he has plac'd us in reference to this World and the Concerns of an Animal Life, that so we may be mutually useful, and that since each single Person is too limited and confin'd to attend to many, much less to all things, we may receive from each other a reciprocal advantage, and why may we not think he has done the like in respect of Truth? That since it is too much for one, our united Strength shou'd be employ'd in the search of her. Especially since the divine Being who contains in himself all Reality and Truth is Infinite in Perfection, and therefore shou'd be Infinitely Ador'd and Lov'd; and If Creatures are by their being so uncapable of rendering to their Incomprehensible Creator an Adoration and Love that's worthy of him, it is but decorous that they shou'd however do as much as they can. All that variety of sublime Truths of Beautiful and Wondrous Objects which surround us, are nothing else but a various display of his unbounded Excellencies, and why shou'd any of 'em pass unobserv'd? Why shou'd not every individual Understanding be in a more especial manner fitted for and employ'd in the disquisition of some particular Truth and Beauty? 'Tis true after all our researches we can no more sufficiently Know GOD than we can worthily Love him, and are as much unable to find out all his Works as we are his Nature, yet this shou'd only prompt us to exert *All* our Powers and to do our best, since even *that* were too little cou'd we possibly do more. We can never offer to him so much Praise as he deserves, and therefore it is but fit that he shou'd have *All* that Mankind can possibly render him. He is indeed immutable in his own Nature, but those discoveries we daily make of his Operations will always afford us somewhat New and Surprizing, for this All-glorious Sun the Author of Life and Light is as inexhaustible a Source of Truth as he is of Joy and Happiness. . . .

IV. As to the *Method* of Thinking, if it be proper for me to say any thing of that, after those better Pens which have treated of it already, it falls in with the Subject I'me now come to, which is, that *Natural Logic* I wou'd propose. I call it natural because I shall not send you further than your Own Minds to learn it, you may if you please take in the assistance of some well chosen Book, but a good Natural Reason after all, is the best Director, without this you will scarce Argue well, tho you had the Choicest Books and Tutors to Instruct you, but with it you may, tho' you happen to be destitute of the other. For as a very Judicious Writer on this Subject (to whose Ingenious Remarks and Rules I am much obliged) well observes, "These Operations (of the Mind) proceed meerly from Nature, and that sometimes more perfectly from those who are altogether ignorant of Logic, than from others who have learn'd it." *(Art of Thinking)*

That which we propose in all our Meditations and Reasonings is, either to deduce some Truth we are in search of, from such Principles as we're already acquainted with; or else, to dispose our Thoughts and Reasonings in such a manner, as to be able to Convince others of those Truths which we our selves are Convinc'd of. Other Designs indeed Men may have, such as the Maintenance of their Own Opinions, Actions and Parties without regard to the Truth and Justice of 'em, or the Seduction of their unwary Neighbours, but these are Mean and Base ones, beneath a Man, much more a Christian, who is or ought to be endow'd with greater Integrity and Ingenuity.

Now Reasoning being nothing else but a Comparison of Ideas, and a deducing of Conclusions from Clear and Evident Principles, it is in the first place requisite that our Ideas be Clear and Just, and our Principles True, else all our Discourse will be Nonsense and Absurdity, Falsehood and Error. And that our Idea may be Right, we have no more to do but to look attentively into our Minds, having as we said above, laid aside all Prejudices and whatever may give a false tincture to our Light, there we shall find a Clear and Lively Representation of what we seek for, unsophisticated with the Dross of false Definitions and unintelligible Expressions. But we must not imagine that a transient view will serve the turn, or that our Eye will be Enlightened if it be not fix'd. For tho' Truth be exceeding bright, yet since our Prejudices and Passions have darkned our Eye-sight, it requires no little Pains and Application of Mind to find her out, the neglect of which Application is the Reason that we have so little Truth, and that the little we have is almost lost in the Rubbish of Error which is mingled with it. And since Truth is so near at hand, since we are not oblig'd to tumble over many Authors, to hunt after every celebrated Genius, but may have it for enquiring after in our own Breasts, are we not inexcusable if we don't obtain it? Are we not unworthy of Compassion if we suffer our Understandings to be overrun with Error? Indeed it seems to me most Reasonable and most agreeable to the Wisdom and Equity of the Divine Operations, that every one shou'd have a Teacher in their own Bosoms, who will if they seriously apply themselves to him, immediately Enlighten them so far as that is necessary, and direct them to such Means as are sufficient for their Instruction both in Humane and Divine Truths; for as to the latter, Reason if it be Right and Solid, will not pretend to be our sole Instructor, but will send us to Divine Revelation when it may be had. . . .

The First and Principal thing therefore to be observed in all the Operations of the Mind is, That we determine nothing about those things of which we have not a Clear Idea, and as Distinct as the Nature of the Subject will permit, for we cannot properly be said to Know any thing which does not Clearly and Evidently appear to us. Whatever we see Distinctly we likewise see Clearly, Distinction always including Clearness, tho this does not necessarily include that, there being many Objects Clear to the view of the Mind, which yet can't be said to be Distinct.

That (to use the Words of a Celebrated Author) may be said to be "Clear which is Present and Manifest to an attentive Mind; so as we say we see Objects Clearly, when being present to our Eyes they sufficiently Act on 'em, and our Eyes are dispos'd to regard 'em. And that Distinct, which is so Clear, Particular, and Different from all other things, that it contains not any thing in it self which appears not manifestly to him who considers it as ought." (*Les Princip. De la Philos. De M. Des Cartes,* Part I, para 45.) Thus we may have a Clear, but not a Distinct and Perfect Idea of God and of our own Souls; their Existence and some of their Properties and Attributes may be Certainly and Indubitably Known, but we can't Know the Nature of our Souls Distinctly, for Reasons too long to be mentioned here, and less that of GOD, because he is Infinite. Now where our Knowledge is Distinct, we may boldly deny of a subject, all that which after a careful Examination we find not in it: But where our Knowledge is only Clear, and not Distinct, tho' we may safely Affirm what we see, yet we can't without a hardy Presumption Deny of it what we see not. And were it not very common to find People both Talking and Writing of things of which they have no Notion, no Clear Idea; nay and determining Dogmatically concerning the intire Nature of those of which they cannot possibly have an Adequate and distinct one, it might seem Impertinent to desire them to speak no farther than they Apprehend. They will tell you Peremptorily of Contradictions and Absurdities in such matters as they themselves must allow they cannot Comprehend, tho others as Sharp sighted as themselves can see no such thing as they complain of.

As Judgments are form'd by the Comparing of Ideas, so Reasoning or Discourse arises from the Comparison or Combination of several Judgments. Nature teaches us when we can't find out what Relation one Idea bears to another by a Simple view or bare Comparison, to seek for a Common Measure or third Idea, which Relating to the other two, we may by Comparing it with each of 'em, discern wherein they agree or differ. Our Invention discovers it self in proposing readily apt Ideas for this Middle Term, our Judgment in making Choice of such as are Clearest and most to our purpose, and the excellency of our Reasoning consists in our Skill and Dexterity in Applying them. . . .

JOHN LOCKE

The Origins of Property

John Locke (1632–1704) was one of the most influential political theorists in western history. His Two Treatises on Government not only inspired the English tradition of parliamentary democracy, but influenced the French Enlightenment through the writings of Montesquieu and, most famously, became the foundation for the American Declaration of Independence and Constitution. Locke was educated at Oxford after which he became a physician. His early intellectual endeavors were devoted to science and he was elected to the Royal Society in 1668. In the employ of the Earl of Shaftesbury, Locke wrote an Essay Concerning Toleration *(1667), which argued for the peaceful coexistence of diverse religious groups in England. He wrote his most important philosophical work,* Essay Concerning Human Understanding *(1689), while recovering his health in France. Locke was actively engaged in domestic politics during the reign of Charles II and he wrote his Two Treatises on Government during the Exclusion Crisis (1679–81) to defend the principles that government originated in the consent of the governed and for their benefit alone. His account of an idyllic state of nature from which man emerged voluntarily to form companionable society was in sharp contrast to the brutal state of nature theorized by Hobbes. Locke was associated with the Whig party in England and he followed Lord Shaftesbury into self-imposed exile in Holland after the accession of James II, returning only after the Revolution of 1688. He served briefly in the government of William III, mostly as a financial adviser, but ill health limited his public career. Locke died in 1704.*

The Second Treatise on Government *(1689) is one of the most enduring works of political theory in the western tradition. Although it was written in 1681 as a polemical tract, Locke attempted to prove his ideas about the nature of government by returning to first principles and stating them in simple, didactic terms. In this selection Locke described the origins of private property and the ways in which government was responsible for protecting it.*

"The Origins of Property," from John Locke, *The Political Writings of John Locke*, edited by David Wootton, copyright © 1993 by David Wootton, 273–286.

CHAPTER FIVE: OF PROPERTY

25. Whether we consider natural reason, which tells us that men, being once born, have a right to their preservation, and consequently to meat and drink, and such other things as nature affords for their subsistence; or revelation, which gives us an account of those grants God made of the world to Adam, and to Noah and his sons, 'tis very clear that God, as King David says (Psalm 115.16), 'has given the earth to the children of men', given it to mankind in common. But this being supposed, it seems to some a very great difficulty how anyone should ever come to have a property in anything. I will not content myself to answer, that if it be difficult to make out property upon a supposition that God gave the world to Adam and his posterity in common, it is impossible that any man, but one universal monarch, should have any property upon a supposition that God gave the world to Adam and his heirs in succession, exclusive of all the rest of his posterity. But I shall endeavour to show how men might come to have a property in several parts of that which God gave to mankind in common, and that without any express compact of all the commoners.

26. God, who hath given the world to men in common, hath also given them reason to make use of it to the best advantage of life and convenience. The earth, and all that is therein, is given to men for the support and comfort of their being. And though all the fruits it naturally produces, and beasts it feeds, belong to mankind in common, as they are produced by the spontaneous hand of nature, and nobody has originally a private dominion, exclusive of the rest of mankind, in any of them, as they are thus in their natural state; yet, being given for the use of men, there must of necessity be a means to appropriate them some way or other before they can be of any use, or at all beneficial to any particular man. The fruit or venison which nourishes the wild Indian, who knows no enclosure, and is still a tenant in common, must be his, and so his (i.e. a part of him) that another can no longer have any right to it, before it can do him any good for the support of his life.

27. Though the earth and all inferior creatures be common to all men, yet every man has a property in his own person. This nobody has any right to but himself. The labour of his body, and the work of his hands, we may say, are properly his. Whatsoever, then, he removes out of the state that nature hath provided and left it in, he hath mixed his labour with, and joined to it something that is his own, and thereby makes it his property. It being by him removed from the common state nature placed it in, it hath by this labour something annexed to it that excludes the

common right of other men. For this labour being the unquestionable property of the labourer, no man but he can have a right to what that is once joined to, at least where there is enough and as good left in common for others.

28. He that is nourished by the acorns he picked up under an oak, or the apples he gathered from the trees in the wood, has certainly appropriated them to himself. Nobody can deny but the nourishment is his. I ask then, When did they begin to be his? When he digested? Or when he ate? Or when he boiled? Or when he brought them home? Or when he picked them up? And 'tis plain if the first gathering made them not his, nothing else could. That labour put a distinction between them and common. That added something to them more than nature, the common mother of all, had done; and so they became his private right. And will anyone say he had no right to those acorns or apples he thus appropriated, because he had not the consent of all mankind to make them his? Was it a robbery thus to assume to himself what belonged to all in common? If such a consent as that was necessary, man had starved, notwithstanding the plenty God had given him. We see in commons, which remain so by compact, that 'tis the taking any part of what is common, and removing it out of the state nature leaves it in, which begins the property; without which the common is of no use. And the taking of this or that part does not depend on the express consent of all the commoners. Thus the grass my horse has bit, the turfs my servant has cut, and the ore I have digged in any place where I have a right to them in common with others become my property, without the assignation or consent of anybody. The labour that was mine, removing them out of that common state they were in, hath fixed my property in them.

29. By making an explicit consent of every commoner necessary to anyone's appropriating to himself any part of what is given in common, children or servants could not cut the meat which their father or master had provided for them in common, without assigning to everyone his peculiar part. Though the water running in the fountain be everyone's, yet who can doubt but that in the pitcher is his only who drew it out? His labour hath taken it out of the hands of nature, where it was common, and belonged equally to all her children, and hath thereby appropriated it to himself.

30. Thus this law of reason makes the deer that Indian's who hath killed it; 'tis allowed to be his goods who hath bestowed his labour upon it, though before it was the common right of everyone. And amongst those who are counted the civilized part of mankind, who have made and multiplied positive laws to determine property, this original law of

nature for the beginning of property in what was before common, still takes place; and by virtue thereof, what fish anyone catches in the ocean, that great and still remaining common of mankind, or what ambergris anyone takes up here is by the labour that removes it out of that common state nature left it in, made his property who takes that pains about it. And even amongst us, the hare that anyone is hunting is thought his who pursues her during the chase. For being a beast that is still looked upon as common, and no man's private possession, whoever has employed so much labour about any of that kind as to find and pursue her has thereby removed her from the state of nature, wherein she was common, and hath begun a property.

31. It will perhaps be objected to this that if gathering the acorns, or other fruits of the earth, etc. makes a right to them, then anyone may engross as much as he will. To which I answer: Not so. The same law of nature that does by this means give us property, does also bound that property too. 'God has given us all things richly' (1 Tim. 6.17) is the voice of reason confirmed by inspiration. But how far has he given it us? To enjoy. As much as anyone can make use of to any advantage of life before it spoils, so much he may by his labour fix a property in. Whatever is beyond this, is more than his share, and belongs to others. Nothing was made by God for man to spoil or destroy. And thus, considering the plenty of natural provisions there was a long time in the world, and the few spenders, and to how small a part of that provision the industry of one man could extend itself, and engross it to the prejudice of others; especially keeping within the bounds, set by reason, of what might serve for his use; there could be then little room for quarrels or contentions about property so established.

32. But the chief matter of property being now not the fruits of the earth, and the beasts that subsist on it, but the earth itself, as that which takes in and carries with it all the rest, I think it is plain that property in that too is acquired as the former. As much land as a man tills, plants, improves, cultivates, and can use the product of, so much is his property. He by his labour does, as it were, enclose it from the common. Nor will it invalidate his right to say 'Everybody else has an equal title to it, and therefore he cannot appropriate, he cannot enclose, without the consent of all his fellow-commoners, all mankind.' God, when he gave the world in common to all mankind, commanded man also to labour, and the penury of his condition required it of him. God and his reason commanded him to subdue the earth, i.e. improve it for the benefit of life, and therein lay out something upon it that was his own, his labour. He that, in obedience to this command of God, subdued, tilled and sowed

any part of it, thereby annexed to it something that was his property, which another had no title to, nor could without injury take from him.

33. Nor was this appropriation of any parcel of land, by improving it, any prejudice to any other man, since there was still enough—and as good—left; and more than the yet unprovided could use. So that, in effect, there was never the less left for others because of his enclosure for himself. For he that leaves as much as another can make use of, does as good as take nothing at all. Nobody could think himself injured by the drinking of another man, though he took a good draught, who had a whole river of the same water left him to quench his thirst. And the case of land and water, where there is enough of both, is perfectly the same.

34. God gave world to men in common; but since he gave it them for their benefit, and the greatest conveniences of life they were capable to draw from it, it cannot be supposed he meant it should always remain common and uncultivated. He gave it to the use of the industrious and rational (and labour was to be his title to it); not to the fancy or covetousness of the quarrelsome and contentious. He that had as good left for his improvement as was already taken up needed not complain, ought not to meddle with what was already improved by another's labour. If he did, 'tis plain he desired the benefit of another's pains, which he had no right to, and not the ground which God had given him in common with others to labour on, and whereof there was as good left as that already possessed, and more than he knew what to do with, or his industry could reach to.

35. 'Tis true, in land that is common, in England, or any other country where there is plenty of people under government, who have money and commerce, no one can enclose or appropriate any part without the consent of all his fellow-commoners: because this is left common by compact, i.e. by the law of the land, which is not to be violated. And though it be common in respect of some men, it is not so to all mankind, but is the joint property of this country, or this parish. Besides, the remainder, after such enclosure, would not be as good to the rest of the commoners as the whole was when they could all make use of the whole; whereas in the beginning and first peopling of the great common of the world, it was quite otherwise. The law man was under was rather *for* appropriating. God commanded, and his wants forced him, to labour. That was his property which could not be taken from him wherever he had fixed it. And hence, subduing or cultivating the earth and having dominion, we see are joined together. The one gave title to the other. So that God, by commanding to subdue, gave authority so far to appropriate. And the condition of human life, which requires labour and materials to work on, necessarily introduces private possessions.

36. The measure of property, nature has well set, by the extent of men's labour and the conveniency of life: no man's labour could subdue or appropriate all, nor could his enjoyment consume more than a small part; so that it was impossible for any man, this way, to entrench upon the right of another, or acquire to himself a property to the prejudice of his neighbour, who would still have room for as good and as large a possession (after the other had taken out his) as before it was appropriated. This measure did confine every man's possession to a very moderate proportion, and such as he might appropriate to himself without injury to anybody, in the first ages of the world when men were more in danger to be lost by wandering from their company in the then vast wilderness of the earth, than to be straitened for want of room to plant in. And the same measure may be allowed still, without prejudice to anybody, as full as the world seems. For supposing a man, or family, in the state they were at first peopling of the world by the children of Adam or Noah; let him plant in some inland, vacant places of America, we shall find that the possessions he could make himself, upon the measures we have given, would not be very large, nor, even to this day, prejudice the rest of mankind, or give them reason to complain, or think themselves injured by this man's encroachment, though the race of men have now spread themselves to all the corners of the world, and do infinitely exceed the small number [which] was at the beginning. Nay, the extent of ground is of so little value, without labour, that I have heard it affirmed that in Spain itself a man may be permitted to plough, sow, and reap without being disturbed, upon land he has no other title to, but only his making use of it. But, on the contrary, the inhabitants think themselves beholden to him, who, by his industry on neglected and consequently waste land, has increased the stock of corn, which they wanted. But be this as it will, which I lay no stress on; this I dare boldly affirm, that the same rule of property, viz. that every man should have as much as he could make use of, would hold still in the world, without straitening anybody, since there is land enough in the world to suffice double the inhabitants, had not the invention of money, and the tacit agreement of men to put a value on it, introduced (by consent) larger possessions, and a right to them; which, how it has done, I shall, by and by, show more at large.

37. This is certain, that in the beginning, before the desire of having more than men needed had altered the intrinsic value of things, which depends only on their usefulness to the life of man; or [men] had agreed that a little piece of yellow metal, which would keep without wasting or decay, should be worth a great piece of flesh, or a whole heap of corn, though men had a right to appropriate by their labour, each one to

himself, as much of the things of nature as he could use; yet this could not be much, nor to the prejudice of others, where the same plenty was still left to those who would use the same industry. *To which let me add, that he who appropriates land to himself by his labour, does not lessen but increase the common stock of mankind. For the provisions serving to the support of human life produced by one acre of enclosed and cultivated land are (to speak much within compass) ten times more than those which are yielded by an acre of land, of an equal richness, lying waste in common. And, therefore, he that encloses land and has a greater plenty of the conveniences of life from ten acres than he could have from an hundred left to nature may truly be said to give ninety acres to mankind. For his labour now supplies him with provisions out of ten acres which were but the product of an hundred lying in common. I have here rated the improved land very low in making its product but as ten to one, when it is much nearer an hundred to one. For I ask whether in the wild woods and uncultivated waste of America, left to nature, without any improvement, tillage or husbandry, a thousand acres yield the needy and wretched inhabitants as many conveniences of life as ten acres of equally fertile land do in Devonshire, where they are well-cultivated.*

Before the appropriation of land, he who gathered as much of the wild fruit, killed, caught, or tamed as many of the beasts as he could, he that so employed his pains about any of the spontaneous products of nature as any way to alter them from the state which nature put them in by placing any of his labour on them, did thereby acquire a property in them. But if they perished in his possession, without their due use; if the fruits rotted or the venison putrified before he could spend it, he offended against the common law of nature, and was liable to be punished; he invaded his neighbour's share, for he had no right further than his use called for any of them and they might serve to afford him conveniences of life.

38. The same measures governed the possession of land too: whatsoever he tilled and reaped, laid up and made use of, before it spoiled, that was his peculiar right; whatsoever he enclosed and could feed and make use of, the cattle and product was also his. But if either the grass of his enclosure rotted on the ground, or the fruit of his planting perished without gathering, and laying up, this part of the earth, notwithstanding his enclosure, was still to be looked on as waste, and might be the possession of any other. Thus, at the beginning, Cain might take as much ground as he could till, and make it his own land, and yet leave enough to Abel's sheep to feed on; a few acres would serve for both their possessions. But as families increased, and industry enlarged their stocks, their

possessions enlarged with the need of them; but yet it was commonly without any fixed property in the ground they made use of, till they incorporated, settled themselves together, and built cities; and then, by consent, they came in time to set out the bounds of their distinct territories, and agree on limits between them and their neighbours, and, by laws within themselves, settled the properties of those of the same society. For we see that in that part of the world which was first inhabited, and therefore like to be best peopled, even as low down as Abraham's time, they wandered with their flocks and their herds, which was their substance, freely up and down; and this Abraham did, in a country where he was a stranger. Whence it is plain that at least a great part of the land lay in common; that the inhabitants valued it not, nor claimed property in any more than they made use of. But when there was not room enough in the same place for their herds to feed together, they, by consent, as Abraham and Lot did (Genesis 13.5), separated, and enlarged their pasture where it best liked them. And for the same reason Esau went from his father and his brother, and planted in Mount Seir (Genesis 36.6).

39. And thus, without supposing any private dominion and property in Adam over all the world, exclusive of all other men, which can no way be proved, nor anyone's property be made out from it, but supposing the world given as it was to the children of men in common, we see how labour could make men distinct titles to several parcels of it, for their private uses; wherein there could be no doubt of right, no room for quarrel.

40. Nor is it so strange as perhaps before consideration it may appear that the property of labour should be able to overbalance the community of land. For 'tis labour indeed that puts the difference of value on everything; and let anyone consider what the difference is between an acre of land planted with tobacco or sugar, sown with wheat or barley; and an acre of the same land lying in common, without any husbandry upon it, and he will find that the improvement of labour makes the far greater part of the value. I think it will be but a very modest computation to say that of the products of the earth useful to the life of man, nine-tenths are the effects of labour; nay, if we will rightly estimate things as they come to our use, and cast up the several expenses about them, what in them is purely owing to nature, and what to labour, we shall find that in most of them 99/100 are wholly to be put on the account of labour.

41. There cannot be a clearer demonstration of anything than several nations of the Americans are of this, who are rich in land, and poor in all the comforts of life; whom nature having furnished as liberally as any other people with the materials of plenty, i.e. a fruitful soil, apt to

produce in abundance what might serve for food, raiment, and delight, yet, for want of improving it by labour, have not one-hundredth part of the conveniences we enjoy; and a king of a large and fruitful territory there feeds, lodges, and is clad worse than a day-labourer in England.

42. To make this a little clearer, let us but trace some of the ordinary provisions of life through their several progresses, before they come to our use, and see how much they receive of their value from human industry. Bread, wine, and cloth are things of daily use and great plenty, yet notwithstanding, acorns, water, and leaves or skins must be our bread, drink, and clothing, did not labour furnish us with these more useful commodities. For whatever bread is more worth than acorns, wine than water, and cloth or silk than leaves, skins, or moss, that is wholly owing to labour and industry. The one of these being the food and raiment which unassisted nature furnishes us with; the other provisions which our industry and pains prepare for us, which how much they exceed the other in value, when anyone hath computed, he will then see how much labour makes the far greater part of the value of things we enjoy in this world; and the ground which produces the materials is scarcely to be reckoned in as any, or at most but a very small part, of it. So little, that even amongst us land that is left wholly to nature, that hath no improvement of pasturage, tillage, or planting, is called, as indeed it is, *waste;* and we shall find the benefit of it amount to little more than nothing. *This shows how much numbers of men are to be preferred to largeness of dominions, and that the increase of lands [i.e. 'hands'?] and the right employing of them is the great art of government. And that prince who shall be so wise and godlike as by established laws of liberty to secure protection and encouragement to the honest industry of mankind against the oppression of power and narrowness of party, will quickly be too hard for his neighbours. But this bye the bye. To return to the argument in hand.*

43. An acre of land that bears here twenty bushels of wheat, and another in America which, with the same husbandry, would do the like, are without doubt of the same natural, intrinsic value. But yet the benefit mankind receives from the one, in a year, is worth £5, and from the other possibly not worth a penny, if all the profit an Indian received from it were to be valued and sold here; at least I may truly say, not 1/1000. 'Tis labour then which puts the greatest part of value upon land, without which it would scarcely be worth anything; 'tis to that we owe the greatest part of all its useful products, for all that the straw, bran, bread of that acre of wheat is more worth than the product of an acre of as good land which lies waste is all the effect of labour. For 'tis not barely the ploughman's pains,

the reaper's and thresher's toil, and the baker's sweat is to be counted into the bread we eat; the labour of those who broke the oxen, who digged and wrought the iron and stones, who felled and framed the timber employed about the plough, mill, oven, or any other utensils, which are a vast number, requisite to this corn, from its being seed to be sown to its being made bread, must all be charged on the account of labour, and received as an effect of that; nature and the earth furnished only the almost worthless materials, as in themselves. 'Twould be a strange catalogue of things that industry provided and made use of about every loaf of bread before it came to our use, if we could trace them: iron, wood, leather, bark, timber, stone, bricks, coals, lime, cloth, dying-drugs, pitch, tar, masts, ropes, and all the materials made use of in the ship that brought any of the commodities made use of by any of the workmen to any part of the work, all which 'twould be almost impossible, at least too long, to reckon up.

44. From all which it is evident that, though the things of nature are given in common, yet man (by being master of himself, and proprietor of his own person and the actions or labour of it) had still in himself the great foundation of property, and that which made up the great part of what he applied to the support or comfort of his being, when invention and arts had improved the conveniences of life, was perfectly his own, and did not belong in common to others.

45. Thus labour, in the beginning, gave a right of property wherever anyone was pleased to employ it upon what was common, which remained a long while the far greater part, and is yet more than mankind makes use of. Men at first, for the most part, contented themselves with what unassisted nature offered to their necessities; and though afterwards, in some parts of the world (where the increase of people and stock, with the use of money, had made land scarce, and so of some value), the several communities settled the bounds of their distinct territories, and by laws within themselves regulated the properties of the private men of their society, and so, by compact and agreement, settled the property which labour and industry began; and the leagues that have been made between several states and kingdoms, either expressly or tacitly disowning all claim and right to the land in the other's possession, have, by common consent, given up their pretences to their natural common right which originally they had to those countries, and so have, by positive agreement, settled a property amongst themselves in distinct parts and parcels of the earth. Yet there are still great tracts of ground to be found which (the inhabitants thereof not having joined with the rest of mankind in the consent of the use of their common money) lie waste, and are more than the people who dwell on it do or can make use of, and

245

so still lie in common. Tho' this can scarce happen amongst that part of mankind that have consented to the use of money.

46. The greatest part of things really useful to the life of man, and such as the necessity of subsisting made the first commoners of the world look after, as it doth the Americans now, are generally things of short duration, such as, if they are not consumed by use, will decay and perish of themselves. Gold, silver, and diamonds are things that fancy or agreement hath put the value on, more than real use and the necessary support of life. Now of those good things which nature hath provided in common, everyone had a right (as hath been said) to as much as he could use, and had a property in all that he could affect with his labour. All that his industry could extend to, to alter from the state nature had put it in, was his. He that gathered a hundred bushels of acorns or apples had thereby a property in them; they were his goods as soon as gathered. He was only to look that he used them before they spoiled; else he took more than his share and robbed others. And indeed it was a foolish thing, as well as dishonest, to hoard up more than he could make use of. If he gave away a part to anybody else, so that it perished not uselessly in his possession, these he also made use of. And if he also bartered away plums that would have rotted in a week for nuts that would last good for his eating a whole year, he did no injury; he wasted not the common stock, destroyed no part of the portion of goods that belonged to others, so long as nothing perished uselessly in his hands. Again, if he would give his nuts for a piece of metal, pleased with its colour, or exchange his sheep for shells, or wool for a sparkling pebble or a diamond, and keep those by him all his life, he invaded not the right of others: he might heap up as much of these durable things as he pleased; the exceeding of the bounds of his just property, not lying in the largeness of his possession, but the perishing of anything uselessly in it.

47. And thus came in the use of money, some lasting thing that men might keep without spoiling, and that by mutual consent men would take in exchange for truly useful but perishable supports of life.

48. And as different degrees of industry were apt to give men possessions in different proportions, so this invention of money gave them the opportunity to continue and enlarge them. For supposing an island separate from all possible commerce with the rest of the world, wherein there were but a hundred families, but there were sheep, horses, and cows, with other useful animals, wholesome fruits, and land enough for corn for a hundred thousand times as many, but nothing in the island, either because of its commonness, or perishableness, fit to supply the place of money: what reason could anyone have there to enlarge his

possessions beyond the use of his family, and a plentiful supply to its consumption, either in what their own industry produced or they could barter for like perishable, useful commodities with others? Where there is not something both lasting and scarce, and so valuable to be hoarded up, there men will not be apt to enlarge their possessions of land, were it never so rich, never so free for them to take. For I ask, what would a man value ten thousand or an hundred thousand acres of excellent land, ready cultivated and well-stocked too with cattle, in the middle of the inland parts of America, where he had no hopes of commerce with other parts of the world, to draw money to him by the sale of the product? It would not be worth the enclosing, and we should see him give up again to the wild common of nature whatever was more than would supply the conveniences of life to be had there for him and his family.

49. Thus in the beginning all the world was America, and more so than that is now, for no such thing as money was anywhere known. Find out something that hath the use and value of money amongst his neighbours, you shall see the same man will begin presently to enlarge his possessions.

50. But since gold and silver, being little useful to the life of man in proportion to food, raiment, and carriage, has its value only from the consent of men, whereof labour yet makes, in great part, the measure, it is plain that men have agreed to disproportionate and unequal possession of the earth, they having by a tacit and voluntary consent found out a way how a man may fairly possess more land than he himself can use of the product, by receiving in exchange for the overplus gold and silver, which may be hoarded up without injury to anyone, these metals not spoiling or decaying in the hands of the possessor. This partage of things in an inequality of private possessions, men have made practicable out of the bounds of society, and without compact, only by putting a value on gold and silver and tacitly agreeing in the use of money. For in governments the laws regulate the right of property, and the possession of land is determined by positive constitutions.

51. And thus, I think, it is very easy to conceive without any difficulty how labour could at first begin a title of property in the common things of nature, and how the spending it upon our uses bounded it. So that there could then be no reason of quarrelling about title, nor any doubt about the largeness of possession it gave. Right and conveniency went together, for as a man had a right to all he could employ his labour upon, so he had no temptation to labour for more than he could make use of. This left no room for controversy about the title, nor for encroachment on the right of others; what portion a man carved to himself was easily seen, and it was useless as well as dishonest to carve himself too much, or take more than he needed.

JOHN LOCKE

The Forms of Government

———

*John Locke (1632–1704) was one of the most influential political theorists in
western history. His* Two Treatises on Government *not only inspired the
English tradition of parliamentary democracy, but influenced the French
Enlightenment through the writings of Montesquieu and, most famously,
became the foundation for the American Declaration of Independence and
Constitution. Locke was educated at Oxford after which he became a
physician. His early intellectual endeavors were devoted to science and he
was elected to the Royal Society in 1668. In the employ of the Earl of
Shaftesbury, Locke wrote an* Essay Concerning Toleration (1667), *which
argued for the peaceful coexistence of diverse religious groups in England.
He wrote his most important philosophical work,* Essay Concerning
Human Understanding (1689), *while recovering his health in France.
Locke was actively engaged in domestic politics during the reign of Charles
II and he wrote his* Two Treatises on Government *during the Exclusion
Crisis (1679–81) to defend the principles that government originated in the
consent of the governed and for their benefit alone. His account of an idyllic state of nature from which man emerged voluntarily to form companionable society was in sharp contrast to the brutal state of nature theorized
by Hobbes. Locke was associated with the Whig party in England and he
followed Lord Shaftesbury into self-imposed exile in Holland after the
accession of James II, returning only after the Revolution of 1688. He
served briefly in the government of William III, mostly as a financial
adviser, but ill health limited his public career. Locke died in 1704.*

The Second Treatise on Government *(1689) is one of the most enduring
works of political theory in the western tradition. Although it was written
in 1681 as a polemical tract, Locke attempted to prove his ideas about the
nature of government by returning to first principles and stating them in
simple, didactic terms. In this selection Locke explores the different forms
that governments take, their nature, and the restraints upon them.*

———

"The Forms of Government," from John Locke, *The Political Writings of John Locke*,
edited by David Wootton, copyright © 1993 by David Wootton, 324–336.

CHAPTER NINE: OF THE ENDS OF POLITICAL SOCIETY AND GOVERNMENT

123. If man in the state of nature be so free as has been said; if he be absolute lord of his own person and possessions, equal to the greatest, and subject to nobody, why will he part with his freedom? Why will he give up this empire, and subject himself to the dominion and control of any other power? To which 'tis obvious to answer that, though in the state of nature he hath such a right, yet the enjoyment of it is very uncertain, and constantly exposed to the invasion of others. For all being kings as much as he, every man his equal, and the greater part no strict observers of equity and justice, the enjoyment of the property he has in this state is very unsafe, very insecure. This makes him willing to quit this condition which, however free, is full of fears and continual dangers. And 'tis not without reason that he seeks out, and is willing to join in society with others who are already united, or have a mind to unite, for the mutual preservation of their lives, liberties, and estates, which I call by the general name *property*.

124. The great and chief end, therefore, of men's uniting into commonwealths, and putting themselves under government, is the preservation of their property, to which in the state of nature there are many things wanting.

First, there wants an established, settled, known law, received and allowed by common consent to be the standard of right and wrong, and the common measure to decide all controversies between them. For though the law of nature be plain and intelligible to all rational creatures; yet men being biased by their interest, as well as ignorant for want of study of it, are not apt to allow of it as a law binding to them in the application of it to their particular cases.

125. Secondly, in the state of nature there wants a known and indifferent judge, with authority to determine all differences according to the established law. For everyone in that state being both judge and executioner of the law of nature, men being partial to themselves, passion and revenge is very apt to carry them too far, and with too much heat, in their own cases; as well as negligence and unconcernedness to make them too remiss in other men's.

126. Thirdly, in the state of nature there often wants power to back and support the sentence when right, and to give it due execution. They who by any injustice offended, will seldom fail, where they are able, by force to make good their injustice. Such resistance many times makes the punishment dangerous, and frequently destructive, to those who attempt it.

127. Thus mankind, notwithstanding all the privileges of the state of nature, being but in an ill condition while they remain in it, are quickly driven into society. Hence it comes to pass that we seldom find any number of men live any time together in this state. The inconveniences that they are therein exposed to, by the irregular and uncertain exercise of the power every man has of punishing the transgressions of others, make them take sanctuary under the established laws of government, and therein seek the preservation of their property. 'Tis this makes them so willingly give up every one his single power of punishing to be exercised by such alone as shall be appointed to it amongst them; and by such rules as the community, or those authorized by them to that purpose, shall agree on. And in this we have the original right and rise of both the legislative and executive power, as well as of the governments and societies themselves.

128. For in the state of nature, to omit the liberty he has of innocent delights, a man has two powers:

The first is to do whatsoever he thinks fit for the preservation of himself and others within the permission of the law of nature; by which law, common to them all, he and all the rest of mankind are one community, make up one society distinct from all other creatures. And were it not for the corruption and viciousness of degenerate men, there would be no need of any other; no necessity that men should separate from this great and natural community, and by positive agreements combine into smaller and divided associations.

The other power a man has in the state of nature is the power to punish the crimes committed against that law. Both these he gives up when he joins in a private, if I may so call it, or particular political society, and incorporates into any commonwealth, separate from the rest of mankind.

129. The first power, viz. of doing whatsoever he thought fit for the preservation of himself, and the rest of mankind, he gives up to be regulated by laws made by the society, so far forth as the preservation of himself and the rest of that society shall require. Which laws of the society in many things confine the liberty he had by the law of nature.

130. Secondly, the power of punishing he wholly gives up, and engages his natural force (which he might before employ in the execution of the law of nature, by his own single authority, as he thought fit) to assist the executive power of the society, as the law thereof shall require. For being now in a new state, wherein he is to enjoy many conveniences from the labour, assistance, and society of others in the same community, as well as protection from its whole strength, he is to part also with as much of his natural liberty in providing for himself as the good, prosperity, and safety

of the society shall require: which is not only necessary, but just, since the other members of the society do the like.

131. But though men when they enter into society give up the equality, liberty, and executive power they had in the state of nature into the hands of the society, to be so far disposed of by the legislative as the good of the society shall require; yet it being only with an intention in everyone the better to preserve himself his liberty and property (for no rational creature can be supposed to change his condition with an intention to be worse), the power of the society, or legislative constituted by them, can never be supposed to extend further than the common good; but is obliged to secure everyone's property by providing against those three defects above-mentioned that made the state of nature so unsafe and uneasy. And so whoever has the legislative or supreme power of any commonwealth is bound to govern by established standing laws, promulgated and known to the people, and not by extemporary decrees; by indifferent and upright judges, who are to decide controversies by those laws; and to employ the force of the community at home only in the execution of such laws, or abroad to prevent or redress foreign injuries, and secure the community from inroads and invasion. And all this to be directed to no other end, but the peace, safety, and public good of the people.

CHAPTER TEN: OF THE FORMS OF A COMMONWEALTH

132. The majority having, as has been showed, upon men's first uniting into society, the whole power of the community naturally in them, may employ all that power in making laws for the community from time to time, and executing those laws by officers of their own appointing; and then the form of the government is a perfect democracy. Or else may put the power of making laws into the hands of a few select men, and their heirs or successors, and then it is an oligarchy. Or else into the hands of one man, and then it is a monarchy; if to him and his heirs, it is an hereditary monarchy; if to him only for life, but upon his death the power only of nominating a successor to return to them, an elective monarchy. And so accordingly of these the community may make compounded and mixed forms of government, as they think good. And if the legislative power be at first given by the majority to one or more persons only for their lives, or any limited time, and then the supreme power to revert to them again, when it is so reverted the community may dispose of it again anew into what hands they please, and so constitute a new form of government. For the form of government depending upon the placing the supreme power, which is the legislative, it being impossible to conceive that an inferior power should prescribe to a

superior, or any but the supreme make laws, according as the power of making laws is placed, such is the form of the commonwealth.

133. By commonwealth I must be understood all along to mean, not a democracy, or any form of government, but any independent community, which the Latins signified by the word *civitas,* to which the word which best answers in our language is commonwealth, and most properly expresses such a society of men, which community or city in English does not, for there may be subordinate communities in a government; and city amongst us has a quite different notion from commonwealth. And therefore, to avoid ambiguity, I crave leave to use the word commonwealth in that sense, in which I find it used by king James the First, and I take it to be its genuine signification; which if anybody dislike, I consent with him to change it for a better.

CHAPTER ELEVEN: OF THE EXTENT OF THE LEGISLATIVE POWER

134. The great end of men's entering into society being the enjoyment of their properties in peace and safety, and the great instrument and means of that being the laws established in that society, the first and fundamental positive law of all commonwealths is the establishing of the legislative power; as the first and fundamental natural law, which is to govern even the legislative itself, is the preservation of the society, and (as far as will consist with the public good) of every person in it. This legislative is not only the supreme power of the commonwealth, but sacred and unalterable in the hands where the community have once placed it; nor can any edict of anybody else, in what form soever conceived, or by what power soever backed, have the force and obligation of a law which has not its sanction from that legislative which the public has chosen and appointed. For without this the law could not have that which is absolutely necessary to its being a law, the consent of the society, over whom nobody can have a power to make laws, but by their own consent, and by authority received from them; and therefore all the obedience which by the most solemn ties anyone can be obliged to pay ultimately terminates in this supreme power, and is directed by those laws which it enacts; nor can any oaths to any foreign power whatsoever, or any domestic subordinate power, discharge any member of the society from his obedience to the legislative, acting pursuant to their trust, nor oblige him to any obedience contrary to the laws so enacted, or further than they do allow; it being ridiculous to imagine one can be tied ultimately to obey any power in the society which is not the supreme.

135. Though the legislative, whether placed in one or more, whether it be always in being or only by intervals, though it be the supreme power in every commonwealth, yet:

First, it is not, nor can possibly be, absolutely arbitrary over the lives and fortunes of the people. For it being but the joint power of every member of the society given up to that person, or assembly, which is legislator, it can be no more than those persons had in a state of nature before they entered into society, and gave up to the community. For nobody can transfer to another more power than he has in himself; and nobody has an absolute arbitrary power over himself, or over any other, to destroy his own life, or take away the life or property of another. A man, as has been proved, cannot subject himself to the arbitrary power of another; and having in the state of nature no arbitrary power over the life, liberty, or possession of another, but only so much as the law of nature gave him for the preservation of himself and the rest of mankind, this is all he doth, or can give up to the commonwealth, and by it to the legislative power, so that the legislative can have no more than this. Their power, in the utmost bounds of it, is limited to the public good of the society. It is a power that hath no other end but preservation, and therefore can never have a right to destroy, enslave, or designedly to impoverish the subjects. The obligations of the law of nature cease not in society, but only in many cases are drawn closer, and have by human laws known penalties annexed to them to enforce their observation. Thus the law of nature stands as an eternal rule to all men, legislators as well as others. The rules that they make for other men's actions must, as well as their own and other men's actions, be conformable to the law of nature, i.e. to the will of God, of which that is a declaration. And the fundamental law of nature being the preservation of mankind, no human sanction can be good or valid against it.

136. Secondly, the legislative, or supreme authority, cannot assume to itself a power to rule by extemporary arbitrary decrees, but is bound to dispense justice and decide the rights of the subject by promulgating standing laws, and known authorized judges. For the law of nature being unwritten, and so nowhere to be found but in the minds of men, they who through passion or interest shall mis-cite or misapply it cannot so easily be convinced of their mistake where there is no established judge; and so it serves not, as it ought, to determine the rights and fence the properties of those that live under it, especially where everyone is judge, interpreter, and executioner of it too, and that in his own case; and he that has right on his side, having ordinarily but his own single strength, hath not force enough to defend himself from injuries, or to punish delinquents.

To avoid these inconveniences which disorder men's properties in the state of nature, men unite into societies, that they may have the united strength of the whole society to secure and defend their properties, and may have standing rules to bound it, by which everyone may know what is his. To this end it is that men give up all their natural power to the society which they enter into, and the community put the legislative power into such hands as they think fit, with this trust, that they shall be governed by declared laws, or else their peace, quiet, and property will still be at the same uncertainty as it was in the state of nature.

137. Absolute arbitrary power, or governing without settled standing laws, can neither of them consist with the ends of society and government, which men would not quit the freedom of the state of nature for, and tie themselves up under, were it not to preserve their lives, liberties, and fortunes; and by stated rules of right and property to secure their peace and quiet. It cannot be supposed that they should intend, had they a power so to do, to give to any one, or more, an absolute arbitrary power over their persons and estates, and put a force into the magistrate's hand to execute his unlimited will arbitrarily upon them. This were to put themselves into a worse condition than the state of nature, wherein they had a liberty to defend their right against the injuries of others, and were upon equal terms of force to maintain it, whether invaded by a single man or many in combination. Whereas by supposing they have given up themselves to the absolute arbitrary power and will of a legislator, they have disarmed themselves, and armed him to make a prey of them when he pleases. He being in a much worse condition who is exposed to the arbitrary power of one man who has the command of 100,000 than he that is exposed to the arbitrary power of 100,000 single men, nobody being secure that his will who has such a command is better than that of other men, though his force be 100,000 times stronger. And therefore, whatever form the commonwealth is under, the ruling power ought to govern by declared and received laws, and not by extemporary dictates and undetermined resolutions. For then mankind will be in a far worse condition than in the state of nature, if they shall have armed one or a few men with the joint power of a multitude, to force them to obey at pleasure the exorbitant and unlimited decrees of their sudden thoughts, or unrestrained and till that moment unknown wills, without having any measures set down which may guide and justify their actions. For all the power the government has being only for the good of the society, as it ought not to be arbitrary and at pleasure, so it ought to be exercised by established and promulgated laws, that both the people may know their duty, and be safe and secure within the limits of

the law, and the rulers too kept within their due bounds, and not to be tempted by the power they have in their hands to employ it to such purposes, and by such measures, as they would not have known, and own not willingly.

138. Thirdly, the supreme power cannot take from any man any part of his property without his own consent. For the preservation of property being the end of government, and that for which men enter into society, it necessarily supposes and requires that the people should have property, without which they must be supposed to lose that by entering into society which was the end for which they entered into it, too gross an absurdity for any man to own. Men therefore in society having property, they have such a right to the goods which by the law of the community are theirs, that nobody hath a right to take their substance, or any part of it, from them without their own consent; without this they have no property at all. For I have truly no property in that which another can by right take from me when he pleases, against my consent. Hence it is a mistake to think that the supreme or legislative power of any commonwealth can do what it will, and dispose of the estates of the subject arbitrarily, or take any part of them at pleasure. This is not much to be feared in governments where the legislative consists, wholly or in part, in assemblies which are variable, whose members upon the dissolution of the assembly are subjects under the common laws of their country, equally with the rest. But in governments where the legislative is in one lasting assembly always in being, or in one man, as in absolute monarchies, there is danger still that they will think themselves to have a distinct interest from the rest of the community, and so will be apt to increase their own riches and power by taking, when they think fit, from the people. For a man's property is not at all secure, though there be good and equitable laws to set the bounds of it, between him and his fellow-subjects, if he who commands those subjects have power to take from any private man what part he pleases of his property, and use and dispose of it as he thinks good.

139. But government, into whatsoever hands it is put, being as I have before showed entrusted with this condition and for this end, that men might have and secure their properties, the prince or senate, however it may have power to make laws for the regulating of property between the subjects one amongst another, yet can never have a power to take to themselves the whole or any part of the subject's property, without their own consent. For this would be in effect to leave them no property at all. And to let us see that even absolute power, where it is necessary, is not arbitrary by being absolute, but is still limited by that reason and confined to those ends which required it in some cases to be absolute, we need look no

further than the common practice of martial discipline. For the preservation of the army, and in it of the whole commonwealth, requires an absolute obedience to the command of every superior officer, and it is justly death to disobey or dispute the most dangerous or unreasonable of them: but yet we see that neither the Sargent that would command a soldier to march up to the mouth of a cannon, or stand in a breach where he is almost sure to perish, can command that soldier to give him one penny of his money; nor the general, that can condemn him to death for deserting his post, or for not obeying the most desperate orders, can yet, with all his absolute power of life and death, dispose of one farthing of that soldier's estate, or seize one jot of his goods; whom yet he can command anything, and hang for the least disobedience. Because such a blind obedience is necessary to that end for which the commander has his power, viz. the preservation of the rest; but the disposing of his goods has nothing to do with it.

140. 'Tis true, governments cannot be supported without great charge, and 'tis fit everyone who enjoys his share of the protection should pay out of his estate his proportion for the maintenance of it. But still it must be with his own consent, i.e. the consent of the majority, giving it either by themselves or their representatives chosen by them. For if anyone shall claim a power to lay and levy taxes on the people by his own authority, and without such consent of the people, he thereby invades the fundamental law of property, and subverts the end of government. For what property have I in that which another may by right take, when he pleases, to himself?

141. Fourthly, the legislative cannot transfer the power of making laws to any other hands. For it being but a delegated power from the people, they who have it cannot pass it over to others. The people alone can appoint the form of the commonwealth, which is by constituting the legislative, and appointing in whose hands that shall be. And when the people have said: We will submit to rules, and be governed by laws made by such men, and in such forms, nobody else can say other men shall make laws for them, nor can the people be bound by any laws but such as are enacted by those whom they have chosen and authorized to make laws for them. The power of the legislative being derived from the people by a positive voluntary grant and institution, can be no other than what that positive grant conveyed, which being only to make laws, and not to make legislators, the legislative can have no power to transfer their authority of making laws, and place it in other hands.

142. These are the bounds which the trust that is put in them by the society, and the law of God and nature, have set to the legislative power of every commonwealth, in all forms of government.

First, they are to govern by promulgated, established laws, not to be varied in particular cases, but to have one rule for rich and poor, for the favourite at court and the country man at plough.

Secondly, these laws also ought to be designed for no other end ultimately but the good of the people.

Thirdly, they must not raise taxes on the property of the people without the consent of the people, given by themselves or their deputies. And this properly concerns only such governments where the legislative is always in being, or at least where the people have not reserved any part of the legislative to deputies, to be from time to time chosen by themselves.

Fourthly, the legislative neither must nor can transfer the power of making laws to anybody else, or place it anywhere but where the people have.

CHAPTER TWELVE: OF THE LEGISLATIVE, EXECUTIVE, AND FEDERATIVE POWER OF THE COMMONWEALTH

143. The legislative power is that which has a right to direct how the force of the commonwealth shall be employed for preserving the community and the members of it. But because those laws which are constantly to be executed, and whose force is always to continue, may be made in a little time, therefore there is no need that the legislative should be always in being, not having always business to do. And because it may be too great a temptation to human frailty, apt to grasp at power, for the same persons who have the power of making laws to have also in their hands the power to execute them, whereby they may exempt themselves from obedience to the laws they make, and suit the law, both in its making and execution, to their own private advantage, and thereby come to have a distinct interest from the rest of the community, contrary to the end of society and government, therefore in well-ordered commonwealths, where the good of the whole is so considered as it ought, the legislative power is put into the hands of diverse persons who, duly assembled, have by themselves, or jointly with others, a power to make laws, which when they have done, being separated again, they are themselves subject to the laws they have made; which is a new and near tie upon them to take care that they make them for the public good.

144. But because the laws, that are at once and in a short time made, have a constant and lasting force, and need a perpetual execution, or an attendance thereunto, therefore 'tis necessary there should be a power

always in being, which should see to the execution of the laws that are made, and remain in force. And thus the legislative and executive power come often to be separated.

145. There is another power in every commonwealth which one may call natural, because it is that which answers to the power every man naturally had before he entered into society. For though in a commonwealth the members of it are distinct persons still in reference to one another, and as such are governed by the laws of the society; yet in reference to the rest of mankind they make one body, which is, as every member of it before was, still in the state of nature with the rest of mankind. Hence it is that the controversies that happen between any man of the society with those that are out of it are managed by the public, and an injury done to a member of their body engages the whole in the reparation of it. So that under this consideration the whole community is one body in the state of nature in respect of all other states or persons out of its community.

146. This therefore contains the power of war and peace, leagues and alliances, and all the transactions with all persons and communities without the commonwealth, and may be called federative, if anyone pleases. So the thing be understood, I am indifferent as to the name.

147. These two powers, executive and federative, though they be really distinct in themselves, yet one comprehending the execution of the municipal laws of the society within itself, upon all that are parts of it; the other the management of the security and interest of the public without, with all those that it may receive benefit or damage from, yet they are always (almost) united. And though this federative power in the well- or ill-management of it be of great moment to the commonwealth, yet it is much less capable to be directed by antecedent, standing, positive laws than the executive; and so must necessarily be left to the prudence and wisdom of those whose hands it is in, to be managed for the public good. For the laws that concern subjects one amongst another, being to direct their actions, may well enough precede them. But what is to be done in reference to foreigners, depending much upon their actions, and the variation of designs and interests, must be left in great part to the prudence of those who have this power committed to them, to be managed by the best of their skill, for the advantage of the commonwealth.

148. Though, as I said, the executive and federative power of every community be really distinct in themselves, yet they are hardly to be separated, and placed, at the same time, in the hands of distinct persons. For both of them requiring the force of the society for their exercise, it is

almost impracticable to place the force of the commonwealth in distinct and not subordinate hands; or that the executive and federative power should be placed in persons that might act separately, whereby the force of the public would be under different commands: which would be apt sometime or other to cause disorder and ruin.

OLAUDAH EQUIANO

Horrors of a Slave Ship

Olaudah Equiano was born around 1745 in what is now Nigeria. Equiano was kidnapped and enslaved at about the age of ten. After a period of bondage in Africa, Equiano was transported to the West Indies, and from there to Virginia, where he was sold to a planter. Resold to an officer in the British navy, Equiano—renamed Gustavo Vassa by his new master— witnessed the hostilities of the Seven Years War aboard a Royal Navy ship. In 1762, the naval officer reneged on an earlier promise to free Equiano, and instead sold him in the West Indies. Equiano was able to purchase his own freedom in 1766, using funds he had earned through personal enter- prise. As a freedman, Equiano was involved in several commercial voyages, sailing as far as the North Pole before he settled in London. There, Equiano converted to Methodism and emerged as an outspoken opponent of the slave trade. He married Susanna Cullen, an Englishwoman, in 1792, and left a sizable estate to their daughter when he died in 1797.

The Interesting Narrative was published in 1789. It was one of a series of works by authors of African birth or descent to appear before the public during this period—writings by James Albert Ukawsaw Gronniosaw, Phyllis Wheatley, and Ignatius Sancho were also published in Britain in the 1770s and 1780s. Like these publications, Equiano's work offered convinc- ing evidence of the intellectual capability of Africans. But as the first first- hand Afro-Briton account to offer an indictment of the slave trade, the Interesting Narrative *was unique. It was praised by Mary Wollstonecraft and John Wesley, and ran through nine English language editions during Equiano's lifetime. In this passage, Equiano described how he was trans- ported aboard a slave ship to the Americas.*

The first object which saluted my eyes when I arrived on the coast was the sea, and a slave-ship, which was then riding at anchor, and waiting for its cargo. These filled me with astonishment, which was soon converted into terror, which I am yet at a loss to describe, nor the then feelings of my mind. When I was carried on board I was immediately handled, and tossed up, to see if I were sound,[1] by some of the crew; and I was now persuaded that I had gotten into a world of bad spirits, and that they were going to kill me.[2] Their complexions too differing so much from ours, their long hair, and the language they spoke, which was very different from any I had ever heard, united to confirm me in this belief. Indeed, such were the horrors of my views and fears at the moment, that, if ten thousand worlds had been my own, I would have freely parted with them all to have exchanged my condition with that of the meanest slave in my own country. When I looked round the ship too, and saw a large furnace of copper boiling, and a multitude of black people of every description chained together, every one of their countenances expressing dejection and sorrow, I no longer doubted of my fate, and, quite over-powered with horror and anguish, I fell motionless on the deck and fainted. When I recovered a little, I found some black people about me who I believed were some of those who brought me on board and had been receiving their pay; they talked to me in order to cheer me, but all in vain. I asked them if we were not to be eaten by those white men with horrible looks, red faces, and long hair.[3] They told me I was not; and one of the crew brought me a small portion of spirituous liquor in a wine glass; but, being afraid of him, I would not take it out of his hand. One of the blacks therefore took it from him and gave it to me, and I took a little down my palate, which, instead of reviving me, as they thought it would, threw me into the greatest consternation at the strange feeling it produced, having never tasted any such liquor before. Soon after this, the blacks who brought me on board went off, and left me abandoned to despair. I now saw myself deprived of all chance of returning to my native country, or even the least glimpse of hope of gaining the shore, which I now considered as friendly: and I even wished for my former slavery in preference to my present situation, which was filled with horrors of every kind, still heightened by my ignorance of what I was to undergo. I was not long suffered to indulge my grief; I was soon put down under the decks, and there I received such a salutation in my nostrils as I had never experienced in my life; so that with the loathsomeness of the stench, and crying together, I became so sick and low that I was not able to eat, nor had I the least desire to taste any thing. I now wished for the last friend, Death, to relieve me; but soon, to my grief, two of the white men offered me eatables; and, on my refusing to eat, one of them held me fast by the hands, and laid me across, I think, the windlass[4] and tied my feet, while the other flogged me severely. I had never experienced any thing of this kind before; and although, not being used to the water, I naturally feared that element the first time I saw it; yet, neverthe-less, could I have got over the nettings,[5] I would have jumped over the side, but I could not; and, besides, the crew used to watch us very closely who were not chained down to the decks, lest we should leap into the water; and I have seen some of these poor African prisoners most severely cut for attempting to do so, and hourly whipped for not eating. This indeed was often the case with myself. In a little time after, amongst the poor chained men, I found some of my own nation, which in a small degree gave ease to my mind. I inquired of these what was to be done with us? they gave me to understand we were to be carried to these white people's country to work for them. I then was a little revived, and thought, if it were no worse than working, my situation was not so des-perate: but still I feared I should be put to death, the white people looked and acted, as I thought, in so savage a manner; for I had never seen among any people such instances of brutal cruelty; and this not only shewn towards us blacks, but also to some of the whites themselves.[6] One white man in particular I saw, when we were permitted to be on deck, flogged so unmercifully with a large rope near the foremast,[7] that he died in consequence of it; and they tossed him over the side as they would have done a brute. This made me fear these people the more; and I expected nothing less than to be treated in the same manner. I could not help expressing my fears and apprehensions to some of my countrymen: I asked them if these people had no country, but lived in this hollow place the ship? they told me they did not, but came from a distant one. "Then," said I, "how comes it in all our country we never heard of them?" They told me, because they lived so very far off. I then asked where were their women? had they any like themselves! I was told they had: "And why," said I, "do we not see them?" they answered, because they were left behind. I asked how the vessel could go? they told me they could not tell; but that there were cloths put upon the masts by the help of the ropes I saw, and then the vessel went on; and the white men had some spell or magic they put in the water when they liked in order to stop the vessel.[8] I was exceedingly amazed at this account, and really thought they were spirits. I therefore wished much to be from amongst them, for I expected they would sacrifice me: but my wishes were vain; for we were so quartered that it was impossible for any of us to make our escape. While we staid on the coast I was mostly on deck; and one day, to my great astonishment, I saw one of these vessels coming in with the sails up. As soon as the whites saw it, they gave a great shout, at which we were amazed; and the more so as the vessel appeared larger by approaching nearer. At last she came to an anchor in my sight, and when

262

the anchor was let go, I and my countrymen who saw it were lost in astonishment to observe the vessel stop; and were now convinced it was done by magic. Soon after this the other ship got her boats[9] out, and they came on board of us, and the people of both ships seemed very glad to see each other. Several of the strangers also shook hands with us black people, and made motions with their hands, signifying, I suppose, we were to go to their country; but we did not understand them. At last, when the ship we were in had got in all her cargo, they made ready with many fearful noises, and we were all put under deck, so that we could not see how they managed the vessel. But this disappointment was the least of my sorrow. The stench of the hold while we were on the coast was so intolerably loathsome, that it was dangerous to remain there for any time, and some of us had been permitted to stay on the deck for the fresh air; but now that the whole ship's cargo were confined together, it became absolutely pestilential. The closeness of the place, and the heat of the climate, added to the number in the ship, which was so crowded that each had scarcely room to turn himself, almost suffocated us. This produced copious perspirations, so that the air soon became unfit for respiration, from a variety of loathsome smells, and brought on a sickness among the slaves, of which many died, thus falling victims to the improvident avarice, as I may call it, of their purchasers. This wretched situation was again aggravated by the galling of the chains, now become insupportable; and the filth of the necessary tubs, into which the children often fell, and were almost suffocated.[10] The shrieks of the women, and the groans of the dying, rendered the whole a scene of horror almost inconceiveable. Happily perhaps for myself I was soon reduced so low here that it was thought necessary to keep me almost always on deck; and from my extreme youth I was not put in fetters. In this situation I expected every hour to share the fate of my companions, some of whom were almost daily brought upon deck at the point of death, which I began to hope would soon put an end to my miseries. Often did I think many of the inhabitants of the deep much more happy than myself; I envied them the freedom they enjoyed, and as often wished I could change my condition for theirs. Every circumstance I met with served only to render my state more painful, and heighten my apprehensions, and my opinion of the cruelty of the whites. One day they had taken a number of fishes; and when they had killed and satisfied themselves with as many as they thought fit, to our astonishment who were on the deck, rather than give any of them to us to eat, as we expected, they tossed the remaining fish into the sea again, although we begged and prayed for some as well as we could, but in vain; and some of my countrymen, being pressed by hunger, took an opportunity, when they thought no one saw them, of trying to get a little privately; but they were discovered, and the attempt procured them some very severe floggings.

One day, when we had a smooth sea, and moderate wind, two of my wearied countrymen, who were chained together (I was near them at the time), preferring death to such a life of misery, somehow made through the nettings, and jumped into the sea: immediately another quite dejected fellow, who, on account of his illness, was suffered to be out of irons, also followed their example; and I believe many more would very soon have done the same, if they had not been prevented by the ship's crew, who were instantly alarmed. Those of us that were the most active were, in a moment, put down under the deck; and there was such a noise and confusion amongst the people of the ship as I never heard before, to stop her, and get the boat out to go after the slaves. However, two of the wretches were drowned, but they got the other, and afterwards flogged him unmercifully, for thus attempting to prefer death to slavery. In this manner we continued to undergo more hardships than I can now relate; hardships which are inseparable from this accursed trade.—Many a time we were near suffocation, from the want of fresh air, which we were often without for whole days together. This, and the stench of the necessary tubs, carried off many. During our passage I first saw flying fishes, which surprised me very much: they used frequently to fly across the ship, and many of them fell on the deck. I also now first saw the use of the quadrant.[11] I had often with astonishment seen the mariners make observations with it, and I could not think what it meant. They at last took notice of my surprise; and one of them, willing to increase it, as well as to gratify my curiosity, made me one day look through it. The clouds appeared to me to be land, which disappeared as they passed along. This heightened my wonder: and I was now more persuaded than ever that I was in another world, and that every thing about me was magic. At last we came in sight of the island of Barbadoes, at which the whites on board gave a great shout, and made many signs of joy to us. We did not know what to think of this; but as the vessel drew nearer we plainly saw the harbour, and other ships of different kinds and sizes: and we soon anchored amongst them off Bridge Town. Many merchants and planters now came on board, though it was in the evening. They put us in separate parcels,[12] and examined us attentively. They also made us jump,[13] and pointed to the land, signifying we were to go there. We thought by this we should be eaten by these ugly men, as they appeared to us; and, when soon after we were all put down under the deck again, there was much dread and trembling among us, and nothing but bitter cries to be heard all the night from these apprehensions, insomuch that at last the white people got some old slaves from the land to pacify us. They told us we were not to be eaten, but to work, and were soon to go on land, where we should see many of our country people. This report eased us much; and sure enough, soon after we were landed, there came to us Africans of all languages. We were conducted immediately to the merchant's yard, where we were all pent up together like so many sheep in a fold, without regard to sex or age. As every object was new to me, every thing I saw filled me with surprise. What struck me first was, that the houses were built with bricks, in stories,[14] and in every other respect different from those in I have seen in Africa:[15] but I was still more astonished on seeing people on horseback. I did not know what this could mean; and indeed I thought these people were full of nothing but magical arts. While I was in this astonishment, one of my fellow prisoners spoke to a countryman of his about the horses, who said they were the same kind they had in their country. I understood them, though they were from a distant part of Africa, and I thought it odd I had not seen any horses there; but afterwards, when I came to converse with different Africans, I found they had many horses amongst them, and much larger than those I then saw. We were not many days in the merchant's custody before we were sold after their usual manner, which is this:—On a signal given, (as the beat of a drum), the buyers rush at once into the yard where the slaves are confined, and make choice of that parcel they like best.[16] The noise and clamour with which this is attended, and the eagerness visible in the countenances of the buyers, serve not a little to increase the apprehensions of the terrified Africans, who may well be supposed to consider them as the ministers of that destruction to which they think themselves devoted.[17] In this manner, without scruple, are relations and friends separated, most of them never to see each other again. I remember in the vessel in which I was brought over, in the men's apartment, there were several brothers, who, in the sale, were sold in different lots; and it was very moving on this occasion to see and hear their cries at parting. O, ye nominal Christians! might not an African ask you, learned you this from your God? who says unto you, Do unto all men as you would men should do unto you? Is it not enough that we are torn from our country and friends to toil for your luxury and lust of gain? Must every tender feeling be likewise sacrificed to your avarice? Are the dearest friends and relations, now rendered more dear by their separation from their kindred, still to be parted from each other, and thus prevented from cheering the gloom of slavery with the small comfort of being together and mingling their sufferings and sorrows? Why are parents to lose their children, brothers their sisters, or husbands their wives? Surely this is a new refinement in cruelty, which, while it has no advantage to atone for it, thus aggravates distress, and adds fresh horrors even to the wretchedness of slavery.

EXPLANATORY NOTES

1. Sound: healthy.
2. These two sentences were revised twice: the 1st ed. reads ". . . into terror when I was carried on board. I was immediately . . ."; the 3rd ed. reads ". . . into terror, which I am yet at a loss to describe; and the then feelings of my mind when carried on board. I was immediately . . ."; the final revision first appears in the 5th ed.
3. Long hair: only ed. 1 reads "loose hair."
4. Windlass: a winch, or crank, used to wind a heavy rope or chain to lift a weight.
5. Nettings: "a sort of fence, formed of an assemblage of ropes, fastened across each other" (William Falconer (1732–1769), *An Universal Dictionary of the Marine* [London, 1784; first published in 1769], hereafter cited in the notes as Falconer). These nettings were placed along the sides of the ship to form a caged enclosure to prevent the slaves from jumping overboard to try to escape or commit suicide.
6. The abolitionists frequently argued that the slave trade brutalized the enslavers as well as the enslaved. The tyrannical captain became almost a stock figure in the literature. The apologists for slavery argued that the trade served as a nursery for seamen. Evidence supports the abolitionists' claims that the trade was even more lethal, on an average percentage basis, for the crews than for the slaves. The Privy Council in 1789 estimated that the average mortality rate for slaves during the middle passage was 12.5 percent. Modern estimates of the mortality rate of 15 percent for slaves mean that of the approximately 10 million Africans taken to the Americas between 1600 and 1900, about 1.5 million died at sea. More than twice that number of African slaves died during the same period either while still in Africa or on their way to the Orient. The mortality rate of the much smaller number of marine slavers is estimated at about 20 percent. For both slaves and enslavers, the death rate varied with length of voyage, time, and age.
7. Foremast: the term *ship* was "particularly applied to a vessel furnished with three masts, each of which is composed of a lower mast, top mast, and top-gallant mast, with the usual machinery thereto belonging. The mast . . . placed at the middle of the ship's length, is called the main-mast, . . . that which is placed in the fore-part, the fore-mast, . . . and that which is towards the stem [the rear] is termed the mizen-mast" (Falconer).
8. Spell or magic: the anchor.

9. Boat: "a small open vessel, conducted on the water by rowing or sailing" (Falconer).
10. Necessary tubs: latrines.
11. Quadrant: "an instrument used to take the altitude of the sun or stars at sea, in order to determine the latitude of the place; or the sun's azimuth, so as to ascertain the magnetical variation" (Falconer).
12. Parcels: groups.
13. Made us jump: as a sign of health and strength.
14. The 1st ed. reads "... the houses were built with stories ..."; the 2nd ed. reads "... the houses were built with bricks and stories ..."; the final revision first appears in the 5th ed.
15. From ... Africa: only ed. 1 reads "from those in Africa."
16. Equiano refers to what was known as the *scramble*, described from the perspective of an observer by Alexander Falconbridge (d. 1792) in *An Account of the Slave Trade on the Coast of Africa* (London, 1788):

> On a day appointed, the negroes were landed, and placed altogether in a large yard, belonging to the merchants to whom the ship was consigned. As soon as the hour agreed on arrived, the doors of the yard were suddenly thrown open, and in rushed a considerable number of purchasers, with all the ferocity of brutes. Some instantly seized such of the negroes as they could conveniently lay hold of with their hands. Others, being prepared with several handkerchiefs tied together, encircled with these as many as they were able. While others, by means of a rope, effected the same purpose. It is scarcely possible to describe the confusion of which this mode of selling is productive. It likewise causes much animosity among the purchasers, who, not unfrequently upon these occasions, fall out and quarrel with each other. The poor astonished negroes were so much terrified by these proceedings, that several of them, through fear, climbed over the walls of the court yard, and ran wild about the town; but were soon hunted down and retaken (34).

Falconbridge's *Account* was written at the behest of the Society for Effecting the Abolition of the Slave Trade, which printed and distributed six thousand copies of it.
17. Devoted: doomed.

ADAM SMITH

The Invisible Hand of the Free Market

———————

Adam Smith is perhaps the most famous and influential economist in European history. A Scot, he was born in Kirkcaldy in 1723 and attended Glasgow University before entering Oxford University in 1740. He returned to Glasgow in 1751, this time as a professor. Smith became a celebrated lecturer, first in logic and later in moral philosophy. Indeed, it was as a moral philosopher that he achieved his earliest fame. His Theory of Moral Sentiments *appeared in 1759 and went through six editions before Smith's death. The work offered a sophisticated treatment of human ethical and social sensibilities, a subject that interested many Enlightenment thinkers. In 1764 Smith resigned his university position and became the tutor to the Duke of Buccleuch. Together they toured France. Already acquainted with important British philosophers such as David Hume, in France Smith met a group of French economic theorists known as the "Physiocrats." Under their influence, Smith began work on* The Wealth of Nations, *today recognized as the first systematic explanation of classical economics. Its theories dominated the nineteenth century and are still widely accepted. In 1778 Smith accepted the post of Commissioner of Customs and returned to Scotland, where he lived a quiet life. He was elected Lord Rector of Glasgow University in 1787. Adam Smith died in 1790 at the age of sixty-seven.*

The Wealth of Nations *(1776) is a virtual manifesto for Britain's emerging manufacturing age. Building on Smith's interests in human sociability and material progress, it brilliantly formulated many fundamentals of classic capitalist economics. The most influential portions of* The Wealth of Nations *explained the fundamental role of labor in determining economic value, and explained the mechanisms by which markets set prices. Smith generally favored the free movement of markets, and rebuked European states for trying to control them. His teachings were thus used to justify policies such as free trade and an end to trade guilds. Adam Smith's faith in the "invisible hand" of the markets has remained a standard feature of* laissez-faire *economics.*

———————

"The Invisible Hand of the Free Market," from *The Wealth of Nations, Books I–III*, by Adam Smith, edited by Andrew Skinner, copyright © 1970 by Andrew Skinner, 157–161.

CHAPTER VII
OF THE NATURAL AND MARKET PRICE OF
COMMODITIES

There is in every society or neighbourhood an ordinary or average rate both of wages and profit in every different employment of labour and stock. This rate is naturally regulated, as I shall show hereafter, partly by the general circumstances of the society, their riches or poverty, their advancing, stationary, or declining condition; and partly by the particular nature of each employment.

There is likewise in every society or neighbourhood an ordinary or average rate of rent, which is regulated too, as I shall show hereafter, partly by the general circumstances of the society or neighbourhood in which the land is situated, and partly by the natural or improved fertility of the land.

These ordinary or average rates may be called the natural rates of wages, profit, and rent, at the time and place in which they commonly prevail.

When the price of any commodity is neither more nor less than what is sufficient to pay the rent of the land, the wages of the labour, and the profits of the stock employed in raising, preparing, and bringing it to market, according to their natural rates, the commodity is then sold for what may be called its natural price.

The commodity is then sold precisely for what it is worth, or for what it really costs the person who brings it to market; for though in common language what is called the prime cost of any commodity does not comprehend the profit of the person who is to sell it again, yet if he sell it at a price which does not allow him the ordinary rate of profit in his neighbourhood, he is evidently a loser by the trade; since by employing his stock in some other way he might have made that profit. His profit, besides, is his revenue, the proper fund of his subsistence. As, while he is preparing and bringing the goods to market, he advances to his workmen their wages, or their subsistence; so he advances to himself, in the same manner, his own subsistence, which is generally suitable to the profit which he may reasonably expect from the sale of his goods. Unless they yield him this profit, therefore, they do not repay him what they may very properly be said to have really cost him.

Though the price, therefore, which leaves him this profit is not always the lowest at which a dealer may sometimes sell his goods, it is the lowest at which he is likely to sell them for any considerable time; at least where there is perfect liberty, or where he may change his trade as often as he pleases.

The actual price at which any commodity is commonly sold is called its market price. It may either be above, or below, or exactly the same with its natural price.

The market price of every particular commodity is regulated by the proportion between the quantity which is actually brought to market, and the demand of those who are willing to pay the natural price of the commodity, or the whole value of the rent, labour, and profit, which must be paid in order to bring it thither. Such people may be called the effectual demanders, and their demand the effectual demand; since it may be sufficient to effectuate the bringing of the commodity to market. It is different from the absolute demand. A very poor man may be said in some sense to have a demand for a coach and six; he might like to have it; but his demand is not an effectual demand, as the commodity can never be brought to market in order to satisfy it.

When the quantity of any commodity which is brought to market falls short of the effectual demand, all those who are willing to pay the whole value of the rent, wages, and profit, which must be paid in order to bring it thither, cannot be supplied with the quantity which they want. Rather than want it altogether, some of them will be willing to give more. A competition will immediately begin among them, and the market price will rise more or less above the natural price, according as either the greatness of the deficiency, or the wealth and wanton luxury of the competitors, happen to animate more or less the eagerness of the competition. Among competitors of equal wealth and luxury the same deficiency will generally occasion a more or less eager competition, according as the acquisition of the commodity happens to be of more or less importance to them. Hence the exorbitant price of the necessaries of life during the blockade of a town or in a famine.

When the quantity brought to market exceeds the effectual demand, it cannot be all sold to those who are willing to pay the whole value of the rent, wages, and profit, which must be paid in order to bring it thither. Some part must be sold to those who are willing to pay less, and the low price which they give for it must reduce the price of the whole. The market price will sink more or less below the natural price, according as the greatness of the excess increases more or less the competition of the sellers, or according as it happens to be more or less important to them to get immediately rid of the commodity. The same excess in the importation of perishable, will occasion a much greater competition than in that of durable commodities; in the importation of oranges, for example, than in that of old iron.

When the quantity brought to market is just sufficient to supply the effectual demand, and no more, the market price naturally comes to be either exactly, or as nearly as can be judged of, the same with the natural price. The whole quantity upon hand can be disposed of for this price, and cannot be disposed of for more. The competition of the different dealers obliges them all to accept of this price, but does not oblige them to accept of less.

The quantity of every commodity brought to market naturally suits itself to the effectual demand. It is the interest of all those who employ their land, labour, or stock, in bringing any commodity to market, that the quantity never should exceed the effectual demand; and it is the interest of all other people that it never should fall short of that demand.

If at any time it exceeds the effectual demand, some of the component parts of its price must be paid below their natural rate. If it is rent, the interest of the landlords will immediately prompt them to withdraw a part of their land; and if it is wages or profit, the interest of the labourers in the one case, and of their employers in the other, will prompt them to withdraw a part of their labour or stock from this employment. The quantity brought to market will soon be no more than sufficient to supply the effectual demand. All the different parts of its price will rise to their natural rate, and the whole price to its natural price.

If, on the contrary, the quantity brought to market should at any time fall short of the effectual demand, some of the component parts of its price must rise above their natural rate. If it is rent, the interest of all other landlords will naturally prompt them to prepare more land for the raising of this commodity; if it is wages or profit, the interest of all other labourers and dealers will soon prompt them to employ more labour and stock in preparing and bringing it to market. The quantity brought thither will soon be sufficient to supply the effectual demand. All the different parts of its price will soon sink to their natural rate, and the whole price to its natural price.

The natural price, therefore, is, as it were, the central price, to which the prices of all commodities are continually gravitating. Different accidents may sometimes keep them suspended a good deal above it, and sometimes force them down even somewhat below it. But whatever may be the obstacles which hinder them from settling in this centre of repose and continuance, they are constantly tending towards it.

. . .

JEAN-JACQUES ROUSSEAU

Freedom in Chains

Born to a Genevan watchmaker in 1712, Jean-Jacques Rousseau became a thinker and author of exceptional power and influence. His impact on everything from revolutionary politics to modern psychology, German idealist philosophy, romantic poetry, the novel, and academic disciplines that analyze culture has given him a remarkable presence in the history of modernity—and in the development of criticisms that persistently accompany it. Rousseau's prodigious writings as a philosopher, novelist, apostle of "natural religion," and autobiographer did not begin until he was nearly forty years old. In 1750 he published the first of his well-known essays, the Discourse on the Arts and Sciences, *in which he argued that Enlightenment—not in spite but because of its aesthetic curiosity and technological advances—would not be the progenitor of universal human fulfillment, but the harbinger of general moral decline and spiritual apathy. Similarly daring arguments found eloquent if often protean expression in the* Discourse on Inequality *(1755), the epistolary novel* La Nouvelle Héloïse *(1760), the novelistic treatise of philosophy known as* Emile or On Education *(1762), the* Social Contract *(1762), and the posthumously published autobiographical writings including the* Confessions, Rousseau Judge of Jean-Jacques *and the* Reveries of the Solitary Walker. *Rousseau's life was as difficult to categorize as his books. The writer of innumerable panegyrics to familial harmony abandoned his five children to a foundling home; the stern advocate of republican virtue and unwavering obedience was repudiated by his native city of Geneva, and he repudiated it in turn; and the sometime critic of imaginative indulgence himself beguiled his readers with the charms of his daydreams. Rousseau died in 1778.*

The Social Contract *is one of the most influential and least understood works in modern political philosophy. Maddeningly elusive in its definition of terms and argumentative structure, it has been considered a founding document of both modern democracy and modern totalitarianism. The scope and depth of its influence on revolutionary politics also has been hotly debated, from the days of the French Revolution to the present. In this passage, Rousseau separated is own arguments from what he believed to be the pernicious assumptions of modern political philosophers like Grotius, and announced that a distinctively Rousseauian freedom is a necessary imperative for all human beings.*

BOOK I

My purpose is to consider if, in political society, there can be any legitimate and sure principle of government, taking men as they are and laws as they might be. In this inquiry I shall try always to bring together what right permits with what interest prescribes so that justice and utility are in no way divided.

I start without seeking to prove the importance of my subject. I may be asked whether I am a prince or a legislator that I should be writing about politics. I answer no: and indeed that that is my reason for doing so. If I were a prince or a legislator I should not waste my time saying what ought to be done; I should do it or keep silent.

Born as I was the citizen of a free state and a member of its sovereign body, the very right to vote imposes on me the duty to instruct myself in public affairs, however little influence my voice may have in them. And whenever I reflect upon governments, I am happy to find that my studies always give me fresh reasons for admiring that of my own country.

CHAPTER 1
THE SUBJECT OF BOOK I

Man was born free, and he is everywhere in chains. Those who think themselves the masters of others are indeed greater slaves than they. How did this transformation come about? I do not know. How can it be made legitimate? That question I believe I can answer.

If I were to consider only force and the effects of force, I should say: 'So long as a people is constrained to obey, and obeys, it does well; but as soon as it can shake off the yoke, and shakes it off, it does better; for since it regains its freedom by the same right as that which removed it, a people is either justified in taking back its freedom, or there is no justifying those who took it away.' But the social order is a sacred right which serves as a basis for all other rights. And as it is not a natural right, it must be one founded on covenants. The problem is to determine what those covenants are. But before we pass on to that question, I must substantiate what I have so far said.

CHAPTER 2
THE FIRST SOCIETIES

The oldest of all societies, and the only natural one, is that of the family; yet children remain tied to their father by nature only so long as they need him for their preservation. As soon as this need ends, the natural bond is dissolved. Once the children are freed from the obedience they owe their father, and the father is freed from his responsibilities towards them, both parties equally regain their independence. If they continue to remain united, it is no longer nature, but their own choice, which unites them; and the family as such is kept in being only by agreement.

This common liberty is a consequence of man's nature. Man's first law is to watch over his own preservation; his first care he owes to himself, and as soon as he reaches the age of reason, he becomes the only judge of the best means to preserve himself; he becomes his own master.

The family may therefore perhaps be seen as the first model of political societies: the head of the state bears the image of the father, the people the image of his children, and all, being born free and equal, surrender their freedom only when they see advantage in doing so. The only difference is that in the family, a father's love for his children repays him for the care he bestows on them, while in the state, where the ruler can have no such feeling for his people, the pleasure of commanding must take the place of love.

Grotius denies that all human government is established for the benefit of the governed, and he cites the example of slavery. His characteristic method of reasoning is always to offer fact as a proof of right.[1] It is possible to imagine a more logical method, but not one more favourable to tyrants.

According to Grotius, therefore, it is doubtful whether humanity belongs to a hundred men, or whether these hundred men belong to humanity, though he seems throughout his book to lean to the first of these views, which is also that of Hobbes. These authors show us the human race divided into herds of cattle, each with a master who preserves it only in order to devour its members.

Just as a shepherd possesses a nature superior to that of his flock, so do those shepherds of men, their rulers, have a nature superior to that of their people. Or so, we are told by Philo, the Emperor Caligula argued, concluding, reasonably enough on this same analogy, that kings were gods or alternatively that the people were animals.

The reasoning of Caligula coincides with that of Hobbes and Grotius. Indeed Aristotle, before any of them, said that men were not at all equal by nature, since some were born for slavery and others born to be masters.

Aristotle was right; but he mistook the effect for the cause. Anyone born in slavery is born for slavery—nothing is more certain. Slaves, in their bondage, lose everything, even the desire to be free. They love their servitude even as the companions of Ulysses loved their life as brutes.[2] But if there are slaves by nature, it is only because there has been slavery against nature. Force made the first slaves; and their cowardice perpetuates their slavery.

I have said nothing of the King Adam or of the Emperor Noah, father of the three great monarchs who shared out the universe between them, like the children of Saturn, with whom some authors have identified them. I hope my readers will be grateful for this moderation, for since I am directly descended from one of those princes, and perhaps in the eldest line, how do I know that if the deeds were checked, I might not find myself the legitimate king of the human race? However that may be, there is no gainsaying that Adam was the king of the world, as was Robinson Crusoe of his island, precisely because he was the sole inhabitant; and the great advantage of such an empire was that the monarch, secure upon his throne, had no occasion to fear rebellions, wars or conspirators.

CHAPTER 3
THE RIGHT OF THE STRONGEST

The strongest man is never strong enough to be master all the time, unless he transforms force into right and obedience into duty. Hence 'the right of the strongest'—a 'right' that sounds like something intended ironically, but is actually laid down as a principle. But shall we never have this phrase explained? Force is a physical power; I do not see how its effects could produce morality. To yield to force is an act of necessity, not of will; it is at best an act of prudence. In what sense can it be a moral duty?

Let us grant, for a moment, that this so-called right exists. I suggest it can only produce a tissue of bewildering nonsense; for once might is made to be right, cause and effect are reversed, and every force which overcomes another force inherits the right which belonged to the vanquished. As soon as man can disobey with impunity, his disobedience becomes legitimate; and as the strongest is always right, the only problem is how to become the strongest. But what can be the validity of a right which perishes with the force on which it rests? If force compels obedience, there is no need to invoke a duty to obey, and if force ceases to compel obedience, there is no longer any obligation. Thus the word 'right' adds nothing to what is said by 'force'; it is meaningless.

'Obey those in power.' If this means 'yield to force' the precept is sound, but superfluous; it will never, I suggest, be violated. All power comes from God, I agree; but so does every disease, and no one forbids us to summon a physician. If I am held up by a robber at the edge of a wood, force compels me to hand over my purse. But if I could somehow contrive to keep the purse from him, would I still be obliged in conscience to surrender it? After all, the pistol in the robber's hand is undoubtedly a *power*.

Surely it must be admitted, then, that might does not make right, and that the duty of obedience is owed only to legitimate powers. Thus we are constantly led back to my original question.

CHAPTER 4
SLAVERY

Since no man has any natural authority over his fellows, and since force alone bestows no right, all legitimate authority among men must be based on covenants.

Grotius says: 'If an individual can alienate his freedom and become the slave of a master, why may not a whole people alienate its freedom and become the subject of a king?' In this remark there are several ambiguous words which call for explanation; but let us confine ourselves to one—to 'alienate'. To alienate is to give or sell. A man who becomes the slave of another does not give himself, he sells himself in return for at least a subsistence. But in return for what could a whole people be said to sell itself? A king, far from nourishing his subjects, draws his nourishment from them; and kings, according to Rabelais, need more than a little nourishment. Do subjects, then, give their persons to the king on condition that he will accept their property as well? If so, I fail to see what they have left to preserve.

It will be said that a despot gives his subjects the assurance of civil tranquillity. Very well, but what does it profit them, if those wars against other powers which result from a despot's ambition, if his insatiable greed, and the oppressive demands of his administration, cause more desolation than civil strife would cause? What do the people gain if their very condition of civil tranquillity is one of their hardships? There is peace in dungeons, but is that enough to make dungeons desirable? The Greeks lived in peace in the cave of Cyclops awaiting their turn to be devoured.

To speak of a man giving himself in return for nothing is to speak of what is absurd, unthinkable; such an action would be illegitimate, void, if only because no one who did it could be in his right mind. To say the same of a whole people is to conjure up a nation of lunatics; and right cannot rest on madness.

Even if each individual could alienate himself, he cannot alienate his children. For they are born men; they are born free; their liberty belongs to them; no one but they themselves has the right to dispose of it. Before they reach the years of discretion, their father may, in their name, make certain rules for their protection and their welfare, but he cannot give away their liberty irrevocably and unconditionally, for such a gift would be contrary to the ends of nature and an abuse of paternal right. Hence, an arbitrary government would be legitimate only if every new generation were able to accept or reject it, and in that case the government would cease to be arbitrary.

To renounce freedom is to renounce one's humanity, one's rights as a man and equally one's duties. There is no possible *quid pro quo* for one who renounces everything; indeed such renunciation is contrary to man's very nature; for if you take away all freedom of the will, you strip a man's actions of all moral significance. Finally, any covenant which stipulated absolute dominion for one party and absolute obedience for the other would be illogical and nugatory. Is it not evident that he who is entitled to demand everything owes nothing? And does not the single fact of there being no reciprocity, no mutual obligation, nullify the act? For what right can my slave have against me? If everything he has belongs to me, his right is *my* right, and it would be nonsense to speak of my having a right *against* myself.

Grotius and the rest claim to find in war another justification for the so-called right of slavery. They argue that the victor's having the right to kill the vanquished implies that the vanquished has the right to purchase his life at the expense of his liberty—a bargain thought to be the more legitimate because it is advantageous to both parties.

But it is clear that this so-called right to kill the vanquished cannot be derived from the state of war. For this reason alone, that men living in their primitive condition of independence have no intercourse regular enough to constitute either a state of peace or a state of war; and men are not naturally enemies. It is conflicts over things, not quarrels between men which constitute war, and the state of war cannot arise from mere personal relations, but only from property relations. Private wars between one man and another can exist neither in a state of nature, where there is no fixed property, nor in society, where everything is under the authority of law.

Private fights, duels, skirmishes, do not constitute any kind of state; and as for the private wars that were permitted by the ordinances of

Louis IX, King of France, and suspended by the Peace of God, these were no more than an abuse of feudal government, an irrational system if there ever was one, and contrary both to natural justice and to all sound polity.

War, then, is not a relation between men, but between states; in war individuals are enemies wholly by chance, not as men, not even as citizens,[3] but only as soldiers; not as members of their country, but only as its defenders. In a word, a state can have as an enemy only another state, not men, because there can be no real relation between things possessing different intrinsic natures.

This principle conforms to the established rules of all times and to the constant practice of every political society. Declarations of war are warnings not so much to governments as to their subjects. The foreigner—whether he is a king, a private person or a whole people—who robs, kills or detains the subjects of another prince without first declaring war against that prince, is not an enemy but a brigand. Even in the midst of war, a just prince, seizing what he can of public property in the enemy's territory, nevertheless respects the persons and possessions of private individuals; he respects the principles on which his own rights are based. Since the aim of war is to subdue a hostile state, a combatant has the right to kill the defenders of that state while they are armed; but as soon as they lay down their arms and surrender, they cease to be either enemies or instruments of the enemy; they become simply men once more, and no one has any longer the right to take their lives. It is sometimes possible to destroy a state without killing a single one of its members, and war gives no right to inflict any more destruction than is necessary for victory. These principles were not invented by Grotius, nor are they founded on the authority of the poets; they are derived from the nature of things; they are based on reason.

The right of conquest has no other foundation than the law of the strongest. And if war gives the conqueror no right to massacre a conquered people, no such right can be invoked to justify their enslavement. Men have the right to kill their enemies only when they cannot enslave them, so the right of enslaving cannot be derived from the right to kill. It would therefore be an iniquitous barter to make the vanquished purchase with their liberty the lives over which the victor has no legitimate claim. An argument basing the right over life and death on the right to enslave, and the right to enslave on the right over life and death, is an argument trapped in a vicious circle.

Even if we assumed that this terrible right of massacre did exist, then slaves of war, or a conquered people, would be under no obligation to obey their master any further than they were forced to do so. By taking an equivalent of his victim's life, the victor shows him no favour; instead of destroying him unprofitably, he destroys him by exploiting him. Hence, far from the victor having acquired some further authority besides that of force over the vanquished, the state of war between them continues; their mutual relation is the effect of war, and the continuation of the rights of war implies that there has been no treaty of peace. An agreement has assuredly been made, but that agreement, far from ending the state of war, presupposes its continuation.

Thus, however we look at the question, the 'right' of slavery is seen to be void; void, not only because it cannot be justified, but also because it is nonsensical, because it has no meaning. The words 'slavery' and 'right' are contradictory, they cancel each other out. Whether as between one man and another, or between one man and a whole people, it would always be absurd to say: 'I hereby make a covenant with you which is wholly at your expense and wholly to my advantage; I will respect it so long as I please and you shall respect it so long as I wish.'

CHAPTER 5
THAT WE MUST ALWAYS GO BACK TO AN ORIGINAL COVENANT

Even if I were to concede all that I have so far refuted, the champions of despotism would be no better off. There will always be a great difference between subduing a multitude and ruling a society. If one man successively enslaved many separate individuals, no matter how numerous, he and they would never bear the aspect of anything but a master and his slaves, not at all that of a people and their ruler; an aggregation, perhaps, but certainly not an association, for they would neither have a common good nor be a body politic. Even if such a man were to enslave half the world, he would remain a private individual, and his interest, always distinct from that of the others, would never be more than a personal interest. When he died, the empire he left would be scattered for lack of any bond of union, even as an oak crumbles and falls into a heap of ashes when fire has consumed it.

'A people,' says Grotius, 'may give itself to a king.' Therefore, according to Grotius a people is a *people* even before the gift to the king is made. The gift itself is a civil act; it presupposes public deliberation. Hence, before considering the act by which a people submits to a king, we ought to scrutinize the act by which people become *a* people, for that act, being necessarily antecedent to the other, is the real foundation of society.

In fact, if there were no earlier agreement, how, unless the election were unanimous, could there be any obligation on the minority to accept the decision of the majority? What right have the hundred who want to have a master to vote on behalf of the ten who do not? The law of majority-voting itself rests on an agreement, and implies that there has been on at least one occasion unanimity

EXPLANATORY NOTES

1. 'Learned researches on public law are often only the history of ancient abuses, and one is misled when one gives oneself the trouble of studying them too closely.' *Traité manuscrit des intérêts de la France avec ses voisins* par M. L. M. d'A. This is exactly what Grotius does. [Rousseau's quotation is from the Marquis d'Argenson. *Trans.*]
2. See a short treatise of Plutarch entitled: *That Animals use Reason.*
3. The Romans, who understood and respected the rights of war better than any other nation, carried their scruples on this subject so far that a citizen was forbidden to volunteer without engaging himself expressly against the enemy and against an enemy specifically named. When the legion in which the younger Cato fought his first campaign under Popilius was re-formed, the elder Cato wrote to Popilius saying that if he wished his son to continue to serve under him, he should administer a fresh military oath, on the grounds that his son's first oath was annulled, and that he could no longer bear arms against the enemy. Cato also wrote to his son warning him not to go into battle without first taking the oath.

   I realize that the siege of Clusium and other incidents from Roman history may be quoted against me, but I am citing laws and customs. No nation has broken its own laws less frequently than the Romans, and no nation has ever had such excellent laws. [Footnote added in the Edition of 1782.]

THE CONSTITUTION COMMITTEE OF THE NATIONAL CONSTITUENT ASSEMBLY

Declaration of the Rights of Man and the Citizen

The founding document of the French Revolution, the Declaration of the Rights of Man and the Citizen was the product of deliberations in the National Assembly, the legislative body that emerged from a chaotic series of developments in the spring and summer of 1789. In May of that year, amid political and economic crises, the Estates-General convened in France for the first time since 1614. From the beginning, members of the Third Estate (the commoners) demanded that all three Estates meet as a unicameral body in which votes would be counted by head. Their refusal to meet as a separate body brought the Estates-General to a standstill. On June 17, the Third Estate voted to name itself the National Assembly. Three days later, denied access to their meeting place, members of the National Assembly gathered at a nearby tennis court and declared their intention of remaining in session until they had written a national constitution. Although he initially refused to recognize the decrees of the National Assembly, a fearful Louis XVI ordered the First and Second Estates to join the unicameral assembly on June 27. During the tumultuous summer of 1789, which was marked by popular revolt and demonstrations, the National Assembly began work on its constitution. On August 26, it produced the Declaration of the Rights of Man and the Citizen. Drawing on a wide range of sources in political theory and targeting specific abuses in French society, the Declaration provided a forceful statement of the National Assembly's political agenda and outlined its basic principles. It served as a preamble to the constitution promulgated in 1791.

The representatives of the French people organized in National Assembly, considering that ignorance, forgetfulness or contempt of the rights of man, are the sole causes of the public miseries and of the corruption of governments, have resolved to set forth in a solemn declaration the natural, inalienable, and sacred rights of man, in order that this declaration, being ever present to all the members of the social body, may unceasingly remind them of their rights and their duties: in order that the acts of the legislative power and those of the executive power may be each moment compared with the aim of every political institution and thereby may be more respected; and in order that the demands of the citizens, grounded henceforth upon simple and incontestable principles, may always take the direction of maintaining the constitution and the welfare of all.

In consequence the National Assembly recognizes and declares, in the presence and under the auspices of the Supreme Being, the following rights of man and citizen.

1. Men are born and remain free and equal in rights. Social distinctions can be based only upon public utility.

2. The aim of every political association is the preservation of the natural and imprescriptible rights of man. These rights are liberty, property, security, and resistance to oppression.

3. The source of all sovereignty is essentially in the nation; no body, no individual can exercise authority that does not proceed from it in plain terms.

4. Liberty consists in the power to do anything that does not injure others; accordingly, the exercise of the natural rights of each man has no limits except those that secure to the other members of society the enjoyment of these same rights. These limits can be determined only by law.

5. The law has the right to forbid only such actions as are injurious to society. Nothing can be forbidden that is not interdicted by the law, and no one can be constrained to do that which it does not order.

6. Law is the expression of the general will. All citizens have the right to take part personally, or by their representatives, in its formation. It must be the same for all, whether it protects or punishes. all citizens being equal in its eyes, are equally eligible to all public dignities, places, and employments, according to their capacities, and without other distinction than that of their virtues and their talents.

7. No man can be accused, arrested, or detained, except in the cases determined by the law and according to the forms that it has prescribed. Those who procure, expedite, execute, or cause to be executed arbitrary orders ought to be punished: but every citizen summoned or seized in virtue of the law ought to render instant obedience; he makes himself guilty by resistance.

8. The law ought to establish only penalties that are strictly and obviously necessary, and no one can be punished except in virtue of a law established and promulgated prior to the offence and legally applied.

9. Every man being presumed innocent until he has been pronounced guilty, if it is thought indispensable to arrest him, all severity that may not be necessary to secure his person ought to be strictly suppressed by law.

10. No one should be disturbed on account of his opinions, even religious, provided their manifestation does not derange the public order established by law.

11. The free communication of ideas and opinions is one of the most precious of the rights of man; every citizen then can freely speak, write, and print, subject to responsibility for the abuse of this freedom in the cases determined by law.

12. The guarantee of the rights of man and citizen requires a public force; this force then is instituted for the advantage of all and not for the personal benefit of those to whom it is entrusted.

13. For the maintenance of the public force and for the expenses of administration a general tax is indispensable; it ought to be equally apportioned among all the citizens according to their means.

14. All the citizens have the right to ascertain, by themselves or by their representatives, the necessity of the public tax, to consent to it freely, to follow the employment of it, and to determine the quota, the assessment, the collection, and the duration of it.

15. Society has the right to call for an account of his administration from every public agent.

16. Any society in which the guarantee of the rights is not secured, or the separation of powers not determined, has no constitution at all.

17. Property being a sacred and inviolable right, no one can be deprived of it, unless a legally established public necessity evidently demands it, under the condition of a just and prior indemnity.

OLYMPE DE GOUGES

Declaration of Women's Rights and Their Omission from the Principles of the French Revolution

Olympe de Gouges (1748?–1793) is best known for her defense of women's rights during the French Revolution and especially her authorship of the Declaration of the Rights of Woman and Citizen *(1791), which highlighted the omission of women in the Revolution's central document* Declaration of the Rights of Man and Citizen *(1789). De Gouges's* Declaration *not only pointed out that the central revolutionary statement of principles forgot women, but also pointed to specific legal concerns that women continued to face. De Gouges focused not only on issues of gender. She also wrote prose works and a play that illuminated the mistreatment of slaves and colored people in general, based on European racist attitudes toward the capability of colored people to hold responsible roles as members of society. Her play,* Black Slavery, or The Happy Shipwreck, *was performed at the* Comédie-Française, *but with opposition to its condemnation of slavery and French racism—its performance was both brief and controversial. De Gouges's moderate political stance as well as her outspoken commitment to feminism and women's political rights led to her death. She was executed in 1793 for being too close to the Girondins (a moderate political faction) while the Jacobins were in power and promoting the execution of Louis XVI and Marie Antoinette toward the success of the Revolution. De Gouges had dedicated her* Declaration *to Marie Antoinette, asking the Queen to concern herself with the hardships of women. On October 29, 1793—just before de Gouges was executed—the National Assembly passed the following resolution effectively ending women's organized political actions: "The clubs and popular societies of women, under whatever denomination, are prohibited."*

This declaration highlighted the omission of women from the general goals of the French Revolution by using the language of the Declaration of the Rights of Man and Citizen *as the basis for its critique. It served as a model for* The Declaration of Sentiments, *from the 1848 Seneca Falls women's rights meeting, which used the language of the* Declaration of Independence *to reveal a similar omission.*

DECLARATION OF THE RIGHTS OF WOMAN AND CITIZEN (1791)

Man, are you capable of being just? It is a woman who asks you this question; at least you will not den her this right. Tell me! Who has given you the sovereign authority to oppress my sex? Your strength? Your talents? Observe the creator in his wisdom; regard nature in all her grandeur, with which you seem to want to compare yourself; and give me, if you dare, an example of this tyrannical empire. (From Paris to Peru, from Rome to Japan, the most stupid animal, in my opinion, is man.) Go back to the animals, consult the elements, study the plants, then glance over all the modifications of organized matter, and cede to the evidence when I offer you the means. Seek, search, and distinguish, if you can, the sexes in the administration of nature. Everywhere you will find them mingled, everywhere they cooperate in harmony with this immortal masterpiece. Only man has fashioned himself a principle out of this exception. Bizarre, blind, bloated by science and degenerate, in this century of enlightenment and wisdom, he, in grossest ignorance, wishes to exercise the command of a despot over a sex that has received every intellectual faculty; he claims to rejoice in the Revolution and claims his rights to equality, at the very least.

DECLARATION OF THE RIGHTS OF WOMAN AND CITIZEN

To be decreed by the National Assembly in its last meetings or in those of the next legislature.

PREAMBLE

The mothers, daughters, and sisters, representatives of the nation, demand to be constituted a national assembly. Considering that ignorance, disregard of or contempt for the rights of women are the only causes of public misfortune and of governmental corruption, they have resolved to set forth in a solemn declaration, the natural, inalienable and sacred rights of woman; to the end that this declaration, constantly held up to all members of society, may always remind them of their rights and duties; to the end that the acts based on women's power and those based on the power of men, being constantly measured against the goal of all political institutions, may be more respected; and so that the demands of female citizens, henceforth founded on simple and indisputable principles, may ever uphold the constitution and good morals, and may contribute to the happiness of all.

Consequently, the sex that is superior in beauty as well as in courage of maternal suffering, recognizes and declares, in the presence and under the auspices of the Supreme Being, the following rights of woman and citizen.

Article One. Woman is born free and remains equal in rights to man. Social distinctions can be founded only on general utility.

II. The goal of every political association is the preservation of the natural and irrevocable rights of Woman and Man. These rights are liberty, property, security, and especially resistance to oppression.

III. The principle of all sovereignty resides essentially in the Nation, which is none other than the union of Woman and Man; no group, no individual can exercise any authority that is not derived expressly from it.

IV. Liberty and Justice consist of rendering to persons those things that belong to them; thus, the exercise of woman's natural rights is limited only by the perpetual tyranny with which man opposes her; these limits must be changed according to the laws of nature and reason.

V. The laws of nature and of reason prohibit all acts harmful to society; whatever is not prohibited by these wise and divine laws cannot be prevented, and no one can be forced to do anything unspecified by the law.

VI. The law should be the expression of the general will: all female and male citizens must participate in its elaboration personally or through their representatives. It should be the same for all; all female and male citizens, being equal in the eyes of the law, should be equally admissible to all public offices, places, and employments, according to their capacities and with no distinctions other than those of their virtues and talents.

VII. No woman is immune; she can be accused, arrested, and detained in such cases as determined by law. Women, like men, must obey these rigorous laws.

VIII. Only punishments strictly and obviously necessary may be established by law. No one may be punished except under a law established and promulgated before the offense occurred, and which is legally applicable to women.

IX. If any woman is declared guilty, then the law must be enforced rigorously.

X. No one should be punished for their opinions. Woman has the right to mount the scaffold; she should likewise have the right to speak in public, provided that her demonstrations do not disrupt public order as established by law.

XI. Free communication of thoughts and opinions is one of the most precious rights of woman, since this liberty assures the legitimate paternity of fathers with regard to their children. Every female citizen can therefore freely say: "I am the mother of a child that belongs to you," without a barbaric prejudice forcing her to conceal the truth; she must also answer for the abuse of this liberty in cases determined by law.

XII. Guarantee of the rights of woman and female citizens requires the existence of public services. Such guarantee should be established for the advantage of everyone, not for the personal benefit of those to whom these services are entrusted.

XIII. For the maintenance of public forces and administrative expenses, the contributions of women and men shall be equal; the woman shares in all forced labor and all painful tasks, therefore she should have the same share in the distribution of positions, tasks, assignments, honors, and industry.

XIV. Female and male citizens have the right to determine the need for public taxes, either by themselves or through their representatives. Female citizens can agree to this only if they are admitted to an equal share not only in wealth but also in public administration, and by determining the proportion and extent of tax collection.

XV. The mass of women, allied for tax purposes to the mass of men, has the right to hold every public official accountable for his administration.

XVI. Any society in which the guarantee of rights is not assured, or the separation of powers determined, has no constitution. The constitution is invalid if the majority of individuals who compose the Nation have not cooperated in writing it.

XVII. The right of property is inviolable and sacred to both sexes, jointly or separately. No one can be deprived of it, since it is a true inheritance of nature except when public necessity, certified by law, clearly requires it, subject to just and prior compensation.

POSTAMBLE

Woman, wake up! The tocsin of reason is sounding throughout the Universe; know your rights. The powerful empire of nature is no longer surrounded by prejudices, fanaticism, superstition and lies. The torch of truth has dispelled all the clouds of stupidity and usurpation. Man enslaved has multiplied his forces; he has had recourse to yours in order to break his own chains. Having become free, he has become unjust toward his mate. Oh Women! Women! when will you cease to be blind? What advantages have you gained in the Revolution? A more marked scorn, a more signal disdain. During centuries of corruption, you reigned only over the weakness of men. Your empire is destroyed; what then remains for you? The proof of man's injustice. The claim of your patrimony founded on the wise decrees of nature—what have you to fear from such a splendid enterprise? The good word of the legislator at the marriage of Canaan? Do you not fear that our French legislators, who are correcting this morality, which was for such a long time appended to the realm of politics but is no longer fashionable, will again say to you, "Women, what do we have in common with you?" You must answer, "Everything!" If, in their weakness, they are obstinate in drawing this conclusion contrary to their principles, you must courageously invoke the force of reason against their vain pretensions of superiority. Unite yourselves under the banner of philosophy; deploy all the energy of your character, and soon you will see these prideful ones, your adoring servants, no longer grovelling at your feet but proud to share with you the treasures of the Supreme Being. Whatever the obstacles that are put in your way, it is in your power to overturn them; you have only to will it. Let us turn now to the frightful picture of what you have been in society; and since there is currently a question of national education, let us see if our wise legislators will think wisely about the education of women.

Women have done more evil than good. They have had their share in coercion and double-dealings. When forcibly abused, they have countered with stratagems; they have had recourse to all the resources of their charms, and the most blameless among them has not hesitated to use them. They have used poison and irons; they have commanded crime and virtue alike. For centuries, the government of France in particular has depended on the nocturnal administration of women; the cabinet had no secrets from their indiscretion: embassy, military command, ministry, presidency, pontificate, cardinalate—one might say everything profane and sacred subject to the foolishness of man has been subordinated to the greed and ambition of the female sex, which was formerly contemptible and respected but, since the revolution, is respectable and yet contemptible.

What could I not say about this paradox! I have only a moment for offering a few remarks, but this moment will attract the attention of the most remote posterity. Under the Old Regime, all were vicious, all were guilty; but could one not perceive the improvement of things, even in the substance of vice? A woman needed only to be beautiful or lovable; when she possessed these two advantages, she saw a hundred fortunes at her feet. If she did not profit from this situation, she had either a bizarre character or a rare philosophy that led her to despise wealth; in such a case she was relegated to the status of a brainless person; the most indecent woman could make herself respected with enough gold; the buying and selling of women was a kind of industry taken for granted in the first rank of society, which, henceforth, will have no credit. If it did, the revolution would be lost, and under the new order we would remain ever corrupt. Still, can reason hide the fact that all other routes to fortune are closed to woman, whom man buys like a slave on the African coast? The difference is great, as we know. The slave commands the master; but if the master sets her free, without compensation, at an age when the slave has lost all her charms, what becomes of this unfortunate creature? A contemptible toy; even the doors of charity are closed to her; she is poor and old, they say; why didn't she know how to make her fortune? Other more touching examples suggest themselves to reason. A young person without experience, seduced by a man she loves, will abandon her parents to follow him; the ungrateful fellow will leave her after a few years, and the older she has grown with him, the more inhuman will his inconstancy be. If she has children, he will abandon her all the same. If he is rich, he will think himself exempt from sharing his fortune with his noble victims. If some commitment binds him to his duties, he will violate its power by using all legal loopholes. If he is married, other commitments lose their rights. What laws then remain to be made in order to destroy vice down to its very roots? One dealing with the sharing of fortunes between men and women, and another with public administration. It is clear that a woman born to a rich family gains a great deal from equal inheritance. But a woman born to a poor family of merit and virtue—what is her fate? Poverty and shame. If she does not excel in music or painting, she cannot be admitted to any public office, even though she might be quite capable. I wish only to give an overview of things. I will examine them more thoroughly in the new edition of my political works, with notes, which I propose to offer to the public in a few days.

I resume my text with regard to morals. Marriage is the tomb of confidence and love. A married woman can, with impunity, present bastards to her husband and the bastards with the fortune that does not belong to them. An unmarried woman has merely a slim right: ancient and inhuman laws have refused her the right to the name and property of the father of her children, and no new laws on this matter have been passed. If my attempt thus to give my sex an honorable and just stability is now considered a paradox on my part, an attempt at the impossible, I must leave to men yet to come the glory of discussing this matter; but meanwhile, one can pave the way through national education, the restoration of morals, and by conjugal contracts.

MODEL FOR A SOCIAL CONTRACT
BETWEEN A MAN AND A WOMAN

We, N & N, of our own free will, unite ourselves for the remainder of our lives and for the duration of our mutual inclinations, according to the following conditions: We intend and desire to pool our fortunes as community property, while nevertheless preserving the right to divide them on behalf of our own children and those we might have with someone else, mutually recognizing that our fortune belongs directly to our children, from whatever bed they might spring, and that all of them have the right to carry the name of the fathers and mothers who have acknowledged them, and we obligate ourselves to subscribe to the law that punishes the renunciation of one's own flesh and blood. We obligate ourselves equally, in case of separation, to divide our fortune, and to set apart the portion belonging to our children as indicated by the law; and in the case of perfect union, the first to die would assign half the property to their children; and if one of us should die without children, the survivor would inherit everything, unless the dying party had disposed of his half of the common wealth in favor of someone else he might deem appropriate.

Here is the general formula for the conjugal agreement I am proposing. Upon reading this unorthodox piece, I envision all the hypocrites, prudes, clergy, and their gang of diabolic followers rising up against me. But would this plan not offer to the wise a moral means of achieving the perfectibility of a happy government? I shall prove it in a few words. A rich and childless epicurean fervently thinks fit to go to his poor neighbor's house to augment his family. Once a law is passed that will authorize the rich man to adopt the poor woman's children, the bonds of society will be strengthened and its morals purified. This law would perhaps save the wealth of the community and check the disorder that leads so many victims into the refuges of shame, servility, and degeneration of human principles, where nature has so long bemoaned its oppression.

May the critics of rational philosophy therefore cease to protest against primitive morals or else go bury themselves in the sources they cite. (Abraham had some very legitimate children with Agar, the servant of his wife.)

I should like a law that protects widows and maidens deceived by the false promises of a man to whom they have become attached; I would like this law to force a fickle-minded man to stand by his agreements or else provide an indemnity proportional to his fortune. Moreover, I would like this law to be rigorous against women, at least against those impudent enough to appeal to a law which they themselves have violated by their own misconduct, if this can be proved. At the same time, I would like prostitutes to be placed in designated quarters, as I discussed in 1788 in *Le Bonheur primitif de l'homme.* It is not the prostitutes who contribute most to the depravation of morals; it is the women of Society. By reeducating the latter, one can modify the former. At first this chain of fraternal union will prove disorderly, but eventually it will result in perfect harmony. I am offering an invincible means of elevating the soul of women; it is for them to join in all the activities of men. If man insists on finding this means impracticable, let him share his fortune with woman, not according to his whim, but according to the wisdom of the law. Prejudice will tumble down; customs and manners will be purified; and nature will recapture all its rights. Add to this the marriage of priests, the reaffirmation of the King on his throne, and the French government will never perish.

MARY WOLLSTONECRAFT

A False System of Education

Mary Wollstonecraft was born in 1759 in England, the oldest daughter of
an abusive gentleman farmer. When she was nineteen, Wollstonecraft left
home to work as a widow's companion in Bath. In 1783 Wollstonecraft, her
sister Everina, and childhood friend Fanny Blood established a successful
school for girls at Newington. There she befriended Richard Price, a radical
who encouraged her political opinions. After the school's fortunes declined,
Wollstonecraft published her first book, Thoughts on the Education of
Daughters (1787), and assumed a position as governess to the daughters of
wealthy Lord Kingsborough. Conflict with Lady Kingsborough led to her
dismissal and Wollstonecraft fled to London, where she published several
works of fiction and became involved with the radical circle that included
William Godwin, Tom Paine, Joseph Priestly, and Henry Fuseli. Traveling
to Paris in December 1792 to observe the progress of the French Revolution, Wollstonecraft began an affair with an American, Gilbert Imlay, who
fathered her daughter Fanny. Abandoned by Imlay several years later,
Wollstonecraft tried to commit suicide by throwing herself into the River
Thames, but was rescued by a passerby. She then resumed both her writing
and her acquaintance with William Godwin. When Wollstonecraft became
pregnant with Godwin's child they married, despite a mutual commitment
to the doctrine of free love. Wollstonecraft died at the age of thirty-eight
from complications related to the birth of her second daughter, the future
Mary Shelley.

A Vindication of the Rights of Woman was released in 1792, at the
height of revolutionary fervor in France, and was read widely on both sides
of the Atlantic. Though Vindication languished after Wollstonecraft's death—
its reputation marred by her unconventional lifestyle—it is now recognized
as a landmark treatise on women's rights. Wollstonecraft's thoughts drew
upon the works of radical thinkers such as Tom Paine, as well as those of
women's education advocates including Catharine Macaulay. Vindication
makes a strong argument for woman's birthright as the intellectual equal of
man, but allows that an inferior education has rendered many women
mentally feeble and vain. Its insistence that culture rather than nature is
the determiner of much gender difference foreshadows later feminist theory.

In her introduction, Wollstonecraft offers an outline of her central argu-
ment and identifies her imagined readership—the middle class. In a later
chapter, she proposes a national system of education intended to remedy
gender inequality.

———————

After considering the historic page, and viewing the living world with anxious solicitude, the most melancholy emotions of sorrowful indignation have depressed my spirits, and I have sighed when obliged to confess that either Nature has made a great difference between man and man, or that the civilization which has hitherto taken place in the world has been very partial. I have turned over various books written on the subject of education, and patiently observed the conduct of parents and the management of schools; but what has been the result?—a profound conviction that the neglected education of my fellow creatures is the grand source of the misery I deplore, and that women, in particular, are rendered weak and wretched by a variety of concurring causes, originating from one hasty conclusion. The conduct and manners of women, in fact, evidently prove that their minds are not in a healthy state; for, like the flowers which are planted in too rich a soil, strength and usefulness are sacrificed to beauty; and the flaunting leaves, after having pleased a fastidious eye, fade, disregarded on the stalk, long before the season when they ought to have arrived at maturity. One cause of this barren blooming I attribute to a false system of education, gathered from the books written on this subject by men who, considering females rather as women than human creatures, have been more anxious to make them alluring mistresses than affectionate wives and rational mothers; and the understanding of the sex has been so bubbled by this specious homage, that the civilized women of the present century, with a few exceptions, are only anxious to inspire love, when they ought to cherish a nobler ambition, and by their abilities and virtues exact respect.

In a treatise, therefore, on female rights and manners, the works which have been particularly written for their improvement must not be overlooked, especially when it is asserted, in direct terms, that the minds of women are enfeebled by false refinement; that the books of instruction, written by men of genius, have had the same tendency as more frivolous productions; and that, in the true style of Mahometanism, they are treated as a kind of subordinate beings, and not as a part of the human species, when improvable reason is allowed to be the dignified distinction which raises men above the brute creation, and puts a natural sceptre in a feeble hand.

Yet, because I am a woman, I would not lead my readers to suppose that I mean violently to agitate the contested question respecting the quality or inferiority of the sex; but as the subject lies in my way, and I cannot pass it over without subjecting the main tendency of my reasoning to misconstruction, I shall stop a moment to deliver, in a few words, my opinion. In the government of the physical world it is observable that the female in point of strength is, in general, inferior to the male. This is the law of Nature; and it does not appear to be suspended or abrogated in favour of woman. A degree of physical superiority cannot, therefore, be denied, and it is a noble prerogative! But not content with this natural pre-eminence, men endeavour to sink us still lower, merely to render us alluring objects for a moment; and women, intoxicated by the adoration which men, under the influence of their senses, pay them, do not seek to obtain a durable interest in their hearts, or to become the friends of the fellow creatures who find amusement in their society.

I am aware of an obvious inference. From every quarter have I heard exclamations against masculine women, but where are they to be found? If by this appellation men mean to inveigh against their ardour in hunting, shooting, and gaming, I shall most cordially join in the cry; but if it be against the imitation of manly virtues, or, more properly speaking, the attainment of those talents and virtues, the exercise of which ennobles the human character, and which raises females in the scale of animal being, when they are comprehensively termed mankind, all those who view them with a philosophic eye must, I should think, wish with me, that they may every day grow more and more masculine.

This discussion naturally divides the subject. I shall first consider women in the grand light of human creatures, who, in common with men, are placed on this earth to unfold their faculties; and afterwards I shall more particularly point out their peculiar designation.

I wish also to steer clear of an error which many respectable writers have fallen into; for the instruction which has hitherto been addressed to women, has rather been applicable to *ladies,* if the little indirect advice that is scattered through 'Sandford and Merton'[1] be excepted; but, addressing my sex in a firmer tone, I pay particular attention to those in the middle class, because they appear to be in the most natural state. Perhaps the seeds of false refinement, immorality, and vanity, have ever been shed by the great. Weak, artificial beings, raised above the common wants and affections of their race, in a premature unnatural manner, undermine the very foundation of virtue, and spread corruption through the whole mass of society! As a class of mankind they have the strongest claim to pity; the education of the rich tends to render them vain and helpless, and the unfolding mind is not strengthened by the practice of those duties which dignify the human character. They only live to amuse themselves, and by the same law which in Nature invariably produces certain effects, they soon only afford barren amusement.

But as I purpose taking a separate view of the different ranks of society, and of the moral character of women in each, this hint is for the present sufficient; and I have only alluded to the subject because it appears to me to be the very essence of an introduction to give a cursory account of the contents of the work it introduces.

My own sex, I hope, will excuse me, if I treat them like rational creatures, instead of flattering their *fascinating* graces, and viewing them as if they were in a state of perpetual childhood, unable to stand alone. I earnestly wish to point out in what true dignity and human happiness consists. I wish to persuade women to endeavour to acquire strength, both of mind and body, and to convince them that the soft phrases, susceptibility of heart, delicacy of sentiment, and refinement of taste, are almost synonymous with epithets of weakness, and that those beings who are only the objects of pity, and that kind of love which has been termed its sister, will soon become objects of contempt.

Dismissing, then, those pretty feminine phrases, which the men condescendingly use to soften our slavish dependence, and despising that weak elegancy of mind, exquisite sensibility, and sweet docility of manners, supposed to be the sexual characteristics of the weaker vessel, I wish to show that elegance is inferior to virtue, that the first object of laudable ambition is to obtain a character as a human being, regardless of the distinction of sex, and that secondary views should be brought to this simple touchstone.

This is a rough sketch of my plan; and should I express my conviction with the energetic emotions that I feel whenever I think of the subject, the dictates of experience and reflection will be felt by some of my readers. Animated by this important object, I shall disdain to cull my phrases or polish my style. I aim at being useful, and sincerity will render me unaffected; for wishing rather to persuade by the force of my arguments than dazzle by the elegance of my language, I shall not waste my time in rounding periods, or in fabricating the turgid bombast of artificial feelings, which, coming from the head, never reach the heart. I shall be employed about things, not words! and, anxious to render my sex more respectable members of society, I shall try to avoid that flowery diction which has slided from essays into novels, and from novels into familiar letters and conversations.

These pretty superlatives, dropping glibly from the tongue, vitiate the taste, and create a kind of sickly delicacy that turns away from simple unadorned truth; and a deluge of false sentiments and overstretched feelings, stifling the natural emotions of the heart, render the domestic pleasures insipid, that ought to sweeten the exercise of those severe duties, which educate a rational and immortal being for a nobler field of action.

The education of women has of late been more attended to than formerly; yet they are still reckoned a frivolous sex, and ridiculed or pitied by the writers who endeavour by satire or instruction to improve them. It is acknowledged that they spend many of the first years of their lives in acquiring a smattering of accomplishments; meanwhile strength of body and mind are sacrificed to libertine notions of beauty, to the desire of establishing themselves—the only way women can rise in the world—by marriage. And this desire making mere animals of them, when they marry they act as such children may be expected to act—they dress, they paint, and nickname God's creatures. Surely these weak beings are only fit for a seraglio! Can they be expected to govern a family with judgement, or take care of the poor babes whom they bring into the world?

If, then, it can be fairly deduced from the present conduct of the sex, from the prevalent fondness for pleasure which takes place of ambition and those nobler passions that open and enlarge the soul, that the instruction which women have hitherto received has only tended, with the constitution of civil society, to render them insignificant objects of desire—mere propagators of fools!—if it can be proved that in aiming to accomplish them, without cultivating their understandings, they are taken out of their sphere of duties, and made ridiculous and useless when the short-lived bloom of beauty is over,[2] I presume that *rational* men will excuse me for endeavouring to persuade them to become more masculine and respectable.

Indeed the word masculine is only a bugbear; there is little reason to fear that women will acquire too much courage or fortitude, for their apparent inferiority with respect to bodily strength must render them in some degree dependent on men in the various relations of life; but why should it be increased by prejudices that give a sex to virtue, and confound simple truths with sensual reveries?

Women are, in fact, so much degraded by mistaken notions of female excellence, that I do not mean to add a paradox when I assert that this artificial weakness produces a propensity to tyrannize, and gives birth to cunning, the natural opponent of strength, which leads them to play off those contemptible infantine airs that undermine esteem even whilst they excite desire. Let men become more chaste and modest, and if women do not grow wiser in the same ratio it will be clear that they have weaker understandings. It seems scarcely necessary to say that I now speak of the sex in general. Many individuals have more sense than their male relatives; and, as nothing preponderates where there is a constant struggle for an equilibrium without it has naturally more gravity, some women govern their husbands without degrading themselves, because intellect will always govern.

. . .

The good effects resulting from attention to private education will ever be very confined, and the parent who really puts his own hand to the plough, will always, in some degree, be disappointed, till education becomes a grand national concern. A man cannot retire into a desert with his child, and if he did he could not bring himself back to childhood, and become the proper friend and playfellow of an infant or youth. And when children are confined to the society of men and women, they very soon acquire that kind of premature manhood which stops the growth of every vigorous power of mind or body. In order to open their faculties they should be excited to think for themselves; and this can only be done by mixing a number of children together, and making them jointly pursue the same objects.

. . .

[T]o improve both sexes they ought, not only in private families, but in public schools, to be educated together. If marriage be the cement of society, mankind should all be educated after the same model, or the intercourse of the sexes will never deserve the name of fellowship, nor will women ever fulfil the peculiar duties of their sex, till they become enlightened citizens, till they become free by being enabled to earn their own subsistence, independent of men; in the same manner, I mean, to prevent misconstruction, as one man is independent of another. Nay, marriage will never be held sacred till women, by being brought up with men, are prepared to be their companions rather than their mistresses; for the mean doublings of cunning will ever render them contemptible, whilst oppression renders them timid. So convinced am I of this truth, that I will venture to predict that virtue will never prevail in society till the virtues of both sexes are founded on reason; and, till the affections common to both are allowed to gain their due strength by the discharge of mutual duties.

. . .

To render this practicable, day-schools for particular ages should be established by Government, in which boys and girls might be educated together. The school for the younger children, from five to nine years of age, ought to be absolutely free and open to all classes.[3] A sufficient number of masters should also be chosen by a select committee in each parish, to whom any complaints of negligence, etc., might be made, if signed by six of the children's parents.

Ushers would then be unnecessary; for I believe experience will ever prove that this kind of subordinate authority is particularly injurious to the morals of youth. What, indeed, can tend to deprave the character more than outward submission and inward contempt? Yet how can boys be expected to treat an usher with respect, when the master seems to consider him in the light of a servant, and almost to countenance the ridicule which becomes the chief amusement of the boys during the play hours?

But nothing of this kind could occur in an elementary day-school, where boys and girls, the rich and poor, should meet together. And to prevent any of the distinctions of vanity, they should be dressed alike, and all obliged to submit to the same discipline, or leave the school. The schoolroom ought to be surrounded by a large piece of ground, in which the children might be usefully exercised, for at this age they should not be confined to any sedentary employment for more than an hour at a time. But these relaxations might all be rendered a part of elementary education, for many things improve and amuse the senses, when introduced as a kind of show, to the principles of which, dryly laid down, children would turn a deaf ear. For instance, botany, mechanics, and astronomy; reading, writing, arithmetic, natural history and some simple experiments in natural philosophy, might fill up the day; but these pursuits should never encroach on gymnastic plays in the open air. The elements of religion, history, the history of man, and politics, might also be taught by conversations in the Socratic form.

After the age of nine, girls and boys, intended for domestic employments, or mechanical trades, ought to be removed to other schools, and receive instruction in some measure appropriated to the destination of each individual, the two sexes being still together in the morning; but in the afternoon the girls should attend a school, where plain work, mantuamaking millinery, etc., would be their employment.

The young people of superior abilities, or fortune, might now be taught, in another school, the dead and living languages, the elements of science, and continue the study of history and politics, on a more extensive scale, which would not exclude polite literature.

Girls and boys still together? I hear some readers ask. Yes. And I should not fear any other consequence than that some early attachment might take place; which, whilst it had the best effect on the moral character of the young people, might not perfectly agree with the views of the parents, for it will be a long time, I fear, before the world will be so far enlightened that parents, only anxious to render their children virtuous, shall allow them to choose companions for life themselves.

Besides, this would be a sure way to promote early marriages, and from early marriages the most salutary physical and moral effects naturally flow. What a different character does a married citizen assume from the selfish coxcomb, who lives but for himself, and who is often afraid to marry lest he should not be able to live in a certain style. Great emergencies excepted, which would rarely occur in a society of which equality was the basis, a man can only be prepared to discharge the duties of public life, by the habitual practice of those inferior ones which form the man.

In this plan of education the constitution of boys would not be ruined by the early debaucheries, which now make men so selfish, or girls rendered weak and vain, by indolence, and frivolous pursuits. But, I presuppose, that such a degree of equality should be established between the sexes as would shut out gallantry and coquetry, yet allow friendship and love to temper the heart for the discharge of higher duties.

These would be schools of morality—and the happiness of man, allowed to flow from the pure springs of duty and affection, what advances might not the human mind make? Society can only be happy and free in proportion as it is virtuous; but the present distinctions, established in society, corrode all private, and blast all public virtue.

. . .

I only drop these observations at present, as hints; rather, indeed as an outline of the plan I mean, than a digested one; but I must add, that I highly approve of one regulation mentioned in the pamphlet[4] already alluded to, that of making the children and youths independent of the masters respecting punishments. They should be tried by their peers, which would be an admirable method of fixing sound principles of justice in the mind, and might have the happiest effect on the temper, which is very soured or irritated by tyranny, till it becomes peevishly cunning, or ferociously overbearing.

My imagination darts forward with benevolent fervour to greet these amiable and respectable groups, in spite of the sneering of cold hearts, who are at liberty to utter, with frigid self-importance, the damning epithet—romantic; the force of which I shall endeavour to blunt by repeating the words of an eloquent moralist: 'I know not whether the allusions of a truly humane heart, whose zeal renders everything easy, be not preferable to that rough and repulsing reason, which always finds an indifference for the public good, the first obstacle to whatever would promote it.'

. . .

My observations on national education are obviously hints; but I principally wish to enforce the necessity of educating the sexes together, to perfect both, and of making children sleep at home that they may learn to love home; yet to make private support, instead of smothering, public affections, they should be sent to school to mix with a number of equals, for only by the jostlings of equality can we form a just opinion of ourselves.

To render mankind more virtuous, and happier of course, both sexes must act from the same principle; but how can that be expected when only one is allowed to see the reasonableness of it? To render also the social compact truly equitable, and in order to spread those enlightening principles, which alone can ameliorate the fate of man, women must be allowed to found their virtue on knowledge, which is scarcely possible unless they be educated by the same pursuits as men. For they are now made so inferior by ignorance and low desires, as not to deserve to be ranked with them; or, by the serpentine wrigglings of cunning, they mount the tree of knowledge, and only acquire sufficient to lead men astray.

. . .

In short, in whatever light I view the subject, reason and experience convince me that the only method of leading women to fulfil their peculiar duties is to free them from all restraint by allowing them to participate in the inherent rights of mankind.

Make them free, and they will quickly become wise and virtuous, as men become more so, for the improvement must be mutual, or the injustice which one-half of the human race are obliged to submit to retorting on their oppressors, the virtue of man will be worm-eaten by the insect whom he keeps under his feet.

Let men take their choice. Man and woman were made for each other, though not to become one being; and if they will not improve women, they will deprave them.

. . .

A man has been termed a microcosm, and every family might also be called a state. States, it is true, have mostly been governed by arts that disgrace the character of man, and the want of a just constitution and equal laws have so perplexed the notions of the worldly wise, that they more than question the reasonableness of contending for the rights of humanity. Thus morality, polluted in the national reservoir, sends off streams of vice to corrupt the constituent parts of the body politic; but should more noble, or rather more just, principles regulate the laws, which ought to be the government of society, and not those who execute them, duty might become the rule of private conduct.

. . . The conclusion which I wish to draw is obvious. Make women rational creatures and free citizens, and they will quickly become good wives and mothers—that is, if men do not neglect the duties of husbands and fathers.

Discussing the advantages which a public and private education combined, as I have sketched, might rationally be expected to produce, I have dwelt most on such as are particularly relative to the female world, because I think the female world oppressed; yet the gangrene, which the vices engendered by oppression have produced, is not confined to the morbid part, but pervades society at large; so that when I wish to see my sex become more like moral agents, my heart bounds with the anticipation of the general diffusion of that sublime contentment which only morality can diffuse.

EXPLANATORY NOTES

1. [Editor's note] *'Sandford and Merton': History of Sanford and Merton,* a children's book by Thomas Day (1748–89). Published in three volumes, 1783, 1787 and 1789. Widely read and admired, it used ideas from Rousseau's *Émile* extensively.
2. [Author's note] A lively writer (I cannot recollect his name) asks what business women turned of forty have to do in the world?
3. [Author's note] Treating this part of the subject, I have borrowed some hints from a very sensible pamphlet, written by the late Bishop of Autun, on 'Public Education'. [Talleyrand]
4. [Editor's note] *The Bishop of Autun's:* Wollstonecraft dedicated *A Vindication of the Rights of Woman* to Talleyrand, late Bishop of Autun.